...ing Game of 1897

...vs Balti...

GLORY FADES AWAY

GLORY

⬥

FADES

⬥

AWAY

—— The ——
Nineteenth-Century
World Series Rediscovered

JERRY LANSCHE

Foreword by John Thorn

Taylor Publishing
Dallas, Texas

Copyright © 1991 by Jerry Lansche

Published by Taylor Publishing Company
        1550 West Mockingbird Lane
        Dallas, Texas 75235

Designed by David Timmons Graphic Design

Library of Congress Cataloging-in-Publication Data

Lansche, Jerry, 1951–
    Glory fades away : the nineteenth-century world series
rediscovered / Jerry Lansche.
        p.   cm.
    Includes bibliographical references and index.
    ISBN 0-87833-726-1 : $19.95
    1. World series (Baseball)—History—19th century.   I. Title.
GV878.4.L36   1990
796.357'646—dc20   90-19540
                                                         CIP

Printed in the United States of America

10 9 8 7 6 5 4 3 2 1

For my mom

ACKNOWLEDGMENTS

I would like to thank my mother, Melba Mae Lansche, for the many hours she selflessly devoted to reading and editing the early drafts of the manuscript. Mom has an unerring eye for misplaced phrases, misspellings, mistakes, and misfires in general. If the reader does not pull up short trying to make sense of some baffling or inane passage, the credit must go, first, to her.

My thanks to a terrific editor and a good friend at Taylor Publishing in Dallas, Jim Donovan—not just for coming up with a really fine title, not just for patiently enduring my endless ideas on how to sell the book, but also for his excellent good ear and unflagging sense of humor.

I would also like to thank my wife, Sonia, for listening to dozens of stories about the nineteenth century, and for supporting me, financially and psychologically, during the months it took to write this book. I may make a baseball fan of her yet. Special thanks to my four-year-old son, Hunter Kenneth Lansche, the light of my life, and whose name I include here simply because I enjoy seeing it in print.

My sincere gratitude goes to Mr. Robert Franklin for his leg up; to Mr. Steve Gietschier of The Sporting News offices in St. Louis; to Mr. Ralph Horton of Horton Publishing Company, St. Louis; to Mr. Frederick Ivor-Campbell of Warren, Rhode Island, for his invaluable help with some of the Boston and Providence games; to Mr. W. Lloyd Johnson, the former executive director of the Society for American Baseball Research (SABR) in Kansas City, Missouri; to the society itself for developing my interest in nineteenth-century baseball; to Mr. John Holway; to Mr. John Thorn; to Prof. David Quentin Voigt; to Messrs. Bill Deane and Gary Van Allen of the National Baseball Hall of Fame and Museum, Inc., in Cooperstown, New York; to Warden Warren of the New Haven Correctional Center; to Mr. Herb Feiler; to Mr. Stephen Holtje; and to Miss Alice Coyle Lunn, a perfectly lovely researcher in Ohio.

I would like to offer a lengthy and heartfelt ovation to the many helpful and patient individuals at the many libraries around the country who were so kind as to assist me in researching material for the book.

And, finally, these acknowledgments would be incomplete without mentioning my father. Charles Kenneth Lansche bequeathed his passion for baseball to his son and, without his tutelage, I would never have written this book. He wasn't particularly interested in nineteenth-century baseball and probably wouldn't have read this volume if anyone else had been its author. But he would have been mighty proud of me for writing it and that thought is comforting. My dad passed away less than a month after the 1987 World Series between the St. Louis Cardinals and the Minnesota Twins.

Like most little boys my age who have lost a father, I still miss him.

—JERRY LANSCHE
November, 1990

A NOTE ON THE BOX SCORES

This book contains box scores revised to reflect modern scoring methods. Trying to make sense of century-old box scores was simultaneously the most and least fun of writing this book. It was easy enough, for example, to change hits to walks in revising box scores for the 1887 World Series, the only year in which bases on balls were counted as hits. And in the early days of baseball, an error was charged to the pitcher for a walk, a wild pitch, a hit batsman, or a balk, and a catcher was penalized for a passed ball or a wide throw to the bag when he tried to throw out a baserunner stealing second. It wasn't much of a problem to expunge these errors from the box scores. But when you are confronted, as I was in a particular game, with four box scores from four different sources, and each box score gives a different number of errors for each team—well, it wasn't always easy.

In some instances, a single was credited as a double if the outfielder booted the ball. I changed that double to a single and an error on the outfielder in the obvious cases.

My hierarchy for determining accurate play-by-play was as follows: In all cases, I gave most weight to the newspaper in the city in which the game was played, to an account written by someone who was actually at the game. Failing that, I gave most credence to the account which appeared in the visiting club's hometown newspaper on the assumption, right or wrong, that the paper sent someone to cover the game or was receiving a report from a special correspondent in the park. Failing that, I chose the best available objective source, whether it was the *New York Clipper*, *The Sporting News*, the *Boston Herald*, or any other publication. In some thirty cases, I was unable to locate a complete play-by-play. I have revised the box scores to the best of my ability. In any event, each box score shown in this book is more accurate than any you have ever seen before. Any mistakes are mine, and mine alone.

CONTENTS

◆

Twenty-four pages of photographs follow page 178

FOREWORD

◆

The World Series: what a breathtakingly presumptuous term that is today, when nearly ninety baseball-playing nations are excluded from the competition and billions of people still have not heard of it. And yet, that presumption pales before the brass of those who coined the term—not in 1903, the year of what has come to be called, stupefyingly, the first "modern World Series," but in the mid-1880s, when baseball was virtually unknown outside North America.

The 1880s, an age of invention and expansion and moral certitude, must have been a wonderful time to be an American (unless, of course, you were poor, black, or female). The Civil War and Reconstruction were behind, and only great things seemed to lie ahead.

Baseball, too, was in a period of invention and expansion in the 1880s—the "Changing Game" sidebars that accompany each chapter of this book testify to the wild shifts in rules and scorekeeping, the declaration of three new leagues, and such innovations as spring training, the chest protector, and sunglasses—and like the budding nation whose pastime it was, baseball was pretty cocksure of itself. Albert Spalding, who in the offseason of 1888-89 would lead a group of ball-players ("the All-American Tourists") on a global mission to spread the gospel of bat and ball, wrote:

> I claim that Base Ball owes its prestige as our National Game to
> the fact that as no other form of sport it is the exponent of
> American Courage, Confidence, Combativeness; American Dash,
> Discipline, Determination; American Energy, Eagerness,
> Enthusiasm; American Pluck, Persistency, Performance; American
> Spirit, Sagacity, Success; American Vim, Vigor, Virility.

Whew! With that sort of patriotic bluster abroad in the land, it was no wonder that the term "World Series" or "World's Championship" would be applied to these internecine skirmishes that were noted by few and witnessed, as in the case of the finale of the 1884 Series, by fewer than 500 people.

Still, putting aside the question of chutzpah, the World Series of the nineteenth century were not mere oddities, nor were they prototypes of the "modern World Series." As Jerry Lansche convincingly argues and joyously displays, the postseason championship of, say, 1889 had as much if not more in common with that of today than the World Series of 1903 or 1919 or 1945. And Lansche has a feeling for the period, a delight in the small details that put you in the park, cheering a slide by Curt Welch or a diving catch by Monte Ward, drinking a phosphate and munching on a pickled egg. Great ideas—like baseball, or cars, or rock and roll— are most interesting in their formation. Perhaps few of the 100 million fans who watch this year's World Series will pause to wonder how this great idea got started . . . but the more thoughtful among them ought to, and now, thanks to this book, they have a way to look it up.

—JOHN THORN

But fame is fleeting as the wind,
and glory fades away . . .

JAMES WILSON,
"Casey's Revenge"

INTRODUCTION

Baseball is the very symbol, the outward and
visible expression of the drive and pride and rush
and struggle of the raging, tearing, booming
nineteenth century.

MARK TWAIN

———————◆———————

The game was baseball. The nineteenth-century brand. And what a game it was, too. The images come alive.

October 6, 1882. On a scrabbly field by the banks of the Ohio River, a bespectacled Will White sets down the fearsome Chicago White Stockings inning after inning. In this, the first post-season matchup between pennant-winning clubs of rival major leagues, White shuts out the White Stockings on eight hits . . . Cincinnati right fielder Harry Wheeler becomes the first goat in a series game the next day as his errant throw to third base lets in the winning run . . .

Two years later, Charles "Old Hoss" Radbourn becomes the first pitcher to win three games in a World Series as he utterly dominates the New York Metropolitans. Radbourn pitches every inning for the Providence Grays and gives up no earned runs, proving, as early as 1884, that good pitching stops good hitting, even in the World Series . . . There is Jerry Denny at third base, gloveless, fielding and perhaps even throwing with either hand . . .

In 1885, flashy-fielding first baseman Charlie Comiskey pounds his glove and glowers in at the hard-hitting Cap Anson, waiting his turn at the plate. Chicago center fielder George Gore, still drunk from the previous night's revelry, is replaced in center field, appropriately, by future evangelist Billy Sunday . . .

In 1887, Detroit Wolverines pitcher Charlie Getzien takes a no-hitter into the ninth inning of Game Six against the St. Louis Browns. The issue of who will win the game is no longer in doubt: Detroit has a 9-0 lead. At one point in the game, nineteen straight Browns are retired, so dominating is Getzien on this day. St. Louis has yet to make a safe hit as the Detroit hurler works to Arlie Latham, the leadoff batter in the ninth. Latham grounds to short and Jack Rowe kicks the ball for an error. A moment later, Bill Gleason hits a hard liner to first baseman Charlie Ganzel. Ganzel is nearly knocked off his feet, but holds onto the ball, and Latham is stranded in no-man's-land, doubled off the bag. Two outs. Tip O'Neill steps to the plate. Tip O'Neill, baseball's best hitter in 1887 with a .435 batting average. Charlie Getzien, Detroit's leading pitcher. St. Louis's best against Detroit's finest. This is the way baseball has always been, the way it will always be.

Getzien delivers.

O'Neill swings.

The ball streaks for right field, Getzien's bid for baseball immortality riding on its wings, and drops in for a single, a few feet shy of the outstretched glove of Ned Hanlon. The bid is ended. The no-hitter has vanished . . .

There are more stories and more names. Some of the names now appear curious or quaint—Lady Baldwin, Sadie McMahon, Cupid Childs, Icebox Chamberlain, Oyster Burns, Chicken Wolf, Boileryard Clarke, and the two Cannonballs, Crane and Titcomb. And some names are those of baseball giants, men who are today enshrined in the Hall of Fame—Mike "King" Kelly, John Montgomery Ward, "Wee Willie" Keeler, John McGraw, Cy Young. But each of these men, in some way great or small, helped give the World Series the grandeur, the pomp, and the luster it enjoys today. Glory fades away, but the accomplishments remain.

The game was baseball.

The nineteenth-century brand.

BASEBALL IN THE
NINETEENTH
CENTURY

◆

By the mid-1830s, people were playing a mixture of cricket, rounders, One Old Cat, and a dozen other games that had been played with a stick and a sphere since the days of the Pharaohs. Whatever form the sport may have taken, America was calling it "base ball." In most games, there was no limit to the number of members on a team and, to the untrained eye of the innocent passerby, a contest might easily resemble a riot more than anything else. By the early 1840s, Alexander Cartwright, a New York surveyor, had applied some semblance of order to the game. Cartwright changed the shape of the field from a rectangle to a diamond, reduced the lineup to nine, placed the bases ninety feet apart, and decreed that the third out would end the inning. He wrote the first rulebook for the game, a slim tome which asked that players be on time and each game be governed by an umpire. And, mercifully, he put an end to the barbarous practice of throwing the ball at the runner in order to put him out. Cartwright and a group of clerks, merchants, and white-collar workers formed the Knickerbocker Base Ball Club and began playing their revolutionary style of baseball, the New York City game. In 1849, the Knickerbockers again led the way when the club introduced team dress.

That those flannel uniforms were topped off by straw hats seemed incongruous to no one.

In 1857, a group of baseball teams around the country formed the National Association of Base Ball Players, and its first order of business was to draft a standard code of playing rules. The National Association also paved the way for the next revolutionary change in baseball when it broke with the Knickerbockers over the issue of charging admission.

During the Civil War, soldiers on both sides of the struggle played baseball during the frequent long periods of battlefield inactivity. (There is an exceptional photograph in the National Baseball Library at the Hall of Fame in Cooperstown, New York, showing Union troops standing in formation at Fort Pulaski in Savannah, Georgia. Their comrades, in uniform, can clearly be seen in the background, playing baseball. The pitcher, in shirtsleeves, is about to deliver the ball while other soldiers look on. Five cannon line a parapet behind the batter and catcher.) There were even rumors that an occasional game was played between North and South troops during truces.

Following the war, the game was transformed from a harmless diversion into one in which the pursuit of victory became the norm. In 1869, the Cincinnati Red Stockings became the first club to acknowledge accepting money for play. The idea of salaried, professional ballplayers rapidly spread throughout the country. Two years later, the National Association of Professional Base Ball Players was formed and the era of amateurism was officially dead. In that first season, competition was fierce. The Athletics of Philadelphia captured the pennant, winning twenty-two games of twenty-nine played, but the Chicago White Stockings and Boston Red Stockings weren't far behind. Boston's record of 22-10 placed it second over Chicago, with a record of 20-9. (Although Chicago's winning percentage was higher, championships were determined at that time by which team won the most games.)

In 1872, things took a turn for the worse in the National Association with the rise of the Boston Red Stockings. Led by their great pitcher, Al Spalding (37-8), Boston finished the season at 39-8, coasting to an easy pennant, 7½ games ahead of Philadelphia in the standings. In 1873, it was Boston by four games; in 1874, Boston by 7½. Competition reached its nadir in 1875 when the amazing Red Stockings won all but eight of the seventy-nine games they played. The Athletics, with a pretty fair record of 53-20, and the Hartfords, with a record of 54-28, weren't even close. The unbalanced competition was wrecking the pennant races, and it was clear something needed to be done.

William Ambrose Hulbert, the owner of the sixth-place Chicago White Stockings, had a plan. Increasingly weary of Boston's domination in the National Association and incensed at player rowdiness and contract-jumping, Hulbert decided to form his own league. But before doing so, he took steps to strengthen his club by pirating Spalding, Cal McVey, Deacon White, and Ross Barnes from Boston, and Cap Anson from Philadelphia. Hulbert was a shrewd businessman and correctly reckoned that the other owners would move against him by suspending his new stars. On February 2, 1876, at the Grand Central Hotel in New York City, Hulbert met with a small group of excited franchise-seekers and formed the National League.

On March 10, Alexander Graham Bell invented the telephone. Six weeks later, on April 22, Boston and Philadelphia played the first game in the history of the National League. Boston won, 6-5, and the two clubs committed a total of somewhere between eighteen and twenty-six errors. On June 24, there was a full slate of games in the National League. One day later—a travel day for the baseball clubs—Lieutenant Colonel George Armstrong Custer and some two hundred members of the Seventh Cavalry were massacred at the Little Bighorn. On August 2, in the only game scheduled in the National League, Hartford beat the Athletics, 15-5, at the Hartford Ball Club Grounds in Connecticut. Out west, in the town of Deadwood in the Dakota Territory, Wild Bill Hickok was shot in the back while playing poker.

Such were the remarkable contrasts of nineteenth-century life.

The country was growing and so was baseball. But growing brought with it growing pains. At the end of the 1876 season, poor fan support prompted the Philadelphia and New York management to forgo a final western road trip, a violation of National League rules. The League summarily expelled the two clubs and, as a result, the 1877 season saw no major league baseball in the two largest eastern cities. It also saw the game's first scandal, as four players on the Louisville club were barred from baseball for life for conspiring to fix games. Following the financially disastrous 1877 season, Louisville, St. Louis, and Hartford disbanded and were replaced by franchises in Providence, Milwaukee, and Indianapolis, the latter two surviving but one year in the League. In 1879, the

League expanded by adding franchises in Troy, Syracuse, Cleveland, and Buffalo. Except for Buffalo, each club lost twice as many games as it won. Within five years, all four would drop from the League.

The first night game on record was played on September 2, 1880, at Nantasket's Sea Foam House in Massachusetts between teams composed of employees from Boston's two largest department stores—Jordan Marsh and Company and R.H. White and Company. The contest was a demonstration by the Northern Electric Light Company of Boston that large areas could be illuminated. NELC thought big in those days—it was its contention that entire cities could be lighted—but the crowd of three hundred, although enjoying the spectacle, was clearly skeptical. This was, after all, only the second year of Edison's incandescent bulb. (It would take another fifty years before the first regular-season, minor league night game took place, on April 28, 1930, between Independence and Muskogee of the Class C Western Association, and another five years before the Cincinnati Reds played the major leagues' first regular-season night game at Crosley Field. The circle would not be completed until 1988 when the Chicago Cubs belatedly installed lights at Wrigley Field.)

The National League careened into the 1880s beset, if not overwhelmed, by troubles. Not for the first time, and not for the last, the owners blamed most of their ills on the players and took steps to broaden their power base by strengthening the reserve system, hardening the rules, and lowering salaries. Players were assessed thirty dollars a year for uniforms, fifty cents a day for board while on the road, and were made to pay for their own laundry and meals. Under the reserve system, a magnate owned a player, lock, stock, and barrel, past, present, and future. A player was contractually bound to his club from one year to the next, could be sold or traded without his consent, and received no share of the sale price. If he broke the rules, failed to perform, or injured himself, the club could tender his release by giving a mere ten days' notice. And because he was, in the final analysis, a mere employee, it was not unusual that a player (pitchers and substitutes especially) be assigned a vacant post selling tickets at the ticket window or taking them at the gate.

In 1880, the average salary in the National League was $1,000, and if ballplayers labored under a benign form of indentured slavery, it was often better employment than they could find elsewhere. Many players were illiterate and most had little formal schooling. Life in the city or on the farm was hard, and a poor but athletic young man at the lower level of the social classes could do far worse than seek a career in baseball. Salaries grew. From 1880 to 1886, the average player's salary had skyrocketed to two thousand dollars. Superstars, such as Fred Dunlap, Bob Caruthers, and Mike "King" Kelly, were earning as much as six thousand dollars for six months' work. A select few, among them St. Louis player-manager Charlie Comiskey, commanded salaries of eight thousand dollars and more. The average college faculty member at this time brought home less than fifteen hundred dollars a year.

Baseball did not ask that a man wear starched shirts or use the proper fork. Baseball did not require the occasional sacrifice of a finger as a job in the stockyards did. Ballplayers did not lose their arms or legs to a runaway threshing machine, the fate of many young farmers. All the game asked was that a man be able to hit a curveball, or throw one.

As a result of such low standards for entry into the game, the 1880s became a tumultuous time for baseball. The general public regarded ballplayers as roughnecks, and the public was right in most cases. Organized ball had begun as a gentleman's sport, but when the element of winning at any cost was introduced to the game everything changed. In 1885, there were a combined total of eight thousand bakeries, grocery stores, and butcher shops in New York and over a hundred thousand saloons and three thousand distilleries spread throughout the rest of the country. Half the male population visited a saloon once a week and major league baseball had its share of hard drinkers—most of them of Irish descent, it seemed. Several who indulged were not at all averse to taking the field with a little alcohol on their breath. A reporter once asked King Kelly if he drank while playing baseball and Kelly replied, "It depends upon the length of the game." Pete Browning, the star outfielder of the Louisville club, actually claimed, "I can't hit the ball until I hit the bottle."

Gambling was another menace to the game. Louisville may have been the only club to have had players expelled for conspiring to fix ballgames, but it was an open secret that more than a few men might "take a day off" in the field in exchange for a handful of silver. A fan could place a bet on his favorite team in the gambling houses, in the pool halls, and even with bookies in the grand-stands. And, as you will see later, the 1919 Chicago "Black Sox" weren't the first team to fix a World Series.

In general, club owners fought this element of rowdyism. But some encouraged it, believing it brought the fans to the park. A few, most notably Chris Von Der Ahe, the very hypocritical owner of the St. Louis Brown Stockings, encouraged rowdyism on the one hand by urging his players to give no quarter and take none, and on the other hand condemned his men publicly when matters spilled over into his personal domain. Von Der Ahe once fined the popular Yank Robinson for insubordination, very nearly bringing about a strike by the Browns. Robinson's crime? He talked back.

If the language was vulgar and the play was rough on the field, it only matched the goings-on in the stands. Crowds were volatile. Beer sales swelled attendance but also caused violence. Fans hurled seat cushions and beer bottles at players and umpires alike while they cursed and derided their favorite targets on the field. In his autobiography, *My Thirty Years in Baseball,* no less an authority on this unruly element than John McGraw, said, "The rowdyism that prevailed in baseball in the earlier days was not entirely due to the players. Fans were just about as rough as the men on the field. In fact, it was their encouragement of rough tactics that egged the players on. An attack on the umpire often was a genuine treat for them. . ."

Indeed, the umpires frequently got the worst of it. In the early days of baseball, only one umpire was assigned to a contest and, because a lone ump could hardly be expected to cover every phase of the game, players would often cheat when the umpire wasn't looking. Every close call on the field occasioned an argument, and although the arbiters were empowered to fine or expel a player who "kicked," this solution did little to improve the problem. Club owners would simply pay the fines. And Heaven help the ump whose judgment calls had gone against the home team. He was often met outside the dressing room by a bloodthirsty mob, seething with vengeance.

The *Spalding Official Base Ball Guides* were full of tales during this time of how rowdyism was hurting the game. To combat this element, ballclubs hired police and provided seating for their aristocratic patrons away from the unwashed masses—the first luxury boxes. A few clubs even offered a special section behind the outfield where a prosperous gentleman and his wife (or lady friend) could enjoy the game from the privacy of his parked carriage. Policemen were detailed to prevent these well-to-do fans from being bothered.

Both on the field and off, the game was undergoing rapid and often mind-numbing changes. On the field, the manager of the Philadelphia Phillies, Harry Wright, instituted pre-game batting and fielding practice. This proved enormously popular with early arrivals to the park and, within a few years, all clubs were holding pre-game warmups. During the 1880s and into the early 1890s, the owners were constantly tinkering with the game, trying to find the correct balance between the offense and defense.

The Spalding was the official ball of both leagues. New balls were put in play only if the old one was lost. Because of their steep price tag of $1.50, baseballs hit into the crowd were always retrieved by the players or umpire. A ball hit out of the park was usually returned by a street urchin who was given a free ticket to the game in exchange. More often than not, the ball that started the game finished the game, prompting the *New York Clipper* to express astonishment that one National League contest had actually required the use of three baseballs.

There were no public-address systems, and no names or numbers on player uniforms. The Providence and Boston clubs sold season tickets for fifteen dollars, and Boston offered a season pass for women at a five-dollar discount.

Substitutions were allowed if a player was injured or became ill, but only when the opposing team agreed!

Umpires were completely on their own and could no longer ask the crowd or players in the game for advice on rulings as they had prior to 1880. On the suggestion of umpire Ben Young, the American Association introduced blue coats and caps and the arbiters were immediately and forever thereafter dubbed the "men in blue." The National League published a list of twenty-four umpires who had league blessing for the 1882 season. On the slate was Charles Briody, starting catcher for the Cleveland Spiders, nicknamed "Alderman" by his teammates in recognition of his fairness.

Umpires were subject to being expelled for the same offenses as players or managers, and Dick Higham of Troy, New York, became the first arbiter in baseball history to receive his ouster for dishonesty. Higham worked a string of games involving the Detroit Wolverines, and every borderline call went against the team. Detroit management, magnificently unconcerned over any fussy laws which forbade tampering with the U.S. mail, intercepted letters from Higham to gamblers and solved the rather simple code in which they were written. Three handwriting experts were called in, each one testifying that Higham had written the letters. Faced with the evidence, Higham confessed. He was expelled from baseball for life, but not without leaving a legacy: Dick Higham was the first umpire to use a mask to protect himself from foul balls.

A club could earn its ouster from the National League for selling beer or liquor, allowing open betting on the grounds, playing on Sunday, allowing non-League clubs to play games on League grounds without permission, or for failing to pay the visitor's share of the gate receipts promptly. National League clubs had already adopted the rule of reserving five players for the coming season. A nineteenth-century version of collusion, the reserve rule allowed clubs to retain the services of a player from year to year without fear of another club signing him. A released player was not free to play for another club for twenty days. A team could use a man who had not signed a League contract as long as he didn't appear in more than five games.

Club owners in the National League agreed not to hire drunk or insubordinate ballplayers whose names were entered on the blacklist. Al Spalding of the Chicago White Stockings even went so far as to make his players sign a pledge of abstinence, then hired private detectives to check on their movements. Spalding once rebuked King Kelly because a detective's report had stated the ballplayer was out to all hours after a game and had been seen drinking lemonade at three A.M. in Chicago's Tenderloin District. Kelly vehemently denied the report. "I never drank a lemonade at that hour in my life," he replied indignantly.

Spalding's Official Base Ball Guide of 1882 rationalized the blacklist in this manner:

> Intemperance had come to be an evil of increased growth in the professional ranks up to 1881, and something was required as an effectual check . . . and if the same determination is shown in adhering to it [the blacklist] that has been exhibited in connection with the penalty for dishonest play, it will not be long before intemperance will have been eliminated from the League ranks.

Alas, it was not to be. Dissipation was a subject on which the *Guide* would continue to harp for a decade.

In 1881, the distance to the mound was increased from forty-five feet to fifty feet. In 1892, a year in which batting averages hovered around .250, teams were still scoring about five runs a game and making an average of three errors a day. To aid the hitters, League owners (in the belief that a high-scoring game drew more fans into the park than a pitchers' duel) once again moved the mound back, this time to the modern figure of sixty feet, six inches. Prior to 1885, pitchers threw underhand. Prior to 1888, a batter could request a pitch to his liking, although the rulesmakers had limited his selection to either a high or low strike. By 1890, nearly all catchers had donned some kind of protective equipment, and most infielders were wearing small fielding gloves, something which had been looked upon a decade earlier as the mark of a sissy.

Not all of the owners' innovations were intelligent. In 1882, the National League color-coded its uniforms by position. Each player wore white pants and a white belt, but different colored jerseys according to the position he played. Pitchers wore light blue jerseys; catchers, scarlet; first basemen, scarlet and white; second basemen, orange and black; third basemen, gray and white; short-stops, maroon; left fielders, white; center fielders, red and white; right fielders, gray; and substitutes, either green or brown. Eventually it occurred to someone that a knowledgeable fan could probably tell a player's position by where he stood on the field, and the idea was scrapped.

And not all of the owners' innovations were well received. In 1883, Cincinnati Reds owner Aaron Stern decided to put numbers on his team's uniforms so the fans might more easily identify their favorite players. The Reds, annoyed and ashamed because everyone knew the uniforms of convicts also bore numbers, balked at the notion and the numbers were soon removed.

Off the field, Joseph Pulitzer instituted a separate sports department for the *New York World*. Baseball, as it turned out, sold newspapers. Imitators were rife. Among these were the *New York Clipper*, Francis Richter's Philadelphia publication, *Sporting Life*, and Alfred and Charles Spink's *The Sporting News*. Concession-aires like "Scorecard Harry" M. Stevens began offering the popular baseball meal of hot dogs and soda pop.

As the major leagues were changing, so was America, and no picture of nineteenth-century baseball can be complete without a glimpse at the era.

In a typical nineteenth-century small town, clothes were mostly homemade, cotton serving for summer attire and wool for winter. A Sunday dress or suit was often bought in a department store or ordered from a catalogue. Everyone wore black high-top shoes.

The showpiece of one's home was the parlor, what we call today the living room. With the shades drawn to prevent the sun from fading the carpet, the parlor was almost always a dark and dreary place. For children, the parlor took on an air of mystery and foreboding. Little ones rarely got a glimpse of the room except when visitors came to call and sit on the high, uncomfortable furniture. Children, of course, sat stiffly at attention and spoke only when spoken to.

The kitchen was often the gathering place for the family. Mother, or for those well-to-do families, the maid, would boil water for cooking or washing in big kettles on a black, wood-burning stove. Two or three times a week, a deliveryman brought huge cakes of ice for the wooden icebox. This barely kept the food from spoiling. There was a steel sink with a pump. Mother did her laundry in a tub and pressed everyone's clothing with a heavy iron she heated on the stove. On Saturday nights, everyone took a bath. (Most people believed the effluvia from one's own bath water caused disease, so bathing was not encouraged. It was acceptable, however, to bathe infants more often than once a week.) Some houses had electric lighting, but most had gas or kerosene lamps. The house itself was heated by cast-iron radiators connected by pipes to the boiler in the cellar. Coal or wood was used for fuel.

Children had many chores to do around the house and had little idle time. The lucky ones played baseball when they got the chance. Children of the rich engaged in more sedate pleasures, such as bicycling. Small-town schools were tiny buildings with all grades taught by the same teacher, in the same room. The boys tended the fire in the stove. Students would stand by their fixed desks and recite lessons and most did not plan on pursuing their education through college or even high school.

A person could mail a letter for two cents. It took six or seven days for the mail to cross the country. Although the telephone had been invented in 1876, few families had one in their homes. Those who did considered it a violation of their privacy when the thing rang. It was unthinkable for a person to speak to someone without benefit of a proper introduction. People had little knowledge of what was happening outside their own town and even less concern. Most families had enough to do providing food, shelter, and clothing for their own needs.

The country had a population of over fifty million in 1880, up from thirty-nine million a decade earlier. One-third of these were laborers and more than four million were industrial workers. During the twenty-year period commencing with the formation of the National Association of Professional Base Ball Players, the United States saw an increase in population to sixty-three million; in most years, from a third to one-half of the increase was due to immigration. Most people in the country were members of the vast middle class, and middle-class life-styles, through appliances and diversions, were undergoing transformation. Americans no longer endured their leisure time suffering the pangs of guilt that told them they were wasting time and that pleasure had no value. Americans wanted more time to themselves and they wanted more things to do in their off-hours. And there seemed to be no end of newfangled devices. In 1870, there were no telephones; in 1890, there were over a million and a half. In 1870, there was no electricity; in 1890, over forty percent of the nation was served by electric power. In 1870, there were no bicycles in America; by 1895, there were ten million.

The nineteenth century was an era of dreams, an age of incredible confidence and unlimited promise. America was growing in wealth, in industry, and in the value of real estate. The country was transforming from a rural-agricultural society to an urban-industrial one, and America was on the move, from East to West, from the farms to the cities. By 1890, only one of every three Americans lived in an urban area and roughly one of every four had moved west of the Mississippi.

"Get money—honestly if you can, but at any rate get money!" So said Henry George in *Progress and Poverty* and thereby summed up a nation's pursuit. Vast corporate bureaucracies were being forged and power was caught up in the hands of a few men as never before. At the outset of the Civil War, there were some three hundred millionaires in the country. In 1892, the *New York Tribune Monthly* listed 4,047 by name. And yet never was there such a startling gap between the rich and the poor. If American life was difficult on the farm, it was unbearable in the cities.

Take New York, for example. Then, as now, anything that life had to offer, good as well as bad, could be found in New York. Most immigrant families were destitute when they debarked from steerage at Castle Garden at the tip of lower Manhattan (replaced in 1892 by Ellis Island). Finding limited opportunities for work, these vast numbers of unskilled immigrants had nowhere else to go but the seaports and industrial cities where jobs were most readily available. Few prospered. Fewer still managed to rise in a society in which money alone influenced social standing. Most families persisted in poverty into the second and third generations and beyond. Many took what meager possessions they had and moved into the city's already overcrowded slums. Manhattan in the 1880s had close to a million and a half residents crammed onto the tiny island, roughly the same population as a century later, but *without* the accommodations of high-rise housing. Garbage pickup was inept and erratic. Street corners were piled high with kitchen slop. Industrial pollution was unimpeded. The city was overridden with crime and tuberculosis and cholera. Residents of the slum-ridden lower tip of Manhattan made up one-half of the city's population but accounted for seventy percent of the city's deaths.

In New York, the slums were the Lower East Side. Around the country, the locations and the names changed, but the living conditions never did. In St. Louis, the slums were Cross Keys and Clabber Alley. In Cleveland, the Flats. In Boston, the North End. Everywhere it was the same. City streets lacked adequate sanitation or drainage. Each horse—and everything in the city was transported by horse—produced between twenty and twenty-five pounds of manure a day, piles of which attracted swarms of flies and gave off a powerful stench. During dry spells, city traffic pounded the manure into a fine dust which blew up a person's nostrils and covered one's clothing and furniture. In these days before air conditioning, heavy clothing brought on thousands of sunstrokes. An 1896 heat wave in New York caused the deaths of some two thousand horses and three thousand human beings.

Inside the tenements, as many as eight persons shared a living room that was ten feet by twelve feet and a single bedroom six feet by eight feet. Ventilation shafts were frequently used as garbage chutes, sending an overpowering odor through the many window-less rooms. The stale air was further befouled by coal stoves which heated the rooms, and by plumbing pipes which emitted sewer gases. In 1880, four of every ten fires in New York were blamed on defective kerosene lamps. In 1882, only two percent of New York's residents had water connections. Those few renters who had water could rarely recognize it as such, polluted as it was. With no legislation governing tenants' rights, some landlords charged rents twenty-five to thirty-five percent higher per square foot than fashionable apartments in uptown New York.

Those who had jobs worked twelve-hour shifts, six days a week, for as little as $1.25 a day. Workmen's compensation was unknown and hundreds died in the factories each year from exposure to heat, dust, and noxious fumes. It was estimated that as many as a million workers were killed annually by job-related accidents. In the railroad industry alone, one of every three hundred workers died on the job, and one in every thirty was injured. Those who had the money to sue for damages were bullied or beaten by management thugs to drop the suit. The rare case which made it to court was invariably decided in favor of the employer.

The state of medicine as practiced in America in the nineteenth century was primitive and, sadly, often fraudulent. Diploma mills were rife. Diagnoses were based on guesswork and if the doctor was wrong, well, the patient died. Operations were performed in the most logical location, the person's home.

Eleven of every twelve families in America had an average yearly income of less than four hundred dollars. A pound of butter cost nineteen cents; bacon, ten cents; fowl, ten to fifteen cents; eggs, fifteen cents a dozen. Rents were eight to twelve dollars a month and living costs were consistently five to seven dollars a month per person. In New York's garment industry, a male worker was unable to support a family on his wages alone, so his wife and children were recruited as well. Women put in an eighty-four-hour work week in the sweatshops at an average of five cents an hour. There were no child labor laws and children, the cheapest of cheap labor, made up approximately one-fifth of the work force. Was it any wonder, then, that a man born in 1880 had an average life expectancy of just forty-three years?

Those who took the horse-drawn streetcar to work traveled on a rolling oven in summer and an icebox in winter. At rush hour, there were often as many as eighty people crammed into a car designed for thirty. Unwashed bodies, reeking of sweat, beer, and tobacco, only served to make the ride more unpleasant. Runaway cars, a common occurrence, terrorized passengers and pedestrians alike. The streetcars were a haven for pickpockets and criminals. When the electric trolley car was introduced in the late 1880s, it was heralded as cheap, fast transportation, but the trolley created constant traffic jams, seldom reached its designed speed of twenty-five miles per hour, and the five- or ten-cent fare was hardly considered a bargain for the average day laborer. The elevated railways were no better. These rattling, wood-burning locomotives belched smoke and cinders which fell on pedestrians below, and kept New Yorkers awake through the night with their incessant noise. With the train windows open, passengers found themselves covered with soot and grime at journey's end.

Until 1890, when reformer Jacob Riis published his shocking book, *How The Other Half Lives*, many people had no awareness of how horrible a life in the slums truly was. New York may have had its brilliant architecture, beautiful music, and elegant private clubs, but it also had thousands of homeless children who slept in the streets during winter and scavenged garbage for an evening meal.

Small wonder, then, that people needed something to take their minds away from the rigors of everyday life. And that something was baseball.

• 1 •

THE BIRTH OF COMPETITION

————————◆————————

From its beginnings in 1876, the National League had enjoyed a monopoly on major league baseball. But League magnates were dismayed to see the specter of competition rear its ugly head in the winter of 1881–1882. The Cincinnati club had been expelled from baseball in 1880 for selling liquor in its park, a violation of League rules, and Justus Thorner, president of the Reds, fumed over the action. The Queen City was a town which boasted twenty-seven breweries and distilleries and if Thorner wanted to hawk J.G. Sohn & Company's beer at the park, well, it seemed like that ought to be his own business. Cincinnati was out West, after all, and life was a little different. The city had a large German population and the Germans liked their beer, especially after spending a six-day week working at the odorous Fifth Street Market or in the coal mines. And they liked their baseball, too, although few professed to understand the game. But so what if they didn't? Thorner would rather have them at the park, buying his tickets and drinking his beer, than having a Sunday picnic or taking a carriage ride into Kentucky.

Of course, that wouldn't be possible in the National League, with its rules against liquor and Sunday baseball, so Thorner and

1882

The Changing Game

◆ ◆ ◆

• The "three-foot rule," which prevented a batter from running outside the baselines on the way to first base, went into effect.

• The penalty for a hurler intentionally hitting a batter with a pitch, a fine imposed and collected on the spot by the umpires, was eliminated. A baserunner could no longer be put out when returning to his base after the batter struck a foul that was not caught on the fly, provided he returned immediately.

• It required seven bad deliveries before a batter was given his base on balls, but with the pitching distance a mere fifty feet, it was nearly impossible to throw that many pitches wide of the plate.

• The best catcher's mask could be purchased at the finest sporting goods store for three dollars, the best catcher's mitt for $2.50, the best willow bat for thirty-five cents.

• Providence Grays outfielder Paul Hines amused the fans and earned some jeering from the opposition when he became the first major league ballplayer to wear sunglasses on the field.

sportswriter O.P. Caylor hit upon a plan. They'd form their own league. Not such a revolutionary idea; William Hulbert had done the same thing just six years earlier. So Thorner and delegates from Brooklyn, Louisville, Pittsburgh, and St. Louis met to form the American Association of Base Ball Clubs, copying the National League's constitution almost word for word. Brooklyn dropped out before the first pitch was thrown, but that franchise was replaced by Baltimore, and a Philadelphia entry threw its hat in the ring just before the season opened. It was no coincidence that four of the six clubs were based in cities which had been members of the original National League: St. Louis, Cincinnati, Philadelphia, and Louisville.

The American Association immediately earned the enmity of the senior circuit by introducing some changes. First of all, the Association would charge only half the League's admission fee to the park. Thorner and his associates reasoned that more people would come to the games if they could afford to, so the American Association dropped the price of a ticket from fifty cents to a quarter. The Monday-through-Saturday crowd was usually composed of well-to-do businessmen—ladies rarely attended the games and laborers were at work—so a suggestion that the Association allow Sunday baseball was immediately embraced. And the Association let its fans bring liquor to the park. If hard liquor wasn't to your liking, or if you left your booze at home, you could always buy a bottle of beer at the game. Of course, it wouldn't do for the players to drink; there would be stiff punishments for those miscreants. The upstart league also introduced a new wrinkle to sports: The team with the best winning percentage would win the pennant, not the club which won the most games.

The American Association was all set to go, but if it was to compete on an equal level with the National League, it needed some professional players. And what was the best source of major league ballplayers? The National League. Will White, who had been a star pitcher for Cincinnati just three years earlier, came over from Detroit and Charles "Pop" Snyder left Boston. Things didn't go as well as they hoped, but there would be more defections in 1883. The Association also culled a number of amateurs and hopefuls from the various high minor leagues throughout the country, among them Bid McPhee and a young Charlie Comiskey, already making a name for himself around first base.

But the American Association posed an even more significant threat to the National League. The six clubs of the Association had a greater population base than the League's eight clubs. This edge in potential fans would prove to be a fact in 1882, as every Association club turned a profit.

The game, as Sherlock Holmes would have said, was afoot.

◆ ◆ ◆

In the greatest stretch drive in the seven-year history of the National League, the White Stockings had won fifteen of their last sixteen games to capture a third straight pennant. Providence, piloted by the legendary Harry Wright, led the league as late as the middle of September, when the White Stockings swept a three-game series from the Grays in Chicago. The teams did not face each other in the remaining few days of the season, and the White Stockings rolled to the pennant by feasting on softer competition.

The Chicagos of 1882 were a powerful team led by first baseman and player-manager Adrian Constantine "Cap" Anson. In his long and distinguished career, Anson was the connecting link between the primitive and modern styles of baseball. When he first broke in with the National Association Athletics of Philadelphia, pitchers stood only forty-five feet from the plate and, for Anson's first fourteen years, no farther than fifty feet. Anson came to the White Stockings in 1876 and remained with the team for the next twenty-two years, all but two of those as the club's manager. More than any other pilot in the nineteenth century, Anson left his mark on the game of baseball. He was the first to coach from the sidelines, the first to coordinate infield and outfield defense, and the first to institute a pitching rotation, although his 1882 "staff" consisted only of Larry Corcoran and Fred Goldsmith. From 1879, his first year at the helm of the White Stockings, until 1892, the club never finished lower than fourth place. Anson's distaste for losing was legendary and he ruled the White Stockings with an iron fist, believing that any player was expendable. Years later, when club owner Al Spalding, eager to unload Mike Kelly, asked Anson if he could spare him, Anson replied, "Sure, spare anybody."

As a player, Anson was the dominant figure of his day. A line-drive contact hitter—he struck out only 294 times in 5,657 at bats—Anson was the first player ever to record three thousand hits. He was a free-swinger and firmly believed a bunt was a sissy thing to do. Anson's name was a household word in Chicago. Charlie Comiskey called him the greatest hitter who ever lived, and there is no doubt that Anson was one of the game's most heralded players. Only twice in his twenty-two-year career, at ages thirty-nine and forty, did the right-handed Anson fail to hit for a .300 average. Three times he led the league in batting average and he retired with a lifetime .334 mark. Never known for his speed, Anson was a big, heavy-set man for his day, standing six feet tall and weighing in at 202 pounds. (The average player stood five feet, nine inches, and weighed 165 pounds.) His ramrod posture and fearless, aggressive demeanor made him a formidable opponent and, while his outspoken ways may have endeared him to Chicago fans, they made him a pariah among National League umpires. Anson was tough, gruff, and abrupt. He said what he meant and he meant what he said and he made a number of bitter enemies in so doing. If Anson had ever stooped to answer his critics, he would have pointed out that he managed and played on five pennant winners while at Chicago and finished second as manager four other times. Anson was voted into the Hall of Fame in 1939.

At short for the White Stockings was Michael Joseph "King" Kelly, one of baseball's legendary players and a perennial fan favorite. It was a common enough occurrence for nineteenth-century ballplayers to be nicknamed King, but Kelly was the only man to whom the nickname stuck. An entire volume could be written about this mustachioed Irishman from Troy, New York. Tall, powerfully built, and very handsome, Kelly wore tailored suits, ascots, and black patent-leather shoes, and was often accompanied on his nightly jaunts by a Japanese valet and a black monkey. His popularity with the fans reached such astounding heights that a famous lithograph showing him sliding into second base replaced Custer's Last Stand behind the bars of many saloons. Of course, you didn't have to admire Mike Kelly in oils. If you celebrated a Chicago victory with a visit to a favorite saloon, the King himself might very well be standing right next to you, oiled up in a different manner.

Kelly had broken in on the sandlots of Paterson, New Jersey, where he played ball for three dollars a week. At the age of twenty-four, he was playing semi-pro ball in Ohio when he was spotted by the National League Cincinnati Reds. The Reds had picked him up for the 1878 season and he had hit for a modest .283 average. The King had spent two years with Cincinnati before moving to Anson's White Stockings where he had already established his reputation for being a hard drinker and big spender. Kelly perfected the hook, fallaway, and head-first slides and even inspired a song, "Slide, Kelly, Slide."

Rules were just something to be gotten around as far as Mike Kelly was concerned. He would frequently cut second base by ten or twenty feet going from first to third or cut third base by a similar distance racing from second to home. When the rules of baseball were changed to allow substitutions, Kelly once jumped off the bench, yelled, "Kelly now catching," and snared a pop fly near the foul line. If he was catching, Kelly would drop his mask where an unsuspecting baserunner was sure to trip over it or, having been hit by a pitch, would limp to first as if in great pain, then promptly steal second base. In the twelfth inning of a game against Boston, with dusk rapidly approaching, Kelly crashed against the outfield fence to apparently make a spectacular inning-ending catch. When a teammate asked how close the ball had come to being a home run, Kelly replied, "How the hell should I know? It went a mile over my head."

In his youth, Connie Mack played against Kelly and later paid high tribute when he compared the right-handed hitter to Ty Cobb. "Like Cobb," Mack said, "Kelly never gave an infielder or catcher anything more than the tip of his toe to tag. He had all of Ty's stuff—the fadeaway, fallaway, and hook slides, and a few so distinctively his own that others could not copy them." As late as 1921, more than a quarter of a century after Kelly had retired, Al Spink of *The Sporting News* was still calling him the greatest ballplayer who ever lived.

Kelly remained with Chicago throughout the 1886 season before Al Spalding, tired of his drunkenness, sold him to the Boston Beaneaters for the then-unheard-of-sum of ten thousand dollars. But in his last year with the White Stockings, Kelly was the team's leading right-handed hitter.

Boston management would also tire of Kelly's intemperance and send him to the Giants in 1893. Kelly was right at home in New York and shrewdly knew what effect good publicity had at contract time. He once held a newspaper aloft in the clubhouse and said to his teammates, "Why don't some of you dubs break a window and get yourselves talked about?" Sadly, Kelly never learned to change or even temper his habits. While with the Giants, he would be suspended for going on a drinking spree when he was supposed to be getting into playing shape at the Turkish baths.

Arguably the most versatile ballplayer of the nineteenth century, Kelly adopted a menacing batting stance in which he stood with his back square to the catcher. He would hold his bat low to the ground, raising it only when the pitcher went into his delivery. Kelly would retire following the 1893 season, having played 759 games in the outfield, 582 games behind the plate, 239 games on the infield, and having appeared as a pitcher twelve times. He stole fifty or more bases at least four times during his career—his high mark was 84 in 1887—and, after retiring from the major leagues in 1893, Kelly surfaced the next season as the player-manager for Allentown in the Pennsylvania State League where he hit .305 in seventy-five games. Later in the year, he went to Yonkers in the Eastern League and hit .377 in fifteen games. Following the season, Kelly contracted pneumonia and died just two months before his thirty-seventh birthday. It was said that over five thousand fans viewed his body as it lay in state in Boston's Elks Hall. Mike "King" Kelly, the game's first superstar, would be voted into the Hall of Fame in 1945.

At third base for the White Stockings was Ned Williamson. Defensively, Williamson was fast on his feet, covered a lot of ground at the hot corner, and was noted for making strong, accurate throws to first base. Because most first basemen, indeed, most fielders, used the "clamshell" catch (wrists together, palms up, fingers outstretched), the ability to deliver the ball waist-high was a sought-after commodity in 1880s baseball. At the plate, Williamson was a good, if not great, hitter, but he was a speedy baserunner, and if there was a better man at sliding in the league it could only have been Mike Kelly. Well read and articulate, unlike most of his contemporaries, Williamson possessed a kind and gentle disposition and was liked by nearly everyone. His only faults, and he shared these with many major leaguers of his era, were that he enjoyed high living and gambling.

The vaunted Chicago pitching staff was composed of Larry Corcoran and Fred Goldsmith, two of the best pitchers in the league. Although the rules restricted pitchers to underhand deliveries, Corcoran, a slight man, had a blazing fastball and excellent control, and had racked up two ten-game winning streaks during the season, including a no-hit victory against Worchester in September. (By 1884, Corcoran would pitch two more no-hitters, becoming the first man in the history of baseball to throw three.) He was ably supported by his teammates: In twenty-three of Corcoran's forty starts, the White Stockings scored six or more runs. The right-handed hurler closed out the season atop the National League in winning percentage (27-13, .675), and earned run average (1.95), and finished fifth in wins and strikeouts (170). His career winning percentage of .663 (177-90) is seventh on the all-time list.

Although the invention of the curveball is generally credited to William "Candy" Cummings (in about 1864), Fred Goldsmith always claimed it was his idea. Goldsmith said he threw a curve in the mid-1860s while a boy in New Haven, Connecticut. He taught the pitch to his teammate Corcoran and, in later years, to New York's Mickey Welch. In 1882, Goldsmith was second in the League to Corcoran in winning percentage (.636), third in victories (28), fourth in earned run average (2.42), and fifth in complete games (44).

The Cincinnati Reds of the newly formed American Association were decided underdogs in the series. Management had lured savvy catcher Charles "Pop" Snyder over from the Boston Red Caps by offering him the job of manager, and the crusty Snyder had pushed, prodded, and coerced his young charges into the first Association pennant. Snyder insisted on good work habits and was a stickler for the fundamentals. (He once fined first baseman Henry Luff five dollars for making a one-handed catch. Luff indignantly quit the team.) Cincinnati took over first place in the Association on June 13 and quickly made a shambles of the pennant race. Playing at a .700 clip for the remainder of the season, the Reds coasted to an 11½-game finish over the second-place Philadelphia Athletics.

The Reds were a weak-hit, good-field team, and they got solid defensive performances from Bid McPhee at second, Warren "Hick" Carpenter at third, and Joe Sommer in left. Each man led the American Association at his position in fielding percentage.

John Alexander "Bid" McPhee, along with Fred Pfeffer of the Chicago White Stockings, would become the finest fielding second baseman of the nineteenth century. The diminutive McPhee appeared in 2,138 major league baseball games, all with Cincinnati, and all but six at second base. He led his league eleven times in double plays turned, nine times in fielding average, and was the only second sacker ever to top five hundred putouts in a single season. In 1886, McPhee put together 529 putouts and 464 assists for a total of 993 chances, a stratospheric number usually reserved for first basemen. Among second basemen, only Frank Frisch has had more chances in a single season and only Eddie Collins leads McPhee in career putouts and total chances. (Both Frisch and Collins, modern-day ballplayers, are in the Hall of Fame. McPhee is not.)

McPhee's accomplishments were all the more incredible when one considers that he played all but four years barehanded. In 1896, the Cincinnati second baseman opened the season with a broken finger and was forced to wear a padded glove to prevent injuring himself further. The results were nothing short of astonishing, in nineteenth-century terms. Using the padded glove, McPhee's errors dropped from thirty-four to fifteen, lowest in the league. His fielding average shot up to .978, a new major league record which eclipsed the old mark for second basemen by a full ten points. It would remain a major league standard for the next twenty-three years.

On the field or off, McPhee was a gentleman. He commanded the respect of his teammates, opposing players, and the fans. And how did the umpires feel about him? In his eighteen-year career, McPhee was never once ejected from a ballgame, a claim few nineteenth-century players could make.

Warren Carpenter, nicknamed "Old Hickory," or just "Hick" for short, was that rarest of athletes, a left-handed third baseman. Baseball historian Lee Allen once called Carpenter the "most skillful of the lefthanded infielders of the last century" and this was not faint praise. The statistics bear Allen out. In 1882, Carpenter was second among Association third basemen in assists (167 to Jack Gleason of St. Louis with 168), and, despite making sixty errors, led the Association in fielding average. And Carpenter wasn't just filling in at third either. In a major league career spanning twelve years and 1,118 games, Old Hickory took his post at the hot corner, 1,059 times.

Joe Sommer played left field for the Reds, one of two positions (the other is right field) traditionally reserved for the weakest fielding members of any ball club. But Joe Sommer was no lightweight with the glove. In 1882, he was one of the best defensive outfielders in the game, leading all Association left fielders in putouts and fielding percentage by a wide margin. Known for his accurate throws, Sommer had an arm like a cannon. In 1887, while playing for the Baltimore Orioles, the left fielder would become the only outfielder in history to register three assists in one inning, all three on throws to home plate. It was Sommer's defensive skills that kept him in the game for twelve years. Offensively, he was a mediocre baserunner and a middling hitter with little extra-base power.

Player-manager Pop Snyder handled the duties behind the plate and, along with pitcher Will White, formed one of the best fielding batteries of the day. Snyder caught seventy of his team's eighty games, quite an accomplishment at a time when catchers played without gloves or any protective equipment, although

Snyder, like most catchers, played some fifteen to fifty feet behind the plate and caught the ball on the bounce. Despite taking this precaution, Snyder had a hand injury and would not appear in the World Series.

It was a good thing the Reds could field because they certainly weren't renowned for their hitting. The only regular who managed a .300 batting average was Carpenter, whose .342 mark was second in the Association only to Pete Browning's .382. The rest of the club featured first baseman Dan Stearns (.257), McPhee (.228), shortstop Chick Fulmer (.281), Snyder (.291), and outfielders Jimmy Macullar (.234) and Harry Wheeler (.250).

The Reds' leading moundsman was the deeply religious Will White, brother of Jim "Deacon" White, who was himself one of the best players in the nineteenth century. Will was an anomaly, a switch-hitting pitcher, and he and brother Jim had formed baseball's first brother battery when Jim had played with Cincinnati in the National League from 1878–1880. Will broke another mold when he became the first bespectacled player in the National League back in 1877, the year he broke in with the Boston Red Caps. White started two of every three games in 1882 and, with a record of 40-12, led the Association in victories, winning percentage (.769), complete games (52), innings pitched (480), and shutouts (8). He was second in games pitched (54), and fourth in earned run average (1.54) and strikeouts (122). White's three best years were 1882–84, when he compiled a 117-52 record with 168 complete games in 171 starts. He finished his career with a lifetime 229-166 mark and today stands tenth on the all-time earned run average list with a mark of 2.28.

Before the World Series could be played, the Reds had to circumvent a major obstacle. American Association president H.D. "Denny" McKnight had forbade play between all Association teams and the National League because he shared the opinion of many team owners that ballplayers did not take exhibition games seriously and this only led to the throwing of games, or "hippodroming." But Cincinnati management, eager for the chance to make some post-season money at the gate, got around the rule, or so it thought, by releasing the players, then re-signing them under special contracts.

In these pre-commissioner days, arrangements for the World Series—number of games, game sites, prize money, and even umpires—were decided upon by the participants.

Because there had been no Cincinnati entry in the National League since 1880, the White Stockings, as a team, had not been to the Queen City in two years. Prior to the Series, Chicago had taken two of three exhibition contests from the New York Metropolitans at the Polo Grounds and, on the evening of October 4, took the Erie train from New York to Cincinnati. The club stayed at the Grand Hotel, located a few minutes from the park.

For Cincinnati fans this was to be a battle of good vs. evil. It was Cincinnati against Chicago, Ohio against Illinois, and the American Association against the National League. Anson and Kelly were the two most popular players in Chicago and everybody knew about *them*. One was a hothead and the other cheated. Most Cincinnatians felt they didn't deserve to be on the same field with the well-mannered Bid McPhee and Will White, a solid church-going man. The championship was greatly ballyhooed in Cincinnati and largely ignored in Chicago, where the Red Stockings were viewed as little more than a minor league team.

On October 6, the White Stockings arrived at Bank Street Grounds for pre-game practice before the ticket office opened at 2:00. Despite the inflated prices of thirty-five and fifty cents, some 2,700 people turned out for the game. Bank Street Grounds was wooden and, like nearly all parks of the era, had no seating in the outfield area. Located at the foot of Bank Street, close to the downtown business district, the ballpark was bounded on the north by Cross Street, on the west by Duck Street, and on the east by Western Avenue. Three blocks north, on Western Street, was the future site of Crosley Field, the home of the Cincinnati Reds from 1912 to 1970. Bank Street Grounds was noted for flooding out during the spring rains each year.

While the Reds took infield practice, Cap Anson coldly regarded the vastly inferior club with his clear blue eyes. He could see why this team was the best in the American Association, but clearly they were no match for his boys. Having piloted the White Stockings to three straight pennants in the National League, Anson was nothing if not arrogant.

Pop Snyder, Anson's counterpart, held a different slant on things. Well aware the visiting White Stockings held his team in contempt, Snyder reasoned that the Reds had nothing to lose and everything to gain with a victory. Precisely at 3:00, Cap Anson, strutting and swaggering, led his team onto the field. Neither Anson nor Snyder spoke to each other as umpire Charles M. Smith flipped a twenty-dollar gold coin to determine who batted first. Snyder called the toss correctly and elected to put his team into the field. His only wish was that he could take his usual place behind the plate, but the hand injury kept him out of action. Phil "Grand-mother" Powers would have to substitute, and that worried Snyder. Powers had worked the plate only ten times all year and had not caught White at all.

There weren't many fans at the Bank Street Grounds who, if they were honest, thought the Reds had much of a chance to win either game. But by the time the sixth inning rolled around, most of these doubting Thomases had changed their minds.

White had put the Chicagos down in order in the first on three harmless fly balls and, with two out in the bottom of the inning, Cincinnati fans got their first thrill when Hick Carpenter hit an easy grounder and Fred Goldsmith muffed the chance by throwing low to Anson at first. Perhaps the White Stockings weren't invincible after all. In the Chicago fourth, Abner Dalrymple singled and decided to test Phil Powers's arm by stealing. But Powers's throw to second was on the money and all Dalrymple could do was walk off the field, his head down. Ned Williamson's triple moments later would have scored the first run of the game.

The Reds mounted a threat in the bottom of the same inning when Carpenter singled and went to second on Dan Stearn's groundout. Chick Fulmer lined a single to left and Carpenter had to hold up at third but the Cincinnati fans were immediately on their feet, cheering for the Reds to bring home the first run. Fulmer lit out to steal and Silver Flint, the Chicago catcher, heaved the ball to second. Tom Burns took the throw but instead of stooping to tag Fulmer, fired the ball to Ned Williamson at third. Carpenter was caught off base and run down and, when McPhee grounded out a moment later, the scoring threat was ended.

White retired the White Stockings in the fifth and sixth and Cincinnati's Harry Wheeler led off the bottom of the sixth for the Reds by popping out to left. But Carpenter singled to center and Stearns followed with a blow to right to give the Reds another first-and-third opportunity. When Chick Fulmer laced one of Goldsmith's next deliveries into center field, just in front of George Gore's glove, the Reds had a 1-0 lead and the noise of applause and stamping feet filled the ballpark. The popular Bid McPhee was next to the plate. He stroked a line drive into the power alley in right-center and by the time Hugh Nicol could get the ball back to the infield, McPhee was standing on third base and the Reds had a three-run lead. Everyone in the park could tell that Goldsmith was rattled and he proved it a moment later when he wild-pitched McPhee home. McPhee accepted his teammates' congratulations and resumed his seat on the players' bench.

Chicago put men on base in the seventh and eighth but failed to score as White bore down. Cincinnati went out one-two-three in the bottom of the eighth and the stage was set for the final frame. The fans were on their feet as White worked to Dalrymple, leading off. The Chicago left fielder grounded up the middle and White got his glove on the ball, but just enough to deflect it so Fulmer was unable to make a play. George Gore lifted a high fly toward right field and Harry Wheeler, after a long run, caught the ball in foul territory for the first out of the inning. But the White Stockings seemed determined to avoid a shutout. Ned Williamson lined a White delivery into right-center between Wheeler and Jimmy Macullar, good for a double. Dalrymple danced off third and Williamson off second as Cap Anson strode to the plate. A natural showman, Anson took several practice swings before assuming his wide-open stance in the batter's box, nearly facing the pitcher. This was the moment White and every baseball fan in Cincinnati had been waiting for. Anson lifted a fly ball into center field and, at the crack of the bat, Dalrymple returned to third to tag up. When Macullar pulled the ball into his chest, Dalrymple streaked for home. The ball reached the plate a split second before Dalrymple did and Powers applied a hard tag for the final out. It took the spectators a moment to realize the game was over and then they burst into one long protracted cheer which seemed to come from everywhere at once. The supermen from Chicago had been defeated and by a 4-0 "Chicago", or shutout, at that! The irony.

Will White finished with an eight-hit shutout. He struck out two and, save for third baseman Ned Williamson who tripled in the fourth and doubled in the ninth, had little trouble with the White Stockings.

Exultant, the *Cincinnati Enquirer* engaged in a bit of good-natured fun with the White Stockings. In a rather splendid example of the florid sportswriting style of the nineteenth century, the paper had this to say about the game:

> Leonidas and his Spartan band treated the Persians many, many years ago at Thermopylae to a terrible surprise. Yesterday history

was repeated, only that it was Will White and his Lilliputian crew
that astonished the Chicagos, the champions of the League, the
great, high-toned and only moral baseball show. . . . 'Twere not,
however, in the minds of the powerful leaders of the League to
entertain for a moment a belief that His Bigness, Sir Gulliver
Anson and colleagues would ever be harried in their efforts to
triumph; but a defeat, Merciful Powers, the thought of such a
visitation was as much undreamed-of as that each member of the
team was to be tendered the Gubernatorial nomination of Illinois.
Subjugation was not so distasteful to the bow-legged—should say,
white-limbed—champions. But ah! to be conquered by an
American nine—arrah musha magrah!

To be sure, arrah musha magrah!

Following such a stirring victory, a standing-room-only crowd
of 3,500 (except for the game on Independence Day, the largest
crowd of the season in Cincinnati), turned out the next day to watch
White work again. Anson was displeased with Goldsmith's effort
the day before and selected Larry Corcoran to pitch the second
game. Cincinnati won the toss and Snyder again elected to start the
game in the field. White appeared weary from working a full nine
innings twenty-four hours earlier, but he retired Dalrymple on a
fly ball to begin the first. Gore grounded to Carpenter and the
usually reliable third baseman fumbled the ball for an error. With
Williamson at the plate, Anson unveiled a new offensive weapon,
the hit-and-run. It worked perfectly. Gore ran for second and Fulmer and McPhee, seeing what they believed was an attempted steal,
closed on the bag. Williamson pushed a safe hit into the hole
McPhee had just vacated and Gore raced for third base. The Reds
had never seen anything like this in the American Association. (The
hit-and-run has variously been attributed to the Boston Beaneaters
and, more popularly, the Baltimore Orioles, but it is clear Cap Anson knew a thing or two about "inside baseball" as early as 1882.)
Right fielder Harry Wheeler, showing off his strong arm, unleashed
a wild throw over Carpenter's head and Gore trotted home with the
game's first run. Williamson pulled into third. Now Cap Anson
came to the plate, eager to atone for his game-ending fly ball of
the prior day. After taking several mighty cuts in the air, Anson
grounded to short. The ball was hit slowly enough to score
Williamson and the Chicagos had a 2-0 lead.

That, as it turned out, was the game. White surrendered only
three more hits in the game and only one of those men, Williamson,

got as far as second base. But for Wheeler's error, White might have shut out the feared White Stockings on two successive days. Chicago's Larry Corcoran pitched a masterful three-hit shutout (all singles) struck out six, and walked one. Carpenter drew a base on balls in the first but was thrown out stealing. Phil Powers singled in the third but was stranded on first. Dan Stearns singled in the fourth but was thrown out when he tried to stretch his hit into a double. And Stearns singled again in the seventh but was also stranded at first.

According to the *Cincinnati Commercial*, umpire Smith worked the games "in splendid style."

By this time, American Association president Denny McKnight had learned of the games and telegraphed Cincinnati, threatening the Reds with expulsion if they continued play. Cincinnati would later be fined a hundred dollars and reprimanded for playing the two games, but remained in the Association until rejoining the National League fold in 1890. The Series ended the 1882 baseball season for the Reds and the ballplayers returned to their homes. Two months later at New York's Hotel Victoria, the leagues signed the National Agreement, which called for an eleven-player reserve limit, territorial rights, and minimum player salaries of one thousand dollars. At least, for the time being, an uneasy truce existed in the baseball world.

Most baseball historians downplay the importance of this first meeting of rival leagues. That does not seem right but, in fairness, to call these two contests the first World Series is more a matter of opinion than fact. The games were of considerable import to the city of Cincinnati, to the Reds and, by implication, to the American Association, however it may have discouraged the meeting officially. But the White Stockings entered the Series feeling the contests were nothing more than mere games of exhibition. After the first day, however, Cap Anson and his men changed their tune. To be upstaged by the Reds would be nothing short of a complete disgrace. In any event, the 1882 games between Cincinnati and Chicago were the first time in baseball history two pennant-winning clubs from two different major league organizations met in a post-season series to determine the championship of the world.

Though the aborted two-game series had been inconclusive, baseball's most colorful and enduring tradition had begun.

GAME ONE—October 6, 1882, at Bank Street Grounds, Cincinnati

CHICAGO	AB	R	H	PO	A	E	CINCINNATI	AB	R	H	PO	A	E
Dalrymple, lf	4	0	2	4	0	0	Sommer, lf	4	0	0	4	0	0
Gore, cf	4	0	1	0	0	0	Wheeler, rf	4	0	0	4	0	0
Williamson, 3b	4	0	2	1	2	0	Carpenter, 3b	4	1	2	2	0	0
Anson, 1b	4	0	1	12	1	0	Stearns, 1b	4	1	1	5	0	1
Burns, 2b	3	0	0	2	5	0	Fulmer, ss	4	1	2	1	4	0
Goldsmith, rf	3	0	1	1	8	1	McPhee, 2b	4	1	3	4	2	0
Corcoran, p	3	0	0	0	0	1	Macullar, cf	3	0	1	2	1	1
Nichol, ss	3	0	0	1	0	0	Powers, c	3	0	0	5	3	0
Flint, c	3	0	1	3	2	0	White, p	3	0	2	0	4	0
	31	0	8	24	18	2		33	4	11	27	14	1

```
CHI    0 0 0   0 0 0   0 0 0  -  0
CIN    0 0 0   0 0 0   4 0 0  -  4
```

Earned runs: CIN 3.   D: Williamson.   T: Williamson, McPhee.   DP: CIN.   Struck out: by White 2; by Corcoran 4.   LOB: CHI 3, CIN 4.   WP: White, Goldsmith,   Balk: Goldsmith.   PB: Flint.   Umpire: C.M. Smith.   Time—1:55.   Att: 2,700.

GAME TWO—October 7, 1882, at Bank Street Grounds, Cincinnati

CHICAGO	AB	R	H	PO	A	E	CINCINNATI	AB	R	H	PO	A	E
Dalrymple, lf	4	0	1	0	1	0	Sommer, lf	4	0	0	4	0	0
Gore, cf	4	1	0	1	0	0	Wheeler, rf	4	0	0	2	0	1
Williamson, 3b	4	1	2	1	3	0	Carpenter, 3b	2	0	0	3	1	1
Anson, 1b	3	0	1	13	0	0	Stearns, 1b	3	0	2	7	0	0
Burns, 2b	3	0	0	2	4	0	Fulmer, ss	3	0	0	0	3	0
Goldsmith, rf	3	0	0	1	0	0	McPhee, 2b	3	0	0	3	1	0
Corcoran, p	3	0	0	0	12	0	Macullar, cf	3	0	0	1	1	0
Nichol, ss	3	0	0	0	1	0	Powers, c	3	0	1	7	0	1
Flint, c	3	0	0	9	1	0	White, p	3	0	0	0	9	0
	30	2	4	27	22	0		28	0	3	27	15	3

```
CHI    2 0 0   0 0 0   0 0 0 - 2
CIN    0 0 0   0 0 0   0 0 0 - 0
```

Earned runs: None.   DP: CIN.   LOB: CIN 2, CHI 1.   Struck out: by White 2; by Corcoran 6.   BB: White 1.   Umpire: C.M. Smith.   Time—1:40.   Att: 3,500.

• 2 •

HOSS RADBOURN
AND THE
PROVIDENCE GRAYS

---◆---

Charles Gardner "Old Hoss" Radbourn wasn't just the ace of the Providence pitching staff, he *was* the pitching staff. The only man to win sixty games in a major league season was a less-than-imposing figure. Standing on the small side, at five feet, nine inches, Radbourn weighed only one hundred sixty-eight pounds. In these early days before the advent of sports medicine, Radbourn treated his pitching arm with hot towels, by flipping an iron ball underhand, and by throwing a baseball the pitching distance several times before the game started. In these pre-slugger days, Radbourn did not have to worry about some latter-day Bucky Dent beating him with a late-inning home run, and would pace himself through the game. As teammate Paul Hines later would say, "Rad had plenty of speed, but he never let it loose until it was absolutely necessary. That's why his arm lasted for so many years." Hoss batted from the left side but threw right-handed, and played the outfield, with occasional starts on the infield when not pitching.

A graduate of Illinois Wesleyan, Hoss had played the infield professionally for three years before he broke in as an outfielder and second baseman with Buffalo in 1880. In his last year in the minors, Radbourn hit .387 with Dubuque in the Northwestern

1884

The Changing Game

◆ ◆ ◆

- Pitchers were now allowed to throw overhand.

- An error was charged to the pitcher for a walk, balk, wild pitch, or hit batsman, and the same logic put an error in the catcher's column for a passed ball. A foul ball caught on one bounce was no longer an out.

- Umpires were now empowered to fine players five dollars on the spot for "kicking," although team captains were exempt from such a fine.

- There were five new teams in the American Association. The New York Metropolitans, often called the Mets, became the first professional team to play its home games in the city of New York. Also joining the Association were the Brooklyn Trolley Dodgers, Toledo Blue Stockings, Indianapolis Blues, and the Washington Nationals.

- The term "fan" was coined by Browns manager Ted Sullivan (or in another version of the story, by team owner Chris Von Der Ahe), who referred to club followers as "fanatics." The rest of the country still commonly called spectators "kranks."

League. Providence manager Jim Bullock converted him into a full-time pitcher in 1881.

Due largely to Radbourn and his screwball, Providence's team ERA was 1.59 in 1884, almost half the league average of 2.98, and nearly a full run lower than second-place Boston's 2.47. Radbourn had started or relieved in fifty of the Grays' fifty-eight victories in 1883, and manager Frank Bancroft planned to spell him more frequently with newcomer Charlie Sweeney during the 1884 season. This did not sit well with the veteran Radbourn, who viewed the twenty-one-year-old youngster more as a threat than a helpmate, and the two quickly became fierce rivals. Sweeney struck out nineteen batters in a game against the Boston Beaneaters on June 7 and when Hugh "One Arm" Daily duplicated the feat a month later, Radbourn taunted Sweeney, saying, "What you did, any pitcher with one arm can do."

The Grays lost their season opener to Cleveland, then reeled off seventeen victories in their next eighteen games. By the end of June, the National League pennant race had become a two-team competition between the Grays and the Beaneaters.

By mid-July Charlie Sweeney had developed arm trouble and Radbourn was doing most of the pitching. On July 16, following a 5-2 Providence loss to the Beaneaters, Radbourn was suspended by club management for lackadaisical play and "insubordination." (Insubordination was a euphemism oft-used for drunkenness.) Radbourn's record at this point of the season was 24-8, but half his losses had come in the last two weeks.

Four days after Radbourn's suspension, Sweeney, with a record of 17-8, got drunk and failed to report for practice. When he finally did appear, just a few minutes before game time with the Philadelphia Phillies, manager Frank Bancroft installed rookie pitcher Joe "Cyclone" Miller in right field, just in case. Sweeney had a 6-2 lead when Bancroft decided to spell him with Miller. Sweeney refused. Bancroft threatened him with suspension and Sweeney said that was fine with him, he could make more money elsewhere. The Grays played the final two innings with only eight men on the field and lost the game when the Phillies scored eight unearned runs in the ninth. Sweeney was expelled from the club and joined St. Louis of the Union Association. (Sweeney compiled a 24-7 record for St. Louis, but was never much of a pitcher thereafter; in 1887, at the age of twenty-four, his career was over. Seven years later, he killed a man in a San Francisco saloon and, although protesting he acted out of self-defense, the former pitcher was sentenced to ten years for manslaughter. He was released shortly before completing his sentence and died of tuberculosis on April 4, 1902, just nine days short of his thirty-ninth birthday.)

Manager Bancroft—his best pitcher on suspension and his second best expelled from the club—correctly reasoned that he was in big trouble. All he had left was Cyclone Miller, an untested rookie. So Radbourn was reinstated, given a raise for the extra duty he was about to put in, and promised his release at the end of the season if he pitched every game from there on. Hoss did almost exactly that, pitching in thirty-five of the next thirty-seven games and playing in the outfield for the other two.

Providence closed out August with fifteen straight wins and opened September with five more to run up a 20-game winning streak. Radbourn had won eighteen times in that stretch. On September 5, in Cleveland, Radbourn sat out a game for the first time since July 23. With the pennant virtually assured, Radbourn worked in only five of the last twelve games of the season as Bancroft rested him in preparation for the World Series. On October 4, the Grays clinched the pennant with a 4-1 win over Buffalo. On the 15th, Radbourn captured his sixtieth victory, blanking the Philadelphia Phillies before an admiring home crowd, 8-0. It was his eleventh shutout of the year, a season for which he was paid the princely sum of three thousand dollars.

During the regular season, New York Metropolitans Manager Jim Mutrie had challenged the Providence Grays to an exhibition game to be played August 15.*

When the day of the game arrived, the Grays were in New York all right, but playing the Gothams, not the Mets, having declined the invitation. In September, when it was apparent that Providence and New York would win their respective pennants, Mutrie wired manager Frank Bancroft and challenged the Grays to a two-game, post-season championship, one game in New York and one in Providence. But Bancroft again declined. Riled, Mutrie took his case to the New York newspapers, popping off that the Grays were afraid of American Association competition, afraid of his Mets. Bancroft finally agreed to a three-game series to be played at the enemy Polo Grounds and under Association rules. The two

---

* There had been no 1883 World Series, although the American Association champion Philadelphia Athletics were scheduled to meet the National League's Boston Beaneaters late in October. But the A's lost seven of their first eight post-season exhibition contests and Philadelphia manager Lew Simmons politely cancelled the Series, no doubt saving his boys further embarrassment.

clubs put up a thousand-dollar purse which was held by Alfred Wright, baseball editor of the *New York Clipper*. (Although they had drawn well at the gate, the victorious St. Louis Maroons of the newly formed Union Association were icily ignored for post-season consideration.)

The Providence Grays were not a particularly good hitting team. They ranked fifth in batting and slugging average and had only one .300 hitter—Paul Hines at .302. But a veteran lineup and good pitching carried the team to the 1884 World Series. The club began the year with Paul Revere Radford, a promising second-year man, replacing John Cassidy in right field. Center fielder Hines, perhaps the first deaf man to play in the major leagues, had been with the team since its entry into the National League in 1878 and would be the only member of the Grays to play for Providence in all eight years of its existence. Second baseman Jack Farrell and Joe Start joined the club in 1879.

Joe Start was a veteran of the old National Association and already thirty-six years old when he came over from the White Stockings but, next to Hines, he was the club's most consistent hitter. Nicknamed "Old Reliable" for his fielding ability, Start began his professional career with the amateur Enterprise Club of New York in 1860. He turned professional sometime around 1867 and, when he retired following the 1886 season, had been in the game for twenty-seven years, an unusually long career for a nineteenth-century ballplayer. Start bore a remarkable resemblance to the present-day actor Robert Conrad. In 1884, he was captain of the Providence team.

Radbourn and catcher Barney Gilligan were in their fourth year with the Grays and Gilligan shared his duties behind the plate at various times during the year with three other catchers—Miah Murray, Charlie Bassett, and Sandy Nava. Nava described himself as a Spaniard and, in the quaint manner of the day, was frequently accused of being black because of his dark complexion. At third was Jeremiah "Jerry" Denny, also in his fourth year with the club. Denny was a slick-fielding third baseman with good range and an annoying habit of throwing the ball away on easy plays.

The Grays' shortstop was Arthur Irwin. Irwin is credited by some baseball historians with introducing the fielder's glove. Prior to 1885, an occasional infielder had worn protection of some kind, almost always a skintight and flesh-colored glove so the fans wouldn't see how unmanly he was. To protect a broken finger,

Irwin devised a padded glove which he continued to use long after his digit had healed, much to the surprise of his teammates and the other real men around the league. But then, Art Irwin was a man of many surprises. In July 1921, while journeying by ship from New York to Boston, Irwin would somehow fall overboard and drown. A few weeks following his death, it was discovered that the former shortstop had a wife and children in both cities. He had kept this charade alive for over thirty years.

The New York Metropolitans, on the other hand, were a very good offensive team. During the 1884 season, the Mets scored nine or more runs thirty-four times, although only two regulars hit for a .300 average—Dave Orr (.354) and Dude Esterbrook (.314). James "Chief" Roseman just missed the mark at .298.

Dave Orr, the Mets' first baseman, was the first player to accumulate three hundred total bases in a single season and one of only four nineteenth-century hitters to retire with a slugging average of over .500. The others are Dan Brouthers, Ed Delahanty, and Sam Thompson. Brouthers, Delahanty, and Thompson are in the Hall of Fame while Orr has been overlooked. A huge man at five feet, eleven inches, and two-hundred fifty pounds, Orr was still at the top of his game in 1890 when he suffered a stroke and was partially paralyzed during an exhibition game at Renova, Pennsylvania. Fearing his playing days were over at the age of thirty-one, Orr went to Hot Springs, Arkansas, in 1891 and attempted a comeback, but it was not to be. The stroke had ended his major league career after only eight years. Following his retirement, Orr would labor as a stonecutter, a stagehand, and, when Ebbets Field was being built, he was named the park's caretaker. When the Brooklyn Feds opened their season in 1914, Orr was in charge of the press box. The following summer, he died of heart disease.

The rest of the Mets' infield featured John "Dasher" Troy at second, Thomas "Dude" Esterbrook at third, and John "Candy" Nelson at short. These three men would win no Gold Gloves for their fielding ability. Behind the plate was the weak-hitting Bill Holbert, a fair catcher with a strong arm. Holbert loved to gun runners down trying to steal and had the assists to prove it. Unfortunately, his right arm was often as inaccurate as it was strong as Holbert topped all National League catchers in errors for the year.

The Mets had a two-man pitching staff, Tim Keefe and Jack Lynch. Keefe, with a record of 37-17, was the superior pitcher but Lynch had a slight edge in 1884 with a 37-14 mark.

Jack Lynch began his major league career with Buffalo in 1881 and came to the Mets in 1883. After a mediocre record of 13-15 in 1883, Lynch burst from the gate in 1884, winning fourteen consecutive games in one stretch. He finished the season atop the Association in winning percentage (.725) and tied for second in victories with his teammate.

Timothy John Keefe, nicknamed "Sir Timothy" by his teammates for his aristocratic ways, was the son of Irish immigrants. Keefe had pitched for Utica, New Bedford, and Albany in the National Association before coming to Troy in 1880. The Trojans never finished above .500 in Keefe's three years with the team and his record of 42-59 reflects that fact. Keefe was transferred to New York in 1883 and responded with the first of six consecutive seasons in which he would win thirty or more games. Sir Timothy was a man who finished what he started: From 1880 through 1888, he started 444 games and completed all but eight. In four of those nine years, Keefe finished every game he started. The big right-hander was a very sensitive man and would miss several weeks of the 1887 season because of a nervous breakdown suffered after beaning Jack Burdock on the temple. When Keefe retired following the 1893 season, only Pud Galvin had more victories. Today, he stands eighth on the all-time victory list with 344 wins, and third in complete games with 558. He was elected to the Hall of Fame in 1964.

Mutrie, the Metropolitans' manager, had never appeared in a major league baseball game. Mutrie had arrived in New York in the summer of 1880 and, with the backing of John B. Day, leased the Polo Grounds in Manhattan and formed the minor league New York Metropolitans. In late October of 1882, the Mets were granted membership in the American Association, replacing the defunct Troy Trojans. The Mets had finished fourth in their Association debut but gave the city of New York its first pennant in 1884. Mutrie would go on in later years to lead the New York Giants to National League championships in 1888 and 1889, thus becoming the first pilot ever to win pennants in two leagues. His lifetime winning percentage of .611 is exceeded only by Joe McCarthy's .614. Popular with his players, Mutrie was always dressed to the nines in gloves, spats, and a black silk top hat as he managed his club from the players' bench. On special occasions, Mutrie would appear at the ballpark decked out in a formal black coat and cravat, his saber mustache waxed to a fare-thee-well.

The temperature was in the low fifties and a cold wind blew through the Polo Grounds as 2,500 spectators turned out for Game One on Thursday, October 23, 1884. As an added inducement for coming to the park, each of the patrons was given a steel engraving of all the prominent players, donated by Mr. Pierre Lorillard. This made up, in part, for the victory parade which had been cancelled because of rain the night before.

The Mets played on the west diamond (sometimes called Metropolitan Stadium) at the Polo Grounds, an enormous wooden ballpark featuring two fields, located just north of Central Park. The National League Giants (then called the Gothams) played on the more fashionable east diamond, with a green field and a fine grandstand.

The Polo Grounds had opened for baseball on September 29, 1880, but was not occupied by a major league team until the Mets played their first game here on May 12, 1883. At first there was no fence between the fields but later a short fence in front of the left-field bleachers was erected and a canvas barrier was added, separating the two diamonds. The Mets' side was perhaps the worst major league ballpark in the history of the game. The ground was uneven and stadium planners had used garbage as a landfill, prompting pitcher Jack Lynch's comment that "a player may . . . go down for a grounder and come up with six months of malaria." Despite lower ticket prices and the availability of beer at the park, Association fans stayed away in droves and, even though they won the pennant, the Metropolitans lost close to eight thousand dollars in 1884.

Early arrivals at the park could watch Hoss Radbourn going through his usual warmup exercises, first lobbing the ball twenty feet away from the plate and eventually working up to soft throws from short center field. A few pitches from the mound and he was ready to go.

Umpire John Kelly called for play to begin at 3:00. Kelly had not yet earned his nickname of "Honest John," but would do so in 1889 when he supposedly turned down ten thousand dollars to shade decisions for the Boston Beaneaters. Kelly was a colorful character as, apparently, many Irishmen of the day were. In 1884, he umpired games in all three leagues. Two years later, he would be the "referee" (a kind of tie-breaking umpire) in one of the World Series games between the St. Louis Browns and Chicago White Stockings—about as high an honor as could be accorded an umpire of those days. In later years, Kelly would work as a boxing referee and, ironically, open a gambling house in New York in the late 1890s.

As he eyed New York's leadoff hitter, Candy Nelson, Radbourn was confident of victory. He'd taken the measure of the best the League had to offer during the season and was blithely unconcerned about the caliber of men an American Association team could put on the field. Nelson hit an easy grounder to Jerry Denny at third, and Denny nonchalantly threw the ball wide of Joe Start at first. Disgusted, Radbourn fired the ball plateward and got Brady to lift a pop foul to Barney Gilligan for the first out of the game. Dude Esterbrook gave Denny a chance to redeem himself and, with Radbourn's fierce eyes on him all the way, Denny threw the runner out at first. Radbourn wild-pitched Nelson to third, then bore down and struck out the dangerous Chief Roseman.

The teams changed sides and Tim Keefe took the mound, still fuming over the change in his batterymate. Jim Mutrie was starting Charley Reipschlager behind the plate instead of Bill Holbert, mainly to get Reipschlager's stronger bat in the lineup. Keefe was uncomfortable with the twenty-year-old giving the signs and started the game poorly by hitting both Paul Hines and Cliff Carroll with pitches. (The decision to play the games under Association rules had ironically paid immediate dividends for the National League's Grays, whose league rules did not award first base to a hit batsman.) Unnerved, Keefe uncorked a wild pitch which advanced both runners. A second wild pitch scored Hines and when Carroll raced home on a passed ball by Reipschlager, Keefe forgot to cover the plate. His worst nightmares were coming true.

Radbourn surrendered a one-out single to Dasher Troy in the second but struck out Reipschlager and Ed Kennedy to end the inning. In the third, Old Hoss gave the Mets a taste of his ability when he fanned Keefe, Nelson, and Brady. Keefe went out in the bottom of the inning and gave up a one-out single to Paul Hines. Still having trouble making connections with Reipschlager, Keefe's next delivery escaped his catcher and Hines motored down to second. Two successive wild pitches brought him home with the Gray's third run.

Through six innings, Keefe had allowed only one hit, but his inability to mesh with his new batterymate had given Providence a 3-0 lead. In the seventh, the Grays broke the game wide open. After Joe Start struck out, Jack Farrell doubled and Art Irwin tripled to make the score 4-0. Singles by Barney Gilligan and Jerry Denny and a run-scoring groundout by Paul Radford gave Providence a convincing 6-0 victory. Radbourn was never in trouble and finished with a two-hit shutout. He faced just thirty batters in the game, walked two, and struck out nine. Dasher Troy and Tim Keefe got the only hits, both singles.

Game Two was played the next day, and the weather was so cold that only two thousand fans turned out. Jack Remsen of the Brooklyn Trolley Dodgers was the umpire. Providence manager Frank Bancroft had originally intended to let Paul Radford pitch, but changed his mind and went with the man who had brought the Grays to the Series; so it was Radbourn and Keefe again. Keefe was somewhat mollified by the return of Bill Holbert behind the plate.

Neither club threatened through the first four innings, but Grays' second baseman Jack Farrell singled with one out in the fifth and raced to third on Barney Gilligan's two-out double. The throw into second appeared to have nailed Gilligan but Remsen called the runner safe and, although the Mets protested, it was to no avail. A favorable call would have ended the inning. Still upset, Keefe served up a fat pitch to the next batter, Jerry Denny, and Denny smashed a home run—the first in Series history—over the short fence in front of the left field bleachers to give the Grays a 3-0 lead.

In the bottom of the inning, the Mets tallied their first run of the Series to avoid a second shutout. Leadoff batter Chief Roseman beat out an infield single to short. Art Irwin retrieved the ball and, turning, saw that Roseman had taken a wide turn around first base. He fired the ball to Joe Start but the throw was wild and Roseman went all the way to third. One out later, Roseman scored when second baseman Jack Farrell bobbled Dasher Troy's ground ball.

Providence pushed across two more runs in the top of the eighth, but it was too dark to finish the inning and the score reverted to 3-1. Radbourn surrendered only three hits in the game, struck out six, walked no one, and allowed no earned runs for the second successive day. In sixteen innings of work, Hoss had given up only five hits, all singles, and no earned runs.

The Grays and Mets had previously decided to donate the profits for the final two games to the players, and when only five hundred fans showed up on the 25th for the third game, Providence manager Bancroft balked at playing. A northwest wind swept across the park and the Polo Grounds was even colder than the previous two days. The Grays, for their part, simply wanted to go home but were finally persuaded to take the field when Mutrie offered them their choice of umpires. With such a tantalizing offer, the Grays ensured themselves of a victory by selecting Tim Keefe! Rookie Buck Becannon became the starting pitcher for the Mets. Becannon's experience on the mound was limited. In 1884, he had pitched in only one game for New York, working six innings and giving up two hits for a victory.

Charlie Reipschlager was back behind the plate for Game Three* and had an inning to remember in the first. Leadoff batter Paul Hines drew a base on balls from the inexperienced Becannon. A moment later, one of Becannon's deliveries skittered off Reipschlager's hand for a passed ball. Reipschlager pounced on the ball, which had gone just a few feet, and made a hurried throw to second. The ball soared high over the bag and into center field, with Hines making third easily. Cliff Carroll grounded out but Radbourn hit a sacrifice fly to Steve Brady in right and the Grays led, 1-0. The Grays scored twice in the second and maintained their three-run lead until the fifth when they scored four times to take a commanding 7-0 lead. Providence pounded Becannon for nine hits and eleven runs over six innings and won easily, 11-2. The Mets scored unearned runs in the fifth and sixth and, following the conclusion of the inning, the clubs ended the game by mutual consent. Darkness was coming on and, considering the way Radbourn was pitching, it might have taken New York months to make up a nine-run deficit.

Old Hoss finished the game with a six-hitter. His numbers for the Series were positively incredible: In twenty-two innings, Radbourn had surrendered ten singles and a double, walked no one, and struck out seventeen. His earned run average was a perfect 0.00. As a team, the Mets batted .143, and only Dude Esterbrook and Chief Roseman were able to solve the Providence right-hander for more than one hit.

Radbourn was the toast of Providence over the winter, but his celebrity was short-lived. In 1885, he careened to twenty-six wins,

---

* An unusual sidelight of the third game was the appearance of a "Foster" at second base for the Metropolitans. No Foster is listed as having played for the Mets in 1884, and because there were no hard and fast roster rules for these early World Series games, his identity remains unknown.

and when the Grays disbanded following the 1885 season, Hoss was awarded to the Boston Beaneaters. He never approached the success he enjoyed in 1884. In 1890, he jumped to the Boston Players' League team, then signed on for one last major league fling with Cincinnati in 1891 before retiring in mid-season. In his twelve-year playing career, Radbourn started 503 games and finished 489 for a record of 309-191, numbers good enough to earn him entrance to the Hall of Fame in 1939.

Following his retirement, Radbourn suffered several financial setbacks before opening a billiards parlor in Bloomington, Illinois. He lost an eye in a hunting accident and became morose over his disfigurement. He spent the last few months of his life in the back room of the hall, drinking heavily until his death at the age of forty-two.

◆ ◆ ◆

GAME ONE—October 23, 1884, at the Polo Grounds, New York

NEW YORK	AB	R	H	BI	E	PROVIDENCE	AB	R	H	BI	E
Nelson, ss	4	0	0	0	0	Hines, cf	4	2	1	0	0
Brady, rf	4	0	0	0	0	Carroll, lf	3	1	0	0	0
Esterbrook, 3b	4	0	0	0	0	Radbourn, p	4	0	0	0	0
Roseman, cf	3	0	0	0	0	Start, 1b	4	0	0	1	0
Orr, 1b	3	0	0	0	0	Farrell, 2b	3	1	1	0	0
Troy, 2b	3	0	1	0	0	Irwin, ss	3	1	1	1	1
Reipschlager, c	3	0	0	0	0	Gilligan, c	3	1	1	1	0
Kennedy, lf	3	0	0	0	0	Denny, 3b	3	0	1	0	1
Keefe, p	3	0	1	0	0	Radford, rf	3	0	0	1	0
	30	0	2	0	0		30	6	5	4	2

```
NY     0 0 0   0 0 0   0 0 0 - 0
PROV   2 0 1   0 0 0   3 0 x - 6
```

D: Farrell. T: Irwin. DP: PROV. SF: Start. Struck out: Radbourn 9, Keefe 8. PB: Reipschlager 2, Gilligan 1. WP: Radbourn 2, Keefe 3. HBP: Hines, Carroll (by Keefe). Umpire: John Kelly. Time—1:55. Att: 2,500.

GAME TWO—October 24, 1884, at the Polo Grounds, New York

NEW YORK	AB	R	H	BI	E	PROVIDENCE	AB	R	H	BI	E
Nelson, ss	3	0	1	0	0	Hines, cf	2	0	0	0	0
Brady, rf	3	0	0	0	0	Carroll, lf	3	0	0	0	0
Esterbrook, 3b	3	0	1	0	0	Radbourn, p	3	0	0	0	0
Roseman, cf	3	1	1	0	0	Start, 1b	3	0	1	0	0
Orr, 1b	3	0	0	0	0	Farrell, 2b	3	1	2	0	2
Troy, 2b	2	0	0	0	0	Irwin, ss	3	0	0	0	1
Holbert, c	2	0	0	0	0	Gilligan, c	3	1	1	0	0
Kennedy, lf	2	0	0	0	0	Denny, 3b	3	1	1	3	0
Keefe, p	2	0	0	0	0	Radford, rf	2	0	0	0	0
	23	1	3	0	0		25	3	5	3	3

```
PROV  0 0 0   0 3 0   0 – 3
NY    0 0 0   0 1 0   0 – 1
```

D: Gilligan.   HR: Denny.   SB: Kennedy, Esterbrook.   DP: NY 1, PROV. 1.   BB: Keefe 1.   Struck out: Keefe 4, Radbourn 6.   WP: Keefe.   Umpire: Remsen.   Time—1:30. Att: 1,000.

GAME THREE—October 25, 1884, at the Polo Grounds, New York

NEW YORK	AB	R	H	BI	E	PROVIDENCE	AB	R	H	BI	E
Nelson, ss	3	0	0	0	0	Hines, cf	2	3	1	0	0
Brady, rf	3	1	0	0	1	Carroll, lf	4	1	1	1	0
Esterbrook, 3b	3	0	2	0	2	Radbourn, p	3	1	1	N/A	0
Roseman, cf	3	0	2	N/A	0	Start, 1b	3	0	0	N/A	0
Orr, 1b	3	0	1	N/A	0	Farrell, 2b	3	1	1	N/A	0
Foster, 2b	3	0	0	0	1	Irwin, ss	3	1	1	N/A	0
Reipschlager, c	2	1	0	0	1	Gilligan, c	3	1	2	N/A	0
Kennedy, lf	2	0	0	0	0	Denny, 3b	3	2	2	N/A	0
Becannon, p	2	0	1	1	0	Radford, rf	2	1	0	N/A	0
	24	2	6	N/A	5		26	11	9	N/A	0

```
PROV  1 2 0   0 4 4 – 11
NY    0 0 0   0 1 1 –  2
```

D: Esterbrook.   T: Denny.   SF: Radbourn.   DP: PROV.   BB: Becannon 3, Radbourn 1.   Struck out: Radbourn 1, Becannon 1.   PB: Reipschlager 2.   WP: Radbourn 1, Becannon 1.   Umpire: Timothy Keefe.   Time—1:20.   Att. 500.

· 3 ·

THE DISPUTED
CHAMPIONSHIP

◆

The portly, bulbous-nosed Christian Frederick Wilhelm Von Der Ahe, owner of the St. Louis Browns, was easily the most colorful figure in the ten-year history of the American Association. Born in 1851 in Hille, Germany, Von Der Ahe emigrated to the United States and opened a meat-packing plant and beer garden in St. Louis years later. Von Der Ahe viewed baseball as an excellent medium for hyping beer sales—St. Louis baseball hasn't changed that much in a hundred years—and purchased Sportsman's Park for $6,500. The aging park had been used by the National Association Brown Stockings in 1875, and by the National League Brown Stockings in 1876-77, but no major league team had graced the field since the Boston Red Caps and Indianapolis Blues had played a three-game series there in 1878. Von Der Ahe had horse races and fireworks displays in the park, booked minor league and semiprofessional exhibition games, and bided his time, waiting for his chance to break into the ranks of the major leagues. That opportunity came along when the American Association was born and the St. Louis Brown Stockings were made a charter member.

Chris Von Der Ahe has been portrayed in most popular histories as a clown and a vulgarian. And some of his actions were

1885

The Changing Game

◆ ◆ ◆

• Major league owners reduced the number of balls required for a walk from seven to six and ruled that a portion of the bat could be flat, to improve bunting.

• Official batting and pitching statistics were changed to include all performances in ties and in games which were suspended before a full nine innings had been played.

• The St. Louis Union club, now calling itself the Maroons, merged with the Cleveland Spiders and joined the National League.

• National League and American Association owners established an arbitrary contract ceiling of $2,000, sparking the creation of the Brotherhood of Professional Base Ball Players, the brainchild of New York Giants shortstop John Montgomery Ward.

unusual, of that there can be little doubt. He once named a string of apartment houses he owned after the star players on his team. He built a life-sized statue of himself and placed it in the ballpark — a self-serving tribute which future club owners like Charlie Finley and George Steinbrenner somehow managed to resist. Perhaps strangest of all, Von Der Ahe would often take a game's cash receipts to the bank in a wheelbarrow, flanked by security guards armed with rifles.

But if legend has portrayed this garishly dressed German-American as a buffoon, the facts are somewhat different. Chris Von Der Ahe was a shrewd businessman, a daring entrepreneur, and a man who truly loved baseball, although like so many of his former countrymen, he did not understand the game completely. Giving a group of visiting businessmen a tour of the park one day, Von Der Ahe proudly boasted that he had the biggest diamond in the world. His manager, Charlie Comiskey, gently pulled him aside and pointed out that all baseball diamonds were the same size. Von Der Ahe apologized to the group for his gaffe, but recovered to insist that his park had the biggest infield!

But Von Der Ahe had an elementary understanding of, and a crude logic about, the game. At a time when baseball rules said a ball landing foul *after* it left the park was not a home run, Von Der Ahe correctly observed that the rule made little sense.

This self-made man promoted the Browns with the flair of a twentieth-century huckster, outfitting the players in colorful silk uniforms and sending the team on parade from its hotel to the park in open carriages. He was the first owner to install a ladies' room in his ballpark. Von Der Ahe fined his players constantly, mostly for lack of discipline or unprofessional behavior on the field. The Browns' popular third baseman, Arlie Latham, once had to cough up twenty-five dollars for "singing and otherwise acting up" during a game. In 1889, Von Der Ahe nearly precipitated a players' strike by the entire team when he dunned William "Yank" Robinson for insubordination.

The owner's later life, unfortunately, would be filled with setbacks and disappointments. Harried by lawyers in the 1890s— once, undergoing the indignity of being kidnapped by detectives who brought him east to face a lawsuit—the big German would eventually be stripped of his franchise, deserted by his second wife (who accused him of adultery), and disowned by his son. He probably would have died penniless had it not been for financial assistance from Comiskey, who never forgot his former boss's kindness.

But in 1885, Von Der Ahe was on top of the world. His Browns had risen from a fourth-place finish in 1884 to their first pennant, all in just the fourth year of operation. The American Association got nearly a two-week jump on the National League, opening its season on April 18. The Browns lost five of their first eleven games before launching a twenty-game winning streak which gave them, as it developed, an insurmountable eight-game lead. When the season ended, St. Louis' sixteen-game lead over the second-place Reds was the largest margin of victory in the history of either the National League or the American Association.

Most of the club's success was due to player-manager Charlie Comiskey. At sportswriter Al Spink's suggestion, Von Der Ahe had hired Charles Albert Comiskey, a former Chicago sandlot player, as his first baseman in 1882. Comiskey had become the club's manager late in 1883 but the twenty-four-year-old was succeeded the next year by Jimmy Williams. The Browns finished in fourth place, and Von Der Ahe, convinced the club was better than that, gave Comiskey the job a second time. In the six years Comiskey managed at St. Louis, the Browns never finished lower than second.

As a ballplayer, Charlie Comiskey had pioneered the art of playing off the bag; while with Dubuque in 1880, he was one of the earliest players in the game to see the wisdom of having the pitcher cover first. The "Old Roman" made a study of hitters and would position his players where he thought the batter would hit the ball. As the manager or in the field, Comiskey encouraged aggressiveness and umpire-baiting, and quickly established his team as the "bad boys" of the American Association. Following his retirement as a player in 1894, Comiskey would become the owner of the Western League St. Paul club and president of the American League Chicago White Sox in 1901. For the next thirty years, he would be one of baseball's most prominent owners. His penuriousness would be the central cause of his 1919 club's conspiring with gamblers to throw the World Series. Comiskey was voted into the Hall of Fame in 1939, eight years after his death.

The Browns' opponents in the 1885 World Series were the Chicago White Stockings. Following a shoulder injury to ace pitcher Larry Corcoran, John Clarkson was pressed into extra mound duty and responded with a thirteen-game winning streak, after which he reeled off twelve victories in his next fourteen starts. White Stockings president Al Spalding purchased the contract of veteran Jim McCormick from the Providence Grays and McCormick strung together fourteen straight wins, bringing Chicago back to Congress Street Grounds to face the New York Giants in a do-or-die four-game series late in September. The White Stockings won the first three contests before dropping the finale. They clinched the pennant in their next game.

If the White Stockings were confident, they had every reason to be. Led by player-manager Cap Anson, Chicago exhibited a more potent offense than any other team in the National League, leading second-place New York in runs scored by 143. The White Stockings had more home runs than any other two teams combined, and four of the six National League leaders in home runs wore Chicago uniforms.

If the club had a weakness, and it most certainly did, it was defense, or lack of same. The famed "Stone Wall" infield of Anson at first, Fred Pfeffer at second, and Tom Burns at short had led the league in errors, the double-play combination accounting for 184 alone. Ned Williamson was only the second-worst third baseman in the league, but he could be excused. Philadelphia's Joe Mulvey had set a torrid pace with 62 miscues to top the circuit for the second successive year. Add to this the White Stockings' leading moundsman, John Clarkson, who led the league in errors for a pitcher, and you have an up-the-middle defense which would drive a manager to drink. To say the Chicago infield was a sieve would be an insult to the sieve.

This was the third season Anson, Pfeffer, Burns, and Williamson had played together. The famed Stone Wall Infield would remain intact from 1883 through 1889 and eventually grow to become legend. In 1886, Burns would move to third and Williamson to short.

The White Stockings had recruited twenty-two-year-old Fred Pfeffer to play short for a nine-game exhibition series in October 1882, and manager Anson was so impressed with the youngster's sure hands that he offered him a contract immediately. Anson's good eye for a prospect was rewarded as Pfeffer soon turned into one of the top pivot men in the game. Pfeffer led the league in putouts for eight straight years, from 1884 through 1891, a mark exceeded only when Nellie Fox led the American League nine straight times in the 1950s. Pfeffer topped the circuit seven times in total chances per game, six times in double plays turned, and four times in assists. He established a National League putout record for second basemen which lasted twenty-eight years, and even today Pfeffer is tied with his contemporary, Bid McPhee, in career chances per game. Pfeffer committed a lot of errors in his sixteen-year career but many of those can be attributed to his vast range and aggressiveness in the field. Pfeffer got to many ground balls that eluded other second sackers of the era, and threw men out on hits that other second basemen could only stop. Never a top-notch hitter (his lifetime batting average was only .255), Pfeffer nevertheless had a fair amount of power and was an excellent baserunner.

Of his teammate, Cap Anson once said, "Fred knew the game of baseball and he played it with his head as well as his hands. There wasn't a minute of the game that he wasn't on the job and he had more tricks up his sleeve than any other of his contemporaries."

King Kelly, who played with Pfeffer for four years, commented on Pfeffer's defensive ability when he said he was "the greatest second baseman of them all. All you had to do was throw anywhere near the bag and he would get it—high, wide, or on the ground. What a man he was to make a return throw! Why, he could lay on his stomach and throw a hundred yards."

The Chicago White Stockings had recently moved into their new park, the Congress Street Grounds (later called West Side Park). It was located at Congress and Loomis streets in a middle-class neighborhood, a fifteen-minute carriage ride from downtown Chicago. The park was a major league showplace, featured seating for ten thousand fans, private roof boxes, facilities for cycling, track, and lawn tennis, and a toilet with a private entrance for ladies. Long and bathtub-shaped, like the Polo Grounds, Congress Street Grounds boasted a twelve-foot-high brick fence around the perimeter. It was 560 feet to dead center field. Eight years later, the park would be torn down to make room for the site of the Columbian Exposition.

An intense rivalry already existed between the two midwestern cities of Chicago and St. Louis, and prospects looked good for a financially successful World Series. Both teams put up five hundred dollars as a purse, the money to be held by the editor of *The Mirror of American Sports*, a newspaper of the time. The first game was to be played at Chicago's Congress Street Grounds; the next three in St. Louis' Sportsman's Park; Game Five at Pittsburgh's American Association Recreation Park; Games Six and Seven at Cincinnati's Base Ball Grounds; Game Eight at Baltimore's Union Park; Games Nine and Ten at Philadelphia's Jefferson Street Grounds; and the final two contests at Brooklyn's Washington Park. The fact that most of the twelve games were to be played under American Association rules and (excepting the first game) on Association grounds would later prove to be a bone of contention. But at the beginning of the Series, at least, the National League was exhibiting the same arrogance it had shown in the first two World Series by giving the junior circuit every possible advantage.

On the mound for the White Stockings were John Clarkson and Jim McCormick. Clarkson had a dazzling fastball and when he lost his speed later in his career, he added a mystifying "drop" pitch and an even more baffling changeup.

John Gibson Clarkson had pitched for the National League Worcester team in 1882 and spent the next two years with Saginaw of the Northwestern League before signing with Chicago in 1885. He would win twenty-five games or more each year from 1885 through 1892 and finish his career with a lifetime record of 326-177. With 485 complete games, he stands eighth on the all-time list. Clarkson would help Chicago to three straight pennants before being sold to Boston in 1888 for ten thousand dollars. Released by the Beaneaters in June 1892 because of recurring arm trouble, he would pitch for Cleveland through the end of 1894. When his twelve-year career ended in 1894, Clarkson had led the National League in no fewer than twenty-four different pitching categories. He entered the Hall of Fame in 1963.

The slight right-hander—Clarkson stood 5'10" and weighed 155 pounds—had a year to remember in 1885, his first full season in the majors, as he dominated the National League by a wide margin in wins (53), strikeouts (318), innings pitched (623), appearances (70), complete games (68), and shutouts (10). He trailed only Tim Keefe and Mickey Welch in earned run average. When Clarkson beat Boston on September 18 for his fiftieth win, he joined Hoss Radbourn (60-12 in 1884) and Guy Hecker (52-20 in 1884) as the only pitchers to ever post more than fifty wins in a season.

Cap Anson provided an insight into Clarkson's personality when he said, "Clarkson was one of the greatest pitchers of all time, certainly the best Chicago ever had. Many regard him as the greatest, but not many know of his peculiar temperament and the amount of encouragement needed to keep him going. Scold him, find fault with him, and he could not pitch at all. Praise him, and he was unbeatable. In knowing what kind of a ball a batter could not hit, and his ability to serve up that kind of ball, I don't think I have ever seen the equal of Clarkson."

When Clarkson wasn't on the mound, the Scottish-born Jim McCormick would handle the pitching duties. His fourteen straight victories from July through September had complemented Clarkson's fine work. After arriving from the Providence Grays, the portly right-hander won twenty of his twenty-four starts.

The 1885 Chicago White Stockings were a poor fielding team, but their counterparts from the American Association, the St. Louis Browns, were anything but. The Browns led the Association in fielding percentage, and their starting eight made 105 fewer errors than Chicago's starting eight. St. Louis also had the Association's second most potent offense and gave up 114 fewer runs than any of its competitors.

The Browns' infield was Comiskey at first, Sam Barkley at second, Bill Gleason at short, and Arlie Latham at third. Barkley was an undistinguished second baseman whose position on the club would be taken by newcomer Yank Robinson in 1886.

Bill Gleason was a rough-and-tumble ballplayer, a slap hitter who was adept at reaching base by being hit with the pitch. A native of St. Louis, Gleason was immensely popular with the hometown crowd as much for his aggressive style of play as for his base coaching. But Gleason was detested by opposing players for his ability to break up the double play at second (not a common practice of the day), and in the field, he was not above slamming a knee or a hip into a passing baserunner.

But as well liked as Gleason was, it is doubtful there was a more popular player in St. Louis in the 1880s than third baseman Arlie Latham. Nicknamed "The Freshest Man On Earth," Walter Arlington "Arlie" Latham managed to do a little of everything in a baseball career which spanned three-quarters of a century. He had begun his career playing semipro baseball in Stoneham, Massachusetts, at the age of fifteen, had a brief fling at the major league level with Boston in 1880, and found himself with the St. Louis Browns in 1883.

A diminutive third baseman—he weighed only 150 pounds—Latham was the game's first great basestealer. When he retired (for the first time) in 1899, Latham had a career total of 678 stolen bases. Speedster Billy Hamilton retired two years later with a total of 937, but records for stolen bases were not accurately kept until 1887 and Latham's lifetime totals are probably closer to between 850 and 900. He stole forty or more bases nine times—Hamilton stole forty or more ten times—and scored one hundred or more runs nine times.

Latham's private life was a shambles. His first wife attempted suicide and his second wife sued him for divorce on grounds of perversion, desertion, and infidelity. But in the field, Arlie Latham helped provide just the spark the St. Louis Browns needed to become the strongest club in the history of the American Association and one of the best of the nineteenth century.

A standout performer at third base, Latham possessed one of the strongest arms in baseball until he injured it in a throwing contest with teammate Albert "Doc" Bushong in 1887. Even today, over eighty years after his retirement, Latham ranks sixth in total chances, eighth in assists, and twelfth in putouts among all third basemen. In 1909, Latham became baseball's first full-time coach when he joined the New York Giants. He even managed to appear in four games, two at second base, becoming the oldest man (at age forty-nine) in major league history to steal a base. With his coaching help, the 1911 Giants established a record 347 stolen bases.

After hanging up his spikes for good, Latham umpired for three seasons and later moved to England where he lived for seventeen years. In England, he would become the Administrator of baseball (a position not unlike our present-day office of commissioner) and form a close friendship with the Prince of Wales. Latham spent the last sixteen years of his life working for major league baseball clubs in the New York area. He was the press box attendant for the New York Yankees when he died in the winter of 1952 at age ninety-two.

The pitching staff of the St. Louis Browns was Bob Caruthers and Dave Foutz. Bob Caruthers was an immensely talented pitcher who had overcome all manner of diversity to become a success. As a boy, he was sickly and the family doctor recommended outdoor exercise, so Caruthers took up baseball. A small man (just 5'7" and 137 pounds), Caruthers nonetheless had a muscular physique. Von Der Ahe had taken some pains to acquire the right-hander, purchasing the Minneapolis minor league franchise to do so, but the acquisition paid off. In his career, only four years of which were spent with the Browns, Caruthers ran up a lifetime record of 218-97. His winning percentage of .692 ranks first on the all-time list, but like many deserving nineteenth-century players, he is not in the Hall of Fame. In 1885, he led the Association in ERA (2.07), winning percentage (.755), and victories (40).

Following the 1885 season, Caruthers and batterymate Doc Bushong would take a vacation to Paris, from where the pitcher and Browns owner Chris Von Der Ahe engaged in some transatlantic sniping over his salary for the upcoming 1886 season. (From this escapade came Caruthers's nickname of "Parisian Bob.") When not pitching, Caruthers would play right field, well enough to compile a .282 lifetime batting average. A well-rounded ballplayer, Caruthers was also an excellent baserunner. In 1893, he would quit pitching altogether, moving to the outfield for a few games before retiring from major league baseball. The next year, Caruthers was back in Grand Rapids, where his career began, hitting .333 in 132 games. After two more years of minor league ball, Caruthers became an umpire for four seasons. He was umpiring in the Three-I League in 1911 when he suffered a nervous collapse. He died the same year.

The other half of the Browns' pitching staff, Dave Foutz, was no slouch either. Born in Carroll County, Maryland, Foutz had left home at an early age to pan for gold in Colorado. He played amateur baseball for the Leadville Blues and racked up an astounding record of 40-1 in 1882. Foutz broke into organized baseball with the Bay City franchise of the Northwestern League, and his contract was purchased by the St. Louis Brown Stockings when Bay City folded in 1884. Despite recurring bouts with malaria, Foutz was an immediate success in his first season with St. Louis, compiling a 15-6 mark with a sparkling 2.18 earned run average.

The lanky Foutz, who stood 6'2" and weighed 161 pounds, soon earned the nickname "Scissors." He fielded his position well, was an excellent hitter (lifetime batting average .277), and a good baserunner. Completely unflappable on the mound, his calm demeanor made him a leader by quiet example. In 1885, Foutz's record was an eye-popping 33-14 for St. Louis, and his career mark of 147-66 ranks second in winning percentage only to Caruthers on the all-time list.

As a kind of payroll-reduction plan, Chris Von Der Ahe would sell Foutz and Caruthers to Brooklyn in 1888. Harried by salary demands that shot his payroll over $40,000, the Browns' owner would give up the two pitchers who would finish first and second on the all-time winning percentage list. Of course, Von Der Ahe had no way of predicting the future, but that was no defense. At the close of the 1887 season, Caruthers had a career mark of 106-38 (.746) and Foutz of 114-48 (.704). For the years 1884 through 1887, Caruthers and Foutz won exactly two of every three games the Browns played.

Chicago was a rugged, dynamic, growing city in 1885, unashamed of its faults and its vulgarity. The first permanent dwellings in Chicago were established around 1773, but the settlement remained sparse until the Potawatomi Indians were driven from the area in 1832. By 1837, the population had reached 4,000 and the community was incorporated as a city. In 1871, the Chicago Fire had destroyed nearly four square miles of central Chicago—nearly one-third of the entire area—but although damages were estimated at over $300 million, the city was quickly rebuilt.

The heart of the great city was the Loop. The elevated railways had begun running in January 1882, and between 1885 and 1894, twenty-one skyscrapers would make their appearance in the Loop. State Street remained the primary retail street, with such famous department stores as Marshall Field's and Carson Pirie Scott, while the carriage trade patronized the fashionable specialty shops located along Michigan Avenue. With nine theaters, the Loop was the place to go in Chicago for culture.

But the city had its dark side as well—the vice districts of Little Cheyenne, the Badlands, Satan's Mile, Dead Man's Alley, the Black Hole, Hell's Half Acre, and the Levee—filled with saloons, gambling houses, whorehouses, and streetwalkers for those too cheap or lazy to visit the brothels.

At the southern end of Whiskey Row was Mickey Finn's Lone Star Saloon. Finn, a former pickpocket, would serve unsuspecting patrons the "Mickey Finn Special," a mixture of raw whiskey, snuff-soaked water, and a voodoo powder he swore he bought from a witch doctor. The victim would be rendered unconscious and Finn would rifle his pockets before dumping him unceremoniously into the street.

On Clark, Dearborn, State, and Randolph streets—just a few minutes' ride from the ballpark—a sport could bet his wages on that afternoon's contest at any one of thirty gaming houses.

Chicago took its gambling and its baseball seriously.

The World Series got off to a false start on October 14 at Congress Street Grounds when the White Stockings and Brown Stockings played eight innings to a 5-5 tie. Before the game began, members of both clubs engaged in a throwing and running contest, a common event for the times. Fred Pfeffer ran the bases in 15 3/4 seconds, defeating King Kelly, George Gore, Ned Williamson, Abner Dalrymple, and Bob Caruthers. Ned Williamson threw a baseball 133 yards, one foot, and four inches, beating Pfeffer, Dalrymple, Doc Bushong, and Yank Robinson. Williamson's long throw delighted the paying crowd of two thousand.

Umpire David F. Sullivan called the teams to the field at 3:15, and Chicago won the coin toss, electing to bat first. On the mound for St. Louis was Bob Caruthers. His opposite number was John Clarkson, Chicago's leading pitcher.

The Browns drew first blood when Charlie Comiskey scored the first run of the game in the second inning with the aid of three Chicago errors. The White Stockings tied the score in similar fashion in the fourth when King Kelly singled and came around on two St. Louis fumbles. In the bottom of the inning, the Browns took what appeared to be a commanding lead when singles by James "Tip" O'Neill, Yank Robinson, Arlie Latham, and Caruthers combined with three Chicago errors for four runs. Clarkson and Caruthers were near-perfect for the next three innings and the score was still 5-1 when Chicago came to bat in the eighth. Darkness was fast approaching and Caruthers anticipated the game would be suspended at any time. Working hurriedly, the St. Louis right-hander issued a base on balls to George Gore. Kelly and Anson followed with singles to pull Chicago within three runs. Eager to get the third out of the inning and perhaps the final out of the game, Caruthers served up a pitch to Fred Pfeffer which was just a little too good. Pfeffer connected for a long home run over the left-field fence and the score was tied. Caruthers was correct in one respect: At the conclusion of the inning, umpire Sullivan called the contest when it became too dark to continue.

Cap Anson was furious.

Not just because his boys had come within a hair of losing the first game of the Series. That was bad enough. What was worse, Anson was certain that George Gore had been drinking before he arrived at the ballpark. Drunk or not, Gore had played indifferently and Anson angrily told him he wouldn't be accompanying the team to St. Louis. He suspended Gore for the balance of the Series, then told reserve outfielder Billy Sunday to get ready to play center field in Gore's absence.

Billy Sunday had been plucked off a Marshalltown, Iowa, sandlot in 1883 by fellow resident Cap Anson, who had scouted the twenty-two-year-old youngster on the recommendation of Anson's aunt. Taken straight to the White Stockings, Sunday proved to be only a fair hitter, but he had blinding speed. He stole 236 bases in his short career, his high mark of eighty-four coming in 1890, and was one of the first ballplayers to circle the bases in fourteen seconds from a standing start. An undisciplined, free-swinging hitter, Sunday drew only 134 walks in 499 career games and only once—in 1887—did his batting average rise above .260. His lifetime mark of .248 is less than impressive. But Sunday was a playmaker, a showman, the kind of ballplayer who led by example. According to legend, his conversion to Christianity occurred when he was enjoying a drink with Mike Kelly and Ned Williamson in a Chicago saloon at the corner of State and Madison in 1887. Sunday heard the hymns from an outdoor meeting and followed the singers to the Pacific Garden Mission. He would continue to play baseball (although not on Sundays) through the 1890 season, but would give up drinking, smoking, card playing, and the theater. In stark contrast to many of his contemporaries, Sunday would pass his free time giving talks at the local YMCA. Sunday would spend the last few games of his career with the Philadelphia Phillies, and despite a contract offer calling for $3,500 for 1891, elected to quit baseball and organize religious activities at the Chicago YMCA for eighty-three dollars a month.

The clubs arrived in St. Louis by train early the next morning. St. Louis was a city rich in ethnic divisions: The south side of the city was predominantly German, while much of the large west-central area (known as The Hill) was Italian. St. Louis was a leading commercial hub, the greatest manufacturer of chewing tobacco in the world, and second only to Chicago as a railroad center. Budweiser, first marketed in 1876, was already the most popular beer in the city, not to mention the midwest. While in town, the White Stockings might have taken one of the cable street railways out to Forest Park or the Missouri Botanical Gardens. And a trip to St. Louis would hardly be complete without having dinner at Tony Faust's Oyster House and Saloon.

By 2:00, both teams had arrived at Sportsman's Park, located at Grand Boulevard and Dodier Street, a wooden stadium which featured a short right-field fence (285 feet), a distant left-field fence (350 feet), and a remote center-field fence (460 feet). This would be the setting for the next three games.

Browns' catcher Doc Bushong had injured his hand in the first game, so Yank Robinson was pressed into duty behind the plate. In many ways, Robinson was the glue that held together the pennant-winning St. Louis clubs of the mid-1880s. In 1882, Robinson had been playing semipro baseball in Boston when the Detroit Wolverines came into town for a series with the Boston Red Caps. The regular shortstop for the Wolverines, Mike McGeary, was injured, and Detroit manager Frank Bancroft asked Robinson if he could fill in. Robinson had stayed with the club for the rest of the year, played minor league ball in 1883, and joined the Baltimore Unions in 1884. At Baltimore, Robinson had played three infield positions, caught, and appeared in eleven games as a pitcher. Chris Von Der Ahe was so impressed with the young man's versatility that he signed him in 1885 for $2,100, pretty good money for a ballplayer with only two years' experience. During the season, Robinson had spelled injured left fielder Tip O'Neill for nearly three months, played each infield position except shortstop, and had even caught five games. Playing several positions was nothing unusual in the nineteenth century, but Robinson's ability to play everywhere was. Charlie Comiskey was so taken with the young man that he would sell Sam Barkley following the season and install Robinson as his regular second baseman for 1886.

In the field, Robinson was agile, smart, and got rid of the ball quickly. He showed good range in knocking down ground balls and made accurate throws to all bases. Ambidextrous (and barehanded) Robinson nailed many a surprised runner at third base by throwing across his chest with his left hand. In his ten-year career, he would play every position except center field. At the plate, the short and stocky Robinson was a weak, opposite-field hitter with little power. He made up for this deficiency with an amazing talent for bunting safely, drew bases on balls in clusters, and was a daring runner who always took the extra base.

Game Two of the 1885 Series was a disgrace. Umpire Sullivan called for play to begin at 3:15 with a disappointing crowd of only three thousand fans in the stands. The White Stockings won the coin toss and Anson again elected to bat his team first. The starting pitchers were Jim McCormick and Dave Foutz. Bob Caruthers, who frequently played right field when he wasn't pitching, was given the day off and Hugh Nicol started in his place. For the White Stockings, pitcher John Clarkson was in right field.

Foutz retired the first Chicago batter, Abner Dalrymple, on an easy ground ball, but Billy Sunday singled and went to second when a Foutz fastball ticked off Robinson's glove for a passed ball. King Kelly grounded a single into center field and when Curt Welch bobbled the ball, Sunday raced home with the first run of the game.

Bill Gleason led off the Browns' half of the inning with a ringing double to center field. Welch grounded to third but the ball went right through Ned Williamson's legs for an error. Sam Barkley sacrificed Welch to second and when Charlie Comiskey connected with a pitch, Gleason streaked for home. Fred Pfeffer fielded Comiskey's grounder cleanly and made an ill-advised throw home. The relay was perfect but Kelly had no one to tag. Gleason had long since scored and was heading for the bench. The Browns had Chicago on the run now. Capitalizing on his team's momentum, Comiskey stole second base and when Pfeffer booted the late throw from Kelly, Welch raced home and Comiskey slid into third. When a Clarkson fastball eluded Kelly, Comiskey scored the third run of the inning. The crowd was ecstatic. What a start for the Browns!

The White Stockings put a marker on the scoreboard in the second but the Browns equalled that with a run in the fourth. Several of umpire Dave Sullivan's early decisions had gone against St. Louis and by the top of the sixth inning, the partisan crowd was brewing for trouble. Billy Sunday started the sixth with a double over Hugh Nicol's head in right, and went to third on a wild pitch a moment later. Kelly grounded to Gleason and was easily retired at first, but Sullivan, who had his eye on Sunday coming home, neglected to watch the play at first. When he called Kelly safe, Comiskey exploded. Seconds later, the ump was beset by an angry crowd of St. Louis ballplayers. Comiskey called Sullivan every name in the book and threatened to take his club off the field if he didn't reverse the decision at once. For the next fifteen minutes, Sullivan repeatedly told Comiskey to get his men back in position and finally said that if the Browns weren't ready to play in two minutes, he'd forfeit the game to Chicago. To punctuate his threat, the beleaguered umpire pulled out a pocket watch. That had the desired effect, as the Browns took their places. Cap Anson, who had watched all this in great amusement, strolled to the plate for Chicago.

Before Anson could even swing at the ball, Kelly stole second. With the tying run in scoring position, Anson's competitive ire was aroused, and he singled to center to knot the score. Pfeffer hit a medium pop fly to right field. Nicol dropped the ball but recovered in time to force Anson. Pfeffer stole second and went to third on a passed ball, and what happened next caused all hell to break loose. Ned Williamson grounded a pitch into foul territory behind first, but the ball spun back onto the playing field. Comiskey picked it up and nonchalantly tossed to Barkley who had moved over to cover first. Williamson, running from the moment the ball hit the bat, easily beat the throw as Pfeffer scored the go-ahead run. When Comiskey realized what had happened, he argued that Sullivan had shouted "foul ball" and the runners should be made to return to their bases. Sullivan agreed and was sending Pfeffer to third and Williamson back to the plate when King Kelly and Cap Anson left their seats on the players' bench and angrily advanced on the ump.

Fearing that either one of the bully boys from Chicago might give him a pummeling, Sullivan reversed his reversal and earned the enmity of nearly everyone. Nearly two hundred fans jumped onto the field and made their way straight for the umpire but were forcibly restrained by the police. Just about the time constables could get the diamond cleared, a second crowd of men descended from the grandstands and milled onto the playing field. The White Stockings, fearing for their safety, wielded baseball bats as weapons. At this point, Sullivan and the Chicago ballplayers were escorted from the field by the police. Later that evening, from the relative safety of his hotel room, Sullivan declared the game forfeited to Chicago. The Browns contested the decision, arguing they were not the first team to leave the field and would not have left at all if not forced off by the crowd. Comiskey claimed the game had to be decided at the park and correctly pointed out that forfeits were not generally awarded from hotel rooms.

Sullivan later acknowledged that he had tried to do his best but had had an off day. Then, as now, the umpire's decision stood, and so did the forfeit.

Another small crowd of three thousand fans turned out at Sportsman's Park on October 16 for the third game of the Series. The Browns had "fired" Sullivan and umpiring in his place was a local man, one Harry McCaffrey. McCaffrey had been a former pitcher for the American Cincinnati Reds and was acceptable to Anson and the White Stockings. Chicago won the toss and chose to bat first for the third consecutive game, the first played under National League rules. The White Stockings scored a single run at the outset and gave an awful exhibition of baseball in the bottom of the first. Leadoff batter Bill Gleason singled and Curt Welch lifted a pop fly for King Kelly in right field. Kelly dropped the easy chance but recovered in time to force Gleason at second. Welch stole second and went to third on a passed ball, and Sam Barkley fanned for the second out of the inning. It looked as if Clarkson was out of danger when Charlie Comiskey hit an easy fly ball to left. But the ball skittered off Dalrymple's hands and Welch, running all the way, scored easily. Dalrymple's error opened the floodgates. Yank Robinson drew a base on balls, and a wild pitch advanced the runners into scoring position. Tip O'Neill laced a single to center to give St. Louis a 3-1 lead, and pulled into second on Sunday's late throw to the plate. A double by Arlie Latham and a triple by Bob Caruthers gave St. Louis a five-run inning. The Browns were never headed and won the game easily, 7-4.

Game Four was delayed forty-five minutes because Chicago manager Cap Anson petulantly refused to allow McCaffrey to umpire. Second baseman Fred Dunlap of the National League St. Louis Maroons was in town watching the games, and Anson asked if he would work the game but Dunlap demurred. At last, William Medart, a local sportsman and rabid Browns fan, was persuaded to leave his seat in the grandstand and umpire the game. In the early going, the hometown crowd couldn't have been happier with Medart's work, and for good reason: Every close play was decided in favor of the Browns. By game's end, however, everyone in the park was unhappy with Medart and his blatant favoritism. Even Charlie Comiskey admitted his team had been outplayed.

The whole Series was taking on the look of a circus show by now, so much so that Anson gave Clarkson (due to play right field) the day off and substituted James "Bug" Holliday, a seventeen-year-old amateur St. Louisan ballplayer who would not reach the major leagues until 1889. Holliday went 0-for-4 at the plate and made an error in right field on one of two balls hit his way. He does, however, hold the distinction of being the first and only nonprofessional player to appear in a World Series.

The Browns scored once in the bottom of the third but fell behind when the White Stockings came back with two in the fifth, despite a terrible ruling by Medart on a play in which he called Tom Burns out at third on a pickoff play. Burns had led off with a single, went to second on a passed ball, and to third when Jim McCormick reached on an error. McCormick bluffed a steal of second, attempting to draw a throw from Robinson, but the catcher pumped once then fired the ball to Latham at third. Medart, who probably hadn't seen the play at all, called Burns out. Abner Dalrymple salvaged the inning for the White Stockings with a two-run homer over the right-field fence. The score remained 2-1, Chicago, until the

Browns batted in the bottom of the eighth. Arlie Latham singled, went to second on a passed ball, and scored the tying run on Bob Caruthers's single. Kelly let another of McCormick's deliveries get past him, and Caruthers wound up on second. Bill Gleason hit an easy comebacker to McCormick who whirled and found Caruthers trapped off second. Parisian Bob was eventually run down, but in the confusion Gleason managed to take second on the play. Ned Williamson then made a dazzling stop of Curt Welch's grounder but his throw to first was too late and Gleason never slowed again, crossing the plate with the lead run.

Now trailing, 3-2, Chicago came to bat in the ninth. Ned Williamson grounded out but Tom Burns reached base on an error by Sam Barkley. Jim McCormick lifted a pop fly behind first, but Charlie Comiskey dropped the ball and the White Stockings had two men on base. Before flipping the ball back to the pitcher, Comiskey playfully tagged McCormick, who was standing with one foot on the bag. To the amazement of everyone in the park, and to the utter consternation of the White Stockings, Medart called McCormick out. The 195-pound pitcher advanced menacingly on the umpire, but Cap Anson hurried onto the field and stepped between the two, saving Medart from a beating. Billy Sunday, in a decidedly non-Christian show of emotion, doubled up his fists and called the umpire a liar but was prevented from launching a blow when King Kelly intervened. Bug Holliday, poor Bug Holliday, was the next batter and he fouled to third, ending the game.

The teams journeyed to Recreation Park at Pennsylvania and Allegheny avenues in Pittsburgh for the fifth game on the 22nd. The weather was chilly and no more than five hundred people attended the game. Sometime during the four open dates, Anson had telegraphed "Honest John" Kelly, one of the most respected umpires in the game, and Kelly made the trip to Pittsburgh to work the final three games of the Series. The White Stockings jumped on Dave Foutz for four first-inning runs and cruised to an easy 9-2 win behind John Clarkson's four-hit pitching. Umpire Kelly called the game at the end of seven innings because of darkness.

From Pittsburgh, it was on to the Cincinnati Base Ball Grounds and a second 9-2 victory for the White Stockings, the game played under American Association rules. Before the contest began, umpire Kelly made an announcement to the Cincinnati crowd that both clubs had agreed Game Seven would decide the championship. Fifteen hundred fans watched an extraordinary job of pitching as

Chicago's Jim McCormick shut down the vaunted St. Louis offense on just two hits. Except for McCormick's performance, the game featured undistinguished work on both sides. The White Stockings made ten errors, St. Louis eight, and both sides played rather listlessly. An anonymous sportswriter for the Cincinnati *Commercial Gazette*, in a witty style completely unlike that of any other publication of the day, had this to say about the Browns' play:

> Spectators who saw the Browns play in their championship games could hardly realize that it was the same club playing yesterday. Every mother's son of them seemed to be witless save Bushong . . . and whenever a man got to first he stood there like a tethered cow . . . Barkley, Comisky, [sic], Robinson and O'Neil [sic] hugged the base as though it were an ark of life everlasting to them . . .

To this point in the Series, six games had been played. The first game was a tie, the third and fourth games were St. Louis victories, and the fifth and sixth games had gone to Chicago. The only remaining question was the second game. Was it a forfeit? Did it count?

On the evening of the 23rd, prior to the seventh game, Anson and Comiskey met and agreed to ignore the forfeited game. With back-to-back 9-2 victories under his belt, Anson felt certain the White Stockings were playing up to their potential. With a competent umpire in the field and knowing Game Seven would be played under National League rules, the White Stockings manager was confident his club would carry the day. To the press, he gave this quote: "We will not even claim the forfeited game. We each have two victories now and the winner of today's game will be the winner of the series."

Clarkson was due to pitch for Chicago but when he unaccountably arrived on the field five minutes after game time, McCormick was already in the box. Dave Foutz worked for the Browns. The White Stockings took a 2-0 lead in the first on a single by Billy Sunday, a double by King Kelly, and a Sam Barkley error, but the Browns overtook them in the third. Curt Welch lined an RBI triple into left, then scored when Dalrymple's throw to the infield went wild. Barkley atoned for his first-inning error with a single, raced to third on a safety by Comiskey, and scored the tie-breaker when Yank Robinson forced Comiskey. Robinson stole second and came all the way around on a passed ball by the Chicago catcher, Frank "Silver" Flint. The Browns pounded McCormick for five hits in a wild fourth inning which featured two errors by Anson, wild throws by Dalrymple and Williamson, and two more passed balls by Flint. St. Louis had finally discovered the secret of hitting McCormick: Rather than flail away at his high fastballs and tantalizingly slow curves, the Browns were calling for nothing but low pitches. The same clever writer from the Cincinnati *Commercial Gazette* described the scene thusly:

> There was no scratch hitting either. The ball cracked like a rifle shot, and went on a line to the outfield. The crowd of fifteen hundred spectators went wild over the St. Louis men's batting and cheered loudly every time a hit was made. One fellow yelled, "Buckle up your harness, Mac," and then everybody (no, not *every*body, but *nearly* everybody) cheered again. Mac showed an ugly humor over it at first, but finally recovered his good nature and took it with a six-inch standing smile.

The final score was 13-4, and the Series was over. Cap Anson was the leading batter for the White Stockings with a .423 batting average, followed closely by Fred Pfeffer at .407. Only one St. Louis regular managed to top the .300 mark and that was Arlie Latham at .318.

White Stockings president Al Spalding, who apparently had lost his voice in the eight days between the second and seventh games, now angrily commented, "Does anyone suppose that if there had been so much as that at stake that I should have consented to the games being played in American Association cities, upon their grounds, and under the authority of their umpires?" Spalding seems also to have suffered a convenient lapse in memory, forgetting that the first game took place in a National League park, that at least three of the contests were played under League rules, and that it was none other than his own manager who chose the umpire for the final and decisive three games. All available evidence points to the inescapable conclusion that Al Spalding was a sore loser.

The baseball world regarded the St. Louis Browns as champions, and rightly so. Chris Von Der Ahe delighted in telling anyone who came within ten feet that his Browns were the best team in the country. Well, maybe not everyone. For public consumption at least, Von Der Ahe agreed with Al Spalding that the Series had ended in a tie, thus cheating his players out of their share of the $1,000 prize money. On October 28, the editor of *The Mirror of American Sports* returned five hundred dollars to Von Der Ahe and five hundred dollars to Spalding.

GAME ONE—October 14, 1885, at Congress Street Grounds, Chicago

ST. LOUIS	AB	R	H	PO	A	E	CHICAGO	AB	R	H	PO	A	E
Gleason, ss	4	0	0	1	3	1	Dalrymple, 1f	4	0	0	1	0	0
Welch, cf	4	0	1	1	0	0	Gore, cf	3	1	0	0	0	1
Barkley, 2b	4	0	0	3	4	0	Kelly, rf	4	2	1	1	0	0
Comiskey, 1b	4	1	1	11	0	1	Anson, 1b	4	1	2	8	0	1
O'Neill, lf	4	1	1	0	0	0	Pfeffer, 2b	4	1	2	2	2	1
Robinson, rf	4	1	2	0	0	0	Williamson, 3b	3	0	0	2	2	2
Latham, 3b	4	1	1	2	0	0	Burns, ss	4	0	0	1	2	1
Caruthers, p	3	1	0	0	8	2	Clarkson, p	3	0	0	1	13	2
Bushong, c	3	0	1	6	0	1	Flint, c	3	0	1	8	4	3
	34	5	7	24	15	5		32	5	6	24	23	11

```
CHI   0 0 0   1 0 0   0 4 – 5
STL   0 1 0   4 0 0   0 0 – 5
```

Earned runs: CHI 3. 2B: Welch. HR: Pfeffer. PB: Flint 1, Bushong 1. BB: Caruthers 2. Struck out: Clarkson 8, Caruthers 6. DP: CHI. Umpire: David F. Sullivan. Att: 2,000.

GAME TWO—October 15, 1885, at Sportsman's Park, St. Louis

CHICAGO	AB	R	H	PO	A	E	ST. LOUIS	AB	R	H	PO	A	E
Dalrymple, lf	3	0	0	3	0	0	Gleason, ss	3	1	1	1	2	1
Sunday, cf	3	2	3	0	0	0	Welch, cf	3	1	0	1	0	0
Kelly, c	3	1	1	4	2	1	Barkley, 2b	2	0	0	3	3	0
Anson, 1b	3	0	1	7	0	0	Comiskey, 1b	2	1	0	7	0	1
Pfeffer, 2b	3	2	1	0	2	2	Robinson, c	2	0	0	4	1	0
Williamson, 3b	2	0	0	0	4	1	O'Neill, lf	2	1	0	0	0	0
Burns, ss	2	0	0	0	1	1	Latham, 3b	2	0	1	0	1	0
McCormick, p	2	0	0	1	6	0	Foutz, p	2	0	0	0	2	1
Clarkson, rf	2	0	0	0	0	0	Nicol, rf	2	0	0	0	1	1
	23	5	6	15	15	5		20	4	2	16*	10	4

*Only one man out in sixth inning

```
CHI   1 1 0   0 0 3 – 5
STL   3 0 0   1 0 x – 4
```

Earned runs: CHI 1. 2B: Gleason, Latham, Sunday, Pfeffer. DP: STL. BB: Foutz 1. Struck out: Foutz 2, McCormick 3. PB: Robinson 3, Kelly 1. WP: Foutz 1. Umpire: David F. Sullivan. Att: 3,000.

GAME THREE—October 16, 1885, at Sportsman's Park, St. Louis

CHICAGO	AB	R	H	PO	A	E	ST. LOUIS	AB	R	H	PO	A	E
Dalrymple, lf	4	0	1	1	0	1	Gleason, ss	4	0	1	1	4	1
Sunday, cf	3	1	0	3	0	0	Welch, cf	4	1	0	2	0	0
Kelly, rf	4	0	1	1	1	0	Barkley, 2b	4	0	0	4	1	0
Anson, 1b	4	1	1	9	1	1	Comiskey, 1b	4	1	0	9	0	0
Pfeffer, 2b	4	0	2	3	3	1	Robinson, rf	3	1	0	3	0	0
Williamson, 3b	4	0	0	0	2	2	O'Neill, lf	4	2	2	0	0	1
Burns, ss	4	1	1	1	1	2	Latham, 3b	4	2	3	0	1	0
Clarkson, p	4	1	2	1	3	2	Caruthers, p	3	0	2	0	8	1
Flint, c	4	0	0	5	2	3	Bushong, c	3	0	0	8	2	1
	35	4	8	24	13	12		33	7	8	27	16	4

```
CHI   1 1 1   0 0 0   0 0 1 – 4
STL   5 0 0   0 0 2   0 0 x – 7
```

Earned runs: STL 2, CHI 2.   2B: Latham 2, Kelly, Clarkson.   3B. Caruthers, Burns. BB: Caruthers 1, Clarkson 1.   Struck out: Caruthers 7, Clarkson 5.   PB: Flint. WP: Clarkson 4.   DP: CHI.   Umpire: Harry McCaffrey.   Time—1:40.   Att: 3,000.

GAME FOUR—October 17, 1885, at Sportsman's Park, St. Louis

CHICAGO	AB	R	H	PO	A	E	ST. LOUIS	AB	R	H	PO	A	E
Dalrymple, lf	4	1	1	1	0	0	Gleason, ss	4	1	0	1	1	0
Sunday, cf	4	0	1	1	0	0	Welch, cf	4	0	1	1	1	0
Kelly, c	4	0	1	3	1	1	Barkley, 2b	4	0	0	7	5	4
Anson, 1b	3	0	1	11	0	0	Comiskey, 1b	3	0	1	9	1	2
Pfeffer, 2b	4	0	1	4	3	1	Robinson, c	3	0	0	5	3	0
Williamson, 3b	3	0	1	3	5	0	O'Neill, lf	3	0	1	0	0	0
Burns, ss	4	0	1	0	1	0	Latham, 3b	3	2	2	4	0	1
McCormick, p	4	1	1	0	5	0	Foutz, p	3	0	0	0	5	0
Holliday, rf	4	0	0	1	0	1	Caruthers, rf	3	0	1	0	0	0
	34	2	8	24	15	3		30	3	6	27	16	7

```
CHI   0 0 0   0 2 0   0 0 0 – 2
STL   0 0 1   0 0 0   0 2 x – 3
```

Earned runs: STL 1.   2B: Sunday.   HR: Dalrymple.   LOB: CHI 3, STL 7.   BB: Foutz 1.   Struck out: Foutz 4, McCormick 3.   PB: Kelly 3, Robinson 2.   DP: STL 1, CHI 2.   Umpire: William Medart.   Time—1:50.   Att: 3,000.

GAME FIVE—October 22, 1885, at Recreation Park, Pittsburgh

ST. LOUIS	AB	R	H	PO	A	E		CHICAGO	AB	R	H	PO	A	E
Gleason, ss	3	0	2	0	3	1		Dalrymple, lf	3	2	3	1	0	0
Welch, cf	3	0	0	1	0	1		Sunday, cf	4	1	0	0	0	0
Barkley, 2b	3	0	0	4	2	1		Kelly, rf	2	2	1	0	0	0
Comiskey, 1b	3	2	2	8	0	1		Anson, 1b	3	2	3	13	0	0
O'Neill, lf	3	0	0	1	0	0		Pfeffer, 2b	4	0	0	1	6	0
Robinson, c	3	0	0	4	3	1		Williamson, ss	4	1	0	1	1	0
Latham, 3b	2	0	0	1	2	1		Burns, 3b	4	1	0	1	3	0
Foutz, p	3	0	0	1	3	0		McCormick, p	3	0	0	0	4	0
Caruthers, rf	2	0	0	1	0	1		Flint, c	3	0	0	4	0	1
	25	2	4	21	13	7			30	9	7	21	14	1

```
STL   0 1 0   0 0 0   1 – 2
CHI   4 0 0   1 1 0   3 – 9
```

Earned runs: CHI 1.   3B: Anson.   DP: CHI.   BB: Clarkson 2, Foutz 5.   Struck out: Clarkson 4, Foutz 4.   PB: Flint.   WP: Foutz.   Umpire: John Kelly.   Att: 500.

◆ ◆ ◆

GAME SIX—October 23, 1885, at Cincinnati Base Ball Grounds, Cincinnati

ST. LOUIS	AB	R	H	PO	A	E		CHICAGO	AB	R	H	PO	A	E
Gleason, ss	4	1	0	2	2	1		Dalrymple, lf	5	1	2	4	0	1
Welch, cf	4	0	0	2	2	2		Sunday, cf	4	0	1	1	0	0
Barkley, 2b	3	1	0	3	3	0		Kelly, c	5	2	2	7	3	2
Comiskey, 1b	4	0	1	8	2	1		Anson, 1b	5	3	1	5	0	4
Robinson, rf	4	0	1	3	2	1		Pfeffer, 2b	4	2	3	3	3	1
O'Neill, lf	4	0	0	1	0	0		Williamson, ss	4	0	1	2	3	0
Latham, 3b	4	0	0	2	1	2		Burns, 3b	3	1	0	2	0	0
Caruthers, p	4	0	0	1	1	1		McCormick, p	4	0	1	0	2	0
Bushong, c	3	0	0	5	2	0		Clarkson, cf	4	0	0	3	0	2
	34	2	2	27	15	8			38	9	11	27	11	10

```
CHI   2 0 0   1 1 1   0 4 0 – 9
STL   0 0 2   0 0 0   0 0 0 – 2
```

Earned runs: CHI 4.   2B: Dalrymple 2, Anson.   3B: Kelly.   BB: McCormick 1, Caruthers 2.   Struck out: McCormick 6.   DP: STL.   PB: Kelly.   Umpire: John Kelly.   Time—1:40.   Att: 1,500.

♦ ♦ ♦

GAME SEVEN—October 24, 1885, at Cincinnati Base Ball Grounds, Cincinnati

CHICAGO	AB	R	H	PO	A	E	ST. LOUIS	AB	R	H	PO	A	E
Dalrymple, lf	3	0	0	1	1	2	Gleason, ss	4	2	2	3	3	1
Sunday, cf	4	1	1	3	0	0	Welch, cf	5	3	2	2	0	0
Kelly, rf	4	2	2	2	0	1	Barkley, 2b	3	2	2	3	3	2
Anson, 1b	4	1	2	7	2	4	Comiskey, 1b	4	1	2	10	0	1
Pfeffer, 2b	4	0	2	4	3	0	Robinson, rf	4	3	1	1	0	1
Williamson, ss	3	0	0	2	6	2	O'Neill, lf	4	0	1	0	0	0
Burns, 3b	4	0	0	0	1	2	Latham, 3b	3	0	0	1	3	0
McCormick, p	4	0	1	0	5	3	Foutz, p	4	1	2	0	6	2
Flint, c	4	0	1	2	3	3	Bushong, c	4	1	1	4	1	3
	34	4	9	21	21	17		35	13	13	24	16	10

```
CHI   2 0 0   0 2 0   0 0 -  4
STL   0 0 4   6 2 1   0 x - 13
```

Earned runs: STL 4.   2B: Kelly 2.   3B: Welch, Robinson.   DP: STL.   BB: McCormick 3, Foutz 2.   Struck out: McCormick 1, Foutz 4.   PB: Flint 3, Bushong 2. Umpire: John Kelly.   Time—1:50.   Att: 1,200.

◆ 4 ◆

CURT WELCH AND THE $15,000 SLIDE

◆

A. G. Spalding, President
Chicago League Club
Chicago

Dear Sir,

The championship season is fast approaching an end, and it now seems reasonably sure that the Chicago White Stockings and St. Louis Brown Stockings will win the championship of their respective associations. I therefore take this opportunity of challenging your team, on behalf of the Browns, for a series of contests to be known as the World's Championship Series. It is immaterial to me whether the series be composed of five, seven or nine games. I would respectfully suggest, however, that it would be better from a financial standpoint to play the entire series on the two home grounds, and not travel around as we did last season. I would like to hear from you at your earliest convenience, in order that the dates and other details may be arranged.

I am yours respectfully,

C. Von Der Ahe
St. Louis
September 26, 1886

1886

The Changing Game

◆ ◆ ◆

• *The pitcher's box was reduced to four feet by seven feet.*

• *The number of bad pitches required for a base on balls was reduced from seven to six.*

• *A stolen base was scored any time a runner advanced an extra base on a hit or an out, so that a man going from first to third on a single, for example, was given credit for a theft.*

• *Chest protectors for catchers and umpires were becoming more common. The fielder's glove, still thought unmanly, was not widely used, although catchers often wore a protective glove on both hands.*

• *The home team was no longer obligated to announce its starting lineup before a game, a rule change instituted because Chicago player-manager Cap Anson would often wait to see if anyone got on base in the first inning before deciding whether to bat.*

• *Cincinnati Reds owner Aaron Stern instituted the idea of Ladies' Day.*

• *The Providence Grays and Buffalo Bisons withdrew from the National League and were replaced by the Kansas City Cowboys and Washington Senators.*

O ne of baseball's pioneers, the pious Albert Spalding was, in his later days, more concerned with the Almighty Dollar than with Almighty God.

Pitcher-turned-owner Spalding accepted the challenge but asked for a nine-game series, and suggested that the clubs play for winner-take-all stakes. Von Der Ahe accepted the all-or-nothing proposition, and asked that the Series be limited to seven games because the Browns already had a commitment to play a city championship series with the National League St. Louis Maroons. (This arrangement made the 1886 World Series the first to be played under the modern best-of-seven format.) If a seventh game was necessary, it would be played in a neutral city decided upon by the two clubs. Von Der Ahe had already stated a preference for Cincinnati. If either team swept the first four games, a fifth game would be played for exhibition only. Both owners would cover their own expenses and the club winning the Series would pay the umpires.

The two teams that met in the 1886 World Series were virtually unchanged from the year before. The Browns had released Sam Barkley to make room for the versatile Yank Robinson at second, and Nat Hudson had joined the pitching staff, but otherwise, this was the same team which had won the 1885 American Association pennant.

The St. Louis Browns won two of every three games they played in 1886 and were easily the best team in the Association, finishing a whopping twelve games ahead of their closest competition. The club's offense was nothing less than incredible. St. Louis outscored its opponents by a staggering 352 runs—944 to 592, or an average of 2½ more runs per game than its opponents— becoming the first team in the history of major league baseball to break the nine hundred-runs barrier. The Browns led the Association in doubles (206) and slugging average (.360), and their team batting average of .273 was ten points higher than any other club in the Association and a full sixty-nine points higher than the last-place Baltimore Orioles.

Two of the Browns' three leading batsmen were Tip O'Neill and Curt Welch.

James "Tip" O'Neill was one of the most feared hitters of his day and yet he began his career in 1883 as a pitcher with the New

York Giants. O'Neill's record was a sad 5-12 and his batting average of .197 gave no indication he would ultimately compile a career mark of .326. Dissatisfied, the Giants released him at the end of the year and O'Neill signed with the St. Louis Browns. The club's opening day pitcher in 1884, O'Neill ran up an 11-4 record for the year, but his control was poor and he had developed a sore arm. At manager Jimmy Williams's suggestion, O'Neill was converted to the outfield in the latter part of the season. He responded with a .276 average. In 1885, O'Neill was tearing up the league when a June 13 collision on the basepaths sidelined him until September. Still, he finished the year with a .350 batting average. In his first full and healthy year, 1886, O'Neill began to develop into a capable defensive outfielder with deceptive speed on the bases, but an utter lack of sliding talent would cost him many an extra base in his career. In 1887, this right-handed pull hitter would become the only man in major league history to lead a league in doubles (52), triples (19), and home runs (14) in the same season. He also topped the Association in hits (225), runs (167), slugging average (.691), and batting average (.435). It is a certainty that O'Neill was among the league leaders in runs batted in and stolen bases as well. (Official records were not kept for RBIs, and stolen base records are unreliable.) Regarded by his contemporaries as a gentleman, O'Neill retired from baseball following the 1892 season. He died of a heart attack on New Year's Eve in 1915.

Center fielder Curt Welch was one of the best defensive outfielders of the nineteenth century and revolutionized his position by being one of the first outfielders to turn his back on the batted ball and run to the spot where he thought it was going to come down. More than any other center fielder of his era, Welch played very shallow and reveled in robbing batters of Texas Leaguers by making headlong diving catches just beyond the infield. And heaven help the headstrong baserunner who thought he could take an extra base on Welch's throwing arm.

One of the best basestealers of the nineteenth century, Welch was a smart hitter who drew a fair number of walks and was quite adept at getting hit by pitches. His aggressive style of play and constant umpire-baiting was a perfect fit for the rowdy St. Louis Browns. Vulgar and nearly illiterate, Welch's heavy drinking brought about a premature retirement at the age of thirty-one, and he died of alcoholism in his hometown of East Liverpool, Ohio, three years later.

Defensively, only the Pittsburgh Alleghenies (.917) led the Browns (.915) in fielding percentage. Welch and catcher Doc Bushong led the Association in fielding at their respective positions.

The St. Louis pitching staff had been greatly strengthened by the addition of right-hander Nat Hudson. Hudson's rookie mark of 16-10 was impressive, and his twenty-nine starts gave Dave Foutz and Bob Caruthers an occasional day off during the season, making the duo that much tougher on the days they worked. Caruthers's record had fallen from 40-13 in 1885 to 30-14 (with ten fewer starts), but Dave Foutz picked up the slack. Starting eleven more games than he had in 1885, Foutz improved his record from 33-14 to 41-16.

For the White Stockings, who clinched the pennant on the last day of the season, there were a few minor changes. Rookie Jimmy Ryan had taken over right field, relegating King Kelly to utility duties, and rookie Jocko Flynn had been added to the team's pitching staff.

The White Stockings were a better defensive team in 1886, but they still had ample room for improvement. First baseman Cap Anson, second baseman Fred Pfeffer, third baseman Ned Williamson, catcher Silver Flint, and pitcher John Clarkson led the league in errors at their respective positions. Flint's feat was of particularly herculean proportions, considering that he spent just fifty-four games behind the plate. But, more than any other National League club, the White Stockings could afford to be a little sloppy defensively. They had the League's most feared offense. Chicago scored 900 runs—the first team in the eleven-year history of the National League to do so—and outscored its opponents by 345 runs. The White Stockings led the league in doubles (198), triples (87), and slugging average (.401), and narrowly lost the league lead to Detroit in homers (by one) and batting average (by .001).

John Clarkson made fifteen fewer starts in 1886, yet still finished with an impressive mark of 35-17, leading the league in strikeouts (340), finishing second in wins, third in earned run average (2.41), and fifth in complete games (50). Right-hander Jim McCormick made fourteen more starts than in 1885, won ten of them, and ran up an equally impressive record of 31-11. McCormick finished fourth in wins and winning percentage (.738), and it was his sixteen-game winning streak early in the year which kept the White Stockings alive in the pennant race with the Detroit Wolverines.

Rounding out the staff was the diminutive John "Jocko" Flynn, who stood 5′6½″ and weighed only 143 pounds. In his major league debut, he went 24-6 to lead the league in winning percentage (.800). Flynn caused quite a sensation in Chicago, and the White Stockings were expecting great things from the twenty-two-year-old youngster, but the following season he would play only one game in the outfield for the White Stockings, then mysteriously vanish forever from the roll calls of major league baseball.

The Browns boarded the Vandalia Special, garishly decorated with banners reading, "ST. LOUIS BROWNS, CHAMPIONS OF 1885 AND 1886," on the evening of Sunday, October 17, bound for Chicago. Dave Foutz was so confident on his team's chances that he reportedly wagered a large sum of money on his club before leaving St. Louis. The team arrived in Chicago early Monday morning, checked into the Clifton House, and departed for the ballpark the next afternoon. The weather was cold and raw but five thousand fans turned out at Congress Street Grounds to watch Game One. Umpires John Kelly, Joe Quest, Gracie Pearce, and John McQuaid met prior to game time and drew lots to determine who would work the game. McQuaid won. Starting pitchers were Dave Foutz and John Clarkson, and the game was played under National League rules.

Austin's First Regiment Band played the teams onto the field and McQuaid called for play to begin promptly at 3:00. Cap Anson, still smarting from his club's defeat in the 1885 Series, won the coin toss and elected to put the White Stockings on defense. The irrepressible Arlie Latham was the first batter for the Browns. Latham intentionally bunted several of Clarkson's deliveries foul before taking a full cut and going down on strikes. Right fielder Bob Caruthers followed with an easy grounder to Fred Pfeffer at second and Clarkson struck out the dangerous Tip O'Neill to end the inning.

The 1886 World Series had begun.

Without fanfare, the White Stockings came in for their first time at bat and immediately roughed up Dave Foutz for two runs and what proved to be the game. Leadoff batter George Gore worked Foutz for a base on balls but was forced at second when King Kelly grounded out. Kelly took second on a passed ball and scored on Cap Anson's single to center. When Curt Welch's return throw to the infield was wild, Anson went to third. A single by Fred Pfeffer gave Chicago its second run and provided all the offense John Clarkson would need. The White Stockings scored a single run in the sixth and three more in the eighth, but those runs were just icing on the cake. Clarkson was never in trouble and finished with a five-hit, 6-0 shutout. He walked only one batter and struck out ten. There was nothing in the game to give Association fans any hope that the Browns were on equal footing with the White Stockings.

The only disagreeable feature of the contest was the unusual bitterness the Chicago crowd directed at the Browns. Spectators jeered and booed St. Louis unmercifully, and at one point the heckling was "directed" by Chicago newspaper reporters seated in the press box. One fan made enough trouble all by himself that he earned an ejection from the ballpark from umpire McQuaid.

In St. Louis, a crowd had gathered outside the offices of the St. Louis *Globe-Democrat* to get results of the game. Under an article entitled "Local Enthusiasm Still Alive" and published in the next day's edition, the paper had this to say about Bob Caruthers, playing right field for the Browns:

> In front of the GLOBE-DEMOCRAT the crowd extended out to the street car tracks, and such expressions as "Bobby's got the heart disease bad," were frequent.

Caruthers, who weighed only 138 pounds, was a sickly man who suffered from heart disease. He went 0-for-4 in the game.

Receipts for the first game totaled $2,002 and were deposited in banks in Chicago and St. Louis, to be awarded after the Series ended. A reported ten thousand dollars in wagers went from St. Louis to Chicago after the first game. Fans who wished to place a bet on the Browns for Game Two had to put up seven dollars to win ten. A fellow named Dick Roche offered $1,000 to anyone else's $400 that the Browns wouldn't win a game the entire Series. (For Roche's sake, one can only hope he found no takers.)

For Game Two, on the 19th, a new plan of having a referee and two umpires was implemented for the first time in Series play. The umpires drew lots again and John Kelly was chosen as the referee. Chicago then drew John McQuaid's name and St. Louis drew Joe Quest. Although this was the first time in history three umpires were used for a Series game, in reality, the experiment was nothing more than a two-umpire system. Kelly umpired behind the pitcher with the bases empty, and with men on, he moved behind second. Quest called balls and strikes when St. Louis was in the field and McQuaid worked the plate when Chicago was on defense.

The weather was much warmer as the clubs took the field before nine thousand fans. The Browns had a team photograph taken at home plate before the game began. Starting pitchers were Bob Caruthers and Jim McCormick.

The three-umpire system paid dividends for St. Louis in the very first inning. Browns leadoff batter Arlie Latham coaxed a base on balls and a moment later was picked off by McCormick. McQuaid called Latham out but was immediately overruled by Kelly. Neither team questioned the decision.

Latham stole second but was absentmindedly standing off the bag when Bob Caruthers struck out. Catcher King Kelly dropped the third strike, but instead of throwing to first to retire the batter, he fired the ball to Pfeffer at second and Latham was tagged out. The next batter, Tip O'Neill, shot McCormick's second delivery down among a line of parked carriages in left field. By the time Abner Dalrymple could retrieve the ball, Caruthers had scored and O'Neill was racing to the plate with an inside-the-park home run. The Browns scored two more runs in the fourth to take a 4-0 lead, and O'Neill legged out his second inside-the-park home run on the first pitch from McCormick in the fifth. This marked the first time in World Series history that a batter had struck two home runs in the same game. Two more runs in the fifth and a five-run explosion in the seventh put the Browns safely on top by a 12-0 margin. Because it was growing dark, the game was called at the conclusion of eight innings by mutual agreement.

The crowd, perhaps silenced by such a resounding defeat of its home club, was much better behaved than the day before and the only incident to mar the game occurred on the field. In the seventh inning, with Curt Welch on second, Yank Robinson singled. As Welch was crossing the plate, his arm accidentally brushed against Jim McCormick, who was backing up the plate. McCormick took umbrage and struck Welch on the neck from behind, knocking off his cap. Welch, the same height as McCormick but twenty pounds lighter, turned on his attacker but wisely declined to fight. McCormick was hissed by the hometown crowd.

Bob Caruthers pitched a masterful game. George Gore's single, leading off the bottom of the first, was the only hit the White Stockings would make in the game, and Caruthers allowed only five baserunners the rest of the way. Anson followed Gore's hit with a one-out walk, but both runners were stranded. Jimmy Ryan reached on an error in the second, but Caruthers retired the next fifteen men before walking Ned Williamson in the seventh. Tom Burns struck out in the same inning but reached first when Doc Bushong dropped the third strike. Gore reached base when Arlie Latham bobbled his grounder in the eighth. "Parisian Bob" finished with a one-hitter, struck out eight, and after the game, was presented with a gold-headed cane from friends and admirers in Chicago.

The only kick either team had against the umpiring occurred in the third inning when, with Tip O'Neill on first, Bill Gleason grounded a foul ball to Cap Anson at first. O'Neill leisurely returned to the base and on his way back was tagged by Anson. The game was being played under League rules, which stipulated a batter had to return to his base immediately after a foul hit, but referee Kelly nonetheless declared O'Neill safe. Despite this minor incident, the umpiring experiment was a resounding success and both clubs vowed to present it to the rules committee in November.

Not for the last time in the Series, the Chicago crowd was somewhat disgusted with Arlie Latham's coaching antics during the game. The Chicago *Inter-Ocean* vilified the Browns' third baseman:

> One feature of the St. Louis game might be eliminated with success, and that is the disgusting mouthings of the clown Latham. There was a universal sentiment of disgust expressed by the crowd that left the ball park at the close of the game at this hoodlum's obscene talk on the ball field. One well known merchant remarked that he never would attend another game that Latham played in. The roughest element that ever attends a ball game in this city could not condone the offense of such a player as Latham. Pres. Spalding should insist upon his being silenced; such coarse mouthings may pass in St. Louis, but will not be tolerated in Chicago.

The *Chicago Tribune* agreed:

> Latham's senseless and everlasting chatter was the only really disagreeable feature of yesterday's game. If the League managers were forced to listen to his incessant bellowing it is safe to predict they would formulate a rule to prevent it on the League grounds.

Not surprisingly, the St. Louis *Post-Dispatch* held a different view on the matter:

> The only man on the Browns' side who failed to get a hit was Latham, but he more than made up for his weakness at the bat by his excellent coaching.

Browns owner Chris Von Der Ahe spent the evening in his hotel room answering dozens of congratulatory telegrams. The Mermod & Jaccard Jewelry Company of St. Louis, still in business today, wired the following:

> Chris Von Der Ahe, President, St. Louis Browns
> Chicago, Ill.
>
> Glorious! We shall present a solid gold monogram scarf-pin to each of the nine and the manager of the St. Louis Browns if they win the championship and we know they will.
>
> Mermod & Jaccard Jewelry Co.

Cap Anson and Fred Pfeffer angrily denied reports the Chicago players had been drinking heavily the night before and that this was the reason for their lopsided loss. Rumors now began to circulate to the effect that Chicago was hippodroming to prolong the Series and increase gate receipts.

Flushed with success over his one-hit performance, Bob Caruthers begged Chris Von Der Ahe to let him start Game Three the next day and, much to Von Der Ahe's regret, he acceded to the request. The Browns won the coin toss for the first time in the Series and elected to play on defense. Despite an early-morning rain, the field was in good playing condition and six thousand fans were in the park. Only one umpire, Kelly, worked this game.

Caruthers immediately showed the effects of pitching without rest when he walked George Gore and King Kelly in the first. Cap Anson sacrificed both runners along and, still struggling to find his control, Caruthers walked Fred Pfeffer and Ned Williamson, forcing in the first run of the game. Tom Burns's groundout scored Kelly and put the White Stockings up, 2-0.

The Browns cut the lead in half in the second on singles by Curt Welch, Yank Robinson, and Doc Bushong, and in the fourth inning, St. Louis extracted a measure of revenge for McCormick's rough tactics the day before. With Yank Robinson on third, Doc

Bushong flew out to Gore in center field. After watching Gore make the catch, Robinson streaked for home. Gore's throw to the plate was on line and Kelly had the ball in his hands as Robinson attempted to score. Yank ran headlong into the catcher and as the players fell to the ground, Kelly was spiked in the face but held the ball for the out. Although banged up, both men stayed in the game.

The White Stockings scored at least once in every inning from the fourth through the eighth and won going away, 11-4. Caruthers was completely ineffective and was pounded for twelve hits, including a double by Jimmy Ryan, a triple by Tom Burns, a fifth-inning solo home run by King Kelly, and an eighth-inning, two-run blast by George Gore. Clarkson didn't exactly mystify the Browns, who banged out eight hits against the right-hander until he was replaced on the mound in the eighth inning by shortstop Ned Williamson.

In the next day's account of the game, the *Chicago Tribune* excoriated Arlie Latham for his coaching. Latham's constant chatter was, according to the *Tribune*:

> . . . just the sort of thing to catch a country crowd—the kind of a crowd that thinks a circus clown is a humorist. The green young men who were up here to send the defeat of the Browns by innings to the St. Louis papers were also impressed as are the other rustics with the idea that Latham was funny.

To be fair, Latham's coaching antics were pretty heavy-handed. His constant chatter and taunts made him no new friends in Chicago, and when he replaced Bushong behind the plate in the seventh, the *Tribune* remarked that it was a "relief to the spectators when this young man was put in a place where he couldn't inflict his yawp on the crowd." Within a year, Latham's free-spirited coaching would cause baseball rulesmakers to mark out specified boxes for coaches.

Umpire John Kelly pronounced the three-man umpiring scheme an unqualified success. "An umpire who stands behind the pitcher," said Kelly, "can see plays upon the bases which are utterly invisible to a man behind the bat and as a matter of course can give decisions which in ninety-nine cases out of a hundred will be perfectly correct." Kelly went on to provide a glimpse of the importance of calling balls and strikes when he added, "So far as umpiring the balls and strikes is concerned, a player from each of the playing nines can umpire almost as well as anybody. I consider that a ball player who can't answer this purpose is not worth hiring."

The clubs departed Chicago for St. Louis after the game and registered at the fashionable Lindell Hotel upon arriving from Union Depot. President Al Spalding stayed behind in Chicago, attending to business. Manager Cap Anson took two extra players with him to St. Louis: Mark Baldwin, a pitcher who had won thirty-nine games in the minor leagues in 1886 and had been signed for the upcoming 1887 season; and Lew Hardie, a reserve catcher who saw action in sixteen regular-season games. At the Lindell Hotel that evening, Anson was asked why Jim McCormick did not accompany the club to St. Louis. He replied, "He's got the rheumatism and stayed at home."

Club secretary John A. Brown elaborated on McCormick's troubles. "The fact is, the trouble doesn't lie in his arm at all, but in his legs. Rheumatism struck him last spring and compelled him to lay off ten days at the Hot Springs. He's got the same trouble in his feet now, and can't get around at all for a ball player."

McCormick would be lost to the White Stockings for the remaining games of the 1886 World Series.

Anson took the occasion to respond to charges of hippodroming. Testily, he told a reporter from the St. Louis *Post-Dispatch*, "There are always a few men everywhere who are anxious to throw dirt at people when they find themselves out. I can tell you now positively that these games are for blood, every one of them. I was present when the agreement was made in Spalding's office, and I heard all that passed. I know that the receipts are deposited in the First National Bank of Chicago and that if we win the series we will get half of it. That is what we are playing for, and I suppose such is the case with the St. Louis club . . ."

Shortstop Bill Gleason managed to get off a rather long opinion in the *Post-Dispatch* on the selection of Caruthers for the third game. "It was dead wrong to put him in," Gleason said. "We all wanted Hudson and we made a special request that Hudson be pitcher. Caruthers insisted on going in, and why they put him in I don't know. Hudson was anxious to pitch and understood he was going to until the last minute. From the very start we all knew how the thing was going, and when the Chicagos took four bases on balls, that settled it. Even then it was not too late, and I heard that Mr. Von Der Ahe told Comiskey to bring Hudson in from the field, but why it wasn't done I don't know."

For Von Der Ahe's part, he was dissatisfied with the club's showing and told the players so in a scathing tirade.

Several Chicago players were seen in gambling halls on the morning of Game Four. Plenty of money was being placed on the White Stockings to win the game that afternoon.

The teams took the field at Sportsman's Park for practice at 2:30 and Game Four began promptly at 3:15 with Joe Quest as the umpire. Despite weather cold enough to force spectators to wear overcoats, a capacity crowd of ten thousand filled the stands. The Browns won the coin toss and sent Chicago to bat. St. Louis starting pitcher Dave Foutz got off to a rocky start in the first inning when he gave up a single to George Gore and walked the next batter, King Kelly. Cap Anson hit a liner to Bill Gleason, but the little shortstop bobbled the ball for an error, and the White Stockings had a bases-loaded, none-out opportunity. Still unable to locate the plate, Foutz walked Fred Pfeffer to force in the first run of the game. Ned Williamson's sacrifice fly to right plated Kelly, and both Anson and Pfeffer advanced a base on the throw to the plate. When catcher Doc Bushong threw down to Yank Robinson in an attempt to nail Pfeffer at second, Anson broke from third. Robinson's throw to the plate was wide and Anson tallied the third run of the inning. Satisfied that his club was at the top of its game, Anson couldn't help but feel the White Stockings would easily take the Browns.

In the second, St. Louis started making some noise. Bill Gleason reached base when Fred Pfeffer fumbled his grounder. Charlie Comiskey gave Pfeffer a chance to atone for his error when he sent an easy grounder at the second baseman, but the ball went right through Pfeffer's legs and everyone was safe. Curt Welch's ground-out forced Comiskey, and with Yank Robinson at the plate, Welch broke for second. Kelly threw down and shortstop Williamson applied the tag, but Gleason streaked home on the delayed steal. The White Stockings had been caught napping and it cost them a run.

In the third, the Browns continued to rally. Bob Caruthers reached on a Ned Williamson error and Tip O'Neill followed with a long triple into the right-field crowd. O'Neill was thrown out trying to stretch his hit into an inside-the-park home run, but St. Louis had pulled to within one run.

If Cap Anson had begun to think he had underestimated the American Association club, his suspicions were confirmed in the St. Louis fifth. With one out, Doc Bushong drew a walk and took second on Arlie Latham's single. Bob Caruthers popped out to bring the dangerous Tip O'Neill to the plate. Before O'Neill batted, catcher King Kelly walked out to Clarkson for a short conversation. The Chicago hurler resumed his spot in the pitchers' box and intentionally threw four pitches well outside the strike zone to O'Neill. Anson called time and told Clarkson to throw the ball over the plate but Clarkson ignored the advice and finished giving O'Neill the intentional walk, the first such free pass in the history of the World Series, and perhaps the earliest example of an intentional base on balls in baseball history. Clarkson's strategy looked as if it was going to pay off when he fired his next two deliveries past Bill Gleason for called strikes. One swing from ending the inning, Gleason grounded the next pitch through the left side, scoring Bushong and Latham, and giving the Browns a 4-3 lead. Charlie Comiskey's ground single to left brought O'Neill home. The White Stockings had their hands full.

Chicago tied the game in the top of the sixth on an RBI triple by Abner Dalrymple and a single by Clarkson, but the Browns rallied in the bottom of the inning for three runs and the game. With one out, Yank Robinson walked and went to second on Bushong's single to left. Robinson stole third and Arlie Latham coaxed a base on balls to load the bases. Caruthers lifted a high pop fly to Williamson at short, but Williamson dropped the ball and Robinson scurried home with the lead run. Williamson recovered to force Latham at second, but Clarkson issued his second intentional walk of the game to Tip O'Neill and Gleason came to the plate with another two-out opportunity. The St. Louis shortstop responded to the pressure again, this time with a line single into center field. Bushong and Caruthers came home with two insurance runs to make the score 8-5, St. Louis. The White Stockings batted in their half of the seventh, but the game was halted because of darkness before the Browns could take their cuts again.

At the Lindell Hotel that evening, the White Stockings, with the exception of Cap Anson, seemed strangely undisturbed by their loss. The team stood around smoking big black cigars, toasting each other with champagne, and joking with reporters. Clarkson, although the losing pitcher, was in especially good humor. Shortstop Ned Williamson smiled enigmatically and said, "Yes sir, they beat us today on the level," and King Kelly told funny stories to a group of friends. Not surprisingly, the team's unusual behavior caused a resurrection of the charges of hippodroming.

Chicago secretary Brown told the St. Louis *Post-Dispatch,* "Spalding, Von Der Ahe, myself, and the players all know that these games are as square as they can be, and it really is so absurd to even think of anything else that it makes us sick to hear this bosh about the series being fixed. It is thousands of dollars for the players and I assure you that our boys will win the next two games if they can, and I feel pretty certain that the St. Louis Club have made up their minds to do the same thing."

Taunted by a *Post-Dispatch* reporter, Anson was asked how it was possible the much-superior White Stockings could have lost the game. "Didn't you see it yourself?" Anson angrily retorted. "Wasn't you there?" When the reporter replied that he was, Anson snapped, "Well, then you know as much as I do about it."

The weather had improved a bit and another capacity crowd turned out for the fifth game the next day. Gracie Pearce was due to umpire, but when he failed to arrive at the park, McQuaid was chosen as his successor. Manager Charlie Comiskey chose Nat Hudson to start for the Browns, and Cap Anson wrote in Mark Baldwin's name. Comiskey objected that it was the White Stockings of 1886 they were playing and not a future nine, and umpire McQuaid concurred, striking Baldwin's name from the lineup. Anson elected instead to start shortstop Ned Williamson. Anson's refusal to start Flynn, if Flynn was healthy, was nothing less than an open declaration that the White Stockings were not giving their best effort in order to prolong the Series and line their pockets. Anson might have been taking his cue from President Spalding, who was often fond of saying, "In this business, everything goes."

Chicago batted first and failed to score against Hudson, despite receiving two-out walks to Fred Pfeffer and Anson and a passed ball. In the bottom of the inning, the Browns greeted Williamson like an old friend. The shortstop-turned-pitcher had trouble locating the plate and walked leadoff batter Arlie Latham, who immediately stole second and scored when Bob Caruthers slapped a single to right. Caruthers anticipated a throw home and tried to take the extra base but was thrown out by Jimmy Ryan. Tip O'Neill touched Williamson for a single, made second on catcher Flint's passed ball, and Bill Gleason, rapidly becoming the hero of the Series for the Browns, laced a single to left, scoring

O'Neill with the second run of the inning. Like Caruthers, Gleason was thrown out at second trying to take an extra base.

The White Stockings got on the scoreboard in the top of the second when Jimmy Ryan was hit by a pitch, stole second, and scored on Abner Dalrymple's single. Displeased with Williamson's performance on the mound, Anson sent Jimmy Ryan to the hill and shuffled his defense. Williamson resumed his position at short, Tom Burns went to right, and Kelly took over at third base. History has failed to record whether Ryan or leadoff hitter Curt Welch was more surprised when Welch struck out, but Ryan's good fortune was short-lived. Yank Robinson singled and took second on the first of four wild pitches Ryan would make. Charlie Hudson struck out but had to be retired at first when Flint dropped the third strike. Robinson went to third on the play and later scored on Ryan's second wild pitch of the inning.

The White Stockings pulled to within one with a run in the third, but St. Louis routed Ryan in the bottom of the inning. Leadoff batter Bob Caruthers started the damage with a triple. Tip O'Neill struck out, but Flint momentarily lost the third strike and Caruthers scored as O'Neill was thrown out at first. A walk to Bill Gleason was followed by doubles from Charlie Comiskey and Curt Welch, and St. Louis had a four-run lead. Welch took an extra base on Tom Burns's throw to the plate, and when Flint made an ill-advised throw to Kelly at third, the ball bounded into left field for an error. Welch came home with the fourth run of the inning and the Browns led, 7-2.

The White Stockings scored a singleton in the fourth but St. Louis batted Ryan around for three insurance runs in a wild sixth inning. With one out, Nat Hudson tripled over the head of George Gore, then scored on a passed ball. Doc Bushong drew a base on balls but was forced at second on Arlie Latham's grounder. Ryan's third wild pitch of the game sent Latham all the way to third from where he scored on Bob Caruthers's single. Caruthers gained two bases on another wild pitch and scored when Flint's throw to third was wild. Tip O'Neill and Bill Gleason followed with singles and the Browns might have batted for the rest of the afternoon had O'Neill not been thrown out at third. After the White Stockings took their cuts in the seventh, umpire John McQuaid called the game because of darkness. The Browns had a decisive 10-3 win and a three-games-to-two lead in the Series.

The *Chicago News* of October 23 made an outright allegation of cheating when it said:

> It would be a hard task for a Chicago man to attempt to regard with any degree of good humor the performances of the Chicago Base Ball Club at St. Louis yesterday. Admitting that base ball is a business conducted for pecuniary profit, there still can be no palliation for the offense of brazenly giving away a game as the game was given away yesterday in St. Louis . . . The base ball series in Chicago was cleverly worked; the public felt that it was being humbugged, but the hippodrome was so artistically played that there really was no inclination to cry out against it. In St. Louis, however, the pins have been set up awkwardly and the wires have been worked bunglingly . . . Yesterday the Chicagos started in with a seeming determination to prevent at the very outset every possibility of winning. The champion League club, having in its membership such pitchers as Clarkson, McCormick, Flynn and Baldwin, disdained the services of all these gentlemen and put in the box the very estimable short stop of the nine . . . We have a higher opinion of the forbearance of the St. Louis public than we have had before. We presume to say that if such a shameless farce had been attempted here in Chicago the conspirators and co[-]conspirators would have been hooted off the field. That the whole business is understood in this city is evident in the common talk upon the streets and in the tone of proceedings at the pool-rooms last night. Odds of 20 percent were given on the Chicagos winning . . .

Al Spalding, finished with whatever business had detained him in Chicago, had arrived in St. Louis and prevailed upon Chris Von Der Ahe to start the sixth game at an earlier time, so all nine innings could be played. The Browns' owner, eager for his first clear-cut world championship, agreed.

Umpire Gracie Pearce arrived and took his position. The game began at 2:18, with John Clarkson working against Bob Caruthers. It was Chicago's turn to win and the White Stockings went about their business doing so. In the top of the second, Caruthers walked leadoff hitter Fred Pfeffer, who stole second and took third on a passed ball. Pitching under pressure, Caruthers struck out Ned Williamson and Tom Burns, but Jimmy Ryan came through with a clutch RBI single. Chicago added a second run in the fourth when Pfeffer deposited a Caruthers fastball into the right-field bleachers for a solo home run. In the sixth, Pfeffer again proved the catalyst as he grounded a pitch through Yank Robinson's legs and raced to third when right fielder Dave Foutz let the ball slip past him. A sacrifice fly by Ned Williamson gave Chicago a 3-0 lead.

And St. Louis? Entering the bottom of the seventh inning, the Browns had yet to reach Clarkson for a hit and their only base-runner had been Tip O'Neill, who drew a two-out walk back in the first. It looked to be a certainty that Chicago would tie the Series with a win in Game Six.

Tip O'Neill doubled to center for the Browns' first hit in the seventh but killed any possible rally when he unwisely tried to stretch his hit into a triple and was nailed at third by George Gore's strong throw. Things were still proceeding according to Chicago's plan when Clarkson took the mound in the eighth. But Charlie Comiskey singled and Tom Burns was guilty of a two-base error when he threw wildly to Anson at first on Curt Welch's slow ground ball. A sacrifice fly to deep center by Dave Foutz gave the Browns their first run and sent Welch to third. Yank Robinson popped up for the second out of the inning, but Doc Bushong worked Clarkson for a base on balls, bringing Arlie Latham to the plate.

No charges of hippodroming had been levelled against St. Louis, and Arlie Latham wasn't ready to be the first Brown Stocking accused of slacking off. Before he stepped to the plate, The Freshest Man On Earth turned to the hometown crowd and said, "Don't get nervous folks, I'll tie it up." (Shades of Babe Ruth.) On Clarkson's next pitch, Latham screamed a liner into right field past a surprised Abner Dalrymple, who had misjudged the force of the hit. The ball rolled to the wall for a triple, tying the score at three-all.

Although Clarkson went on to retire the side, the White Stockings were visibly shaken. This wasn't at all the way things were supposed to go.

Bob Caruthers started the ninth by striking out Ned Williamson, then surrendered a double to Tom Burns. Ryan sacrificed the potential winning run to third but Caruthers fanned Abner Dalrymple to end the threat. The Browns went out one-two-three in the bottom of the inning.

In the tenth, Caruthers struck out Clarkson and retired Gore and Kelly on harmless fly balls to left. Curt Welch, the first batter for the Browns in the bottom of the inning, leaned into a Clarkson delivery and was hit by the pitch. As Welch trotted to first, Cap Anson protested to umpire Pearce that he had made no effort to get out of the ball's way and should be sent back to the plate. Pearce agreed. Welch shrugged his shoulders, stepped into the batter's box, and lined Clarkson's next pitch into center field for a base hit. Dave Foutz grounded an infield single to Williamson at short, and Yank Robinson's sacrifice bunt moved both runners into scoring position. With Welch dancing down the third-base line, Clarkson took a gamble by quick-pitching Doc Bushong. The delivery was well over catcher Kelly's head and glanced off his glove before bounding away. Kelly made no effort to retrieve the ball and Welch came home with a showy and altogether unnecessary slide—one which became known as the "$15,000 Slide," a reference to the Series receipts which, in reality, totaled a little less than fourteen thousand dollars.

St. Louis fans rushed onto the field and carried the Browns into their dressing room. A crowd estimated at over three thousand lingered at the park, cheering the club until each member finally left. Nothing quite like this had ever been seen in St. Louis before.

The White Stockings were full of recriminations for Abner Dalrymple, whose poor judgment of Arlie Latham's triple had allowed the Browns to tie the score in the eighth inning. One unnamed member of the club said that "Ryan or Gore would have smothered it." Club president Al Spalding said, "Dal ought to have caught that ball," and looked at King Kelly for confirmation. Kelly, no great admirer of Spalding, was reluctant to say anything against Dalrymple and defiantly refused to take the cue. "I don't know about his catching it," he answered.

Receipts of the final game amounted to $2,500, bringing the Series total to $13,920.10, all going to the Browns. Despite charging half the admission price of the Chicago ballpark, the Browns netted almost eight hundred dollars more for the three games in St. Louis, and each member of the team received $580 for winning the Series. Spalding was reportedly so angered by the Series defeat that he refused to pay train fare home for the players.

After the game, Von Der Ahe sent a note to Spalding suggesting that the exhibition game scheduled for Cincinnati be played. Spalding's reply was short: "We must decline with our compliments. We know when we have had enough."

The following morning, Spalding sent Von Der Ahe a letter which said, in part:

The series of games for the world's championship between the St. Louis and Chicago clubs having been played, and your club having won that title, I am prepared to endorse over to you the entire gross gate receipts of all the games played, now on deposit to our joint account in the Chicago National Bank of Chicago [sic] and the Boatmen's Savings Bank of St. Louis. Please send me a statement of the amount in the St. Louis bank and I will endorse the same and return to you at once with the amount on deposit in the Chicago bank. The Chicago Club extend their congratulations to the champions of the world, and look to the near future for a return of the same.

The next day, during a game between the St. Louis Browns and St. Louis Maroons, play was stopped in the fifth inning so that New York sportsman Erastus Wiman could present the Browns with a solid silver trophy and a large floral arrangement in the shape of a baseball diamond. The trophy immediately went on display in the window of the Mermod & Jaccard Jewelry Company store at Fourth and Locust streets. King Kelly, who was in the crowd with Ned Williamson and Silver Flint, made the presentation:

Ladies and gentlemen. It is my honor on this occasion to present to your champion club this floral tribute. They have earned it. They have beaten our club, the Chicago club, fairly [applause] and they have beaten us on the dead rattle [applause]. I can say you have treated us well here, and we hope to meet you again in the future [cheers].

The St. Louis *Republican* had the last word. In late October, the paper commented that "Chicago should confine itself to the slaughter of hogs as a popular amusement" because "baseball seems to require more headwork."

GAME ONE—October 18, 1886, at Congress Street Grounds, Chicago

ST. LOUIS	AB	R	H	BI	E	CHICAGO	AB	R	H	BI	E
Latham, 3b	4	0	1	0	1	Gore, cf	2	0	0	0	1
Caruthers, rf	4	0	0	0	0	Kelly, c	4	1	1	0	1
O'Neill, lf	4	0	0	0	0	Anson, 1b	4	2	3	1	0
Gleason, ss	4	0	0	0	1	Pfeffer, 2b	4	2	3	2	0
Comiskey, 1b	4	0	2	0	0	Williamson, ss	4	1	1	1	0
Welch, cf	3	0	0	0	1	Burns, 3b	4	0	0	0	1
Foutz, p	3	0	0	0	0	Ryan, rf	4	0	1	0	0
Robinson, 2b	3	0	2	0	2	Dalrymple, lf	4	0	1	0	0
Bushong, c	3	0	0	0	0	Clarkson, p	4	0	0	0	0
	32	0	5	0	5		34	6	10	4	3

```
STL   0 0 0   0 0 0   0 0 0 - 0
CHI   2 0 0   0 0 1   0 3 x - 6
```

2B: Dalrymple. T: Robinson, Wiliamson. SB: Pfeffer. BB: Clarkson 2, Foutz 2. Struck out: Clarkson 7, Foutz 7. Umpire: McQuaid. Time—1:55. Att: 5,000.

GAME TWO—October 19, 1886, at Congress Street Grounds, Chicago

ST. LOUIS	AB	R	H	BI	E	CHICAGO	AB	R	H	BI	E
Latham, 3b	4	1	0	0	2	Gore, cf	4	0	1	0	0
Caruthers, p	5	2	2	1	0	Kelly, c-ss	4	0	0	0	1
O'Neill, lf	4	2	3	4	0	Anson, 1b	3	0	0	0	1
Gleason, ss	5	1	1	0	0	Pfeffer, 2b	3	0	0	0	1
Comiskey, 1b	5	0	2	0	1	Williamson, ss-c	2	0	0	0	0
Welch, cf	4	2	2	0	0	Burns, 3b	3	0	0	0	3
Foutz, rf	5	2	2	1	0	Ryan, rf	3	0	0	0	0
Bushong, c	4	1	1	2	0	Dalrymple, lf	3	0	0	0	1
Robinson, 2b	4	1	1	0	0	McCormick, p	3	0	0	0	0
	40	12	14	8	3		28	0	1	0	7

```
CHI   0 0 0   0 0 0   0 0 -  0
STL   2 0 0   2 3 0   5 0 - 12
```

2B: Bushong, Caruthers. 3B: Caruthers, Foutz. HR: O'Neill 2. SB: Latham, Gleason, Welch. SAC: Latham. LOB: CHI 3, STL 5. BB: McCormick 3, Caruthers 2. Struck out: Caruthers 8, McCormick 5. PB: Bushong. DP: CHI. Umpires: Kelly, McQuaid, Quest. Time—1:40. Att: 9,000.

GAME THREE—October 20, 1886, at Congress Street Grounds, Chicago

ST. LOUIS	AB	R	H	BI	E	CHICAGO	AB	R	H	BI	E
Latham, 3b	5	0	1	1	0	Gore, cf	4	3	2	2	2
Caruthers, p	3	0	1	0	0	Kelly, c	4	2	3	1	0
O'Neill, lf	3	0	1	0	0	Anson, 1b	5	0	0	0	0
Gleason, ss	4	0	0	0	0	Pfeffer, 2b	4	1	0	1	0
Comiskey, 1b	4	0	0	0	1	Wiliamson, ss	3	1	1	1	0
Welch, cf	3	2	3	0	0	Burns, 3b	4	2	2	1	0
Robinson, 2b	4	2	2	1	1	Ryan, rf	4	1	2	1	0
Hudson, rf	4	0	0	0	0	Dalrymple, lf	4	1	1	0	1
Bushong, c	4	0	1	0	0	Clarkson, p	4	0	0	0	0
	34	4	9	2	2		36	11	11	7	3

```
CHI   2 0 0   1 1 2   3 2 - 11
STL   0 1 0   0 0 2   0 1 -  4
```

D: Welch, Ryan.   T: Burns.   HR: Gore, Kelly.   SAC: Anson.   SF: Ryan.   LOB: STL 9, CHI 6.   DP: CHI.   BB: Clarkson 3, Caruthers 4.   Struck out: Clarkson 5, Caruthers 1.   PB: Kelly 4.   WP: Clarkson 2.   Umpire: John Kelly.   Time—2:05. Att: 6,000.

GAME FOUR—October 21, 1886, at Sportsman's Park, St. Louis

CHICAGO	AB	R	H	BI	E	ST. LOUIS	AB	R	H	BI	E
Gore, cf	4	1	1	0	0	Latham, 3b	3	1	1	0	1
Kelly, c	3	1	0	0	1	Caruthers, rf	4	2	0	1	0
Anson, 1b	3	1	1	0	0	O'Neill, lf	2	1	1	1	0
Pfeffer, 2b	3	0	0	1	2	Gleason, ss	4	1	2	3	1
Williamson, ss	3	0	0	1	1	Comiskey, 1b	4	0	1	1	0
Burns, 3b	3	0	2	0	1	Welch, cf	3	0	0	0	0
Ryan, rf	3	1	0	0	0	Foutz, p	3	0	1	0	0
Dalrymple, lf	3	1	1	1	0	Robinson, 2b	1	1	0	0	0
Clarkson, p	3	0	1	1	0	Bushong, c	2	2	1	0	0
	28	5	6	4	5		26	8	7	6	2

```
CHI   3 0 0   0 0 2   0 - 5
STL   0 1 1   0 3 3   x - 8
```

D: Foutz, Burns.   T: Dalrymple, O'Neill.   SB: Pfeffer, Anson 2, Robinson.   SF: Williamson.   LOB: STL 4, CHI 5.   BB: Foutz 4, Clarkson 6.   Struck out: Clarkson 3, Foutz 2.   Umpire: Quest.   Time—1:50.   Att: 10,000.

GAME FIVE—October 22, 1886, at Sportsman's Park, St. Louis

CHICAGO	AB	R	H	BI	E	ST. LOUIS	AB	R	H	BI	E
Gore, cf	4	0	0	0	0	Latham, 3b	3	2	0	0	0
Kelly, ss	4	0	1	0	0	Caruthers, rf	4	2	3	2	0
Anson, 1b	2	0	1	0	0	O'Neill, lf	4	1	2	0	0
Pfeffer, 2b	3	1	0	0	0	Gleason, ss	3	1	2	1	0
Williamson, p-rf	2	0	0	0	0	Comiskey, 1b	3	1	1	1	0
Burns, 3b	3	0	0	0	0	Welch, cf	3	1	1	1	0
Ryan, rf-p	3	2	1	0	0	Robinson, 2b	3	1	1	0	1
Dalrymple, lf	3	0	0	1	0	Hudson, p	2	1	1	0	0
Flint, c	3	0	0	1	2	Bushong, c	1	0	0	0	0
	27	3	3	2	2		26	10	11	5	1

```
CHI   0 1 1   1 0 0   0 - 3
STL   2 1 4   0 0 3   x - 10
```

D: Comiskey, Welch.   T: Caruthers, Hudson.   SB: Ryan, Dalrymple, Pfeffer, Williamson, Ryan, Kelly, Latham.   HBP: Ryan (Hudson).   BB: Hudson 4, Williamson 5. Struck out: Williamson 3, Hudson 2.   PB: Flint 2.   WP: Ryan 4.   LOB: STL 3, CHI 6. SAC: Flint.   Umpires: Kelly, McQuaid, Quest.   Time—1:45.   Att: 10,000.

GAME SIX—October 23, 1886, at Sportsman's Park, St. Louis

CHICAGO	AB	R	H	BI	E	ST. LOUIS	AB	R	H	BI	E
Gore, cf	5	0	0	0	0	Latham, 3b	4	0	1	2	1
Kelly, c	5	0	0	0	0	Caruthers, p	4	0	0	0	0
Anson, 1b	4	0	0	0	0	O'Neill, lf	3	0	1	0	0
Pfeffer, 2b	4	3	2	1	0	Gleason, ss	4	0	0	0	0
Williamson, ss	4	0	0	1	0	Comiskey, 1b	4	1	1	0	0
Burns, 3b	4	0	2	0	1	Welch, cf	4	2	1	0	0
Ryan, rf	3	0	1	1	0	Foutz, rf	4	0	0	1	1
Dalrymple, lf	4	0	1	0	0	Robinson, 2b	4	0	0	0	1
Clarkson, p	4	0	0	0	0	Bushong, c	2	1	0	0	0
	37	3	6	3	1		33	4	4	3	3

```
CHI   0 1 0   1 0 1   0 0 0   0 - 3
STL   0 0 0   0 0 0   0 3 0   1 - 4
```

D: O'Neill, Burns.   T: Latham.   HR: Pfeffer.   SAC: Robinson, Ryan.   SF: Williamson, Foutz.   LOB: STL 2, CHI 6.   BB: Clarkson 2.   Struck out: Clarkson 9, Caruthers 5.   PB: Bushong.   WP: Caruthers, Clarkson.   Umpire: Pearce. Time—2:20.   Att: 10,000.

• 5 •

THE SERIES THAT WENT ON FOREVER

◆

The most ambitious of all the nineteenth-century World Series was, ironically, the least profitable as well.

The Detroit Wolverines began the season with a grim determination to win the pennant they had narrowly missed in 1886. Winning nineteen of their first twenty-one games, the Wolverines roared to an early lead, faltered, and found themselves tied with the defending champion White Stockings on August 15. But Detroit ace Charlie Getzien won three games in the next five days and the Wolverines were never seriously threatened again.

At the end of the season, Wolverines owner and pharmaceuticals magnate Frederick Stearns challenged Browns owner Chris Von Der Ahe to a best-of-fifteen series to determine the baseball championship of the world. The Browns, riding the crest of an early-season fifteen-game winning streak, had coasted to a very profitable third straight Association pennant.

Von Der Ahe had recovered nearly twenty percent of his club payroll for the six games with the White Stockings in 1886, and he incorrectly assumed a fifteen-game series would be a financial windfall. Stearns suggested that the gate be divided after each game, with the winning club receiving seventy-five percent of the

1887

The Changing Game

◆ ◆ ◆

• Batters could no longer request a high or low pitch.

• The number of bad pitches required for a walk was reduced to five, and the number of strikes required for a strikeout was increased to four. A walk was counted as a base hit and a time at bat.

• The pitcher's box was reduced to four feet by five feet, six inches, and a hurler was now required to keep one foot on the rear line of his position and the ball in plain sight of the umpire at all times.

• An error was no longer given for a walk, a balk, a wild pitch, or a hit batsman. The catcher was also relieved of any defensive liability for a passed ball. Hit batsmen were now awarded first base with no time at bat being charged.

• In the National League, the St. Louis Maroons and Kansas City Blues were replaced by the Indianapolis Hoosiers and the Pittsburgh Alleghenies, which transferred from the American Association. The Alleghenies were replaced in the American Association by the Cleveland Spiders.

• Cap Anson originated spring training when, eager for his club to get off to a fast start, he took the White Stockings to Hot Springs, Arkansas, to prepare for a pre-season meeting with the St. Louis Browns.

• St. Louis first baseman Charlie Comiskey became the first ballplayer to be paid for an endorsement when he recommended Menell's Penetrating Oil.

net receipts—after travel and hotel expenses were deducted—and Von Der Ahe eagerly agreed. Both owners put up six hundred dollars to be awarded to the team winning the Series. If the Browns won the championship, each player's share would be about a hundred dollars. But Stearns offered his club an extra incentive: If the Wolverines won, he would sweeten the pot by four hundred dollars per man. Stearns's generosity and Von Der Ahe's penny-pinching would play a large part in the Series outcome.

The Wolverines were a worthy representative of the National League. They set a League record with 969 runs scored, led the circuit in doubles (213), triples (126), slugging average (.436), and fielding percentage (.925); and with fifty-nine round-trippers, the club finished second only to the Chicago White Stockings in that category. Detroit's team batting average of .299 was twenty points higher than its nearest competition.

The Wolverines were led by hard-hitting right fielder Sam Thompson and first baseman Dan Brouthers. In 1887, Thompson led the National League in at bats (545), hits (203), triples (23), batting average (.372), slugging average (.571), total bases (311), and runs batted in. His 166 RBIs were sixty-two more than New York's Roger Connor, who finished second. Thompson would play in the majors another twelve years and lose a batting title to Jesse Burkett in 1894, despite hitting for a .404 mark. He was elected to the Hall of Fame in 1974.

Dan Brouthers had begun his professional career as a pitcher and first baseman. In 1882 and 1883, he became the first man to win back-to-back batting titles when he hit .368 and .374, respectively, for Buffalo. In his career, Brouthers would lead the league in batting four times and tie for the league lead one other year. His lifetime .343 batting average is ninth on the all-time list. After he left the majors in 1896, Brouthers would hook up with Springfield in the Eastern League, where he led all batters with a .415 mark. He was still playing ball in the high minor leagues at the age of forty-one and five years later, in 1904, Brouthers appeared in two games for the New York Giants. In 1887, the left-handed power hitter led the National League in doubles (36) and runs scored (153), finished second in slugging average (.562) and total bases (281), third in batting average (.338), fourth in runs batted in (101), and tied for fifth place in homers (12)

The Wolverines had a five-man pitching staff—Charlie Getzien (29-13), Charles "Lady" Baldwin (13-10), George "Stump"

Weidman (13-7 with the Wolverines before he was sent to the New York Metropolitans in mid-season), Pete Conway (8-9), and Larry Twitchell (11-1).

German-born Charlie Getzien grew up in Chicago and entered organized baseball with Grand Rapids of the Northwestern League in 1883. Getzien was 14-12 in his organized baseball debut, improved to 27-4 in 1884, and when the club folded in early August, he was sold to the last-place Detroit Wolverines. Getzien began his major league career by losing his first eight games, but finished at 5-12 for the year. In 1887, he got off to another bad start but manager Bill Watkins liked what he saw and had the luxury of staying with the youngster as the Wolverines grabbed an early lead in the National League pennant race. When hot weather came, Getzien seemed to find his stride.

Getzien had a pronounced skip in his delivery, plenty of speed, and an excellent drop pitch. He had no peer in his mastery of the curve and changeup. Depending on which story you prefer, Getzien received his nickname (Pretzels) either because of his excellent curveball, or because of the position batters frequently found themselves in after swinging at the difficult pitch. In 1887, Getzien led the National League in winning percentage (.690) and finished third in wins.

Lady Baldwin's unusual nickname arose because of his unusual behavior—unusual, that is to say, for a nineteenth-century ballplayer. Baldwin neither drank, smoked, nor cursed. In 1886, he had nearly single-handedly brought the Wolverines their first pennant when he won forty-two of the club's games, made fifty-six starts, and worked 487 innings. In 1887, Baldwin had difficulty adjusting to the new rule which required that pitchers keep one foot on the back line of the box while taking only one step before delivering the ball. That, coupled with a weary arm, made him virtually ineffective in the early months of the season. On July 27, Baldwin was sent home without pay, his record a disappointing 6-9. He rejoined the club in August and won seven of his last eight games, helping spur the Wolverines to the pennant. But after starting five games in the World Series, his arm was completely dead. Baldwin would make only fifteen more appearances at the major league level and three more in the high minors before retiring from the game.

Larry Twitchell was a big right-handed thrower who had made a little enough impression on Detroit fans in 1886 when he made his debut with an 0-2 record and a 6.48 earned run average in four starts. In 1887, used in spots by manager Bill Watkins, Twitchell compiled an 11-1 record in fifteen starts and cut his earned run average by over two runs a game. His .917 winning percentage would easily have been the best mark in the League had he had enough decisions to qualify. When not pitching, Twitchell played left field for the Wolverines and hit .333 with some power.

The Browns, not satisfied with their record 900-plus runs in 1886, accomplished the seemingly impossible feat of breaking the 1,100-run mark while winning their third consecutive pennant. Their 1,131 runs scored worked out to an average of 8.33 per game against their opponents' 5.64, a margin of 2.69 runs a game. The Browns' regular starting lineup scored an astounding 954 runs—left fielder Tip O'Neill (167), third baseman Arlie Latham (163), first baseman Charlie Comiskey (139), shortstop Bill Gleason (135), second baseman Yank Robinson (102), right fielder Bob Caruthers (102), center fielder Curt Welch (98), and catcher Jack Boyle (48).

A St. Louis ballplayer either led the American Association or was near the top in every offensive or pitching category. O'Neill's batting average of .435 easily outdistanced Pete Browning's .402; Bob Caruthers was fifth with a .357 mark. O'Neill led the league in home runs with fourteen; Caruthers was tied for third with eight. O'Neill was first in slugging average (.691); Caruthers was third (.547). O'Neill also led the league in hits (225), doubles (52), and triples (19). As a team, the Browns topped the Association in home runs (39), fielding percentage (.916), doubles (261), batting average (.307), slugging average (.413), and stolen bases (581).

Tip O'Neill's .435 batting average in 1887 was the loftiest ever recorded in the twelve-year history of the major leagues and today remains the second highest ever for a right-handed batter. Still, O'Neill's .435 was apparently a fluke—the mark was 107 points higher than his average of 1885, one hundred points higher than he would attain in 1888, and 124 points higher than his career average, with the .435 season factored out. The Canadian-born Irishman hit for the cycle twice during the season, and by any standard you would care to apply, was the most dangerous batter in all of baseball for this year.

The Browns pitching staff of Bob Caruthers, Dave Foutz, and Silver King was equally stupendous.

Bob Caruthers suffered from occasional bouts of malaria through the 1887 season and, although improving his record, saw his earned run average jump by nearly a run a game, from 2.32 to 3.30. Still, the St. Louis right-hander was fifth in the Association in ERA and his 29-9 record was good enough to lead the league in winning percentage (.763).

Dave Foutz had tailed off considerably from his exceptional year in 1886. Foutz was 23-8 when he broke his thumb on August 14. When he returned to the rotation, he had trouble breaking off his curveball properly and would win only two more decisions. His starts were down from fifty-seven to thirty-eight, his innings pitched dropped from 504 to 339 1/3, and his earned run average ballooned from 2.11 to 3.87. Although he had won twenty-five of his thirty-seven decisions, Foutz's arm was nearly dead.

Silver King was born Charles Frederick Koenig, but St. Louis newspapers shortened his name to King and nicknamed him Silver for his prematurely gray hair. King had broken into organized baseball with St. Joseph of the Western League at the age of eighteen, was bought by Kansas City, and came to the Browns in 1887. King was the best pitcher on the staff in 1887, winning his first seven games and finishing second in winning percentage and third in victories. At season's end, he would demand that Chris Von Der Ahe double his $1,800 salary, a proposition which must have greatly amused the tight-fisted owner. King would threaten to quit baseball and go to work for his father, a bricklayer, but eventually thought better of the idea and inked his contract at a lesser sum. It would not be the last time the right-hander would be involved in a salary dispute. In 1888, he would be the Browns' most reliable pitcher, working a staggering 585.2 innings and compiling a 45-12 record. King was a powerfully built man whose huge hands and long arms aided him immeasurably in his delivery. Stepping from the left side of the pitcher's box to the right side when he delivered, his sideways motion was so extreme that opposing batters constantly complained he was nowhere near his proper mark in the box when the ball left his hand. The introduction of the pitching rubber in 1893 restricted King's delivery and ended his effectiveness. With a record of 8-10 for the year, and facing a salary reduction for 1894, King retired from the game and went into his father's business. In 1896, he would attempt a half-hearted comeback, but hitters no longer feared his sidearm delivery, and after two seasons, he retired for good at the age of twenty-nine.

Admission prices for the 1887 Series were raised to one dollar for general admission and $1.50 for reserved seats. The two-umpire system, such a success in 1886, was used again in 1887, and the combatants selected John Kelly and John Gaffney, the two arbiters generally acknowledged to be the best in the game. Kelly and Gaffney would alternate behind the plate each half-inning and be paid expenses plus two hundred dollars for two weeks' work. All games were played under American Association rules.

The Series opened at Sportsman's Park in St. Louis on Monday, October 10, the final day of the American Association season, with a 6-1 victory for St. Louis. The Wolverines wore white uniform shirts with collars, dark blue pants, and white stockings. The word "Detroit" was embroidered in an arc across the front of the jerseys. The Browns, resplendent in bright red warmup jackets, bright blue uniforms, knickerbockers, and brown stockings, took the field for practice at 2:30 as a drizzling rain and cold wind forced many of the twelve thousand spectators to don their overcoats. The Wolverines were hampered by the loss of Dan Brouthers, who was out with a bad ankle injury. Brouthers would see action in only one of the games and then not until after the Series winner had been decided.

The Browns won the coin toss and took the field at 3:00. The starting pitchers were Bob Caruthers and Charlie Getzien. Detroit went down one-two-three in the top of the first, but Arlie Latham led off the bottom of the inning with a single and quickly stole second base. Bill Gleason walked, both runners moved up on a wild pitch, and singles by Tip O'Neill and Bob Caruthers gave the Browns a 2-0 lead. Four insurance runs in the fifth made an easy winner of Caruthers, who spun a four-hitter, two of the safeties coming off the bat of opposing pitcher Charlie Getzien.

After the game, Detroit center fielder and club captain Ned Hanlon sat in a rocking chair at the Lindell Hotel and had high words of praise for Caruthers's performance. "Caruthers is a mighty fine pitcher," said Hanlon. "He has good curves and his command of the ball is superb. There are plenty of pitchers as speedy as he, but there are few who are graceful in their movements. He pitched a beautiful game and I know that everything I cracked at came right over the plate."

The Detroit *Free Press*, leaving no descriptive phrase un-
turned, commented on the loss:

> Did they beat us? Well, rather. Did the Volunteer beat the Thistle?
> Did J. L. Sullivan beat Paddy Ryan? Did Kalamazoo beat
> Indianapolis? Well, just in proportion did the Browns beat the
> Detroits. They thrashed them out of shape, pounded them back
> into form again, and finally stepped on with both feet and
> crushed into the Mound City mud—outbatted, outfielded and
> outpitched, beaten, whipped, polished off, pulverized,
> demoralized, razzle-dazzled, subjugated.

The weather was still cold on the afternoon of the second
game and the wind was still blowing, but another capacity crowd
overflowed onto Sportsman's Field to watch Dave Foutz square off
against Detroit's Pete Conway. In the second, the Wolverines took
a lead they never relinquished when Charlie Bennett's single drove
in Sam Thompson and Deacon White. Two unearned runs in the
third and another unearned tally in the seventh gave Detroit a 5-0
lead. The Browns broke through against Conway in the bottom
of the seventh when Curt Welch tripled and scored on Yank
Robinson's single. St. Louis added two more runs in the eighth.
Arlie Latham drew a base on balls, stole second, and scored on
Charlie Comiskey's single. Comiskey stole second and when
catcher Bennett's throw went into center field, Comiskey came
home with the club's third and final run of the day.

St. Louis might have scored an additional run in the ninth but
for Dave Foutz's baserunning boner. Under the rule of a "blocked
ball"—a fair ball hit into a standing-room-only crowd—the baserunner could not be put out until the ball was returned to the
pitcher in his box. When Foutz lifted a pop fly into the crowd in
right field in the final inning, he apparently forgot the rule and
stopped at second base. His double put the tying run at the plate
with no one out, but Curt Welch and Jack Boyle fouled out and
Yank Robinson popped to short to end the game.

Toward the close of the contest, local fan Joe Carr presented
Browns catcher Jack Boyle with a gold watch and chain, a gift from
several admiring St. Louis fans for his good work behind the plate
during the season. Boyle had caught in a record forty-four straight
games, quite an accomplishment for the era.

The teams left St. Louis at 7:00 that evening and spent
the next thirteen hours on the Vandalia Special train traveling to

Detroit for the third game of the Series on October 12. Earlier that morning, John Montgomery Ward of the New York Giants had married the well-known actress, Miss Helen Dauvray, and the happy couple planned to honeymoon in San Francisco for the next two months. Helen Dauvray was a regular at the Polo Grounds to watch her favorite team play, and she had persuaded team owners Von Der Ahe and Stearns to pay eight hundred dollars for a trophy to commemorate the Series. The Dauvray Cup was made by Tiffnay's, traveled in its own special car, under guard, and was to be given to the first team winning three successive World Series championships. Miss Dauvray had also commissioned gold medallions for each member of the winning team.

The Browns spent the morning touring the city of Detroit, "where life is worth living," according to the Detroit Board of Commerce. After lunch in the dining car, the clubs dressed on the train and were driven to Recreation Park in horse-drawn hacks, preceded by a local brass band.

Recreation Park had bleachers which extended all the way from left field to the small grandstand behind home plate, and additional bleachers halfway up the first-base line. There were no outfield fences. When the Wolverines were on the road, cricket games were often scheduled on the north end of the field.

The weather was brisk for Game Three, but a capacity crowd of nine thousand fans showed up to see the most exciting match of the Series. Getzien and Caruthers, the starting pitchers for Game One, were rematched in this contest as Detroit took the field. Neither team scored in the first, but in the top of the second, the Browns drew first blood. Charlie Comiskey grounded a hit up the middle and took second on Caruthers's line single to right. Getzien retired Dave Foutz and Curt Welch on harmless fly balls but Yank Robinson came through with a clutch single to center, giving the Browns a 1-0 lead.

Caruthers blanked the Wolverines inning after inning until Detroit came to bat in the last of the eighth. Getzien and Hardy Richardson went down on strikes but Charlie Ganzel reached base when Caruthers fielded his sharp grounder and threw wild to first. Jack Rowe topped a ball down the third-base line and Caruthers, instead of letting the sure-handed Arlie Latham make the play, grabbed the ball, whirled, and threw into short right field for his second error of the inning. First baseman Comiskey scrambled after the elusive sphere and when he finally retrieved it, turned and threw past Arlie Latham at third. Ganzel came home and the score was tied.

Caruthers and Getzien matched each other pitch-for-pitch for the next four frames. The Browns put their first two men on base in the top of the eleventh but Getzien bore down and retired Curt Welch, Yank Robinson, and Doc Bushong in succession to end the threat. In the bottom of the thirteenth, Getzien lifted a pop fly into short right field between Comiskey and Dave Foutz. The two men failed to agree on whose play it should be and the ball dropped in for a single. Getzien went to second and third on groundouts, bringing Jack Rowe to the plate. Rowe smashed a hard grounder to second baseman Yank Robinson, who bobbled the ball and threw low to first. As Rowe landed on the bag, Comiskey dropped the ball. Getzien streaked across the plate with the winning run. The Browns had outhit Detroit by more than a two-to-one margin, but sloppy defensive play had cost them the game.

Betting had been heavy on the third game and the St. Louis *Post-Dispatch* described the scenes at the pool rooms this way:

> . . . humanity was packed so tight that the farthest were shoved up almost to the blackboard. All the passageways were blocked, and . . . betting was practically paralyzed by the inability of either nine to get a man around inning after inning. The crowd just stood and waited in silence like those who watch for a man to drop from a great height.

The *Post-Dispatch* estimated that twelve thousand dollars changed hands on this game alone. The odds were 10-7 that Detroit would win the Series, and 75-to-1 that neither Ed Beatin, Charles "Fatty" Briody, nor Nat Hudson would get the most hits in Game Four.

The Vandalia special left for Pittsburgh at 8:30 that evening. The Detroit ballplayers went to bed early, but the Browns stayed up late playing poker. Teammates Yank Robinson and Curt Welch got into a drunken fistfight over the outcome of one of the hands, leaving Welch with a black-and-blue nose. Following breakfast the next morning, the teams donned their uniforms, and with team owners Von Der Ahe and Stearns leading a makeshift parade, toured the Steel City in horse-drawn hacks before arriving at National League Recreation Park. The crowd of 4,500 included Mayor William McAllin of Pittsburgh and Mayor Pierson of Allegheny.

At the last minute, first baseman Dan Brouthers decided against playing, so Charlie Ganzel took his place in the Wolverines batting order. Detroit's Hardy Richardson doubled to lead off the game, but Silver King retired the next two men he faced and it looked as though the Browns might get out of the inning without any damage. But Sam Thompson doubled, Deacon White reached on an error, and singles by Fred Dunlap and Charlie Bennett put the Wolverines up 4-0. In the second, starting pitcher Lady Baldwin singled, stole second, went to third on a passed ball, and scored on Charlie Ganzel's groundout when Bill Gleason's throw home hit him in the back. Fred Dunlap's triple and a Charlie Bennett sacrifice fly put another run on the board for the Wolverines in the fifth, and two more runs in the sixth made an easy 8-0 winner of Baldwin, who threw a two-hitter. The only St. Louis hits off the lanky left-hander were singles by Tip O'Neill in the first and Yank Robinson in the fourth. The Browns had now gone twenty straight innings without scoring off Detroit pitching.

The Wolverines retired early again that evening, but the Browns resumed their wicked ways, staying up until the early hours of the 14th, smoking cigars and playing some rather spirited hands of poker. When the teams reached New York, they detrained and stayed in hotels for the first time during the Series—the Browns at the Grand Central, the Wolverines at the Victoria.

Game Five was played at the American Association Washington Park in Brooklyn, and by 11:00 that morning the game was sold out. The odds in the Brooklyn gambling houses on St. Louis winning the game were quoted at 5-to-4, although Detroit was still favored to win the Series. Oddsmakers reckoned, correctly as it turned out, that the Browns would not lose four games in a row. A St. Louis man reportedly bet his house against $1,500 put up by a Detroit fan.

There were ten thousand fans in the park, about one-fifth of them women, and a line of parked carriages fringed the outfield. Off in the distance, adventurous men and boys climbed trees to get a free look at the game. A cold northwesterly wind forced the ballplayers to wear long flannels under their uniforms. The game began promptly at 3:00, with Bob Caruthers against Pete Conway. The Browns scored twice in the top of the first on a walk to Latham, a hit batsman, a double steal, and a Tip O'Neill single, but the Wolverines got untracked in the fifth. Fred Dunlap singled— the first hit off Caruthers—and back-to-back doubles by Charlie

Bennett and Ned Hanlon tied the score at two-all. The Browns came right back at Conway in the next half-inning when, with two outs and no one on base, Caruthers and Foutz singled, both men scoring on Curt Welch's long double to left. St. Louis added an insurance tally in the seventh when Tip O'Neill drove in his third run of the game with a sacrifice fly. Bob Caruthers pitched a seven-hitter for his second win of the Series.

The next day, the Browns suffered their second shutout of the Series as Detroit played an almost perfect ballgame in New York's Polo Grounds. Riding in carriages, the clubs entered the park through a gate in the outfield half an hour before the 3:00 game time. The Wolverines started right in on Dave Foutz. The first four men in the lineup singled and the fifth reached on an error to give Detroit a three-run first. An encore performance in the second inning gave the Wolverines an insurmountable 6-0 lead. Foutz was eventually battered for a total of twelve hits and nine runs in the lopsided 9-0 shutout.

Charlie Getzien's performance for the Wolverines matched any in World Series history to date. He walked a man in each of the first two innings, then retired nineteen men in a row before passing Yank Robinson in the eighth. In the ninth, Arlie Latham reached first when Jack Rowe booted his grounder for the first Detroit error of the day, but Bill Gleason lined to Ganzel at first and Latham was doubled off the bag. Getzien was one out away from the first World Series no-hitter; unfortunately, for him, the next batter was Tip O'Neill, who shattered the bid with a clean single to right. Charlie Comiskey followed with an infield hit, but Getzien retired Bob Caruthers to end the game.

In the second inning of this game, Getzien's batterymate Charlie Bennett had split a finger on a foul ball. *The New York Times* presented a rather graphic glimpse into the life of a nineteenth-century catcher:

> It did not seem anything unusual to Bennett or to his fingers. When he held up that battered right hand, with its fingers swollen and spread like a boxing glove, with rags tied around three of them, and a general appearance of having been run over by a freight-car about the entire hand, it did not seem as though there was room to split it in any new place. He went right on with his play . . . though the blood was reddening his hand and could be seen now and then to drip from his fingers. Bennett wears a look of patient suffering on his bronzed features. His hands have

suffered so much that they have probably become case-hardened and ceased to feel . . .

One of the Polo Grounds spectators, a Mr. H. Curtis, manager of the local Spalding sporting goods store, experienced something of a surprise before the game, while he demonstrated a revolver to a potential buyer. According to the *Post-Dispatch* account of October 16:

> Mr. Curtis grasped the handle in his right hand and holding his left hand over the shining barrel pulled the trigger. He was surprised to hear a report and then to discover that the first finger of his left hand had parted company with him. The report of the pistol startled the people in the stand and a rush was made by some people where the unfortunate man stood. He was, apparently, greatly frightened, but said: "I did not know it was loaded."

The careless Mr. Curtis was immediately taken to Harlem Hospital, there to ponder the rules of gun safety.

Fred Stearns, still smarting from what he considered to be a back-stabbing in the division of regular-season road receipts, took the occasion of the sixth-game victory to get off a stinging quote on the integrity of his fellow owners in the same edition of the *Post-Dispatch*:

> I don't like the League and if I win this victory, and I will, I'll make them walk the chalk line, but whether I win it or not I'm going to walk into their meeting this winter and amend the constitution. If they don't agree to it I am going into the Association . . . The Association men are all fine fellows and their clubs play better ball than the League clubs. Then again they don't shake hands with you with their right and rip you up the back with their left . . . You may find me in the League next year and then you may not.

At the Grand Central Hotel that night, Von Der Ahe expressed his displeasure with Bill Gleason's work in the Series and vowed to bench him for the seventh game.

"Gleason is a good enough man and I like him," said Von Der Ahe. "He can bat well enough when there's a man or two on the base, but he makes too many errors, and too costly errors, too. I have stood it just long enough, and I'm going to put a stop to it.

I will lay Gleason off and try Lyons. He is a man that won't do worse than Gleason, if he does not do a great deal better."

Gleason was having a spectacularly bad time in the Series. At the plate, he was 2-for-25 with two runs scored and no runs batted in; in the field, he had handled the ball twenty-one times and made ten errors. It was not his finest hour. Von Der Ahe was true to his word, and rookie shortstop Harry Lyons, who had played only two games for the Browns in 1887—neither of them at the shortstop position—would replace Gleason for the seventh game.

For his part, Gleason was mystified by his poor performance. "I don't know what is the matter with me," he said. "I don't seem to be able to keep my hands on the ball. I know I ought to do it, but sometimes I ain't worth a cent, whilst other times I could stop a cannon ball."

October 16 was an off-day in the World Series but Von Der Ahe, to whom off-days were anathema, scheduled an exhibition game between the Browns and the American Association Brooklyn Trolley Dodgers instead. Before five thousand fans at Ridgewood Park, Nat Hudson was pounded for fifteen hits as St. Louis endured a stinging 10-3 defeat. That evening, the teams departed New York for Game Seven at the National League Philadelphia Baseball Grounds.

A third of the seats in left field were empty and the rear chairs in the pavilion were unoccupied, but the crowd numbered seven thousand, nonetheless, the private boxes holding an unusually large number of women. Many celebrities were on hand for the game, among them Mr. and Mrs. John Montgomery Ward; stage actors Digby Bell and DeWolfe Hopper, famous for reciting "Casey At The Bat"; William Medart, the ill-fated umpire of the fourth game of the 1885 World Series; C.H. Byrne, president of the Brooklyn club; and Francis Richter, editor of *Sporting Life*. The atmosphere was festive and the ballpark was decked out with flags of all nations waving in the warm breeze. A huge banner reading, "DETROIT—CHAMPIONS OF THE LEAGUE FOR 1887" was suspended from the main pole in center field, and the Dauvray Cup was on exhibit at home plate. Detroit was first to take the field for practice and as the players stepped from under the pavilion, the fans whistled, stamped their feet, and applauded loudly. The starting pitchers, Lady Baldwin and Bob Caruthers, gave hope of a good game. Caruthers already had two wins in the Series and Baldwin, in his only appearance so far, had handcuffed the Browns on just two hits.

The Wolverines broke on top in the bottom of the second as Sam Thompson singled, went to second on a wild pitch, and scored on Deacon White's hit. Fred Dunlap's groundout sent White to second. Charlie Bennett struck out, but catcher Doc Bushong dropped the fourth strike. He threw to second base in an attempt to catch White napping, but White dove back into the bag and both runners were safe. A single by Ned Hanlon and sacrifice fly by Baldwin made the score 3-0.

Baldwin was working on a four-hit shutout with two outs in the ninth inning when Tip O'Neill came to the plate. The Browns' most dangerous hitter lofted a little pop fly which just ticked off Baldwin's glove and into foul territory. Given another life, O'Neill lined the next pitch over the center-field fence for a home run, averting a whitewash. Rattled, Baldwin surrendered a double to Charlie Comiskey and a single to Bob Caruthers and suddenly found himself in serious trouble. An extra-base hit would have tied the game, but Dave Foutz flew out to Hardy Richardson in left field. The Wolverines had won their fifth game in seven outings.

By now, Chris Von Der Ahe had lost all confidence in pitcher Dave Foutz. The St. Louis owner was quoted in the *Post-Dispatch* as saying, "I will put in Caruthers to-day and to-morrow and the next day, and the day after that and every day until he can't pitch any more, and after that I don't know what I'm going to do."

Asked if he would put shortstop Bill Gleason back in the starting lineup, Von Der Ahe, showing the effects of his team's collapse, answered, "Yes. That is, I think I will if I am in the same frame of mind that I am in now. I will do it, though. Comiskey and I have not yet thoroughly decided just what we will do in this respect. We both favor it, though."

Comiskey was downhearted and had seemingly given up all hope for the Browns:

> The club is not winning as it should. We are not playing the game we can, although we are playing a good game. I do not believe that Latham ever played the base ball in his life that he is playing now. I do not think that Caruthers ever pitched as he has pitched in these games . . . In fact, individually the team is playing strong ball, but when it comes to a whole we can't win . . . Why, I don't know. There's a screw loose someplace. We play a fielding game that is as good as the other fellow's, and we make more hits than they do, yet they win. I know that they have good pitchers and good fielders, but it breaks my heart to go out on the field to

lose to these fellows when we are beating them at their strongest points. Seems funny, don't it?

The train left Philadelphia that evening after dinner and was due in Boston at 8:30 the following morning, but was delayed en route and did not arrive until shortly before noon. The weather was warm but a cloudy sky threatened rain. The National League South End Grounds was in the process of being renovated, so the eighth game of the Series had to be played at Union Park near Copley Square in Boston's Back Bay. Union Park was a decrepit wooden stadium which had not seen major league baseball since September of 1884. A group of boys who wanted to watch the game for free had set fire to the left-field fence the previous evening, believing repairs could not be completed in time. The field was in wretched condition and the stands, which could hold no more than about three thousand people, were in a state of disrepair. By game time, an overflow crowd ringed the entire playing field.

Silver King was due to start for St. Louis but the ballplayers prevailed upon Von Der Ahe to put Caruthers in the box for the second successive day. Chris Von Der Ahe had had a change of heart and Bill Gleason was back in the starting nine for St. Louis. Pete Conway was scheduled to work for the Wolverines but manager Bill Watkins substituted Charlie Getzien at the last minute. Charlie Bennett showed his spunk by taking his position behind the plate, despite the condition of his right hand, but Dan Brouthers was still missing from the Detroit lineup.

In pre-game ceremonies, Yank Robinson was presented with a gold-headed cane; Hardy Richardson received a floral bouquet. Umpire John Gaffney had stayed with friends in Worcester the night before and was late for the game, so John Kelly worked the first few innings alone. When Gaffney finally arrived, Kelly moved behind the plate.

A drizzling rain began during the first inning and continued throughout the contest. The Browns squeezed a run home on Charlie Comiskey's bunt in the bottom of the first, but the Wolverines took the lead for good in the second. Sam Thompson started the damage with a leadoff home run over the left-field fence and when the inning ended, Detroit had roughed up Caruthers for three singles, a walk, and two more runs for a 3-0 lead. Caruthers, whose post-game treatments for his pitching arm included soaking in scalding hot water for up to two hours, was hit freely from thereon as the Wolverines racked up thirteen hits and a 9-2 victory. Two of the hits were home runs by Thompson. Von Der Ahe's worst nightmares had come true.

A not easily discouraged Arlie Latham sounded off that night to a reporter from the St. Louis *Globe-Democrat*. "That was no game we played today," said Latham. "The men were like a lot of amateurs in a vacant lot. I never saw them go on like that before. It made me sick. It disgusted me. It made me wish I was dead. We were a regular custard pudding for Detroit and they ate us without any sauce. We are not ball-players, we are chumps."

Caruthers, so eager to start without rest, had learned a valuable lesson about pitching on successive days. "I can win from them every other day," he said, "but I'm not made of iron. I'm a man, and I can't do the work."

The *Post-Dispatch* thought it had the answer to the Browns' problems:

> It is gambling. At 8:30 P.M. every Detroit player is in bed. The Browns stay awake all night gambling and fighting and squabbling over the cards. In a recent game Caruthers lost $80, and he was so excited over the loss that he dashed down the pasteboards and cursed the man who invented them. Comiskey stays up all hours playing poker with his men, and the majority of the club never know what sleep means till 2 and 3 o'clock in the morning. Seven o'clock in the morning finds them awake at the poker tables again, and the loss of sleep, combined with the excitement of the game, shows itself in weak, nervous, sulky dispositions and poor eyes when they begin to play ball . . . But there is another thing. Some of the players have been making fools of themselves with strong drink. Club rules are stringent. They absolutely forbid gambling of any kind or drinking of any kind, and it is no wonder that there exists a total disregard for these rules when the captain himself endorses their breach by participating in the breach himself . . . Detroit men meanwhile are as sober as judges, sleep ten hours to the night and play a strong game of ball.

The ninth game was played at Philadelphia's Jefferson Street Grounds, the home of the American Association Athletics, on October 19. The sixteen-year-old park had been the site of the very first National League game on April 22, 1876. Of baseball's existing stadiums in 1887, Jefferson Street Grounds featured one of the most level and well-manicured fields. It had rained earlier in the morning but the groundskeepers had done yeoman's work in getting the field into shape. Threatening clouds promised more bad weather.

The red-jacketed Browns were driven onto the field in carriages and welcomed by warm applause. A moment later, the front-running crowd cheered even louder for the National League Wolverines as they took the field for practice. Dan Brouthers felt up to playing but after taking infield practice, decided against doing so. Charlie Bennett took over first-base duties and Charlie Ganzel moved behind the plate. Pete Conway was the starting pitcher for Detroit and despite Von Der Ahe's promise to work Caruthers every game, Silver King started for the Browns.

The game started at 2:30 and was scoreless until the fourth inning, when the teams traded runs. The Browns took a 2-1 lead in the sixth on a double by Curt Welch and Yank Robinson's single, but Detroit went ahead to stay in the bottom of the seventh. Jack Rowe and Sam Thompson singled and Deacon White squeezed Rowe home to tie the score. After Fred Dunlap struck out, Charlie Bennett laced a single which put Detroit in the lead. The Wolverines added an insurance run in the eighth to make the final score 4-2, and were now within one victory of the World's Championship.

After the game, both clubs accepted an invitation by actor Digby Bell to be his guest for a performance of the play, *The Bellman*, at the Chestnut Street Opera House. Following the late evening at the theater, the clubs boarded the train at 3:00 in the morning for Washington and Game Ten.

Fred Stearns was jubilant over his club's success through the first nine games and now proposed that he and Von Der Ahe each put up five thousand dollars and play a series of five games in New Orleans next spring, winner-take-all. Von Der Ahe hesitated, but immediately agreed to extend this already cumbersome World Series through another three exhibition games—two games in Kansas City on October 27 and 28, and the Series finale in St. Louis on October 29.

St. Louis pitcher Dave Foutz was miffed at the inequity of the players' settlements. "You see how it is," said Foutz. "If we won this series from the best baseball club in the world outside ourselves, we would get our little hundred dollars. If we lost it we wouldn't get a blank cent."

Rain on Thursday, October 20, forced postponement of Game Ten, so an impromptu doubleheader was scheduled for the next day, a morning game at Washington followed by an afternoon game at Baltimore. At 5:00 that evening, the teams left Washington to spend the night in Baltimore before returning to the nation's capital Friday morning.

It was Charlie Getzien against Bob Caruthers at Capitol Park Grounds, more frequently called Swampoodle Grounds, after the section of Washington in which the park was located. The field was soft and muddy after the previous day's rain. Detroit started in on the sore-armed Caruthers like there was no tomorrow. Indeed, for the Browns, there was no tomorrow. Hardy Richardson led off the first inning with a ringing home run over the left-field fence, his first hit off Caruthers in the Series. Charlie Ganzel followed with a single to left and two outs later, aided by an Arlie Latham error, the Wolverines had a 2-0 lead. The Browns tied the score on a bases-loaded, two-out single by Dave Foutz in the bottom of the inning. Detroit took a brief lead in the top of the fifth on Hardy Richardson's RBI single, but St. Louis rolled out its potent offense in the bottom of the inning. Tip O'Neill and Charlie Comiskey started in on Getzien with singles and moved into scoring position on Bob Caruther's sacrifice bunt. Dave Foutz's groundout scored O'Neill with the tying run and Curt Welch's two-out home run over the short left-field fence put the Browns on top, 5-3. St. Louis continued to pour on the heat. Arlie Latham's inside-the-park home run in the sixth gave his club a three-run lead and the Browns broke the game wide open with four runs in the seventh. The final score was 11-4, St. Louis. Charlie Getzien was pounded for nineteen hits, while Caruthers limited the Detroit batters to just nine safeties in recording his third victory of the Series.

At the conclusion of the game, the teams hurriedly departed for the depot to catch the train to Baltimore. After a light lunch in the dining car, they arrived at Union Park at 1:45, preceded by the McNish, Johnson, and Slavin minstrel band. The weather was clear but cold, and there were 2,500 fans on hand. Union Park, home of the American Association Orioles, was situated next to an amusement park which featured band concerts and dancing after ballgames.

The Wolverines needed but one victory to clinch the championship. The club was relaxed and showed its confidence despite injuries to Fred Dunlap and Charlie Bennett. For the second day in a row, Bennett was forced to give up his catching duties in the seventh inning for the less grueling position of first base.

The Browns threatened to blow the game apart in the first inning as they loaded the bases with none out against Lady Baldwin. Charlie Comiskey forced Arlie Latham at the plate for the first out but Bob Caruthers's groundout brought in a run. Dave Foutz one-hopped a grounder to first baseman Charlie Ganzel and Ganzel's throw home forced Tip O'Neill. Baldwin then retired Curt Welch to end the inning. Detroit tied the score in the bottom of the first after two were out. Jack Rowe reached second base when Caruthers dropped his easy fly ball in right field. A couple pitches later, Sam Thompson lifted another easy pop fly, this one for Curt Welch in center. Welch muffed the catch and Rowe trotted home with the tying run. The Browns scored a singleton in the second and held that 2-1 margin until the bottom of the fourth when the Wolverines pounded Foutz for three runs—the big blow, Larry Twitchell's two-run homer. St. Louis scored an unearned run in the fifth to pull within one, but Detroit routed Foutz in the bottom of the inning. Hardy Richardson lined a double off the left-field fence and scored when Bill Gleason let Jack Rowe's soft roller slip through his legs for an error. Sam Thompson singled Rowe to third and when Bob Caruthers's throw to the infield eluded Dave Foutz, Thompson was able to make second. Rowe held at third. Deacon White hit a smash to Bill Gleason, who made a spectacular one-handed stop and launched a throw to the plate. But the ball hit Rowe in the back and he scored as Thompson and White moved up a base. Larry Twitchell's groundout forced Thompson at home before Charlie Bennett drove a long single into center for the final two runs of the inning. The Wolverines had an 8-3 lead and were just four innings away from a World Championship title. St. Louis went out in order in the sixth and four more Detroit runs in the bottom of the inning put the game out of reach. The final score was 13-3.

Lady Baldwin pitched a three-hitter for the Wolverines, and Dave Foutz, more than justifying the lack of confidence shown in him by Chris Von Der Ahe, was racked for ten hits, five for extra bases. The poor playing field at Union Park was held responsible for the thirteen errors committed in the game, eight by the Browns.

The Wolverines had now won eight of the first eleven games and were champions of the world. This little detail resolved, the teams resumed their playing schedule on October 22 at Brooklyn's Washington Park. The final games would be of an exhibition nature.

The weather was frigid at Brooklyn and the crowd was so small it was difficult to make an accurate count, but estimates ran from two hundred to eight hundred people. According to the St. Louis *Post-Dispatch*, "the wind was blowing a hundred miles an hour and from forty different directions." The *Post* may have been indulging in a little hyperbole, but it was cold enough that players on both clubs wore cardigan warmup jackets over their uniforms during the game.

Pete Conway and Silver King were the starting pitchers and Dan Brouthers was in the lineup for the Wolverines, stationed at his familiar first-base position. The Browns took an early lead in a wild first inning. Arlie Latham singled to start the game and stole second base, his tenth theft of the Series. Bill Gleason hit a slow roller to Hardy Richardson at second and was out by a mile at first, but Latham never slowed down and crossed the plate in a blur to give the Browns their first run. Tip O'Neill followed with a hit to right and Charlie Comiskey reached base on Deacon White's fumble. Dave Foutz forced Comiskey and stole second base just before Curt Welch lashed a single to right, scoring both baserunners. Yank Robinson reached on the Wolverines' second error of the inning and Doc Bushong coaxed a base on balls from Conway to load the bases. Silver King helped his own cause with an RBI single but Robinson was thrown out at home to end the inning. St. Louis was never headed and the game was called by the umpires after eighty minutes because of the severe cold. The final score was 5-1.

From Brooklyn, the teams made the long journey back to Detroit for the thirteenth game. The train was due in the city at 9:00 on the morning of October 24, but confusion in the telegraph office had placed its arrival one hour later. As a consequence, Fred Stearns was plenty mad when only a small crowd turned out to greet his conquering heroes. Stearns endeavored to keep his team on the train for the next hour, but many of the ballplayers—much the worse for wear after a long evening spent in celebration— detrained and went uptown to show off Mrs. Ward's gold medals. A few minutes before 10:00, the welcoming committee left for the depot, the first carriage occupied by Detroit's Mayor Chamberlain. The crowd included judges of the civil and criminal courts, distin- guished merchants and lawyers, and prominent citizens. Despite the scarcity of Detroit ballplayers, the welcoming went ahead as scheduled. A banquet dinner in honor of the two clubs was planned for the Russell House later that evening.

While a brass band played popular melodies of the day, the Browns took the field at Recreation Park. The Wolverines waited ten minutes for effect before making their appearance, then were applauded wildly by the four thousand fans in the park. Just before game time, the Spalding Brothers Sporting Goods store of Chicago presented Dan Brouthers with a "zylonite" bat for leading the team in hitting during the season. Charlie Ganzel was given a gold watch and chain from appreciative fans and Charlie Bennett was given the most handsome, albeit least sentimental, gift of all: Five hundred silver dollars in a wheelbarrow, which he good-naturedly pushed around the park to the enthusiastic cheers of the crowd. Lady Baldwin started for Detroit against Bob Caruthers, and Parisian Bob, whose heart was all too apparently not in the game, just lobbed the ball over the plate to give Detroit an easy 6-3 victory.

A rumor leaked out that evening that Detroit second baseman Fred Dunlap had been sold to the New York Giants for five thousand dollars. The rumor of the sale was true, but Dunlap's ultimate destination turned out to be Pittsburgh.

Chris Von Der Ahe now wanted to take Stearns up on his offer to play a best-of-five series, with both clubs putting up five thousand dollars for a purse. Stearns, who had had some time to think over his own idea, demurred.

And the Series relentlessly dragged on. The teams traveled to Chicago's West Side Park on October 25 for the fourteenth game. The temperature was in the twenties, and there were only 378 people in the park. The field was frozen and groundskeepers had to rake the dirt near the baselines before play could begin. Fred Stearns wanted to call the game off but Von Der Ahe argued against disappointing the stalwarts who had shown up. Game time came and went at 2:30 and still neither team had made an appearance. At ten minutes to three, the Browns came out on the field and were welcomed by as much applause as the sparse crowd could muster. The Wolverines, eager to get the game over with, wasted no time starting in on Silver King. Leadoff batter Hardy Richardson slammed a triple into left and scored when Arlie Latham muffed Sy Sutcliffe's easy ground ball. Sutcliffe stole second and went to third when Bill Gleason bobbled Jack Rowe's grounder, and both runners scored on Sam Thompson's long single to center field. Detroit added an unearned run in the fifth. The Browns rallied for two runs in the top of the sixth and St. Louis' Jack Boyle closed out the scoring in the seventh with an RBI single. Charlie Getzien was the winning pitcher, notching his fourth victory in six Series starts. Silver King pitched a credible game, surrendering only four hits, but two of those came in the decisive first inning. The Browns had ten hits, but lost the game, 4-3.

There were no great crowds of happy fans at Union Depot when the Browns arrived in St. Louis on the 26th. At 10:00 that morning, the ballplayers were given a reception at the Southern Hotel, then paraded through the streets of St. Louis on their way to Sportsman's Park. Fred Stearns had calculated a profit of three thousand dollars, after all expenses were paid, but that figure seems suspiciously low when one considers that the receipts for the first twelve games alone amounted to over thirty thousand dollars, and Detroit had won eight of those games.

Expecting a small crowd, St. Louis management had lowered the admission price to twenty-five cents but, not surprisingly, few fans turned out. The Browns battered Lady Baldwin for six hits and seven runs in the first two innings and gave Bob Caruthers an easy 9-2 victory. Play was called at the conclusion of the sixth inning by mutual agreement. Because of the rapidly advancing winter, the three extra games were cancelled and the Series came to a welcome end.

Von Der Ahe, annoyed by his team's poor play, ultimately refused to share so much as one cent of the purse with the ballplayers. Thus, the Browns had played sixteen post-season games for free. Bob Caruthers and Dave Foutz were so disgusted by their owner's penny-pinching antics that they both requested to be traded—Caruthers wanted to go to Cincinnati and Foutz to Brooklyn. Over the winter, Von Der Ahe managed to recoup some of his losses on the Series by selling Caruthers, Foutz, and Doc Bushong to Brooklyn for $8,250, $5,500, and $5,000, respectively. Curt Welch was sold to the Philadelphia Athletics for $3,000. The light-hitting and fumble-fingered Bill Gleason also went to the Athletics, but after his performance in the World Series, the best price Von Der Ahe could coax was $1,000.

Von Der Ahe would have ample opportunity to reflect on the wisdom of breaking up his team.

GAME ONE—October 10, 1887, at Sportsman's Park, St. Louis

ST. LOUIS	AB	R	H	BI	E	DETROIT	AB	R	H	BI	E
Latham, 3b	6	1	3	0	0	Richardson, 3b	4	0	0	0	2
Gleason, ss	5	1	0	0	0	Twitchell, lf	4	0	1	1	0
O'Neill, lf	5	0	2	1	0	Rowe, ss	4	0	0	0	1
Comiskey, 1b	5	1	1	0	0	Thompson, rf	3	0	1	0	0
Caruthers, p	5	0	3	1	0	White, 1b	3	0	0	0	0
Foutz, rf	5	0	0	1	0	Dunlap, 2b	3	0	0	0	0
Welch, cf	5	1	0	0	0	Bennett, c	3	0	0	0	0
Robinson, 2b	5	1	2	1	0	Hanlon, cf	3	0	0	0	0
Bushong, c	5	1	2	1	0	Getzien, p	2	1	2	0	3
	46	6	13	5	0		29	1	4	1	6

```
STL    2 0 0    0 4 0    0 0 0 – 6
DET    0 0 0    0 0 0    0 0 1 – 1
```

D: Getzien, O'Neill.   T: Robinson.   SAC: Foutz.   SF: Foutz.   LOB: STL 14, DET 2. DP: STL 2, DET 2.   BB: Caruthers 1, Getzien 4.   Struck out: Getzien 4, Caruthers 2. WP: Getzien.   HBP: Gleason (Getzien).   SB: Latham, Comiskey, Caruthers.   Umpires: Kelly and Gaffney.   Time—1:50.   Att: 12,000.

GAME TWO—October 11, 1887, at Sportsman's Park, St. Louis

DETROIT	AB	R	H	BI	E	ST. LOUIS	AB	R	H	BI	E
Richardson, lf	5	1	0	0	0	Latham, 3b	4	1	0	0	3
Ganzel, 1b	5	0	1	1	0	Gleason, ss	4	0	1	0	2
Rowe, ss	5	1	1	0	0	O'Neill, lf	4	0	1	0	1
Thompson, rf	4	1	3	0	0	Comiskey, 1b	4	1	1	1	0
White, 3b	4	1	1	1	1	Caruthers, rf	4	0	1	0	0
Dunlap, 2b	4	0	0	0	0	Foutz, p	4	0	1	0	0
Bennett, c	4	0	2	2	1	Welch, cf	4	1	1	0	0
Hanlon, cf	4	1	1	0	0	Robinson, 2b	4	0	1	1	0
Conway, p	4	0	0	0	0	Boyle, c	4	0	0	0	0
	39	5	9	4	2		36	3	7	2	6

```
DET    0 2 2    0 0 0    1 0 0 – 5
STL    0 0 0    0 0 0    1 2 0 – 3
```

D: O'Neill, Foutz.   T: Welch.   SB: White, Latham, Comiskey, Hanlon 2, Richardson. S: Dunlap, Thompson.   BB: Foutz 2, Conway 3.   Struck out: Foutz 4, Conway 2. WP: Foutz 2.   DP: STL 2, DET 1.   LOB: STL 6, DET 7.   Umpires: Kelly and Gaffney. Time—2:00.   Att: 12,000.

GAME THREE—October 12, 1887, at Recreation Park, Detroit

ST. LOUIS	AB	R	H	BI	E	DETROIT	AB	R	H	BI	E
Latham, 3b	6	0	2	0	0	Richardson, lf	6	0	0	0	0
Gleason, ss	6	0	1	0	1	Ganzel, 1b	6	1	1	0	0
O'Neill, lf	6	0	0	0	0	Rowe, ss	6	0	2	0	0
Comiskey, 1b	6	1	2	0	2	Thompson, rf	5	0	0	0	0
Caruthers, p	6	0	2	0	3	White, 3b	5	0	0	0	0
Foutz, rf	6	0	1	0	1	Dunlap, 2b	5	0	0	0	0
Welch, cf	6	0	3	0	0	Bennett, c	4	0	0	0	0
Robinson, 2b	5	0	1	1	0	Hanlon, cf	5	0	1	0	1
Bushong, c	5	0	1	0	0	Getzien, p	5	1	2	0	0
	52	1	13	1	7		47	2	6	0	1

*Two out when winning run scored

```
STL   0 1 0   0 0 0   0 0 0   0 0 0   0 – 1
DET   0 0 0   0 0 0   0 1 0   0 0 0   1 – 2
```

D: Welch.   SB: Getzien, Latham.   LOB: STL 8, DET 2.   BB: Caruthers 1, Getzien 3.
Struck out: Caruthers 3, Getzien 3.   PB: Bushong.   Umpires: Gaffney and Kelly.
Time—2:25.   Att: 9,000.

GAME FOUR—October 13, 1887, at Recreation Park, Pittsburgh

DETROIT	AB	R	H	BI	E	ST. LOUIS	AB	R	H	BI	E
Richardson, lf	5	2	1	0	0	Latham, 3b	4	0	0	0	0
Ganzel, 1b	5	0	1	0	1	Gleason, ss	4	0	0	0	2
Rowe, ss	5	1	1	1	0	O'Neill, lf	4	0	1	0	0
Thompson, rf	5	1	4	2	0	Comiskey, 1b	4	0	0	0	0
White, 3b	5	1	0	0	0	Foutz, rf	4	0	0	0	0
Dunlap, 2b	5	2	3	1	0	Welch, cf	3	0	0	0	0
Bennett, c	5	0	1	2	0	Robinson, 2b	3	0	1	0	1
Hanlon, cf	4	0	0	0	0	Bushong, c	3	0	0	0	0
Baldwin, p	4	1	1	0	0	King, p	3	0	0	0	0
	43	8	12	6	1		32	0	2	0	3

```
DET   4 1 0   0 1 2   0 0 0 – 8
STL   0 0 0   0 0 0   0 0 0 – 0
```

D: Richardson, Thompson 2, Robinson.   T: Dunlap, Rowe.   SB: Dunlap 2,
Richardson, Baldwin, Thompson.   SF: Bennett.   LOB: DET 7, STL 5.   BB: Baldwin 3,
King 1.   Struck out: Baldwin 1, King 1.   PB: Bushong 3.   WP: King.   Umpires: Kelly
and Gaffney.   Time—1:50.   Att: 4,500.

GAME FIVE—October 14, 1887, at Washington Park, Brooklyn

ST. LOUIS	AB	R	H	BI	E	DETROIT	AB	R	H	BI	E
Latham, 3b	4	2	0	0	0	Richardson, lf	4	0	0	0	0
Gleason, ss	5	1	0	0	2	Ganzel, 1b	4	0	1	0	1
O'Neill, lf	5	0	1	3	0	Rowe, ss	4	0	1	0	0
Comiskey, 1b	4	0	0	0	0	Thompson, rf	4	0	1	0	0
Caruthers, p	4	1	1	0	0	White, 3b	4	0	0	0	2
Foutz, rf	4	1	1	0	0	Dunlap, 2b	4	1	2	0	0
Welch, cf	4	0	1	2	0	Bennett, c	4	1	2	1	0
Robinson, 2b	3	0	0	0	0	Hanlon, cf	4	0	1	1	0
Boyle, c	4	0	0	0	1	Conway, p	3	0	0	0	0
	37	5	4	5	3		35	2	8	2	3

```
STL   2 0 0   0 0 2   1 0 0 – 5
DET   0 0 0   0 2 0   0 0 0 – 2
```

D: Welch, Bennett.   SB: Latham, Gleason, Dunlap, Rowe, Hanlon, Robinson.
SF: O'Neill.   HBP: Gleason 2 (Conway).   BB: Caruthers 1, Conway 2.   Struck out:
Caruthers 3, Conway 1.   LOB: STL 7, DET 6.   DP: STL.   WP: Conway 2.   PB: Doyle.
Umpires: Gaffney and Kelly.   Time—1:45.   Att: 10,000.

GAME SIX—October 15, 1887, at the Polo Grounds, New York

DETROIT	AB	R	H	BI	E	ST. LOUIS	AB	R	H	BI	E
Richardson, lf	5	2	2	1	0	Latham, 3b	4	0	0	0	0
Ganzel, 1b	5	2	4	1	0	Gleason, ss	4	0	0	0	3
Rowe, ss	5	1	2	3	1	O'Neill, lf	4	0	1	0	0
Thompson, rf	5	1	1	2	0	Comiskey, 1b	4	0	1	0	0
White, 3b	5	0	1	0	0	Caruthers, rf	4	0	0	0	0
Dunlap, 2b	4	0	1	0	0	Foutz, p	3	0	0	0	0
Bennett, c	3	2	1	0	0	Welch, cf	3	0	0	0	0
Hanlon, cf	4	0	0	0	0	Robinson, 2b	2	0	0	0	1
Getzien, p	3	1	0	0	0	Bushong, c	3	0	0	0	0
	39	9	12	7	1		31	0	2	0	4

```
DET   3 3 0   0 0 0   0 0 3 – 9
STL   0 0 0   0 0 0   0 0 0 – 0
```

T: Richardson.   SB: Latham, Bennett 3, Ganzel, Richardson.   SF: Thompson.
BB: Getzien 3, Foutz 3.   Struck out: Getzien 5, Foutz 2.   DP: STL 2, DET 5.
Umpires: Gaffney and Kelly.   Time—1:55.   Att: 3,000.

GAME SEVEN—October 17, 1887, at Philadelphia Base Ball Grounds, Philadelphia

ST. LOUIS	AB	R	H	BI	E	DETROIT	AB	R	H	BI	E
Latham, 3b	4	0	0	0	0	Richardson, lf	4	0	0	0	0
Lyons, ss	3	0	0	0	0	Ganzel, 1b	4	0	0	0	0
O'Neill, lf	4	1	1	1	0	Rowe, ss	4	0	1	0	0
Comiskey, 1b	4	0	2	0	0	Thompson, rf	3	1	3	0	0
Caruthers, p	4	0	1	0	0	White, 3b	3	1	1	1	1
Foutz, rf	4	0	2	0	0	Dunlap, 2b	3	0	0	0	0
Welch, cf	3	0	0	0	0	Bennett, c	3	1	0	0	1
Robinson, 2b	2	0	1	0	0	Hanlon, cf	3	0	1	1	0
Bushong, c	3	0	0	0	0	Baldwin, p	3	0	0	1	0
	31	1	7	1	0		30	3	6	3	2

```
STL   0 0 0   0 0 0   0 0 1 - 1
DET   0 3 0   0 0 0   0 0 x - 3
```

2B: Comiskey 2, Thompson. HR: O'Neill. SB: Hanlon. SF: Baldwin. DP: DET 2. LOB: STL 5, DET 4. BB: Baldwin 2, Caruthers 1. Struck out: Caruthers 2. PB: Bennett. WP: Caruthers. Umpires: Gaffney and Kelly. Time—1:35. Att: 8,000.

GAME EIGHT—October 18, 1887, at Union Park, Boston

DETROIT	AB	R	H	BI	E	ST. LOUIS	AB	R	H	BI	E
Richardson, lf	5	0	0	0	0	Latham, 3b	4	1	2	0	1
Ganzel, 1b	4	0	0	1	0	Gleason, ss	4	0	0	0	0
Rowe, ss	4	1	2	0	0	O'Neill, lf	4	0	1	0	1
Thompson, rf	5	2	3	2	0	Comiskey, 1b	4	0	1	1	0
White, 3b	4	1	2	1	1	Caruthers, p	4	0	1	0	0
Dunlap, 2b	5	2	0	0	1	Foutz, rf	4	1	1	0	0
Bennett, c	5	1	2	1	0	Welch, cf	4	0	1	0	0
Hanlon, cf	4	1	2	2	0	Robinson, 2b	4	0	3	1	1
Getzien, p	3	1	2	2	1	Bushong, c	4	0	0	0	0
	39	9	13	9	3		36	2	10	2	3

```
DET   0 3 1   0 0 3   2 0 0 - 9
STL   1 0 0   0 0 1   0 0 0 - 2
```

2B: Rowe, White, Hanlon, Getzien, Robinson. 3B: Bennett. HR: Thompson 2. SB: Caruthers, Latham 2, Rowe. SF: Ganzel. HBP: Caruthers (Getzien). DP: STL. LOB: STL 7, DET 6. Struck out: Caruthers 3, Getzien 2. BB: Caruthers 4, Getzien 2. WP: Caruthers 3, Getzien 2. Umpires: Kelly and Gaffney. Time—1:55. Att: 5,000.

GAME NINE—October 19, 1887, at Jefferson Street Grounds, Philadelphia

ST. LOUIS	AB	R	H	BI	E	DETROIT	AB	R	H	BI	E
Latham, 3b	4	0	0	0	0	Richardson, lf	4	1	1	0	0
Gleason ss	4	0	2	0	0	Ganzel, 1b	4	0	0	0	1
O'Neill, lf	4	0	0	0	0	Rowe, ss	3	1	2	1	0
Comiskey, 1b	4	1	2	0	0	Thompson, rf	3	1	1	0	0
Foutz, rf	4	0	1	0	0	White, 3b	3	0	0	1	1
Welch, cf	4	1	2	1	0	Dunlap, 2b	3	0	0	0	0
Robinson, 2b	4	0	1	1	0	Bennett, c	3	0	1	1	0
Boyle, c	4	0	1	0	0	Hanlon, cf	3	1	1	0	0
King, p	4	0	0	0	0	Conway, p	3	0	0	0	0
	36	2	9	2	0		29	4	6	3	2

```
STL   0 0 0   1 0 1   0 0 0 – 2
DET   0 0 0   1 0 0   2 1 x – 4
```

2B: Thompson.   3B: Hanlon.   SB: Thompson.   S: White.   LOB: STL 7, DET 1.
Struck out: King 8, Conway 4.   WP: King.   Umpires: Gaffney and Kelly.   Time—1:40.
Att: 500.

GAME TEN—October 21, 1887, at Swampoodle Grounds, Washington (morning game)

DETROIT	AB	R	H	BI	E	ST. LOUIS	AB	R	H	BI	E
Richardson, lf-2b	4	1	3	2	0	Latham, 3b	5	1	3	1	1
Ganzel, 1b-c	4	0	2	0	0	Gleason, ss	5	0	2	1	1
Rowe, ss	4	1	1	0	0	O'Neill, lf	5	2	2	0	1
Thompson, rf	4	0	0	0	0	Comiskey, 1b	5	3	3	0	0
White, 3b	4	0	1	0	1	Caruthers, p	5	1	1	1	0
Dunlap, 2b	2	0	0	0	0	Foutz, rf	5	1	2	4	0
Twitchell, lf	2	1	0	0	0	Welch, cf	5	2	2	3	0
Bennett, c-1b	4	0	1	1	0	Robinson, 2b	3	0	1	0	0
Hanlon, cf	4	1	0	0	0	Boyle, c	4	1	1	1	1
Getzien, p	4	0	0	0	0		42	11	17	11	4
	36	4	8	3	1						

```
DET   2 0 0   0 1 0   0 0 1 – 4
STL   2 0 0   0 3 1   4 1 x – 11
```

T: Foutz.   HR: Richardson, Welch, Latham.   SB: Hanlon, Latham, Welch, Twitchell.
SAC: Caruthers,   LOB: DET 5, STL 6.   BB: Getzien 3, Caruthers 1.   Struck out:
Caruthers 2.   WP: Caruthers.   Umpires: Gaffney and Kelly.   Time—2:10.   Att: 3,000.

GAME ELEVEN—October 21, 1887, at Union Park, Baltimore (afternoon game)

ST. LOUIS	AB	R	H	BI	E	DETROIT	AB	R	H	BI	E
Latham, 3b	5	0	1	0	0	Richardson, lf	5	3	4	0	1
Gleason, ss	4	1	0	0	2	Ganzel, 1b-c	5	1	0	0	0
O'Neill, lf	4	1	0	0	0	Rowe, ss	5	4	2	2	1
Comiskey, 1b	4	0	1	0	1	Thompson, rf	5	0	1	0	1
Caruthers, rf	4	0	1	1	1	White, 3b	5	2	2	1	1
Foutz, p	4	0	0	0	3	Twitchell, lf	4	2	3	2	0
Welch, cf	3	0	0	0	1	Bennett, c-1b	4	1	1	2	0
Robinson, 2b	2	1	1	0	0	Hanlon, cf	5	0	1	0	0
Boyle, c	4	0	0	0	0	Baldwin, p	5	0	0	0	1
	34	3	4	1	8		43	13	14	7	5

```
STL   1 1 0   0 1 0   0 0 0 –  3
DET   1 0 0   3 4 4   1 0 x – 13
```

2B: Richardson (2), Rowe, Twitchell. HR: Twitchell. SB: Robinson, Latham, Comiskey, Caruthers, Bennett 2, Richardson 2, Thompson. HBP: Twitchell (Foutz); Gleason and Welch (by Baldwin). DP: STL. LOB: STL 7, DET 7. BB: Baldwin 2, Foutz 4. Struck out: Baldwin 2, Foutz 3. WP: Foutz 2. PB: Boyle 2, Hanlon 1. Umpires: Gaffney and Kelly. Time—2:00. Att: 2,500.

GAME TWELVE— October 22, 1887, at Washington Park, Brooklyn

DETROIT	AB	R	H	BI	E	ST. LOUIS	AB	R	H	BI	E
Richardson, lf	3	0	0	0	1	Latham, 3b	4	2	2	0	0
Brouthers, 1b	3	0	2	0	0	Gleason, ss	4	0	1	1	0
Rowe, ss	3	0	1	0	1	O'Neill, lf	4	1	2	1	0
Thompson, rf	3	0	0	0	0	Comiskey, rf	3	0	1	0	0
White, 3b	3	0	0	0	1	Foutz, 1b	3	1	0	0	1
Dunlap, 2b	2	0	0	0	0	Welch, cf	3	1	2	2	0
Ganzel, c	2	1	2	0	1	Robinson, 2b	3	0	0	0	1
Hanlon, cf	3	0	0	0	0	Bushong, c	3	0	0	0	0
Conway, p	2	0	0	0	0	King, p	3	0	1	1	0
Getzien, p	0	0	0	0	0		30	5	9	5	2
	24	1	5	0	4						

```
DET   0 0 0   0 1 0   0 – 1
STL   4 1 0   0 0 0   x – 5
```

2B: Ganzel. SB: Ganzel 2, Latham 2, Foutz, Richardson. DP: STL. LOB: STL 8, DET 4. Struck out: Conway 1, King 1. BB: Conway 2. WP: King, Conway 2. Umpires: Kelly and Gaffney. Time—1:20. Att: 500.

GAME THIRTEEN—October 24, 1887, at Recreation Park, Detroit

ST. LOUIS	AB	R	H	BI	E	DETROIT	AB	R	H	BI	E
Latham, 3b	4	1	0	0	0	Richardson, 2b	5	0	1	0	0
Gleason, ss	4	0	0	0	1	Sutcliffe, 1b	4	0	0	0	2
O'Neill, lf	4	0	0	0	0	Rowe, ss	5	1	2	0	0
Comiskey, 1b	4	1	1	1	0	Thompson, rf	5	1	2	0	0
Caruthers, p	4	0	0	0	0	White, 3b	4	2	3	1	0
Foutz, rf	4	0	1	1	0	Twitchell, lf	4	1	1	0	1
Welch, cf	4	0	0	0	0	Ganzel, c	3	0	0	1	0
Robinson, 2b	3	1	0	0	1	Hanlon, cf	4	1	1	0	0
Bushong, c	3	0	1	0	0	Baldwin, p	4	0	2	1	1
	34	3	3	2	2		38	6	12	3	4

```
DET   0 2 0   1 0 0   1 2 0 - 6
STL   1 0 0   0 1 0   0 0 1 - 3
```

2B: Baldwin.   3B: White.   SB: Thompson, Ganzel, Comiskey, Baldwin, Hanlon.
S: Ganzel.   DP: STL.   LOB: STL 6, DET 6.   BB: Caruthers 2, Baldwin 1.   Struck out:
Caruthers 2, Ganzel 1.   WP: Caruthers 2.   PB: Ganzel, Bushong.   Umpires: Gaffney
and Kelly.   Time—1:55.   Att: 4,000.

GAME FOURTEEN—October 25, 1887, at West Side Park, Chicago

ST. LOUIS	AB	R	H	BI	E	DETROIT	AB	R	H	BI	E
Latham, 3b	4	1	2	0	3	Richardson, 2b	4	1	1	0	0
Gleason, ss	4	0	1	0	1	Sutcliffe, 1b	4	1	1	2	0
O'Neill, lf	4	1	0	0	0	Rowe, ss	4	1	1	0	1
Comiskey, 1b	4	0	2	1	0	Thompson, rf	4	0	1	2	0
Foutz, rf	4	0	0	1	0	White, 3b	4	0	0	0	0
Welch, cf	4	0	0	0	0	Twitchell, lf	3	0	0	0	0
Robinson, 2b	3	1	2	0	1	Ganzel, c	4	0	0	0	0
Boyle, c	4	0	3	1	0	Hanlon, cf	3	0	0	0	0
King, p	4	0	0	0	0	Getzien, p	3	1	0	0	1
	35	3	10	3	5		33	4	4	4	2

```
STL   0 0 0   0 0 2   1 0 0 - 3
DET   3 0 0   0 1 0   0 0 x - 4
```

3B: Richardson.   SB: Comiskey 2, Sutcliffe.   SF: Foutz.   DP: DET.   LOB: DET 4,
STL 3.   BB: Getzien 1.   Struck out: King 9, Getzien 3.   PB: Ganzel.   Umpires: Kelly
and Gaffney.   Time—1:45.   Att: 378.

GAME FIFTEEN—October 26, 1887, at Sportsman's Park, St. Louis

DETROIT	AB	R	H	BI	E	ST. LOUIS	AB	R	H	BI	E
Richardson, lf	4	0	0	0	1	Latham, 3b	4	2	3	1	0
Sutcliffe, 1b-c	3	0	0	0	2	Lyons, ss	4	3	2	2	3
Rowe, ss	3	1	2	0	2	O'Neill, lf	4	1	1	2	0
Thompson, rf	3	0	2	0	0	Comiskey, 1b	4	0	1	1	0
White, 3b	3	0	1	1	1	Caruthers, p	4	0	0	0	0
Twitchell, lf	3	1	0	0	0	Foutz, rf	3	0	0	0	0
Ganzel, c-1b	3	0	1	1	0	Welch, cf	3	0	0	0	1
Hanlon, cf	3	0	1	0	0	Robinson, 2b	2	1	1	0	0
Baldwin, p	3	0	1	0	1	Bushong, c	3	2	2	0	0
	28	2	8	2	7		31	9	10	6	4

```
DET   0 1 1   0 0 0 - 2
STL   3 4 0   1 1 0 - 9
```

2B: Latham.   3B: O'Neill.   SB: Latham.   LOB: DET 6, STL 7.   BB: Caruthers 1, Baldwin 2.   Struck out: Caruthers 2, Baldwin 2.   Umpires: Kelly and Gaffney. Time—1:30.   Att: 800.

· 6 ·

THE BROWNS
BOW OUT

◆

When the 1888 season opened, the St. Louis Browns began their quest to capture a fourth successive Association pennant, something which hadn't been done since the National Association Boston Red Stockings had won four straight times from 1872 through 1875. But for the first four months of the season, the Browns had their hands full trying to stem the onslaught of a rejuvenated Brooklyn club, fortified by the acquisitions of the two former Browns stars, Bob Caruthers and Dave Foutz. In August, St. Louis caught fire, won eighteen of twenty-one, and blew the rest of the Association away. The Browns' record of four straight pennants would stand until the New York Yankees put together five straight championships beginning in 1949. Resting through the final month of the season, the Browns began readying themselves for the upcoming World Series with the surprising New York Giants.

The Giants, a fourth-place club just a year earlier, did little more than mark time until their star pitcher, Tim Keefe, hit his stride. From June 23 through August 14, Keefe won nineteen games and dramatically transformed the National League pennant race. Entering September, the Giants had mounted a seven-game

1888

The Changing Game

◆ ◆ ◆

- The three-strike rule was restored.

- The batter was no longer credited with a base hit and an at bat when he drew a base on balls.

- Baserunners were now allowed an extra base if the batted ball struck an umpire.

- A fair ball hit over the outfield fence was considered only a ground-rule double if the distance from home plate was less than 210 feet.

- A postponed or tie game could be replayed on the grounds of either team.

---

lead. The only issue remaining was the exact date on which the club would clinch the pennant.

The 1888 World Series promised to be a good one. For the third time in the last four years, the Browns had led the American Association in defense, although only one regular, catcher Jack Boyle, had led in fielding percentage at his position. Offensively, the club had slipped from its herculean heights of 1887. St. Louis scored 342 fewer times than the previous year, but balanced that nicely by giving up 260 fewer runs. The team's ERA was a league-leading 2.09. The Browns led the league in home runs (36) and finished a narrow second to hard-slugging Philadelphia in batting average.

• Despite several favorable court rulings, National League clubs could not schedule regular-season games or exhibition contests on Sundays.

• Substitutions were now allowed at the end of an inning. Two players were designated as substitutes and their names were to appear on the scorecard in addition to those of the starting nine. The only time a substitution was allowed before the end of an inning was in the case of injury.

• The Detroit Wolverines became the first club to issue rain checks. Ticket stubs stated, "In case rain interrupts the game before three innings are played, this check will admit the bearer to grounds for the next League game only."

• At the annual meeting of the American Association, $1,200 was set aside to be presented to the team winning the 1888 Association pennant.

Tip O'Neill had another fine year at the plate as he led the Association in hits (177) and batting average (.335), finished third in total bases (236) and slugging average (.446), and fourth in runs batted in (98). Arlie Latham led the Association in stolen bases (109), and Tommy McCarthy (93) finished fourth in the same category.

Silver King had blossomed on the mound, improving his record from 34-11 to 45-21. King topped the Association in wins, games pitched (66), games started (65), complete games (64), innings pitched (585.2), fewest walks per nine innings pitched (1.17), and shutouts (6). He finished second in strikeouts (258) and fewest hits per nine innings (6.72), and third in winning percentage (.682), trailing only teammates Nat Hudson and Elton Chamberlain. His earned run average of 1.64 led second-place Ed Seward by more than a third of a run per game. King was a hometown boy whose record in three years with the Browns was 112-49.

Also on the St. Louis staff were Nat Hudson and Elton Chamberlain, the two men who had been tapped to take over the pitching duties of Bob Caruthers and Dave Foutz. A spot starter in 1887, Hudson had upped his record to 25-10 in 1888, a mark good enough to lead the Association in winning percentage. Elton "Icebox" Chamberlain (so nicknamed because of his extraordinary composure on the mound), was one of three ambidextrous major league pitchers known to have thrown from both sides of the mound during the nineteenth century. The stocky right-hander began the season with Louisville and had compiled a 14-9 record when he was shipped to the Browns in August. From then on, Chamberlain was nearly unbeatable, winning eleven of his thirteen decisions for St. Louis.

Rounding out the pitching staff was Jim Devlin (6-5), an undistinguished left-hander who had filled in with an occasional start.

The only other major change for the Browns saw popular shortstop Bill Gleason go to the Philadelphia Athletics in exchange for reserve second baseman James "Chippy" McGarr. Von Der Ahe, who had never forgiven Gleason his poor performance in the 1887 World Series, had installed the newly acquired Bill White at shortstop. White did little to distinguish himself offensively (.175) but was one of the best defensive shortstops in the Association.

Despite the presence of six future Hall of Famers, the National League New York Giants were a rather mundane defensive and offensive club that won the pennant on the strength of its pitching staff. The team had a substantially lower batting average than the fifth-place Detroit Wolverines (.242 to .263), and its slugging average of .336 was nearly fifty points lower than the hard-hitting Chicago Colts.

The New York outfield featured "Orator Jim" O'Rourke (.274) in left and Mike Tiernan (.293) in right. James Henry O'Rourke had broken in with the Middletown Mansfields of the National Association in 1872, where he hit .287 in limited action. A year later, he was a first-string member of the fabled Boston Red Stockings, the team which won four consecutive pennants in the brief five-year history of the National Association. O'Rourke's good fortune in playing on pennant winners continued when Boston became a charter member of the National League. The stocky outfielder had the distinction of striking the new league's first hit when he stroked a single to left field with two outs in the first inning on opening day of 1876. He was a member of Boston championship clubs in 1877, 1878, and 1880, and a part of the pennant-winning Providence Grays in 1879. O'Rourke was a versatile player in his nineteen-year major league career. He played 1,377 games in the outfield, 249 in the infield, 209 behind the plate, and six on the mound while compiling a lifetime .311 batting average (including his years in the National Association). He retired as an active major leaguer in 1893, became a major league umpire the next year, and managed the Bridgeport team in the Connecticut League from 1895 to 1908. From 1904 through 1907, O'Rourke played three positions for Bridgeport, until retiring once again as an active player, this time at the remarkable age of fifty-five. Two years later, he was named president of the Connecticut League, a position he held until becoming president of the Eastern Association in 1914. To say Jim O'Rourke led an active baseball life would be an understatement. He entered the Hall of Fame in 1945.

Mike Tiernan was born in Trenton, New Jersey, in 1867, across the street from the Trenton State Prison. He started his organized baseball career as a pitcher with Chambersburg of the Keystone League in 1884 and was acquired by New York prior to the 1887 season. The Giants wanted Tiernan to pitch but the youngster had other ideas: He wanted to play the outfield every day. Manager Jim Mutrie finally relented, and Tiernan responded with a .287 batting average in his first year in the majors. Tiernan got his nickname, "Silent Mike," because of his distaste for publicity and his quiet facade on the ball field.

Behind the plate for the Giants was the legendary William Ewing, the dominant catcher of the nineteenth century, known to everyone as Buck. Ewing was the first catcher to crouch behind the batter regularly, and in 1888 was a career .298 hitter. No slouch as a baserunner, he finished his career with at least 336 stolen bases. (Stolen base records are incomplete.)

Monte Ward regarded Buck Ewing as the greatest player of his time. In 1915, Clark Griffith named him the catcher for his all-time all-star team. Francis Richter, longtime editor of the *Reach Guide*, listed Ewing in 1919 as one of the three greatest ballplayers of all time, placing him in the distinguished company of Ty Cobb and Honus Wagner. In the 1930s, *Spalding Guide* editor John Foster named Ewing the catcher on his all-time all-star team and said he was "the greatest all-around player ever connected with the game." Ewing's lifetime batting average was .303 and in 1939, he would become the first backstop to enter the Hall of Fame.

But Ewing and O'Rourke weren't the only future members of the Hall of Fame on the 1888 Giants. Monte Ward, Roger Connor, Mickey Welch, and Tim Keefe have plaques in the Museum as well.

John Montgomery Ward had played one year in the minors before coming to the Providence Grays as a pitcher in 1878. For the first six years of his career, Ward was a full-time pitcher and part-time outfielder/infielder. In five years at Providence, he had pitched a perfect game and run up a record of 146-84. By the time he arrived in New York, his pitching days were numbered. In forty-two appearances with the Giants, Ward was a mediocre 15-17, so he taught himself to switch-hit and became an everyday shortstop. Ward was an accomplished basestealer, with 504 thefts from 1887 until he retired at the age of thirty-four to concentrate solely on his legal practice. He died the day after his sixty-fifth birthday in 1925 and was elected to the Hall of Fame in 1964.

Roger Connor was a big left-handed hitter who came up to Troy in 1880 and instantly became the team's regular third baseman. A year later, he made the move to first base, the position he would occupy for most of his career. Connor was a giant man for his day, standing 6'3" and weighing 220 pounds. A lifetime .318 hitter, he was elected to the Hall of Fame in 1976.

But where the Giants really shone was in the area of pitching. New York's staff of Tim Keefe, Mickey Welch, Cannonball Titcomb, and Cannonball Crane led the league in complete games (136), strikeouts (724), and shutouts (19). The club's earned run average of 1.96 was almost half a run lower than that of the Philadelphia Phillies, second best in the same category.

Tim Keefe was coming off one of the finest years of his career. Relying on changeups and a palmball, Keefe led all National League pitchers in winning percentage (.745), wins (35), ERA (1.74), strikeouts (333), and shutouts (8). He was third in appearances (51) and complete games (51), and fourth in innings pitched (434). Over the past six seasons, his record was an impressive 222-108, for a winning percentage of .673.

Another veteran, Michael Francis Welch, was beginning to show sure signs of decline, but still compiled a 26-19 record and a 1.93 earned run average. "Smiling Mickey"—so nicknamed because of his sunny disposition—had pitched for Auburn and Holyoke in the National Association before coming to Troy in 1880. As a rookie, he won thirty-four games while losing thirty, but his 2.54 ERA held out the promise of greatness. In 1885, his best year, Welch had a 44-11 record, seven shutouts, a 1.66 earned run average, and a seventeen-game winning streak from the middle of July through the fourth of September. After a distinguished career with the Giants, Welch would open the 1892 season by allowing eleven hits and four walks in five innings. His ERA a bloated 14.40, Welch was transferred to the Eastern League Troy franchise where he pitched the rest of the year before retiring. In his career, Welch won twenty or more games nine times, thirty or more games four times, finished 525 of the 549 games he started, and compiled a lifetime record of 311-207. These credentials earned him a plaque in the Hall of Fame in 1973.

Also on the Giants' staff were the twin cannonballs—Ledell "Cannonball" Titcomb, enjoying his first and only good year with a 14-8 record, and Edward "Cannonball" Crane, who rounded out the rotation with a 5-6 mark in 12 starts.

New York's position as America's first city was greatly strengthened by the construction of two of the nineteenth century's Seven Wonders, the Brooklyn Bridge and the Statue of Liberty. Despite these modern wonders, most New Yorkers lived in poverty in the slums of the Lower East Side, eking out a meager living peddling spoiled produce from pushcarts, or working long hours in factory sweatshops. Despite the large numbers of New York's Finest, there was little police presence. The more common neighborhood authority was gangs of Irish-born toughs who protected their own and fought each other for sections of city turf.

Middle- and upper-class residents amused themselves by picnicking at Jerome Park or roller skating at the Olympian Rink on Broadway. A day at Coney Island, complete with a visit to the amusement parks and a viewing of the fireworks display, was relatively inexpensive entertainment. But people thought twice about taking a swim: The city dumped its garbage into the waterway. The more well-to-do took excursion steamers along the banks of the Harlem River or spent a few hours in the sun at New Jersey's Long Beach. A ride in a trotting rig through Central Park included a stopover to see the two newly acquired hippopotamuses at the Zoo, and was a pleasant way to spend a day. Warnings to keep off the grass were strictly enforced and games and sports were frowned upon because they interfered with the more refined pleasure of landscape watching. Of course, one wouldn't want to visit the park

at night. Drunkards, vagrants, robbers, and murderers were a constant danger. Central Park's own designer, Frederick Law Olm-
sted, had recommended as early as 1882 that the grounds be closed
after dark. But the city never discovered a satisfactory method of
buttoning up an eighty-four acre plot.

One of the most popular amusements for New Yorkers was the
sport of baseball. And what could possibly top a World Series game?
On Tuesday, October 16, some five thousand people couldn't think
of a better way to spend the afternoon.

Team owners Chris Von Der Ahe and John B. Day had previously agreed that the first team to win six games would be declared
the champion. The 1888 World Series opened at the Polo Grounds
with a pitchers' duel between Tim Keefe and Silver King. American flag bunting draped the six-foot wooden fence along both sides
of the double-decker Grand Pavilion grandstands. On the outfield
walls were advertisements for McCann's Celebrated Hats; A.G.
Spalding & Bros.; Cross-Cut Cigarets; and Gumpert Brothers Full
Weight 5 cent Cigars. Billboards said, "The Evening-Telegram,
Price 2 Cents"; "Smoke Blackwell's Genuine Durham Tobacco." A
sign on the right-field wall at ground level read, "NO BETTING
ALLOWED ON THESE GROUNDS."

It rained all morning of the sixteenth, but at noon, the winds
veered off to the southwest and took the storm with them. Shortly
thereafter, the opposing managers, Jim Mutrie and Charlie
Comiskey, decided to play the game despite the muddy condition of
the grounds. The Browns were driven onto the field in carriages at
2:30 that afternoon, garbed in their new uniforms, which had been
manufactured by Rawlings Brothers of St. Louis. The caps were
brown-and-white-striped and the pants were white with brown
belts and stockings. The jerseys were also striped and featured sailor
collars and sleeves, the first uniform of its kind ever worn. After
fifteen minutes of practice, the Browns retired and the Giants took
the field, clad in their somber black jerseys.

The two-umpire system was again employed in 1888. In the
first game, John Gaffney worked behind the plate and John Kelly
covered the basepaths. Kelly wore a white flannel shirt with dark
pants, while Gaffney wore a blue cap, blue trousers, and brown shirt.
Neither team had any cause to "kick" about the umpiring during the
game. This would not hold true for the balance of the Series.

At game time, the sky was clear and the sun had dried most of
the diamond. What wasn't dry was covered with sawdust as Silver

King and Tim Keefe, the two aces of the club, prepared to work. The Giants scored the first run of the 1887 World Series in the second when Roger Connor stroked a hit, went to second on Monte Ward's bunt single, to third on a wild pitch, and scored on Mike Slattery's sacrifice fly. Browns center fielder Harry Lyons prevented any more damage in the inning with a dazzling throw to third baseman Arlie Latham to nail Ward, who was attempting to advance on the play. In the next half inning, Latham singled, then heckled Keefe good-naturedly as he danced off first. Keefe was having difficulty concealing his amusement as he delivered the ball to Yank Robinson. Latham stole second and when catcher Buck Ewing's throw to the bag bounced into center field, Latham continued to third, from where he scored the tying run on Tip O'Neill's single.

New York went ahead for good in the bottom of the inning. With two out, Mike Tiernan drew a base on balls, stole second and took off for third as catcher Jack Boyle's throw went into center field. When the ball zipped through the center fielder's legs for an error, Tiernan trotted home with the lead run. King pitched hitless ball the rest of the way, but Tim Keefe gave up only two safeties himself through the final innings and the Browns were unable to mount another threat. The final score was 2-1, New York.

Game Two was played the next day at the Polo Grounds with Icebox Chamberlain starting against Mickey Welch. Heavy morning rain made for another sloppy field and limited the attendance to a little over five thousand. Umpires Kelly and Gaffney switched positions and play began on time at 3:00.

Neither team scored in the first, but St. Louis tallied a single run in the second. With one out, Tommy McCarthy singled and moved to second on a passed ball. Harry Lyons fanned for the second out of the inning, but catcher Buck Ewing dropped the third strike and McCarthy advanced to third when Lyons had to be retired at first. Shortstop Bill White coaxed a base on balls from Welch, then bluffed a break for second, drawing a throw from Ewing. McCarthy scored but White stopped abruptly and sneaked back into first. That was all the offense in the game until the ninth when successive singles by Tip O'Neill, Charlie Comiskey, and Tommy McCarthy, and a sacrifice fly by Bill Lyons accounted for two St. Louis insurance runs. McCarthy apparently forgot there were two umpires on the field in this inning when he tried to score by taking a shortcut directly from second base to home plate. Honest John Kelly signalled him out, and the side was retired. The Giants went out easily in the bottom of the inning and Icebox Chamberlain finished with a five-hit shutout and the first St. Louis win of the Series. The Giants had ample scoring opportunities but were unable to bring anyone around as they stranded runners at third base three times through the first eight innings.

The third game at the Polo Grounds, on the next day, was another close contest decided in the early innings. The weather was colder than it was for the first two games, yet the largest crowd of the Series, 5,780, turned out. Silver King and Tim Keefe were rematched and, for the second time in the Series, Keefe got the better of the deal.

The Giants broke on top in the bottom of the first when Mike Tiernan walked, stole second, and made third on a single by Buck Ewing. Tiernan was nailed at the plate when Danny Richardson grounded out, but Richardson and Ewing worked the double steal successfully and when Monte Ward singled, the Giants had a 2-0 lead. Following the pattern established in his first start, King settled down and pitched creditably the rest of the way, giving up only three more hits, but he surrendered two more runs which put the contest on ice for the Giants. The Browns mounted several threats during the game, but were unable to pull the trigger against Keefe. St. Louis loaded the bases in the fifth and again in the seventh, and a hit in either inning would have dented the 3-0 New York lead, but Arlie Latham was retired both times, leaving a total of six men stranded. The final run for St. Louis came in the ninth when catcher Buck Ewing, to avoid contact with Jack Boyle barreling down from third, stepped back from the plate and allowed Boyle a tainted theft of home. (Under modern scoring rules, this would be considered an uncontested steal, and would not count as a stolen base.) The final score was 4-2.

Tim Keefe finished with eleven strikeouts and a six-hitter in recording his second victory of the Series. Silver King had now worked sixteen innings and surrendered only seven hits, but was winless in both starts.

The most notable feature of this game, and indeed of the Series to date, was the baserunning of the New York Giants. The Giants had run with abandon, challenging the weak arm of Jack Boyle at nearly every opportunity. Through the first three games, New York had fifteen stolen bases; the Browns had five. St. Louis manager Charlie Comiskey benched Boyle after this game and the catcher didn't play again until the ninth game, by which time the Series had already been decided.

Game Four was played at Washington Park in Brooklyn the next day and proved to be the turning point of the Series. Because of a drizzling, freezing rain, attendance was off by nearly half that of the day before. Washington Park was located in a hollow between two hills, and whenever it rained the grounds filled with water. Sawdust was sprinkled on the field to make it playable. Although Brooklyn was an Association town, the crowd favored the Giants, playing tin horns whenever the New Yorkers did anything noteworthy.

With his team ahead 2-1 in the Series, Giants manager Jim Mutrie gave Buck Ewing a day off and started reserve catcher Willard Brown behind the plate. His batterymate was Cannonball Crane, making his first start of the Series. The Browns were the "home" team and Icebox Chamberlain took the mound promptly at 3:00.

The substitution of Brown for Ewing paid dividends in the very first inning for the Giants. With one out, Brown singled and reached second when left fielder Tip O'Neill bobbled the ball. After taking third on a passed ball, Brown scored on Danny Richardson's sacrifice fly. St. Louis tested the New York catcher's throwing arm in the second inning when Harry Lyons singled with two out and attempted to steal second. He was thrown out easily.

The Giants put the game away with four runs in the third inning. Crane singled, went to second on a passed ball, and to third on an infield single by Mike Tiernan. Tiernan promptly stole second and when Yank Robinson booted Danny Richardson's grounder, Crane scored. Tiernan was trapped in a rundown between third and home when Roger Connor grounded to Bill White at short, but successfully eluded the St. Louis defense and wound up back on third, a broad smile on his face. This loaded the bases for Monte Ward, who singled home Tiernan. Jim O'Rourke's two-out single gave the Giants a 5-0 lead. If there was any doubt regarding the outcome of the game or the Series, it was put to rest in this inning. The Browns were clearly overmatched.

St. Louis tallied its first run of the game in the bottom of the inning but the Giants matched that score with one in the fifth. Trailing 6-1 in the eighth, the Browns mounted their last threat of the day. A base on balls to Bill White and a Jocko Milligan single put the first two men on base and a wild pitch moved the runners into scoring position. Crane walked Icebox Chamberlain and when the final pitch eluded Brown, White scored. Arlie Latham tried to catch the New York defense napping with a surprise bunt but Crane fielded the ball cleanly and threw to Brown, retiring Milligan at the plate. Yank Robinson's sacrifice fly brought Chamberlain home with the second run of the inning and Latham stole second, but the uprising ended when Latham tried to push his luck and was nailed trying to purloin third. The play was close and the crowd booed the call.

The Giants continued their thievery on the basepaths with four stolen bases off Browns catcher Jocko Milligan. New York's Willard Brown was more successful, throwing out three St. Louis baserunners.

Umpires John Gaffney (on the basepaths) and John Kelly (at the plate) were, in this game and in the Series so far, particularly hard on the Browns. Both men were jeered and hissed by the Brooklyn crowd for showing apparent favoritism to the Giants. The St. Louis *Post-Dispatch* thought it knew the reason for the arbiters' partiality:

> It is a fact that [John] Kelly is going to open a restaurant and
> saloon in New York, with Mike Kelly [a native New Yorker] as a
> partner. As he will depend on the base-ball patrons for his trade it
> is not likely he will not [sic] antagonize them by giving a decision
> against their pets.

Needless to say, the rules against fraternization were somewhat more relaxed a century ago.

The fifth game in five days, and the first in good weather, was played on October 20. It was clear, cool, and cloudless, as nine thousand fans turned out for Game Five, the last contest to be played at this location of the Polo Grounds. Every seat in the house was taken and the crowd stood three-deep around the field to watch the third duel between staff aces Tim Keefe and the hardluck Silver King.

New York jumped on top in the first. Leadoff batter Mike Tiernan singled, went to second when Tommy McCarthy's throw back to the infield was wild, and scored on Danny Richardson's hit to center. But the Browns rebounded with a vengeance in the third. With one out, Jocko Milligan and Silver King hit back-to-back singles. Arlie Latham attempted to sacrifice and bunted a one-hopper right back to Tim Keefe, but Keefe's throw to first hit

Latham in the back and Milligan came home with the tying run. Before first baseman Roger Connor could retrieve the ball, Latham was on second and King on third. Yank Robinson's single to center gave the Browns a 3-1 lead. St. Louis added to its margin in the sixth when Latham singled and stole second, went to third on a groundout, and scored when Robinson squeezed him home.

New York was finally being reined in on the basepaths. Jocko Milligan threw out Danny Richardson attempting to steal in the first and prevented a New York rally in the fourth when he nailed both Roger Connor and Monte Ward. Jim O'Rourke attempted to score on a short passed ball in the fifth, but Milligan stood his ground and tagged him out at the plate.

It looked as though Silver King was finally going to win a game when New York batted in the eighth, trailing, 4-1. But Giants newcomer Art Whitney led off the inning with a single to center. Tim Keefe grounded to Yank Robinson and was retired easily at first. Charlie Comiskey fired the ball to shortstop Bill White in a hurried attempt to nail Whitney, who had taken a wide swing around second base, but White dropped the ball and this costly error opened the floodgates. Mike Tiernan's single made the score 4-2, St. Louis, and when Buck Ewing tripled over Tommy McCarthy's head in right, the Giants had pulled to within a run. Danny Richardson then hit a come-backer to Silver King, but King booted the easy chance. He recovered in time to throw Richardson out at first, but the damage had been done. Ewing touched home plate to tie the score and the crowd celebrated by throwing hats and umbrellas into the air. When Roger Connor followed with a triple to right, the Giants had the lead run on third. Here, it is safe to say, the Browns simply fell apart.

Monte Ward lifted a high pop fly between Yank Robinson and Harry Lyons in shallow center field for what should have been the third out of the inning. Robinson backed out and Lyons raced in, but the two collided and the ball fell in safely for a single. Connor scored and the Giants led, 5-4. Dazed by the collision, Lyons was unable to continue, so Comiskey took his place in center field. Boyle entered the game at first base. Robinson remained unconscious for five minutes, but eventually recovered to stay in the game. When play resumed, Ward stole second and continued on to third when Milligan's throw was wild. He scored a moment later on King's wild pitch. Mike Slattery popped out to second to end the carnage.

Yank Robinson took his place in the batter's box in the ninth inning but the game was called because of darkness before he could swing the bat. The Giants now had a commanding four-to-one lead in the Series and Tim Keefe was 3-0, with all three decisions coming at the expense of Silver King.

At the Grand Central Hotel that evening, a local doctor ordered Harry Lyons to remain in bed for a month. Fearing a possible rupture, the oft-injured Lyons (who missed several weeks early in the season after being hit in the stomach by a pitched ball) announced his retirement from baseball, a remark which proved to be premature by three years. Second-year man Ed Herr replaced the center fielder for the rest of the Series. A frantic Chris Von Der Ahe sent a telegram to pitcher Nat Hudson, pleading with him to join the team but Hudson, a man of independent means, was enjoying the waters at Hot Springs, Arkansas, and did not bother to reply.

After a day off, the Series resumed at the Philadelphia Baseball Grounds on October 22, with Mickey Welch pitted against Icebox Chamberlain. Despite a small crowd, the cream of the baseball world turned out for the game. Among the spectators were Mr. and Mrs. Harry Wright; Philadelphia Phillies Charlie Buffinton, Sid Farrar, Charlie Bastian, and Dan Casey; Harry Stovey from the Philadelphia Athletics and his manager, Bill Sharsig; Fred Dunlap of the Pittsburgh Pirates; umpire Billy McLean, the ex-pugilist; Mrs. Monte Ward; and Mr. and Mrs. A.J. Reach. Reach would make a one-handed grab of a foul ball during the game, for which he was roundly applauded by the crowd.

Play began at 3:00, and the Browns showed some of their old fire when they jumped on Welch in the bottom of the first. With one out, Yank Robinson tripled to center. Tip O'Neill grounded to Danny Richardson, who threw home in plenty of time to retire Robinson. Robinson and Ewing collided and umpire John Kelly shouted, "Out!" only to reverse himself a split second later when Ewing dropped the ball. Ewing kicked, but the decision stood. Charlie Comiskey drew a base on balls, a wild pitch advanced both runners, and Tommy McCarthy's single gave the Browns a 3-0 lead. St. Louis added a run in the third on another RBI single by McCarthy, and the Giants made the score 4-1 when Ewing and Richardson worked the double steal in the fourth.

Icebox Chamberlain had given up only two hits through the first five innings and promptly retired Welch and Tiernan in the sixth before he suddenly lost his effectiveness. A Buck Ewing single preceded Danny Richardson's RBI triple and after Roger Connor walked and stole second, Monte Ward doubled to right to tie the score at four-all.

The Browns had blown a three-run lead for the second successive game, but things would get worse. In the seventh, Arlie Latham threw Jim O'Rourke's grounder away and a hit by Mickey Welch put the Giants on top, 5-4. Singles from Tiernan and Ewing accounted for two more runs as New York increased its lead to 7-4. The Giants added five insurance runs in the eighth on five hits, a walk, and two errors by Browns first baseman Charlie Comiskey. Ten of New York's fifteen hits came after the sixth inning. Mickey Welch, after surrendering two safeties in the first inning, gave up only one more through the next seven and retired thirteen straight batters before Arlie Latham reached on an error and later scored in the eighth. The game was then halted by the umpires because of darkness, with the final score 12-5. The Giants were within one victory of the championship and the Browns, as every baseball fan in the country had learned by now, were clearly outclassed.

The journey from Philadelphia to St. Louis was fraught with drama. When the train stopped at Pittsburgh, former Browns player Curt Welch was waiting with a few pointed remarks on the quality of the umpiring in the Series. He charged John Kelly with out-and-out favoritism and accused him of wagering on the Giants to win the Series. Chris Von Der Ahe then entered the fray, claiming *both* umpires had bet on the Giants. By the time the train arrived in St. Louis, the Associated Press news flash had reached Gaffney and Kelly.

"I don't care about anyone's opinion of my work," said Gaffney. "But I do object to being called crooked, and I will quit the business before taking any more of that."

Kelly claimed, "If Gaffney won't umpire any more games, I won't either."

Reporters thronged Union Depot when the clubs arrived on October 23, and a makeshift press conference was held. Von Der Ahe claimed he had been misquoted and emphatically denied any wrongdoing by the two umpires. Mollified, Gaffney and Kelly agreed to continue working, and the teams met at Sportsman's Park in St. Louis for Game Seven on the 24th, the first time the Giants had played in St. Louis since the 1886 season. Starting pitchers were Silver King and Cannonball Crane.

The Browns elected to play on defense at the outset of the game, and the Giants looked like they were going to make short work of St. Louis and the Series as they lit into Silver King in the second inning. Consecutive singles by Jim O'Rourke, Mike Slattery, Art Whitney, and Willard Brown, plus a groundout by pitcher Cannonball Crane, gave New York a 3-0 lead. But the Browns struck back in the fourth, their first run of the game coming when Tommy McCarthy reached on an infield single, stole second, and scored on a Monte Ward error. Bill White walked, Jocko Milligan singled, and when the ball eluded center fielder Mike Slattery, two runs came in and the score was tied. New York regained the lead in the sixth on a walk to Roger Connor and an Art Whitney triple, and Whitney came home a moment later when Series goat Bill White booted an easy ground ball for what should have been the third out of the inning.

The Browns were down to their last six outs, and maybe less, when they came to the plate against Crane in the eighth inning. Darkness was falling and Giants catcher Buck Ewing had already made it abundantly clear that he thought the game should be called. On the heels of Von Der Ahe's non-accusation, however, John Gaffney was showing every conceivable fairness to the home team and allowed the game to continue. Tip O'Neill walked and advanced to third on two passed balls when Ewing had trouble picking up Crane's deliveries. Charlie Comiskey's triple pulled the Browns to within one and when center fielder Mike Slattery dropped Tommy McCarthy's fly ball in the twilight, the score was tied once again. McCarthy stole second and advanced another base on Ewing's third passed ball of the inning. Monte Ward booted Ed Herr's grounder and when Herr stole second base, the Browns had the lead runs on second and third with no one out. And it wasn't getting any lighter outside. Shortstop Bill White redeemed himself to some extent for his poor defensive play in the Series by slamming a double to right to put St. Louis ahead, 7-5.

The Giants made one last attempt to tie the score before darkness could end the game. In the bottom of the eighth inning, Buck Ewing singled and went to second on Mike Slattery's one-out bloop single. The two runners then worked the double steal successfully. Art Whitney fouled out to Milligan and Pat Murphy fanned, but strike three bounced off Milligan's chest protector and into the air. The crowd of five thousand watched anxiously as Milligan lunged desperately and caught the ball before it touched the ground. Silver King, although pitching his worst game of the Series, finally had a victory, and the Browns had staved off a New York championship for at least another day.

The Giants were hard-hit by injuries in the loss. In the seventh inning, Roger Connor wrenched his knee and had to be replaced at first base by Buck Ewing. In the eighth, Willard Brown split a finger and reserve catcher Pat Murphy entered the game behind the plate. But with New York needing only one victory for the championship, neither injury would play a significant part in the Series.

The weather was warm on the 25th and at 2:30, half an hour before game time, there were over fifteen hundred fans in the ballpark. By 3:00, attendance had swelled to nearly five thousand, each St. Louis "krank" eager to believe the Browns still had a fighting chance. Cowbells and tin horns were the order of the day, but as it developed, the partisan crowd had little chance to use either.

The starting pitchers were Icebox Chamberlain and Tim Keefe, but more important for the Giants, Buck Ewing was back in the lineup. And Ewing put on quite a display of his hitting prowess over the first three innings. His one-out solo home run in the first gave New York a lead it never relinquished, and his bases-loaded triple in the third put the Giants up, 4-0. An RBI single by Art Whitney increased the margin to five runs in the fourth. St. Louis scored single runs in the fourth and seventh but still trailed by three as it batted in the eighth. The never-say-die Arlie Latham singled to lead off the inning and promptly stole second. A few moments later, Buck Ewing tried a pickoff play but his throw went into center field and Latham motored around to third. Tip O'Neill's sacrifice fly narrowed the Giants' lead to 5-3 with one inning to go.

Chamberlain took the mound for the final inning and immediately got into a jam when leadoff batter Monte Ward laced a single to center. One out later, George Gore singled to left but Ward, fearing Tip O'Neill's strong arm, held at second. No matter. Mike Slattery lined an RBI single into center, and when the ball two-hopped away from Ed Herr, Gore went to third and Slattery to second. A single by Art Whitney made the score 8-3. Tim Keefe coaxed a base on balls from Chamberlain and Mike Tiernan strolled to the plate. Tiernan watched a pair of Chamberlain's deliveries go by, then lined a three-run homer into the right-field stands to cap off the scoring.

The final score left the fans shaking their heads in wonder that the Browns had managed to win any of the games at all.

Tim Keefe, with a five-hitter, had his fourth win of the Series. In thirty-five innings, Sir Timothy had allowed only eighteen hits (all except one were singles) and had a sparkling earned run average of 0.51.

The normally reserved *New York Times* crowed:

> It was an awful revelation to the crowd. They did not expect to see the Browns win at that late stage of the game, nor did they expect to see the Giants make a spectacle of them, but these Giants are bold, bad men, and they are liable to do almost anything . . . All the game lacked to make it a first-class funeral was the music. The corpse was there, for no well-conducted funeral is without a corpse.

After the contest ended, Monte Ward and Cannonball Crane left for San Francisco to accompany Al Spalding on his tour of Australia. Willard Brown and Buck Ewing left for home.

The 1888 World Series was officially over. It was decided that the three remaining games scheduled for Sportsman's Park would still be played, for exhibition and for the gate receipts.

The ninth game, on October 26, resulted in a free-hitting victory for the Browns. In pre-game ceremonies, each member of the Giants was presented with a gold scarf pin by super-fan General Arthur "Hi Hi" Dixwell of Boston. Umpire John Kelly had returned to New York, leaving John Gaffney to umpire the final three games alone.

The one thousand fans at Sportsman's Park got their money's worth as Silver King took the mound against New York's Bill George, a 3-1 performer during the regular season. Tip O'Neill's sacrifice fly gave St. Louis a 1-0 lead in the top of the first, and the Browns combined four hits, three stolen bases, and three New York errors for a four-run explosion in the second. The Giants entered the spirit of fun in the bottom of the inning when they tallied three runs on five clean hits off King, who was less than enthusiastic about pitching. In the third, four hits and a base on balls put five more runs in New York's column, giving the Giants an 8-5 lead. King was through for the day, having allowed nine hits, a walk, and eight runs in three innings pitched. He was replaced on the mound by spot starter Jim Devlin. Tommy McCarthy's RBI single and an error by Art Whitney pulled the Browns to within a run in the fifth. RBI hits from Charlie Comiskey and Jack Boyle put St. Louis on top, 9-8, in the seventh, but the Giants came back to tie the score in the bottom of the inning on a double by Danny Richardson, a sacrifice bunt by Mike Slattery, and Art Whitney's fielder's choice. Richardson's third double of the game plated Jim O'Rourke and George Gore in the bottom of the eighth and gave the Giants an 11-9 lead.

Yank Robinson was the first batter for the Browns in the ninth and he lifted a routine fly ball for Gore in left. Tip O'Neill popped out to shortstop Gil Hatfield, and the Browns were down to their last batter, manager Charlie Comiskey. Within one out of a victory, Bill George playfully tipped his hat to teammates Tim Keefe and Roger Connor, who were applauding him from the bench. But Comiskey and Tommy McCarthy hit back-to-back singles, then worked the double steal successfully and, suddenly, George found himself staring at Jack Boyle, with the tying runs on second and third. Incensed at George's histrionics, Boyle drove the next pitch on a line into left-center field for a triple, both runners scoring, and the game was tied. When the Giants went out in order in the bottom of the ninth, the contest went into extra innings.

Jocko Milligan led off the St. Louis tenth with a ringing single to center and went to second and third on successive groundouts. Yank Robinson drew a base on balls and Tip O'Neill hammered one of Boyle's next deliveries into the left-field stands for a three-run homer and what proved to be the game as the Browns won, 14-11.

That evening, both clubs attended a play in specially decorated reserve boxes at the Grand Opera House in St. Louis.

The tenth game of the Series had originally been slated for Cincinnati but was rescheduled as a players' benefit game at Sportsman's Park. The Browns were still playing to win, but the Giants, as evidenced by their starting lineup, clearly just wanted to have some fun. Right fielder Mike Tiernan and catcher Pat Murphy were playing their normal positions but left fielder George Gore and third baseman Art Whitney had changed places on the field. Jim O'Rourke, who had been filling in for the injured Roger Connor at first, took a turn at second base, while pitcher Bill George played first. Mike Slattery started in center but moved to second base later in the game. Reserve infielder Gil Hatfield started at second but replaced Cannonball Titcomb on the mound in the fifth.

The Giants took an early 4-1 lead off Icebox Chamberlain but the Browns routed Titcomb for five runs in the fourth to go ahead. Hatfield fared no better than Titcomb as St. Louis racked up twelve runs over the final four innings for an easy 18-7 victory.

The Browns and Giants played another exhibition game the next day, also for the financial benefit of the players, as warm weather brought over three thousand people into Sportsman's Park. Tim Keefe, Mickey Welch, and Bill George all took turns on the mound for the Giants and no member of the trio was accused of overexerting himself. Bill White's double gave St. Louis its first run in the second and a single by substitute catcher Tom Dolan, playing his last game for a major league team, increased the Browns' margin to 2-0. St. Louis put another run on the board in the third and scored unearned runs in the sixth, seventh, and eighth to win easily, 6-0. Silver King went the distance for the Browns with a six-hit shutout.

Browns shortstop Bill White was made the goat of the Series and vilified by the St. Louis press. On the 29th, the St. Louis *Post-Dispatch* said:

> The weakness of the Browns in the short stop's position was simply appalling, and the loss of no less than three games in the series can be directly attributed to his poor work. He could not fill the bill. It was as weak work as was ever seen. The Browns themselves were astonished by his poor work . . . White's fielding average in the first nine games was .787. His batting average was .096. He struck out nine times and stole one base. If ever one man lost an important series, it was this man White. Had the Browns had a strong man in his place the result of the series might have been entirely different.

Whether White was offered a contract for 1889 or simply retired at the end of the season is unknown, but he never donned a major league uniform again.

The eighteen members of the New York team each received two hundred dollars for winning the Series, twenty-eight dollars for the benefit game on the 27th, and one hundred dollars for the benefit game on the 28th. Chris Von Der Ahe received and pocketed the $1,200 Association money for winning the 1888 pennant and withheld the benefit game proceeds from his players. Not content with this thievery, Von Der Ahe then added insult to injury by referring to his charges as "chumps."

Including the 1887 World Series and two exhibition contests, the Browns had now played twenty-seven post-season games for free.

New York manager Jim Mutrie had become the first man to pilot teams from two leagues to the World Series—the New York Metropolitans in 1884 and the New York Giants this year. After the games ended, Mutrie finished forever the clumsy idea of meaningless post-series exhibition games.

"If I ever engage in another World Series," said Mutrie, "the ball will stop rolling just as soon as the series is decided."

GAME ONE—October 16, 1888, at the Polo Grounds, New York

ST. LOUIS	AB	R	H	BI	E	NEW YORK	AB	R	H	BI	E
Latham, 3b	3	1	0	0	1	Tiernan, rf	3	1	0	0	1
Robinson, 2b	4	0	1	0	0	Ewing, c	3	0	0	0	1
O'Neill, lf	4	0	1	1	0	Richardson, 2b	3	0	0	0	0
Comiskey, 1b	4	0	0	0	0	Connor, 1b	3	1	1	0	0
McCarthy, rf	4	0	0	0	0	Ward, ss	3	0	1	0	0
Lyons, cf	4	0	0	0	1	Slattery, cf	3	0	0	1	0
White, ss	4	0	0	0	1	O'Rourke, lf	3	0	0	0	0
Boyle, c	3	0	1	0	1	Whitney, 3b	3	0	0	0	0
King, p	3	0	0	0	0	Keefe, p	3	0	0	0	1
	33	1	3	1	4		27	2	2	1	3

```
STL   0 0 1   0 0 0   0 0 0 - 1
NY    0 1 1   0 0 0   0 0 x - 2
```

SB: Latham, Tiernan, Ewing 2, O'Rourke, Robinson 2.   SF: Slattery.   BB: Keefe 1, King 1.   Struck out: Keefe 9, King 3.   WP: King.   PB: Ewing.   Umpires: Gaffney and Kelly.   Time—2:00.   Att: 4,876.

◆ ◆ ◆

GAME TWO—October 17, 1888, at the Polo Grounds, New York

ST. LOUIS	AB	R	H	BI	E	NEW YORK	AB	R	H	BI	E
Latham, 3b	4	0	0	0	0	Tiernan, rf*	3	0	2	0	0
Robinson, 2b	2	0	0	0	0	Ewing, c	4	0	0	0	0
O'Neill, lf	4	1	1	0	1	Richardson, 2b	3	0	1	0	0
Comiskey, 1b	4	1	2	0	0	Connor, 1b	3	0	0	0	0
McCarthy, rf	4	1	2	1	0	Ward, ss	4	0	0	0	0
Lyons, cf	4	0	0	1	0	Slattery, cf	4	0	0	0	0
White, ss	3	0	0	0	1	O'Rourke, lf	4	0	1	0	0
Milligan, c	3	0	2	0	0	Whitney, 3b	4	0	0	0	0
Chamberlain, p	3	0	0	0	0	Welch, p	3	0	1	0	0
	31	3	7	2	2		32	0	5	0	0

* Tiernan called out for interference

```
STL   0 1 0   0 0 0   0 0 2 – 3
NY    0 0 0   0 0 0   0 0 0 – 0
```

D: Milligan 2.   SB: Richardson, Connor, McCarthy, Tiernan, Ewing.   SF: Lyons.
DP: STL 1, NY 1.   BB: Welch 3, Chamberlain 3.   Struck out: Welch 3, Chamberlain 1.
WP: Chamberlain.   PB: Ewing.   Umpires: Kelly and Gaffney.   Time—1:40.   Att: 5,575.

◆ ◆ ◆

GAME THREE—October 18, 1888, at the Polo Grounds, New York

ST. LOUIS	AB	R	H	BI	E	NEW YORK	AB	R	H	BI	E
Latham, 3b	5	0	1	0	0	Tiernan, rf	2	0	0	0	0
Robinson, 2b	4	1	0	0	0	Ewing, c	4	1	1	0	0
O'Neill, lf	4	0	2	0	0	Richardson, 2b	4	1	0	0	0
Comiskey, 1b	4	0	0	1	0	Connor, 1b	3	0	0	0	1
McCarthy, rf	4	0	0	0	0	Ward, ss	3	1	2	2	0
Lyons, cf	3	0	1	0	0	Slattery, cf	3	1	1	1	0
White, ss	4	0	0	0	1	O'Rourke, lf	3	0	0	0	0
Boyle, c	2	1	1	0	1	Whitney, 3b	3	0	1	1	0
King, p	3	0	0	0	0	Keefe, p	3	0	0	0	0
	33	2	5	1	2		28	4	5	4	1

```
STL   0 0 0   0 0 0   0 1 1 – 2
NY    2 0 0   1 0 0   1 0 x – 4
```

D: O'Neill.   SB: Tiernan, Ewing, Richardson, Ward 3, Slattery, Boyle.   SF: Whitney.
DP: NY.   BB: Keefe 4, King 2.   Struck out: Keefe 11, King 2.   WP: Keefe.   PB: Ewing.
Umpires: Kelly and Gaffney.   Time—2:05.   Att: 5,850.

GAME FOUR—October 19, 1888, at Washington Park, Brooklyn

ST. LOUIS	AB	R	H	BI	E	NEW YORK	AB	R	H	BI	E
Latham, 3b	4	0	2	1	0	Tiernan, rf	4	1	1	0	0
Robinson, 2b	4	0	1	1	1	Brown, c*	5	1	1	0	0
O'Neill, lf	4	0	0	0	1	Richardson, 2b	4	1	0	2	0
Comiskey, 1b	4	0	1	0	0	Connor, 1b	4	2	2	0	0
McCarthy, rf	4	0	0	0	0	Ward, ss	4	0	2	2	0
Lyons, cf	3	0	1	0	0	Slattery, cf	4	0	0	0	0
White, ss	2	1	0	0	0	O'Rourke, lf	2	0	1	2	0
Milligan, c	3	1	2	0	0	Whitney, 3b	4	0	0	0	0
Chamberlain, p	2	1	0	0	0	Crane, p	4	1	1	0	0
	30	3	7	2	2		35	6	8	6	0

* Brown declared out on appeal

```
NY    1 0 4   0 1 0   0 0 0 – 6
STL   0 0 1   0 0 0   0 2 0 – 3
```

D: Connor, Comiskey.   T: Connor.   SB: Tiernan, Ward, Connor, O'Rourke, Latham.
SF: Richardson, Robinson.   BB: Chamberlain 4, Crane 2.   Struck out: Chamberlain 4,
Crane 8.   WP: Chamberlain, Crane 2.   PB: Milligan 2.   Umpires: Kelly and Gaffney.
Time—2:00.   Att: 3,062.

GAME FIVE—October 20, 1888, at the Polo Grounds, New York

ST. LOUIS	AB	R	H	BI	E	NEW YORK	AB	R	H	BI	E
Latham, 3b	3	2	1	0	0	Tiernan, rf	4	2	2	1	0
Robinson, 2b	3	0	1	2	0	Ewing, c	4	1	1	1	1
O'Neill, lf	3	0	0	1	0	Richardson, 2b	4	0	1	2	0
Comiskey, 1b	3	0	1	0	1	Connor, 1b	4	1	2	0	0
McCarthy, rf	3	0	0	0	1	Ward, ss	3	1	1	1	0
Lyons, cf	3	0	0	0	0	Slattery, cf	4	0	0	0	0
White, ss	3	0	0	0	2	O'Rourke, lf	3	0	1	0	0
Milligan, c	2	1	1	0	1	Whitney, 3b	2	1	1	0	0
King, p	3	1	1	0	0	Keefe, p	3	0	0	0	1
	26	4	5	3	5		31	6	9	5	2

```
STL   0 0 3   0 0 1   0 0 – 4
NY    1 0 0   0 0 0   0 5 – 6
```

T: Connor, Ewing.   SB: Latham, Ward 2, Slattery.   SAC: O'Neill.   DP: NY 2.
BB: King 2, Keefe 1.   Struck out: Keefe 2, King 3.   WP: King.   PB: Milligan 2, Ewing.
Umpires: Gaffney and Kelly.   Time—1:50.   Att: 9,124.

GAME SIX—October 22, 1888, at Philadelphia Base Ball Grounds, Philadelphia

NEW YORK	AB	R	H	BI	E	ST. LOUIS	AB	R	H	BI	E
Tiernan, rf	5	1	2	0	0	Latham, 3b	3	1	0	0	1
Ewing, c	5	2	3	3	0	Robinson, 2b	3	2	1	1	2
Richardson, 2b	4	1	1	1	0	O'Neill, lf	2	1	0	0	0
Connor, 1b	4	2	1	1	1	Comiskey, 1b	3	1	0	0	2
Ward, ss	4	1	1	3	0	McCarthy, rf	3	0	2	3	0
Slattery, cf	4	0	0	0	0	Herr, cf	3	0	0	0	0
O'Rourke, lf	4	2	2	0	0	White, ss	3	0	0	0	0
Whitney, 3b	4	1	1	1	0	Milligan, c	2	0	0	0	0
Welch, p	4	2	1	2	0	Chamberlain, p	3	0	0	0	0
	38	12	12	11	1		25	5	3	4	5

```
NY    0 0 0   1 0 3   3 5 - 12
STL   3 0 1   0 0 0   0 1 -  5
```

D: Ward.   T: Richardson, Connor, Robinson.   SB: Connor, McCarthy, Latham 2.
SF: Robinson.   BB: Chamberlain 2, Welch 6.   Struck out: Chamberlain 3, Welch 2.
Umpires: Gaffney and Kelly.   Time—1:39.   Att: 3,281.

GAME SEVEN—October 24, 1888, at Sportsman's Park, St. Louis

ST. LOUIS	AB	R	H	BI	E	NEW YORK	AB	R	H	BI	E
Latham, 3b	4	0	0	0	1	Tiernan, rf	4	0	1	0	0
Robinson, 2b	3	0	0	0	1	Ward, ss	4	0	2	0	2
O'Neill, lf	2	1	0	0	0	Richardson, 2b	4	0	0	0	0
Comiskey, 1b	4	1	2	1	0	Connor, 1b	2	1	1	0	0
McCarthy, rf	4	2	1	1	0	O'Rourke, lf	3	1	1	0	0
Herr, cf	4	2	1	0	0	Slattery, cf	4	1	2	0	3
White, ss	3	1	2	2	1	Whitney, 3b	4	2	2	3	0
Milligan, c	4	0	2	1	1	Brown, c	3	0	2	0	0
King, p	4	0	0	0	0	Crane, p	3	0	0	1	0
	32	7	8	5	4	Ewing, 1b	1	0	1	0	0
						Murphy, c	1	0	0	0	0
							33	5	12	4	5

```
STL   0 0 0   3 0 0   0 4 - 7
NY    0 3 0   0 0 2   0 0 - 5
```

D: White.   T: Comiskey, Whitney.   SB: Latham, McCarthy 2, Herr, Connor, Ward,
Ewing, Slattery.   DP: STL.   BB: Crane 4, King 2.   Struck out: Crane 4, King 5.
WP: Crane.   PB: Murphy 3, Milligan.   Umpires: Gaffney and Kelly.   Time—1:52.
Att: 4,624.

GAME EIGHT—October 25, 1888, at Sportsman's Park, St. Louis

ST. LOUIS	AB	R	H	BI	E	NEW YORK	AB	R	H	BI	E
Latham, 3b	3	1	1	0	1	Tiernan, rf	4	2	1	3	0
Robinson, 2b	3	0	0	0	0	Ewing, c	5	1	3	4	1
O'Neill, lf	4	1	1	1	0	Richardson, 2b	5	0	0	0	0
Comiskey, 1b	4	0	1	0	0	Ward, ss	4	1	2	0	0
McCarthy, rf	4	1	1	1	0	O'Rourke, 1b	4	0	1	0	1
Herr, cf	4	0	0	0	1	Gore, lf	4	1	1	0	0
White, ss	4	0	0	0	0	Slattery, cf	4	2	2	1	0
Milligan, c	3	0	1	1	0	Whitney, 3b	4	2	3	3	0
Chamberlain, p	2	0	0	0	0	Keefe, p	2	2	1	0	0
	31	3	5	3	2		36	11	14	11	2

```
NY    1 0 3   1 0 0   0 0 6 – 11
STL   0 0 0   1 0 0   1 1 0 –  3
```

D: Slattery. T: Ewing. HR: Ewing, Tiernan. SB: Latham 2, Chamberlain, Slattery.
SF: O'Neill. HBP: Robinson (Keefe). BB: Keefe 2, Chamberlain 3. Struck out: Keefe
11, Chamberlain 3. PB: Ewing 3. WP: Keefe. DP: NY 1, STL 2. Umpires: Kelly and
Gaffney. Time—2:10. Att: 4,865.

GAME NINE—October 26, 1888, at Sportsman's Park, St. Louis

ST. LOUIS	AB	R	H	BI	E	NEW YORK	AB	R	H	BI	E
Latham, 3b	5	2	1	1	0	Tiernan, rf	5	0	2	0	0
Robinson, 2b	5	3	3	1	0	O'Rourke, 1b	5	1	0	0	0
O'Neill, lf	4	1	1	4	0	Gore, lf	5	2	2	0	0
Comiskey, c-1b	6	2	3	1	0	Richardson, 2b	4	3	3	1	1
McCarthy, rf	5	3	2	1	0	Slattery, cf	5	2	2	1	0
Boyle, cf	5	1	3	3	0	Whitney, 3b	5	1	2	3	2
White, ss	5	1	1	1	1	Hatfield, ss	5	1	1	1	0
Milligan, c-1b	5	1	1	0	0	Murphy, c	5	1	1	1	1
King, p	2	0	0	0	0	George, p	5	0	1	2	1
Devlin, p	3	0	0	0	0		44	11	14	9	5
	45	14	15	12	1						

```
STL   1 4 0   0 2 0   2 0 2   3 – 14
NY    0 3 5   0 0 0   1 2 0   0 – 11
```

D: Richardson 3, Robinson 2. TP: Boyle. HR: O'Neill. SAC: Slattery. SF: O'Neill.
SB: Slattery, Boyle, White, Latham, Comiskey 3, McCarthy. DP: STL. BB: King 1,
Devlin 1, George 3. Struck out: King 2, Devlin 4, George 4. WP: King, Devlin. PB:
Murphy. Umpire: Gaffney. Time—2:20. Att: 711.

GAME TEN—October 27, 1888, at Sportsman's Park, St. Louis

ST. LOUIS	AB	R	H	PO	A	E	NEW YORK	AB	R	H	PO	A	E
Latham, 3b	6	3	4	0	2	0	Tiernan, rf	4	1	2	2	0	1
Robinson, 2b	5	1	2	6	2	0	O'Rourke, ss	5	0	1	1	4	0
O'Neill, lf	5	3	3	3	0	1	Gore, 3b	2	2	2	1	1	2
Comiskey, 1b	5	1	1	10	1	0	George, 1b	4	2	2	10	1	2
McCarthy, rf	6	3	2	2	0	0	Slattery, cf-2b	4	0	1	4	3	1
Boyle, cf	6	2	2	2	0	0	Whitney, lf	4	0	2	1	0	0
White, ss	4	1	2	1	4	2	Hatfield, 2b-p	3	1	1	2	4	1
Milligan, c	3	2	1	3	3	0	Murphy, c	4	0	0	4	1	1
Chamberlain, p	3	2	0	0	1	0	Titcomb, p-cf	4	1	2	1	5	0
	43	18	17	27	13	3		34	7	13	26	19	8

```
STL    0 1 0   5 0 5   4 2 1 – 18
NY     3 1 0   0 0 0   0 2 1 –  7
```

Earned runs: STL 10, NY 7.   2B: Gore, Titcomb.   HR: McCarthy, O'Neill, George. DP: STL 3.   Struck out: Latham 2, Robinson, O'Neill, George.   BB: Robinson, O'Neill, Milligan, Chamberlain 2, Tiernan, Gore 2, Hatfield.   HBP: Comiskey (Titcomb).   WP: Titcomb 1, Hatfield 2, Chamberlain 1.   Umpire: Gaffney.   Time—2:00.   Att: 400 (estimated).

GAME ELEVEN—October 28, 1888, at Sportsman's Park, St. Louis

ST. LOUIS	R	H	PO	A	E	NEW YORK	R	H	PO	A	E
Latham, 3b	0	1	3	2	0	Tiernan, rf-ss	0	1	1	0	0
Robinson, 2b	1	1	3	3	0	Gore, 1b	0	2	15	0	2
O'Neill, lf	0	1	1	0	0	Titcomb, lf-ss-rf	0	0	2	0	2
Comiskey, 1b	1	1	11	0	0	Slattery, 2b	0	1	1	7	1
McCarthy, rf	2	0	0	0	0	George, ss-p	0	2	1	10	1
Boyle, cf	0	0	2	0	0	Hatfield, 3b	0	0	1	1	0
White, ss	1	2	1	3	0	Murphy, c	0	0	4	1	1
Dolan, c	1	1	6	3	0	Welch, cf-p-lf	0	0	0	0	0
King, p	0	1	0	6	0	Keefe, p-cf	0	0	2	0	0
	6	8	27	17	0		0	6	27	19	7

```
STL    0 2 1   0 0 1   1 1 0 – 6
NY     0 0 0   0 0 0   0 0 0 – 0
```

D: White, Robinson.   HBP: McCarthy.   DP: NY 1, STL 2.   PB: Murphy 2.   WP: George.   Umpire: Devlin.   Time—2:25.   Att: 3,000.

• 7 •

WE WUZ ROBBED!

———————◆———————

"Gunner" McGunnigle was in the right place at the right time.

A mediocre pitcher a decade earlier, Bill McGunnigle was tapped to manage the Trolley Dodgers and had the good fortune to arrive close on the heels of Brooklyn's acquisition of standout pitcher Bob Caruthers. Mc-Gunnigle took over a listless sixth-place ballclub and piloted the team to second place, 6½ games behind the St. Louis Browns. In 1889, in only his second full year as the Bridegrooms' manager, he won the big prize in the American Association.

Fire gutted Brooklyn's home field, Washington Park, and the Dodgers played their first month's home games at Ridgewood Park in Queens. Without the home-field advantage, Brooklyn played listlessly, and the Browns, seeking an unprecedented fifth straight pennant, carved out an early lead which they maintained until late August. It was about this time that the Trolley Dodgers acquired a new nickname—the Bridegrooms. Several players were married within a short time and for the sake of the race, abstained from sex during the pennant drive.

Early in September, the Browns began a disastrous East Coast swing as Brooklyn, winning relentlessly, took over the lead for

1889

The Changing Game

♦ ♦ ♦

• Four balls now constituted a walk.

• The sacrifice bunt was officially recognized, but the batter was still credited with a time at bat.

• George Wright's sensible suggestion that a batter be allowed to overrun first base on a hit without being tagged out on returning was incorporated into the rules of the game.

• New York Giants pitcher Mickey Welch became the first pinch-hitter in National League history. He struck out.

• Following the 1888 season, the Brush Classification Plan, named after Indianapolis owner John T. Brush, had been put into effect. The plan called for players to be graded on a scale from "A" to "E," with an "A" ballplayer receiving a maximum salary of $2,500 and an "E" player receiving the minimum of $1,000.

good. On September 6, before the largest non-holiday crowd (16,974) ever to attend a ballgame in Brooklyn, the Browns and Bridegrooms began a three-game series at Ridgewood Park. The skies were already overcast when the game got under way at 4:00, and the Browns were leading, 4–2, when the contest entered the ninth inning. Charlie Comiskey protested to umpire (and former pitcher) Fred Goldsmith that it was too dark to continue, but Goldsmith disagreed, so Comiskey, in protest, pulled the Browns off the field. Goldsmith gave the players five minutes to return, then forfeited the game to the Bridegrooms.

That evening, Von Der Ahe flatly stated that his team would play no more games in Brooklyn. The Bridegrooms' fans were an unruly mob, said Von Der Ahe, and Brooklyn management had failed to provide adequate police protection for the Browns. Second, added Von Der Ahe, these fans intimidated the umpires to the extent that it was impossible for the arbiters to work a fair game; if they wanted to escape the ballpark unharmed, they gave all the close decisions to the Bridegrooms. On the 7th, Von Der Ahe and Comiskey kept the Browns in their hotel rooms and refused to go to the park. Between fifteen and twenty thousand people showed up at the park, but the only action they saw was Fred Goldsmith awarding the game to Brooklyn by a second forfeit. No game was played the following day.

On September 23, at a special meeting of the American Association owners, Goldsmith was dismissed and, to the amazement of Brooklynites, his decision on the September 6 game was reversed, the win now going to St. Louis. The forfeit of the seventh still stood, but no decision was made on the game of the eighth.

By the end of September, the Browns trailed Brooklyn by 4½ games. Beginning in October, St. Louis reeled off a ten-game winning streak, but the Brooklyn lead was too large to overcome. Brooklyn edged the Browns at the wire, dashing St. Louis hopes.

The 1889 Bridegrooms had all the elements of a championship team. They led the American Association in fielding percentage (.928) and runs scored (995), finished second in runs allowed (680), and had a healthy team batting average of .263, third in the league. Only two of the club's regulars hit .300 or better—right fielder Thomas "Oyster" Burns (.304) and left fielder Darby O'Brien (.300)—but Dave Foutz, undergoing a conversion from pitcher to first base, hit for a respectable .277 mark and finished second in the league with 113 runs batted in. Brooklyn's leadoff batter O'Brien was the team catalyst and, like St. Louis third baseman Arlie Latham, one of the noisiest coaches in the game. The big Irishman had 170 hits, drew sixty-one walks, scored 146 runs, and stole ninety-one bases, trailing only Billy Hamilton in that regard.

The Brooklyn pitching staff was led by the remarkable "Parisian Bob" Caruthers, enjoying his last great year in the majors. Caruthers led all American Association pitchers in games won (40), winning percentage (.784), and shutouts (7), and finished third in appearances (56), and fifth in complete games (46).

Following Caruthers in the Brooklyn rotation was veteran Adonis Terry, who had finally begun to fulfill the promise of his strong right arm. With a 22-15 record, Terry supplemented his work on the mound by batting an even .300 with a .450 slugging average.

The final two members of the Grooms' staff were Tom Lovett and Mickey Hughes. Lovett was back in the big leagues for the first time since 1885, and ran up a convincing record of 17-10 despite a rather loud ERA of 4.32. Hughes had shown great promise as a rookie in 1888 when he finished fourth in earned run average and won twenty-five games. In 1889, however, Association batters had caught up to the diminutive right-hander's fastball. His record fell to 9-8 and his ERA more than doubled, to 4.35.

The New York Giants won the National League pennant on the last day of the season. It was the closest race in the League since 1883.

The Bridegrooms were up against a strong New York team, whose mainstay was catcher Buck Ewing. Defensively, Ewing had had a glorious season. He led the league in putouts (524), assists (149), double plays (10), total chances per game (7.4), and finished second in fielding percentage (.937) to Charlie Bennett (.955) of the Boston Beaneaters, although Ewing had 180 more chances. At the plate, Ewing battered National League pitchers for a .327 average, scored ninety-seven runs and drove in eighty-seven.

But Ewing wasn't the only good hitter on this hard-hitting club. First baseman Roger Connor (.317), right fielder Mike Tiernan (.335), center fielder George Gore (.305), and left fielder Orator Jim O'Rourke (.327) had all attained the coveted .300 mark.

Roger Connor led the National League in 1889 in RBIs (130) and slugging average (.528), finished second in triples (17), third in total bases (262), and tied with Mike Tiernan for fourth place in batting average. Tiernan was first in the league in runs scored (147) and fourth in slugging average (.501).

A measure of the respect in which both Mike Tiernan and Roger Connor were held by opposing pitchers was that the two men finished first and second in walks, with ninety-six and ninety-three, respectively.

The Giants led the National League in runs scored (935), triples (77), and batting average (.282), and the team slugging average of .394 was seventeen points higher than that of their nearest competition, the third-place Chicago Colts. But defensively (except for Buck Ewing), the Giants were a mediocre to poor club.

Manager Jim Mutrie's pitching staff was still headed by veterans Mickey Welch and Tim Keefe, each hurler coming off his last good season. Keefe (28-13) had another fine year as he finished first in fewest hits per nine innings (7.66), first in most strikeouts per nine innings (5.17), second in strikeouts (209) and victories, third in winning percentage (.683) and appearances (47), and fifth in earned run average (3.31). Welch (27-12) was second in winning percentage (.692), third in earned run average (3.02), and tied for third in wins and complete games (39).

Rounding out the staff were pitchers Edward "Cannonball" Crane and Hank O'Day. Crane finished the 1889 season with a 14-10 record, his first year in double figures, and had twenty-three complete games in twenty-five starts.

But Hank O'Day was the real star of the pennant drive. In the first six years of his major league career, O'Day had labored for second-division clubs, as his career record of 39-96 would attest. Coming to New York from the Washington Senators (where his record was a dismal 2-10) in mid-season, O'Day was 9-1 in ten appearances down the stretch to help carry the Giants to their second consecutive pennant.

The 1889 World Series was notable for two "firsts": It was the first of many Series encounters between teams from New York and Brooklyn. And it was the first and only World Series in the new Polo Grounds, also known as Manhattan Field.

Team owners John B. Day (New York) and Charles H. Byrne (Brooklyn) met in the offices of the *Sporting Times* on October 17 and decided that regular admission ticket prices would be fifty cents and grandstand seats would cost a quarter. They further agreed that the championship would be a best-of-eleven contest. Giants manager Jim Mutrie had already expressed his intentions to end the Series when either team won a sixth game.

It would not be until 1898 that Long Island and Staten Island were merged with the boroughs of Manhattan, Brooklyn, the Bronx, and Queens to become New York City. In 1889, an intense rivalry existed between New York and Brooklyn, nicknamed City of the Churches for its religious diversity, yet inexplicably, only about nine thousand fans turned out at the new Polo Grounds for

Game One of the 1889 World Series. In a park which boasted seating for fifteen thousand, this was a disappointing crowd.

In the early 1700s, a strip of land at the northern tip of Manhattan Island had been granted by King George I to an Englishman named John Gardiner. One of Gardiner's descendants had married James J. Coogan. Coogan farmed on the land and his tillable acres became known as Coogan's Hollow; an overlooking series of rocky cliffs was known as Coogan's Bluff. Coogan's Hollow became the site of team owner John B. Day's Polo Grounds. But the city of New York had decided that the old Polo Grounds would be a perfectly dandy place for a thoroughfare—a decision, some said, brought on because several aldermen hadn't been given enough free passes to games—so the world-champion New York Giants had to build a new ballpark. The new Polo Grounds, located at 155th Street and Eighth Avenue, featured the steepest and longest embankment ever seen in the major leagues, running through center and right field.

The opposing clubs had chosen two umpires to work the Series. The Giants had picked John Gaffney, an American Association umpire, on the strength of his excellent reputation. The Bridegrooms had selected Tom Lynch to be Gaffney's partner, but Lynch's asking price of eight hundred dollars was deemed too steep for club owners Day and Byrne, so Bob "Death to Flying Things" Ferguson, also an American Association ump, was substituted.

Fair weather and a cloudless sky greeted the players on October 18 as Gaffney and Ferguson called for play to begin at 3:07. Tim Keefe and Adonis Terry were the starting pitchers. Brooklyn manager Bill McGunnigle was so optimistic of victory, he confessed before the game that his players felt no fear of Keefe.

When Terry's first pitch to George Gore was wide of the plate, umpire Ferguson called out, "Ball one!" in such a stentorian voice that the crowd applauded. Terry retired Gore, Mike Tiernan, and Buck Ewing in one-two-three fashion, and the Brooklyn contingent at the park waved white handkerchiefs in approval.

In the bottom of the inning, the Bridegrooms beat up on Keefe with a vengeance. Leadoff batter Darby O'Brien was the lucky recipient of a bad-hop single to right and Hub Collins followed with a double to left. Oyster Burns, a strong clutch hitter, lashed a ringing single into right field, scoring both runners, and Brooklyn had a quick 2-0 edge. Dave Foutz and George Pinckney were retired, but singles by Bob Clark and Adonis Terry and a double by John "Pop" Corkhill gave the Grooms what looked to be a commanding 5-0 lead. Brooklynites in the crowd yelled themselves hoarse, while the New York contingent cheered, "Keefe, don't weaken!"

The Giants struck back for two runs in the top of the second. Roger Connor reached first on Hub Collins's error and came around to score when Oyster Burns narrowly missed Danny Richardson's fly ball to right. Richardson's hit went for a triple and Jim O'Rourke's sacrifice fly made the score 5-2, Brooklyn. Collins atoned for his error in the bottom of the inning with a solo home run.

The Giants closed the gap to 6-4 in the fourth but wasted an opportunity to tie the game. Buck Ewing led off the inning with a double, then committed an unpardonable baseball sin when he was thrown out stealing third for the first out of the inning. Monte Ward and Roger Connor walked but Ward, too, was thrown out stealing third. The next batter, Danny Richardson, launched a fastball into deep center field. Pop Corkhill raced up the steep incline but crashed against the wall, the ball falling from his glove. Corkhill was dazed and his vision was blurred. By the time he recovered, Connor had scored and Richardson had crossed the plate with an inside-the-park home run. If the Giants baserunners had practiced a more conservative running game, the score would have been tied.

Corkhill was forced to leave the game and catcher-outfielder Joe Visner took his place in center field.

In the fifth, a walk to Tim Keefe, a sacrifice bunt, a passed ball, and Monte Ward's single pulled New York within a run at 6-5. The Giants appeared to have Brooklyn on the run.

As the seventh inning opened, New York fans in the crowd shouted, "Stretch for luck!" and those in the grandstand rose. Tim Keefe grounded out to start the inning, but Gore and Tiernan singled. Both runners advanced a base on third baseman George Pinckney's fine running catch of Buck Ewing's pop fly into short left field. Monte Ward's ground single to left scored Gore and Tiernan, and gave the Giants the lead for the first time, 7-6. New York partisans leaped to their feet, waving hats and hands and cheering wildly. When Darby O'Brien booted the ball in left, Ward steamed into second. A moment later, the official scorer put a second "E" next to O'Brien's name when the left fielder dropped Roger Connor's line drive. Ward scored and the Giants now led by two. The lumbering Connor took everyone by surprise with a steal of second and later scored on Danny Richardson's single. Richardson came home on Jim O'Rourke's triple to give New York a five-run inning and a 10-6 lead.

Darkness was coming on fast and the crowd was convinced that when Keefe disposed of the Bridegrooms in the bottom of the inning, the umpires would call the game.

But Brooklyn wasn't finished yet. Singles by Collins and Burns, a double by Dave Foutz, and a sacrifice fly by Pinckney cut the Giants' margin to 10-8 after seven innings. Unfortunately, for the Bridegrooms, it looked as though it would be too dark to start play in the eighth. The players went to the bench and resignedly began putting on their jackets, thinking the game was over, but were surprised to hear umpire Ferguson order them back onto the field. Buck Ewing protested vigorously, pointing out that the electric lights on the elevated train had already been turned on. Ferguson was having none of it, however, and the game proceeded. Despite singles by Tim Keefe and Mike Tiernan in the top of the eighth, the Giants ran themselves out of a possible big inning when Tiernan, thinking there were already two out, was doubled off first base on Buck Ewing's pop fly to short. Ewing lodged another futile protest with Ferguson before play resumed in the bottom of the inning, but the umpire turned a deaf ear and the Bridegrooms came to the plate.

Pop Corkhill singled, but Germany Smith fouled to third for the first out of the inning. O'Brien singled Corkhill to third and both runners scored when Hub Collins drove a double over the head of left fielder Jim O'Rourke, unable to see the ball. The score was tied. Oyster Burns launched a drive into center and when George Gore was unable to locate the ball, it rolled to the wall for another double. Collins was so overjoyed, he turned a handspring at the plate after scoring the lead run. Dave Foutz, trying desperately to make the third out and end the inning (and, he hoped, the game), swung at Keefe's first pitch and lined a double past a flat-footed Art Whitney at third. Burns scored and while Buck Ewing was yammering at Ferguson over the injustice of it all, Foutz continued to run until he was tagged out by Monte Ward, who had taken the throw in from O'Rourke. Brooklyn now led, 12-10, and the result meeting his satisfaction, Ferguson finally halted play. Had he called the game any earlier, the score would have reverted to the last inning and the Giants would have won. In fact, most of the fans were unsure at exactly what point the game *had* been called and many left the park not knowing which team had won.

In its weekly edition a few days later, the *Sporting News* questioned the umpires' objectivity, saying:

> When the St. Louis Browns were robbed at Brooklyn this summer, certain of the New York reporters denied the allegation and gave us the laugh. Now, however, that the New York Club is being given the same dose given the Browns, these same reporters change their tune. Now loud enough to be heard from one end of the country to the other they shout "Murder."

> . . . Gaffney, who was associated with Ferguson, did fairly well under the circumstances. He tried to be impartial but it could easily be seen that he had a leaning toward the Association team. But Ferguson made no effort whatever to conceal his favoritism. He was unreasonable and inconsistent in the decisions which he rendered. He was so unfair in his rulings on balls and strikes, that even the imperturbable Keefe became disgusted. The adherents of the Brooklyn team admitted plainly that Ferguson was displaying the worst kind of favoritism, and denizens of the bleachers could only with difficulty restrain themselves from jumping on the field and giving a forcible demonstration of their displeasure.

Buck Ewing didn't mince any words. "Two umpires," he said, "and neither one with sand enough to award the game on its merits."

The *Boston Herald* said it was "pretty safe to predict that he [Ferguson] will not again be called upon to umpire in the series." The paper was correct on that score. Ferguson was out and after some dickering, Tom Lynch was paid a king's ransom of six hundred dollars to help Gaffney umpire the remaining games of the Series.

Despite his considerable pitching credentials, Tim Keefe had gotten bombed for sixteen hits—among them six doubles and a home run—and twelve runs, ten earned. Manager Jim Mutrie was so disgusted by Keefe's performance that he refused to start him in any of the remaining games of the Series. The only other action Keefe would see came in the seventh game as he came on in relief of Cannonball Crane to protect a four-run lead. Brooklyn's Adonis Terry had shown little more ability than Keefe. Even though he had surrendered four fewer hits then Keefe, Terry had issued five bases on balls.

Although the Giants protested, the game went into the record book and the Bridegrooms had a 12-10 victory and a one-game lead in the Series.

The Series shifted to the other side of the six-year-old Brooklyn Bridge for Game Two at Washington Park the next day. The Bridegrooms' ball yard was located on an uneven stretch of land at Third Street and Fourth Avenue in the Red Hook section of South Brooklyn, near the Bay Ridge Railroad tracks and Gowanus Canal. The park had opened for minor league play in May 1883, and was named after General George Washington, whose Revolutionary War headquarters had been located nearby.

Brooklyn fans choked the turnstiles for two hours before play began, and at game time, every available seat at the park was filled. Spectators eager for a free view of the game crowded onto the steep embankments encircling the grounds, and the more adventurous freeloaders flirted with broken limbs by climbing fences and telephone poles. When all heads were counted, the crowd was the second largest in the history of Washington Park and the largest World Series crowd to date—a paid attendance of 16,172. Hundreds of fans bought standing room behind the ropes which encircled the outfield and foul territory, and hundreds more reclined on the embankment which surrounded the ballpark. Dozens perched on the outfield fences, getting a free look at the game. Estimates of the number of ladies in the crowd ran as high as five thousand. Mother Nature had once again smiled upon the two clubs: The weather was mild and clear and perfect for baseball.

As the Giants left their carriages at the upper end of the grounds to walk to their bench, they were met with polite applause from the Brooklyn crowd. The Bridegrooms, wearing white hats with two broad red stripes, and dressed in their white uniforms with red trim, received a much warmer welcome a few minutes later. Umpire Tom Lynch, nattily attired in his familiar gray woolen suit, took the field with John Gaffney, who wore a more flamboyant wine-colored outfit. Lynch worked the plate, Gaffney took his position at first, and Bob Ferguson observed the contest in quiet anonymity from the reporters' box.

Following pre-game practice, Lynch called for action to begin a little after 3:00, and the Giants quickly scored a tainted run in the top of the first. With a two-strike count, leadoff batter George Gore singled, then went to second on a wild pitch. The bulky Gore reached third when catcher Joe Visner dropped a third strike with

Mike Tiernan at the plate, and came home, puffing and panting, when Buck Ewing sizzled a line drive off starting pitcher Bob Caruthers's leg. This was the signal for a crescendo of applause from the New Yorkers in the crowd.

The Bridegrooms tied the score in the bottom of the inning on a disputed walk to Darby O'Brien followed by singles from Hub Collins and Dave Foutz.

Art Whitney squeezed Roger Connor home with a New York run in the second, but the Bridegrooms tied the score again when Caruthers walked, went to second on Danny Richardson's error, and came home on two successive groundouts. New York took the lead for good in the third when Jim O'Rourke singled, stole second, and scored on Germany Smith's throwing error. The Giants added to their margin with a single run in the fourth and two in the fifth, and the game ended in a 6-2 victory. When the final out was recorded, happy Giants' kranks swarmed onto the field, congratulating each other and shaking hands with the New York ballplayers. But most of the huge crowd at Washington Park went home bitterly disappointed.

Crane had settled down after the second inning, allowing the Bridegrooms just two more hits. His teammates' defensive·play helped him considerably, as the Giants turned three double plays in the game. Brooklyn had put its leadoff man on base in five of the nine innings, but only two of those men came around to score, and the Bridegrooms' baserunning was even worse. Pop Corkhill was picked off third in the second inning, Joe Visner was thrown out stealing in the fourth, and Darby O'Brien was picked off first in the fifth. To add to Brooklyn's embarrassment, Dave Foutz's single in the sixth was turned into an 8-4 fielder's choice when the baserunner, Oyster Burns, thought the ball was going to be caught and failed to break from first.

The Giants, who had stolen two bases in the first game, ran wild against the hapless Joe Visner in Game Two. Tiernan and Ward both stole a base, while O'Rourke and Gore stole two apiece. Brooklyn speedster Darby O'Brien finally broke through with his team's first theft against Buck Ewing in the eighth inning. After the game, Ewing was given three cheers by the crowd for his excellent work and even umpire Ferguson showed with which team his affection lay when he said, "There's a great ball player. He is without an equal as a ball player. He plays with his hands and head, particularly the head. Buck was one of my pupils, and I am proud of him."

Sunday, October 20, was an open date in the Series. The Giants took advantage of the day off, but the Bridegrooms played an exhibition game at Ridgewood Park against the Baltimore Orioles, scoring four unearned runs in the ninth for a 6-2 victory.

A driving rain blanketed New York all day on Monday, October 21, postponing Game Three. That evening, the Giants attended a benefit performance at the Broadway Theatre at Broadway and Forty-First Street. As the curtain opened, the players were seen seated on stage with a large sign reading "LEAGUE CHAMPIONS, 1889-90" suspended above them. The sign slipped when it was lowered and nearly fell on the team. Receipts from the performance netted each player $190.

Threatening clouds on Tuesday, October 22, kept the Polo Grounds attendance to only 5,181. The starting pitchers were Mickey Hughes and Mickey Welch.

"It's a hundred dollars to a toothpick that we win today," Buck Ewing told reporters confidently.

Hughes got off to a terrible start in the first inning and was fortunate to escape only two runs down. With one out, Mike Tiernan singled, took second on a passed ball, and scored on Buck Ewing's hit. Ewing went to second on the throw to the plate and when Monte Ward bunted safely, the Giants had men on first and third, one out, and the promise of a big inning. Ward was thrown out stealing second, but big Roger Connor prolonged the inning by drawing a base on balls. Danny Richardson's hard liner ticked off George Pinckney's glove at third for the second run of the inning. Hughes dug himself an even deeper hole when he walked Jim O'Rourke to load the bases, but he retired light-hitting third baseman Art Whitney on a popout to end the inning. Six straight batters had reached base safely, but the Giants had only two runs to show for their efforts. When New York left the bases jammed again in the second inning, the momentum appeared to swing over to the Bridegrooms.

In the bottom of the second, Brooklyn's Dave Foutz walked and scored on George Pinckney's double. Pinckney went to third on Monte Ward's error and came home with the tying run on Pop Corkhill's sacrifice fly. An inning later, with men on first and second, Oyster Burns hit a sharp liner to George Gore in center field. Mickey Hughes was trapped off second base and Gore had an easy double play in front of him, but he took his eye off the ball and it skittered off his glove. With the bases loaded, a Dave Foutz single plated Hughes and Collins and gave Brooklyn a 4-2 lead. One out later, Bob Clark singled to bring Burns home. The Bridegrooms seemed to have matters well in hand when Pop Corkhill's two-strike leadoff home run in the fourth put Brooklyn up 6-2.

The partisan New York crowd responded with riotous applause when veteran Jim O'Rourke belted a three-run homer over the left-field fence to help the Giants close the gap to 6-5 in the fifth inning. Following O'Rourke's home run, New York catcher Buck Ewing notified umpire Tom Lynch that his manager intended to replace Welch with Hank O'Day at the end of the inning. Unfortunately, for the Giants, Welch had nothing left and the Bridegrooms touched him for two runs. Doubles by Bob Clark and Germany Smith and a single by Pop Corkhill put the Grooms up 8-5.

But the world-champion Giants weren't about to roll over. In the sixth, a Mike Tiernan triple, singles by Monte Ward and Danny Richardson, and a Germany Smith error, brought in two more runs to again pull New York within one run of a tie.

Bob Caruthers relieved Mickey Hughes in the eighth and retired three of New York's most dangerous hitters—Tiernan, Ewing, and Ward—on a fly ball and two strikeouts. Brooklynites in the stands took heart at Caruthers's excellent start.

The Bridegrooms began a stalling game when the top of the order came to the plate in the bottom of the inning. Darby O'Brien refused to swing at any of O'Day's offerings and eventually coaxed a base on balls. After watching several O'Day deliveries go by, Hub Collins, the next hitter, sacrificed O'Brien to second. Oyster Burns kept the bat on his shoulder and was called out on strikes, and Dave Foutz made the final out of the inning when he grounded out to first. From the bench, Bob Caruthers directed a steady stream of invectives toward Gaffney for not calling the game because of darkness. In the stands, minor league manager Jim Cudworth repeatedly lighted small pieces of paper, holding them over his head as a not-too-subtle message to Gaffney that it was too dark to play. Over the last two innings, the Bridegrooms delayed the game at least fifteen minutes with these tactics and were booed roundly by the Polo Grounds fans.

The score was 8-7, Brooklyn, as the Giants came to bat in the top of the ninth inning. Roger Connor grounded an infield single, then was forced at second by Danny Richardson. Experiencing more than a little trouble seeing his catcher in the dark, Caruthers hit a wild streak and walked Jim O'Rourke and Art Whitney to load the bases. Another brief diatribe against Gaffney followed before Caruthers resumed his place in the pitcher's box and delivered a called strike to Hank O'Day. After being harangued by the Brooklyn club for the next twenty minutes to no avail, umpire Gaffney suddenly decided it was too dark to play and ended the game, generously awarding the win to Brooklyn. Buck Ewing flew off the bench and was headed straight for Gaffney when he was restrained by his teammates. The Bridegrooms had a second, albeit tainted, victory. It seemed as though the Giants just couldn't play long enough to win.

Giants manager Jim Mutrie was disgusted with Brooklyn's efforts to delay the game. "The days of such tactics are gone by," he said, "and it comes with poor grace from the Brooklyn men to resort to them. Such methods are disgusting and do not tend to elevate the national pastime. The Brooklyns played like schoolboys. I would sooner lose a game than win as they did this afternoon."

Giants owner John Day said that he was surprised by the work of umpire John Gaffney and thought the arbiter was either "incompetent" or "crooked."

The weather took a turn toward winter on the 23rd as the temperature dropped below forty degrees and a savage wind blew through Washington Park. A slim crowd of three thousand settled in their seats to watch the weirdest game of the 1889 World Series. The starting pitchers were Cannonball Crane and Adonis Terry as umpire Tom Lynch called for play to begin at 2:52.

Crane got off to a rocky start, walking Brooklyn leadoff batter Darby O'Brien in the bottom of the first. The speedy O'Brien broke for second and the Giants decided to play a spirited game of Chase The Ball. Buck Ewing's throw skidded past Monte Ward into center field for an error. O'Brien took a short turn past second and watched happily as the ball squibbed through center fielder George Gore's legs. By the time Gore had retrieved the elusive horsehide, O'Brien was seated on the Brooklyn bench and the Bridegrooms led, 1-0. Crane retired Hub Collins and Oyster Burns, but Dave Foutz drew a walk and stole second base. George Pinckney lifted a seemingly innocuous pop foul to his counterpart at third base, Art Whitney, but Whitney dropped the ball for the third error of the inning. Given a reprieve, Pinckney singled to center to drive in Foutz. With two unearned runs, the Bridegrooms and Adonis Terry had a 2-0 lead.

The Giants scored once in the third, but poor defense let in two more Brooklyn runs in the bottom of the inning. Darby O'Brien was once again the instigator, this time with a leadoff single to center. Hub Collins bunted safely and Oyster Burns grounded to short for what should have been the first out of the inning. Monte Ward's throw to first was on line, but Roger Connor dropped the ball and the bases were loaded. O'Brien scored on a forceout, Collins came home on a wild pitch, and the Bridegrooms led, 4-1.

The Giants cut the lead to 4-2 in the fourth, but the real fun began the next inning. With an 0-1 count, Buck Ewing watched one of Terry's deliveries sail wide of the plate and was stunned to hear umpire Lynch call, "Strike two!" Ewing, suffering through a poor offensive series, left the batter's box and engaged in a lively conversation with Lynch for several minutes. When he finally stepped back in, he struck out, and in frustration, flung his bat twenty feet in the air. There were more incidents to come.

The Bridegrooms took a commanding lead in the bottom of the fifth. With one out, Hub Collins singled, stole second, and came around to score when Art Whitney bobbled a grounder off the bat of Oyster Burns. Crane muffed a pickoff play, sending Burns to third, and Dave Foutz's single drove him in. Foutz later scored on Bob Clark's safety. The three-run inning gave Brooklyn a 7-2 lead.

Adonis Terry was rolling along with a four-hitter as he worked to the Giants in the sixth. Dark shadows had spread around the park and lights in neighboring houses were being turned on as the Giants suddenly came alive. Jim O'Rourke doubled to left and Art Whitney bunted safely to put men on first and third. Cannonball Crane and George Gore hit back-to-back triples to make the score 7-5, Brooklyn, before Mike Tiernan went down on strikes for the first out of the inning. Buck Ewing hit a one-hopper right back to Adonis Terry, who came home with the throw, but the ball hit Gore in the back. The not-so-impartial Mr. Gaffney refused to let the rules stand in his way and improperly called Gore out for being hit by a thrown ball. Understandably, the Giants raised something of a ruckus. Ewing had made second on the play, but was now sent back to first and the Giants' rally was in danger of being quelled. But Monte Ward singled Ewing to third and the two baserunners attempted a double steal. Catcher Bob Clark trapped Ewing in a rundown, then threw the ball into left field. Ewing scored easily and Ward raced for the plate. Darby O'Brien's throw to the infield was wild and hit Jim O'Rourke on the Giants' bench. Ward trotted home with the tying run. Brooklyn protested vigorously and Gaffney was persuaded to send Ward back to third.

Buck Ewing had finally seen enough and challenged Gaffney, "If you decide against us," Ewing shouted, "I will take my men from the field. You know perfectly well that Ward is entitled to his run. Gore, too, should have been allowed to score. I don't propose to be bulldozed any longer."

Gaffney then reversed his decision, claiming Ward would have scored even if the throw had not hit O'Rourke. Once again, the Bridegrooms kicked, and when the brouhaha ended, a full twenty-two minutes had elapsed. Connor struck out to end the inning and several Brooklyn players pleaded with the umpiring crew to call the game. By now, there was no argument on either side that it was too dark to continue play.

But the game went on. Corkhill, leading off for the Bridegrooms in the bottom of the inning, could barely see Cannonball Crane's deliveries and struck out. Germany Smith hit a soft pop fly to second baseman Danny Richardson, but Richardson dropped the ball for an error, later claiming he couldn't see, either. Smith stole second and went to third when Buck Ewing dropped strike three with Darby O'Brien at the plate. There were two outs now and Crane, who found it nearly impossible to see home plate, walked Hub Collins. Up stepped Oyster Burns, who slashed at an invisible 0-1 delivery and drove the pitch into left field for an apparent tie-breaking single. Disgusted, left fielder Jim O'Rourke ignored the ball and began trotting in to the clubhouse. Burns's drive rolled to the wall for a home run and the umpires delivered the Bridegrooms from danger by calling the game because of darkness with the score 10-7 in favor of Brooklyn. The Bridegrooms had taken their third cheap victory with another substantial assist from umpires Gaffney and Lynch.*

Giants owner John B. Day was beside himself at this latest treachery on the part of the umpires. That evening, in a confron-

---

* Contemporary newspaper reports listed the final result as 10-7, and all box scores reflected the eight runs scored by the two teams in the sixth inning. Nevertheless, a 10-7 final is out of the question using any logical scoring method. If Jim O'Rourke, and presumably the rest of the Giants, left the field during play, the game should have been forfeited to Brooklyn. But not all newspaper accounts agree that O'Rourke actually abandoned his position. If, on the other hand, the umpires had called the game on account of darkness before the sixth inning was completed, then the score should have reverted to the last full inning, the fifth. A suspended game would have made the final score 7-2, Brooklyn.

tation with Bridegrooms owner Charles H. Byrne, Day said, "The games will begin at 2:30 o'clock hereafter or my team will not play. We don't care to run any chance of losing another game on account of darkness or intentional delays. And more than this," he added, "I want to see umpires Gaffney and Lynch in your office at 1:30 o'clock tomorrow. I would like you to be there too. This thing has gone far enough and must be stopped. This kind of ball playing and umpiring is enough to kill the game."

Day concluded by saying, "I don't mind losing games on their merit, but I do mind being robbed of them."

The next day, Day had lost little of his outrage. Angrily, he informed Byrne, "Three times have we lost in this series by trickery and we shall do so no more. Unless the Brooklyn club plays on its merits, the same as the New Yorks are doing, the series will end at once. I want only what belongs to me and I will have it or know the reason why. If the Brooklyns resort any longer to the dirty tactics that have characterized them in the games already played, and if the umpires continue to favor Brooklyn, the series will end with today's game. I will not allow my team to compete against a club that insists on playing dirty ball."

Team captain Buck Ewing echoed Day's feelings. "I am sick and tired of the methods resorted to by the Brooklyns . . . Their work throughout has been of the sneaky order. They have made use of tactics that my men would not stoop to." Warming to his subject, Ewing offered a comment on the umpiring crew of Gaffney and Lynch. "I don't know what to make of them," he said. "In every game they have handicapped us, but it must be stopped. In the future Gaffney and Lynch will have to umpire the games strictly on their merits or I will know the reason why. It's an outrage the way we have been treated."

Horrified by the specter of lost profits, Byrne hastily agreed to the new starting time. The Bridegrooms had a three-to-one edge in the Series, he reasoned, and could afford to be generous.

A small crowd of 2,901 turned out on a miserably cold and windy afternoon at Washington Park the next day to watch Bob Caruthers go against Cannonball Crane, making his second start in as many days. Buck Ewing had been given the day off because of a finger injury and reserve catcher Willard Brown, a fair hitter but a defensive liability, was substituted behind the plate. Caruthers disposed of the Giants in the first two innings but lost his curveball as the New Yorkers came at him in earnest in the third.

Art Whitney was given a gift triple when Pop Corkhill narrowly missed a shoetop catch of his fly ball in center field. Whitney scored a moment later on a passed ball. Cannonball Crane grounded out, but George Gore walked, and Mike Tiernan and Willard Brown followed with singles to make the score 2-0. Oyster Burns's two-base error on Monte Ward's pop fly allowed Tiernan to score and sent Brown to third. One out later, Danny Richardson singled on the infield and Brown came home to give the Giants a 4-0 lead.

Bob Caruthers's fourth-inning RBI single gave the Bridegrooms their first run of the game, but New York enjoyed a second four-run inning in the next half-frame. Roger Connor's triple brought the first two runs home and Danny Richardson followed with a wind-blown, inside-the-park home run to give the Giants a commanding 8-1 lead.

In the sixth, Brooklyn's first-string catcher, Bob Clark, sprained his ankle running to first on a single, and his services were lost to the Bridegrooms for the rest of the Series. He was replaced by veteran Doc Bushong.

The Giants increased their lead to 10-3 when Cannonball Crane slugged a two-run homer in the eighth inning. In the ninth, substitute catcher Willard Brown rounded out the scoring when he captured his third RBI of the day with an inside-the-park home run to right-center field. New York had an easy 11-3 victory and Bob Caruthers was touched for his second loss of the young Series. Cannonball Crane went the distance for New York to earn the win.

That evening, officers and players of the Brooklyn organization were treated to a sumptuous dinner in the assembly rooms of the Brooklyn Academy of Music. New York district attorney Ridgway gave a short talk on "Brooklyn, the Cradle of Baseball," which was followed by Henry Chadwick's discussion of "Baseball in Ye Olden Times."

A new hero took center stage for Game Six in the person of New York pitcher Hank O'Day. George Gore had taken ill during the night and was replaced in center field by reserve outfielder Mike Slattery. Brooklyn's Germany Smith was also under the weather and was substituted for at short by James "Jumbo" Davis, a hulking third baseman who had played the 1889 season for the St. Louis Browns. The Giants apparently voiced no objection to his insertion at short.

Played at the Polo Grounds on a cloudy, cold day, Game Six was unquestionably the best contest of the Series, also the most poorly attended. Because of frigid temperatures and threatening rain, attendance was only 2,556. Both managers had ordered their players not to question any of the umpires' calls during the game, and this was the first contest uninterrupted by arguments.

The Grooms broke on top in the second inning. George Pinckney grounded a single on the infield but was thrown out by Jim O'Rourke when he tried to advance to third on Joe Visner's single to left. Visner made second on the throw in and scored a moment later on a single by pitcher Adonis Terry. Pop Corkhill hit safely to short right, but New York escaped any further damage when Terry was doubled off second by Jumbo Davis's line drive to short. Indeed, line-drive double plays seemed to be the order of the day. The Giants would lose Danny Richardson on the basepaths when he was doubled off third base on Jim O'Rourke's line drive in the second; an inning later, pitcher Hank O'Day would be trapped off first when Mike Slattery lined out to third; Adonis Terry would ground into a more routine 4-6-3 double play in the fourth.

In the seventh, Giants fans took their stretch for luck but none was forthcoming. Monte Ward and Roger Connor hit easy grounders and Danny Richardson struck out.

Entering the bottom of the ninth, Hank O'Day was working on a nifty six-hitter and had given up only one hit since the third. Unfortunately, he was on the wrong end of a 1-0 score. Adonis Terry had surrendered only three hits, none since the fifth, and seemed confident of throwing the Series' first shutout. It looked even darker for the Giants when Mike Tiernan lined out to center and Buck Ewing grounded to short, and it looked positively hopeless when Monte Ward watched Terry's first two pitches sail past for called strikes. But the veteran Ward lined a ringing single into right field to keep the Giants' hopes alive, then proceeded almost single-handedly to tie the score by stealing second and third base on successive pitches from Terry to Roger Connor. Ward, playing to the crowd, tipped his cap several times, and danced off third, bluffing a steal of home. When Connor rose to the challenge with a clutch single, knotting the score at one-all, the crowd cheered so loudly and for so long that the umpires were forced to delay the game until they could be heard. From the New York bench came the voice of Buck Ewing, shouting, "We've got you now!" Brooklyn manager

Bill McGunnigle paced nervously in front of the Brooklyn bench as Connor stole second and third, but Danny Richardson grounded to short, sending the game into extra innings.

In the tenth, Mike Slattery turned in the play of the game as he raced up the incline to the deepest part of center field and made a dazzling, running catch of Darby O'Brien's two-out fly ball. Slattery crashed into the wall and took a moment to recover, but the catch prevented what would surely have been a game-winning, inside-the-park home run.

Slattery continued his heroics in the bottom of the eleventh when he led off with a single to left. Buck Ewing hit to the right side of the infield, advancing the baserunner to second. With Monte Ward at the plate, Slattery, a so-so basestealer, lit out for third. Trying to protect the runner, Ward swung feebly at the pitch and hit a slow grounder to short. Jumbo Davis, playing a position with which he was unfamiliar, had some difficulty getting the throw away, and Ward flashed across first just ahead of the ball. Slattery never even slowed down and came home with the winning run.

The Series was tied at three games apiece.

Brooklyn's Adonis Terry, in spite of pitching a seven-hitter and walking only two, took the bitter defeat, his first of the Series. Pitching in and out of trouble all afternoon, Hank O'Day garnered his first win, despite walking five and surrendering six hits. Only the pesky George Pinckney, who reached base three times in the game, was able to touch O'Day for an extra-base hit, a harmless, two-out double in the sixth.

The next day, a drizzling rain fell until about noon, making the field at the Polo Grounds wet and soggy for Game Seven. Rain checks were issued for the first time in World Series history, and when umpire John Gaffney called for play to begin at 2:18, there were threatening clouds overhead and not so much as a hint of a breeze.

Cannonball Crane made his fourth start in eight days, and his teammates struck for the first run of the game against Tom Lovett in the bottom of the first. Mike Slattery reached on George Pinckney's error, went to second on a groundout, and scored on Buck Ewing's single to center. The turning point of the 1889 World Series came in the New York second when the Giants blew the Bridegrooms apart.

Jim O'Rourke started the fun with a double to left. One out later, Crane and Slattery walked to load the bases. Mike Tiernan's single drove in O'Rourke and Crane, and sent Slattery to third from where he scored on Buck Ewing's single. Roger Connor's double made the score 5-0, Giants. Danny Richardson got the sweet part of his bat on a Lovett fastball and rode the pitch over the left-field fence for a three-run homer to put New York up, 8-0. Jim O'Rourke batted for the second time and his solo home run over the center-field fence gave the Giants a 9-0 lead and an eight-run inning—the biggest single scoring outburst in nineteenth-century World Series history. O'Rourke's blast was the longest at the Polo Grounds to that time.

The Bridegrooms, down but not out, rallied with four runs of their own in the third. With the bases loaded, Dave Foutz drew a walk to force in the first run of the inning and George Pinckney singled for two more. Foutz came home on Germany Smith's grounder to cut the Giants' lead to 9-4.

In the top of the fifth, the Bridegrooms narrowed the gap to 9-7. With the bases loaded and one out, Germany Smith lined a fastball into the left-field seats for an apparent grand-slam home run. Smith broke into a nineteenth-century version of a home run trot, while O'Rourke watched helplessly as the ball bounced from seat to seat in the empty stands. O'Rourke then jumped the short fence, retrieved the ball, and heaved it toward the infield. Monte Ward relayed the throw to Ewing who tagged Smith out at the plate. Brooklyn protested vigorously, but umpire Gaffney, who had apparently been preoccupied watching the runners circle the bases, said he hadn't seen the ball go into the seats and the play stood.

The Giants touched relief pitcher Bob Caruthers for single runs in the sixth and seventh to pad their lead to 11-7. Electric lights were coming on throughout the city as Brooklyn went down one-two-three in the ninth. New York had hung on for the victory and Tim Keefe had garnered a "save" with three innings of scoreless relief.

It rained on October 27, an off-day in the Series, and the playing field at Washington Park was wet and muddy and filled with shallow sinkholes on the 28th. Bridegrooms owner Charles Byrne suggested that the game be postponed until the next day, but John Day was eager to wind up the Series and declined the offer. The weather was frigid and only 2,584 people turned out to see Adonis Terry take the mound against the durable Cannonball Crane.

Mike Slattery started matters off for the Giants by reaching on an error when shortstop Jumbo Smith slipped going for his ground ball. Mike Tiernan singled Slattery to second and Buck Ewing moved both runners up a base with a groundout to first. Monte Ward bunted successfully but, unaccountably, both Slattery and Tiernan held their bases and the sacks were jammed. Roger Connor smashed a sharp single to right and when Oyster Burns tumbled to the wet turf trying to glove the ball, both Slattery and Tiernan scored. Ward moved to third and Connor to second when Burns launched a strong throw home in a belated attempt to retire Tiernan. Danny Richardson's single to left scored Ward and Connor, and Richardson went to second on O'Brien's throw home. A stolen base, coupled with Jim O'Rourke's sacrifice fly, gave the Giants a quick 5-0 lead.

The poor playing conditions led to two Brooklyn runs in the bottom of the inning as Hub Collins walked and Mike Slattery slipped trying for a shoetop catch on Dave Foutz's pop fly. The ball rolled to the Fourth Avenue gate in the center-field wall for an inside-the-park home run.

In the second, New York continued its newly acquired habit of scoring runs in bunches. With one out, Slattery walked and Tiernan singled. Buck Ewing's double put the Giants ahead, 7-2. Monte Ward laid down his second bunt single of the day and stole second. Connor singled to right for his fourth RBI of the game and New York led, 9-2. The Giants added a run in the third and two in the fourth for a very comfortable 12-2 lead.

Dave Foutz relieved Terry in the top of the fifth inning and Terry moved over to play first base. Foutz had appeared in twelve games during the 1889 season, winning three and losing none, but was a little rusty nevertheless. He held the Giants at bay in his first inning of work, but Mike Tiernan hit a long home run into the parked carriages outside center field to lead off the sixth. Buck Ewing, who had broken out of his hitting slump with a 3-for-5 performance in the previous game, banged out his second double of this contest and went to third on a passed ball. Monte Ward walked and when ball four was a wild pitch, Ewing scored and Ward made second. Roger Connor hit a high fly ball to deep left field and when O'Brien took his time returning the ball to the infield, Ward raced around to score the Giants' fifteenth run.

Crane had given up only two hits through the first seven innings, and saddled with the security blanket of a big lead, grew a bit lackadaisical. With two out in the eighth, Hub Collins coaxed a base on balls—the fifth walk off Crane—and scored on Oyster

Burns's inside-the-park home run over Mike Slattery's head in center. New York added another run in the top of the ninth, and in the bottom of the inning, Crane surrendered a one-out single to Adonis Terry. Pop Corkhill reached on an error, and Darby O'Brien's triple scored both men. His club leading by ten runs, Ewing moved well back of the plate, the better to handle Crane's fastballs, and Darby O'Brien stole home for the final tally of the day. When Hub Collins grounded to short, the game was over. The Giants had a convincing 16-7 victory and a 5-3 lead in the series. A win at the Polo Grounds the next day would clinch the championship.

By now, most Brooklyn fans had come to the inevitable conclusion that their club was woefully overmatched. The Giants had won four straight games, three decisively, and except for Game Six, the Bridegrooms had been blown out in the early innings. Few Brooklynites harbored any optimism that the Grooms could win the next three games and capture the world championship title.

Hank O'Day took the hill against Adonis Terry on October 29. The weather was cold and most disagreeable, but attendance was up slightly to 3,067. Brooklyn's last gasp came in the first inning when Darby O'Brien walked, Hub Collins beat out an infield single, and Oyster Burns doubled to the left-field embankment to put the Bridegrooms up 2-0. Those were the last runs Brooklyn would score in the Series. The Giants countered with a run of their own in the bottom of the inning when Mike Tiernan doubled and Monte Ward drove him home with a triple.

Brooklyn had a number of scoring opportunities but squandered them all. The Bridegrooms put runners on second and third with two out in the third and again in the fifth, but failed to score either time. They put men on first and third with two out in the fourth, and had men in scoring position in the second and seventh, but couldn't push anyone across. The man responsible for their offensive malaise was Giants pitcher Hank O'Day. After his shaky first-inning start, O'Day settled down and allowed only two more singles the remainder of the game, only one of those after the second, and no hits at all after the fifth. Most of the trouble was of his own making—seven walks kept enough Bridegrooms on base to make the partisan Giants crowd more than a bit nervous. Fellow Illinoisan (and fellow Irishman) Darby O'Brien was O'Day's particular favorite: O'Brien walked four times in the game.

New York tied the score in the sixth when Monte Ward singled, stole second, moved to third on a groundout, and came home on Danny Richardson's sacrifice fly to center. Considering how much offense the Giants had shown in the past two games, the manner in which they scored what proved to be the winning run was ironic. Hank O'Day drew a base on balls to lead off the seventh and was forced at second by Slattery. Mike Tiernan fouled to Pinckney for the second out of the inning, then Slattery stole second base. Buck Ewing struck out on a pitch over his head, but when the ball eluded veteran backstop Doc Bushong, Slattery came all the way around to score.

Brooklyn was down to its last three outs when Germany Smith reached on an error in the ninth. Doc Bushong then laced a screaming line drive, but it went right into Art Whitney's hands at third, and Smith was doubled off first base. In his excitement over the potential Series victory, O'Day again lost the plate and walked Darby O'Brien. O'Brien immediately broke for second, but Buck Ewing cut him down and the Series was over. Led by manager Jim Mutrie, the small crowd chanted the Giants' battle cry, "We are the people!" and crowded onto the diamond.

New York had won an unprecedented five straight games, a winning streak which will never be equalled under today's best-of-seven format. When the Giants met the next day in President Day's office, their winning shares came to about five hundred dollars each.

The usually reserved *New York Times* crowed, "New Yorkers ought to feel proud of their baseball nine. The Giants have once more proved their supremacy in diamond field matters and again claim the distinction of being the world's champions. It is the highest honor that can be bestowed upon a baseball club. . ."

Following the game, super-fan General "Hi Hi" Dixwell of Boston presented each member of the Giants with a scarfpin and was rewarded with applause and three cheers from the players.

Although they had been defeated, the Bridegrooms recognized the contributions of manager Bill McGunnigle. In appreciation of his efforts, each member of the club chipped in and presented their pilot with a gold watch and chain and a diamond-studded locket. First baseman Dave Foutz gave a short, sentimental speech which ended with the words, "Hoping your heart will beat long after the machinery of this watch has rusted into dust, we remain your friends and admirers, the Brooklyn Baseball Club."

It was difficult to isolate a single hero in the Series. Cannonball Crane was a possible choice with four victories, three in succession. But to say Crane was effective against the Bridegrooms would be an exaggeration. In 38-2/3 innings, he had allowed over sixty baserunners and had an earned run average of 3.72. Monte Ward was another likely candidate, with his .417 batting average and only two errors in fifty-three chances. Jim O'Rourke's .389 batting mark and .722 slugging average would give him some claim to the title, and second baseman Danny Richardson would merit consideration with a .657 slugging average, three home runs, and eight RBIs. Roger Connor had a more-than-respectable .343 mark and led all batters with twelve runs batted in.

But the logical choice was pitcher Hank O'Day. O'Day pitched and won the only two low-scoring contests of the championship—Game Six, which allowed the Giants to tie the Series, and Game Nine, the deciding contest. In twenty-three innings, O'Day had given up ten hits, fourteen walks, and only three earned runs. His ERA was a sparkling 1.17 and the Bridegrooms' batting average was a microscopic .135 with O'Day on the hill.

The 1889 championship Series probably marked the high point for nineteenth-century baseball, and it certainly marked the high point of the nineteenth-century World Series. Eight days after the season ended, members of the Brotherhood of Professional Base Ball Players formally announced their plans to withdraw from the two major leagues and form their own players' league.

There would be only one more World Series between competing leagues in the nineteenth century, and within two years, the American Association would be disbanded. The 1890 season would be one of the most disastrous in baseball history, scarring owners, players, and fans alike.

◆ ◆ ◆

GAME ONE—October 18, 1889, at the Polo Grounds, New York

BROOKLYN	AB	R	H	BI	E	NEW YORK	AB	R	H	BI	E
O'Brien, lf	5	2	2	0	2	Gore, cf	5	1	1	0	0
Collins, 2b	5	4	3	1	1	Tiernan, rf	5	1	2	0	0
Burns, rf	5	3	4	2	0	Ewing, c	4	0	1	0	0
Foutz, 1b	5	0	2	1	0	Ward, ss	2	1	2	3	0
Pinckney, 3b	4	0	1	1	0	Connor, 1b	3	3	0	0	0
Clarke, c	4	1	1	1	0	Richardson, 2b	4	3	3	4	0
Terry, p	4	1	1	0	0	O'Rourke, lf	4	0	2	2	0
Corkhill, cf	2	0	1	0	0	Whitney, 3b	4	0	0	0	0
Visner, cf	2	1	1	2	0	Keefe, p	3	1	1	0	0
Smith, ss	4	0	0	0	0		34	10	12	9	0
	40	12	16	8	3						

```
NY    0 2 0   2 1 0   5 0 – 10
BKN   5 1 0   0 0 0   2 4 – 12
```

D: Ewing, Foutz 2, Collins 2, Corkhill, Burns.   T: Richardson, O'Rourke.   HR: Richardson, Collins.   SB: Connor.   SAC: Gore.   SF: O'Rourke, Pinckney.   DP: BKN. BB: Terry 5.   Struck out: Keefe 1, Terry 3.   PB: Clarke.   Umpires: Ferguson and Gaffney.   Time—2:12.   Att: 8,848.

◆ ◆ ◆

GAME TWO—October 19, 1889, at Washington Park, Brooklyn

NEW YORK	AB	R	H	BI	E	BROOKLYN	AB	R	H	BI	E
Gore, cf	4	2	3	0	0	O'Brien, lf	2	1	0	1	0
Tiernan, rf	5	1	1	0	0	Collins, 2b	3	0	1	0	1
Ewing, c	5	0	0	1	0	Burns, rf	4	0	0	0	0
Ward, ss	5	1	1	1	0	Foutz, 1b	3	0	2	1	0
Connor, 1b	4	1	1	0	0	Pinckney, 3b	3	0	0	0	1
Richardson, 2b	4	0	1	0	3	Visner, c	3	0	0	0	1
O'Rourke, lf	4	1	2	0	0	Caruthers, p	2	1	0	0	0
Whitney, 3b	4	0	0	1	0	Corkhill, cf	4	0	1	0	0
Crane, p	4	0	1	0	0	Smith, ss	3	0	0	0	2
	39	6	10	3	3		27	2	4	2	5

```
NY    1 1 1   1 2 0   0 0 0 – 6
BKN   1 1 0   0 0 0   0 0 0 – 2
```

D: Richardson.   SB: Gore 2, O'Rourke 2, Tiernan, Ward, O'Brien.   SAC: Whitney. DP: BKN 1, NY 3.   BB: Caruthers 1, Crane 7.   Struck out: Caruthers 3, Crane 3. PB: Visner.   WP: Caruthers.   HBP: Pinckney (Crane).   Umpires: Gaffney and Lynch. Time—1:53.   Att: 16,172.

The American Association's first champions, the 1882 Cincinnati Reds, featuring the nineteenth century's greatest second baseman, Bid McPhee, and the bespectacled and very bookish-looking Will White. Note the size and shape of the baseball bats and the motley collection of uniforms. (National Baseball Library)

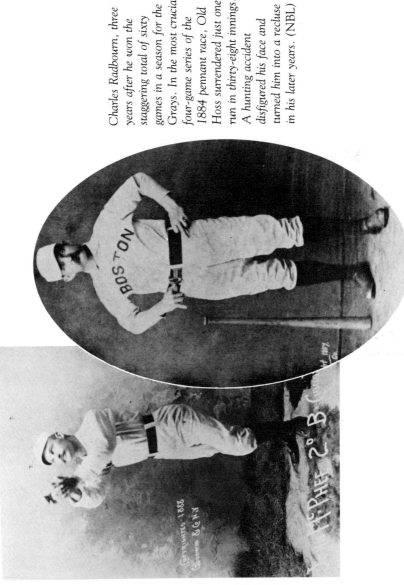

Charles Radbourn, three years after he won the staggering total of sixty games in a season for the Grays. In the most crucial four-game series of the 1884 pennant race, Old Hoss surrendered just one run in thirty-eight innings. A hunting accident disfigured his face and turned him into a recluse in his later years. (NBL)

The greatest defensive second baseman of all time and one of nineteenth-century baseball's true gentlemen, Cincinnati's Bid McPhee refused to use a fielder's glove for a decade after they came into vogue. When he finally relented, his fielding average rose 32 points. (NBL)

Team photo of the 1884 world champion Providence Grays, probably taken at Messer Street Grounds. (Seated, l-r) Barney Gilligan, Paul Radford, and the dark-skinned Sandy Nava. (Standing, l-r) Hoss Radbourn, Charlie Sweeney, Miah Murray, Jerry Denny, Paul Hines, manager Frank Bancroft (in civvies), Joe Start, Charley Bassett, picher John Cattanach (who lasted just one game with the team), Cliff Carroll, Art Irwin, Jack Farrell. (NBL)

One of two cropped versions of the 1885 Chicago White Stockings team photo, featuring Cap Anson (third from left, back row), Mike Kelly (second from right, back row), Jim McCormick (third from right, back row), John Clarkson (second from right, front row), and the clean-shaven Billy Sunday. (NBL)

Chris Von Der Ahe, businessman, booster, buffoon, the Charlie Finley of baseball's Golden Age. (David Q. Voigt)

Charlie Comiskey, in the glory days at St. Louis. (NBL)

The dominant catcher of the nineteenth century, Buck Ewing was fast, too, with at least 336 stolen bases to his credit. As late as the 1930s, Spalding Guide editor John Foster called him the "greatest all-around player ever connected with the game." (NBL)

John Montgomery Ward, the game's first labor leader, followed his own lights and retired at the age of thirty-four to pursue his law practice. (NBL)

The 1889 New York Giants. The long-time rivalry between New York and Brooklyn had its roots not in the twentieth century, but in the 1889 World Series, won by the Giants, six games to three. (NBL)

New York first baseman Roger Connor (shown here in 1887) was a giant man, standing six feet, three inches tall and weighing two-hundred-twenty pounds. Connor's career total of 138 homers stood as a major-league record until surpassed by Ruth in 1921. (NBL)

With 311 career wins, it's hard to believe Mickey Welch ever played second fiddle on the Giants pitching staff. Nicknamed "Smiling Mickey" for his happy-go-lucky disposition, Welch won thirty-four games as a twenty-one-year-old rookie in 1880. (NBL)

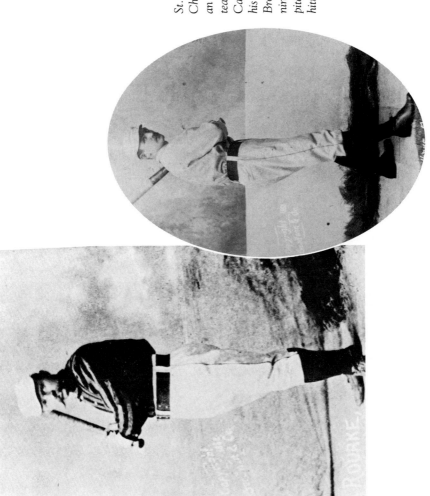

Orator Jim O'Rourke's first seven years in organized baseball were spent with pennant winners. (NBL)

St. Louis Browns owner Chris Von Der Ahe bought an entire minor-league team just to acquire Bob Caruthers, shown here in his later years with Brooklyn. Even in the nineteenth century, pitchers were proud of their hitting ability. (NBL)

Studio portrait of the 1890 National League champion Brooklyn Bridegrooms. (Seated, in front) Michael Hughes. (Seated, l-r) George Pinckney, Bob Caruthers, manager William McGunnigle, Thomas Daly, Tom Lovett. (Standing, l-r) George Smith, John Corkhill, Dave Foutz, Darby O'Brien, Adonis Terry, Oyster Burns. (NBL)

Outfielder Tommy McCarthy saw action on the pennant-winning 1888 St. Louis Brown Stockings and later with the Boston Beaneaters in 1892–93. (NBL)

The profile of Boston's Hugh Duffy, whose .438 batting average in 1894 was the highest ever. On meeting Duffy for the first time, Cap Anson asked, "Where's the rest of you?" Duffy's remarkable baseball career spanned sixty-nine years. (NBL)

The 1892 Boston Beaneaters, who soundly trounced the Cleveland Spiders in the split-season championship series. Cy Young and Jack Stivetts paired up in a scoreless, eleven-inning tie in the Series opener, but the notion of a split season was about as popular with fans in 1892 as it was in 1981. (David Q. Voigt)

Hard-drinking, free-spending Mike "King" Kelly toured the saloons with his pet monkey and a Japanese valet. His flamboyance and versatility endeared him to fans in every city he played. At his death, more than five thousand people viewed his body as it lay in state at Boston's Elks Hall. (NBL)

Boston's boyish-looking Charles Augustus "Kid" Nichols, winner of thirty games or more for seven straight years and the youngest pitcher ever to win three hundred. (NBL)

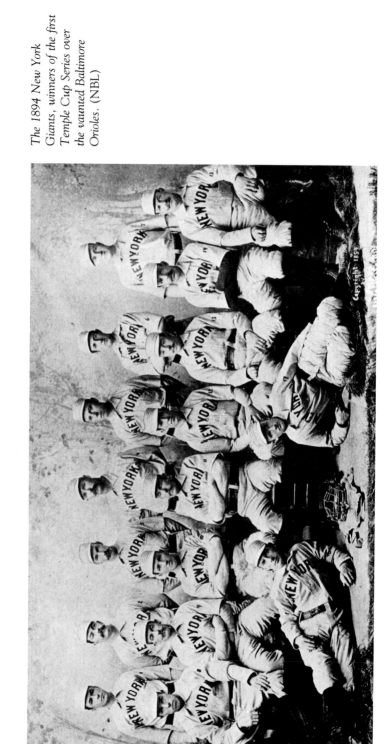

The 1894 New York Giants, winners of the first Temple Cup Series over the vaunted Baltimore Orioles. (NBL)

John J. McGraw, pictured here in 1899 or 1901. The eldest of eight children, four of whom died in childhood, McGraw's mental and physical toughness of character earned him the nickname "Muggsy." Arlie Latham said he ate "gunpowder every morning and washes it down with warm blood." (NBL)

Amos Rusie, of whom sportswriter O.P. Caylor said, "The Giants without Rusie would be like Hamlet without the Melancholy Dane." The Hoosier Thunderbolt might have been the greatest ever if he hadn't been so overworked early in his career. (NBL)

Cleveland's Jesse Burkett was nicknamed "The Crab" for his short temper and sour disposition. "Other players are bigger and huskier," he said, "I have to make up for the difference somehow." Burkett hit .402 for the retooled St. Louis Cardinals in 1899 and didn't even lead the league. (NBL)

The legendary Cy Young—first in wins, losses, games started, complete games, and innings. His career was reborn when he jumped to the American League in 1901, and he retired ten years later only when he was too old and fat to field his position. (NBL)

The 1895 Cleveland Spiders were led by Cy Young who captured three of his club's four victories in the World Series. The Spiders were stoned by angry fans in Baltimore. (NBL)

Wee Willie's talent was so great that he came to the majors as a left-handed third baseman. Cy Young called him his hardest out and John McGraw said that "with the possible exception of Ty Cobb, Willie Keeler was the greatest player of all time." (NBL)

According to most accounts, Ned Hanlon was the real brains behind the success of the pennant-winning 1887 Detroit Wolverines. The first manager to employ platooning consistently, Hanlon frequently wore a silk top hat and spats while managing the team from his place on the bench. (David Q. Voigt)

The 1896 Baltimore Orioles, scamps all. (Front, l-r) Jack Doyle, John McGraw, Willie Keeler, Arlie Pond. (Middle, l-r) Steve Brodie, Bill Hoffer, Joe Kelley, Ned Hanlon, Wilbert Robinson, Hughie Jennings, Heinie Reitz. (Back, l-r) Joe Quinn, Sadie McMahon, Duke Esper, George Hemming, Frank Bowerman, Boileryard Clarke, Jim Donnelly. Note the rebellious attitudes. (NBL)

Shown here in his later years with Detroit, Hughie Jennings was the shortstop of the powerhouse Orioles in the closing years of the nineteenth century. Jennings piloted the Tigers to pennants in his first three seasons, but despite managing the team through 1920, he never won another. (NBL)

When Ned Hanlon began the lengthy project of rebuilding the Orioles in 1892, Wilbert Robinson was the only player he kept. When he retired, Robinson had worked 1,316 games behind the plate, the most of any catcher to that time. (NBL)

Despite winning thirty-eight games for the 1887 Chicago White Stockings, John Clarkson was sold to Boston in the off-season for the incredible sum of ten thousand dollars. (NBL)

The first player to record three thousand hits, Cap Anson had a legendary distaste for losing and played the game so aggressively he believed bunting was for sissies. Fearless, outspoken, despised by umpires, he ruled the Chicago White Stockings with an iron fist. (NBL)

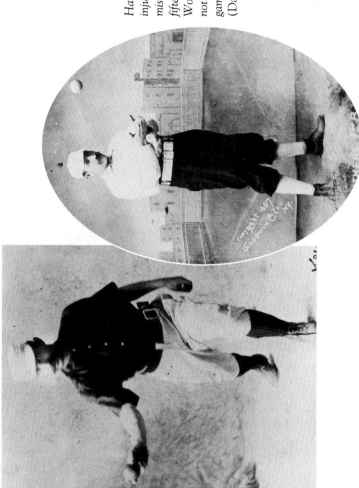

Hampered by an ankle injury, Dan Brouthers missed all but one of the fifteen games of the 1887 World Series. He would not see action in a Series game again until 1894. (David Q. Voigt)

Hall of Famer Tim Keefe was a man who finished what he started. From 1880 to 1889, he pitched 444 games and completed all but eight. (NBL)

Team photo of the Detroit Wolverines, taken one year before they won the 1887 National League pennant and just three years before they disbanded. (NBL)

A rare Joseph Hall cabinet card featuring the 1888 American Association champion St. Louis Brown Stockings. Photo taken at Ridgewood Park or Washington Park, Brooklyn. (Lew Lipset)

GAME THREE—October 22, 1889, at the Polo Grounds, New York

BROOKLYN	AB	R	H	BI	E	NEW YORK	AB	R	H	BI	E
O'Brien, lf	4	0	1	0	0	Gore, cf	5	0	1	0	1
Collins, 2b	5	1	1	0	1	Tiernan, rf	5	2	2	0	0
Burns, rf	4	0	0	0	0	Ewing, c	5	1	1	1	0
Foutz, 1b	4	2	1	2	0	Ward, ss	5	1	3	1	1
Pinckney, 3b	3	1	1	1	0	Connor, 1b	4	1	2	0	0
Clarke, c	4	1	2	1	0	Richardson, 2b	3	1	2	2	0
Corkhill, cf	3	2	2	3	0	O'Rourke, lf	3	1	2	3	0
Smith, ss	4	0	2	1	1	Whitney, 3b	3	0	0	0	0
Hughes, p	3	1	2	0	0	O'Day, p	1	0	0	0	0
Caruthers, p	0	0	0	0	0	Welch, p	3	0	1	0	0
	34	8	12	8	2		37	7	14	7	2

```
NY    2 0 0   0 3 2   0 0 - 7
BKN   0 2 3   1 2 0   0 0 - 8
```

D: Pinckney, Smith 2, Hughes, Clarke, Welch, Gore.   T: Tiernan.   HR: Corkhill, O'Rourke.   SAC: Collins.   SF: Corkhill.   DP: BKN.   BB: O'Day 3, Welch 1, Hughes 4. Struck out: O'Day 3, Welch 3, Hughes 3, Caruthers 2.   WP: Welch.   PB: Ewing, Clarke 2.   Umpires: Lynch and Gaffney.   Time—2:07.   Att: 5,181.

GAME FOUR—October 23, 1889, at Washington Park, Brooklyn

NEW YORK	AB	R	H	BI	E	BROOKLYN	AB	R	H	BI	E
Gore, cf	3	1	2	1	1	O'Brien, lf	3	2	1	0	0
Tiernan, rf	2	0	0	0	0	Collins, 2b	3	3	2	0	0
Ewing, c	4	1	1	1	1	Burns, rf	4	2	1	3	0
Ward, ss	4	1	1	0	0	Foutz, 1b	2	2	1	2	0
Connor, 1b	4	0	1	0	1	Pinckney, 3b	3	0	1	1	0
Richardson, 2b	2	1	0	0	1	Clarke, c	2	0	1	1	1
O'Rourke, lf	2	1	1	0	0	Terry, p	2	0	0	0	0
Whitney, 3b	3	1	2	1	2	Corkhill, cf	3	0	0	0	0
Crane, p	3	1	1	2	1	Smith, ss	3	1	0	0	0
	27	7	9	5	7		25	10	7	7	1

```
NY    0 0 1   1 0 5 -  7
BKN   2 0 2   0 3 3 - 10
```

D: O'Rourke.   T: Crane, Gore.   HR: Burns.   SB: Connor, Ward, Ewing, O'Brien, Foutz, Collins, Smith.   DP: NY.   BB: Crane 5, Terry 5.   Struck out: Crane 5, Terry 5. PB: Ewing.   WP: Terry, Crane.   Umpires: Lynch and Gaffney.   Time—2:10.   Att: 3,045.

◆ ◆ ◆

GAME FIVE—October 24, 1889, at Washington Park, Brooklyn

NEW YORK	AB	R	H	BI	E	BROOKLYN	AB	R	H	BI	E
Gore, cf	4	1	0	0	0	O'Brien, lf	4	0	0	0	0
Tiernan, rf	4	2	1	0	0	Collins, 2b	4	1	1	0	0
Brown, c	5	3	3	2	0	Burns, rf	4	0	1	1	1
Ward, ss	4	0	0	0	0	Foutz, 1b	5	0	1	0	0
Connor, 1b	4	1	1	2	0	Pinckney, 3b	4	1	2	0	0
Richardson, 2b	5	1	2	3	0	Clarke, c	2	1	1	0	0
O'Rourke, lf	5	0	0	0	0	Caruthers, p	4	0	2	1	0
Whitney, 3b	4	2	3	0	0	Corkhill, cf	2	0	0	0	0
Crane, p	4	1	2	2	0	Smith, ss	4	0	0	1	0
	39	11	12	9	0	Bushong, c	1	0	0	0	0
							34	3	8	3	1

```
NY    0 0 4   0 4 0   0 2 1 – 11
BKN   0 0 0   1 1 1   0 0 0 –  3
```

D: Crane, Pinckney, Collins, Burns. T: Whitney, Connor. HR: Richardson, Crane, Brown. SB: Connor, Collins. SAC: Smith. BB: Caruthers 4, Crane 6. Struck out: Crane 7. PB: Clarke 2, Brown. LOB: NY 5, BKN 10. Umpires: Lynch and Gaffney. Time—1:56. Att: 2,901.

◆ ◆ ◆

GAME SIX—October 25, 1889, at the Polo Grounds, New York

BROOKLYN	AB	R	H	BI	E	NEW YORK	AB	R	H	BI	E
O'Brien, lf	4	0	0	0	0	Slattery, cf	5	1	1	0	0
Collins, 2b	4	0	1	0	1	Tiernan, rf	5	0	0	0	0
Burns, rf	4	0	0	0	0	Ewing, c	5	0	1	0	0
Foutz, 1b	5	0	0	0	0	Ward, ss	5	1	2	1	0
Pinckney, 3b	3	0	2	0	0	Connor, 1b	4	0	1	0	0
Visner, c	4	1	1	0	0	Richardson, 2b	3	0	0	0	0
Terry, p	4	0	1	1	0	O'Rourke, lf	4	0	1	0	0
Corkhill, cf	3	0	1	0	0	Whitney, 3b	4	0	1	0	0
Davis, ss	4	0	0	0	0	O'Day, p	3	0	0	0	0
	35	1	6	1	1		38	2	7	1	0

Two out when winning run scored

```
BKN   0 1 0   0 0 0   0 0 0   0 0 – 1
NY    0 0 0   0 0 0   0 0 1   0 1 – 2
```

D: Pinckney, Ewing, Whitney. SB: Collins 2, Corkhill, Richardson, Ward 2, Connor 2. DP: NY 2, BKN 2. BB: O'Day 5, Terry 2. Struck out: O'Day 4, Terry 4. Umpires: Lynch and Gaffney. Time—1:55. Att: 2,556.

GAME SEVEN—October 26, 1889, at the Polo Grounds, New York

BROOKLYN	AB	R	H	BI	E	NEW YORK	AB	R	H	BI	E
O'Brien, lf	4	1	0	0	0	Slattery, cf	4	2	0	1	0
Collins, 2b	4	1	1	0	1	Tiernan, rf	4	2	1	2	0
Burns, rf	2	2	0	0	0	Ewing, c	5	1	3	2	1
Foutz, 1b	4	2	2	1	0	Ward, ss	5	0	1	1	0
Pinckney, 3b	4	0	1	2	1	Connor, 1b	4	1	2	1	0
Corkhill, cf	3	1	0	0	0	Richardson, 2b	5	1	2	2	1
Smith, ss	4	0	1	4	1	O'Rourke, lf	5	2	2	1	0
Bushong, c	4	0	0	0	0	Whitney, 3b	4	1	2	0	1
Lovett, p	1	0	0	0	0	Crane, p	3	1	0	0	0
Caruthers, p	2	0	0	0	0	Keefe, p	1	0	1	0	0
	32	7	5	7	3		40	11	14	10	3

```
BKN   0 4 0   0 0 3   0 0 0 -  7
NY    1 8 0   0 0 1   1 0 x - 11
```

D: O'Rourke, Connor, Whitney, Keefe.   T: Smith.   HR: Richardson, O'Rourke.
SB: O'Brien, Tiernan, Connor.   SAC: Smith.   SF: Slattery.   BB: Crane 9, Keefe 2,
Lovett 2, Caruthers 1.   Struck out: Keefe 2, Lovett 1, Caruthers 1.   PB: Bushong.
HBP: Connor (Lovett).   Umpires: Lynch and Gaffney.   Time—2:14.   Att: 3,312.

GAME EIGHT—October 28, 1889, at Washington Park, Brooklyn

NEW YORK	AB	R	H	BI	E	BROOKLYN	AB	R	H	BI	E
Slattery, cf	3	2	0	0	0	O'Brien, lf	4	1	1	2	0
Tiernan, rf	5	3	3	1	0	Collins, 2b	3	2	0	0	0
Ewing, c	5	2	2	2	0	Burns, rf	4	1	1	2	0
Ward, ss	3	4	3	0	0	Foutz, 1b-p	4	1	1	2	0
Connor, 1b	4	2	3	6	0	Pinckney, 3b	4	0	0	0	0
Richardson, 2b	5	1	1	2	1	Visner, c	3	0	0	0	0
O'Rourke, lf	5	2	2	1	0	Terry, p-1b	4	0	1	0	0
Whitney, 3b	5	0	0	1	0	Corkhill, cf	4	1	0	0	0
Crane, p	5	0	1	1	0	Smith, ss	3	1	1	0	1
	40	16	15	14	1		33	7	5	6	1

```
NY    5 4 1   2 0 3   0 0 1 - 16
BKN   2 0 0   0 0 0   0 2 3 -  7
```

D: Ewing 2.   T: O'Brien, Connor, O'Rourke.   HR: Foutz, Burns, Tiernan.   SB:
O'Brien 2, Richardson, Ward 3.   SF: O'Rourke, Connor.   SAC: Whitney 2.   DP: NY 1,
BKN 1.   BB: Terry 2, Foutz 2, Crane 5.   Struck out: Crane 4, Terry 1, Foutz 2.   PB:
Visner 2.   WP: Foutz.   HBP: Ward (Terry).   Umpires: Lynch and Gaffney.
Time—1:55.   Att: 2,584.

GAME NINE—October 29, 1889, at the Polo Grounds, New York

BROOKLYN	AB	R	H	BI	E	NEW YORK	AB	R	H	BI	E
O'Brien, lf	1	1	0	0	0	Slattery, cf	4	1	1	0	0
Collins, 2b	4	1	2	0	0	Tiernan, rf	3	1	1	0	0
Burns, rf	4	0	1	2	0	Ewing, c	3	0	0	0	1
Foutz, 1b	3	0	0	0	0	Ward, ss	3	1	2	1	1
Pinckney, 3b	3	0	0	0	0	Connor, 1b	4	0	1	0	0
Terry, p	4	0	0	0	0	Richardson, 2b	4	0	0	1	1
Visner, cf	4	0	0	0	0	O'Rourke, lf	4	0	2	0	0
Smith, ss	4	0	1	0	0	Whitney, 3b	4	0	0	0	0
Bushong, c	3	0	0	0	0	O'Day, p	2	0	1	0	1
	30	2	4	2	0		31	3	8	2	4

```
BKN    2 0 0   0 0 0   0 0 0 – 2
NY     1 0 0   0 0 1   1 0 x – 3
```

D: Burns, Tiernan.   T: Ward.   SB: O'Brien, Foutz 2, Smith, Pinckney, Collins, Connor, Ward, O'Rourke, Slattery.   SAC: Whitney.   SF: Richardson.   DP: NY 1, BKN 1.   BB: O'Day 7, Terry 4.   Struck out: O'Day 5, Terry 1.   PB: Ewing 1, Bushong 2.   Umpires: Lynch and Gaffney.   Time—2:02.   Att: 3,647.

◆ 8 ◆

BASEBALL SHOOTS
ITSELF IN THE FOOT

◆

The best baseball in 1890 wasn't
played in the major leagues.
The best team never came
within a mile of the World
Series. The best players were outlaws.

The new Players' League consisted of eight teams composed of
members of the Brotherhood of Professional Base Ball Players,
most of them contract-jumpers from the American Association
and the National League.

The Players' League had declared war on major league baseball, an action which resulted in the most economically disastrous
season in the history of professional baseball. Before the year began, players in both the National League and American Association
were induced to jump their contracts and join teams in the rebel
league. Seventeen percent of the Association players jumped—
weakening an already financially troubled league—and a whopping fifty-three percent of the National League players deserted
their contracts.

The roll call of the outlaw league was impressive, sporting four-
teen future Hall of Famers—Monte Ward, Dan Brouthers, Hoss
Radbourn, King Kelly, Connie Mack, Hugh Duffy, Charlie
Comiskey, Ed Delahanty, Roger Connor, Tim Keefe, Jim O'Rourke,

1890

The Changing Game

◆ ◆ ◆

- A sacrifice hit was no longer charged as a time at bat.

- Only one substitution was allowed per game, per team, except in case of injury.

- An umpire could declare a batter out if he believed the batter was deliberately fouling off pitches.

- The National League lost the Indianapolis Hoosiers and the Washington Senators, who were replaced by two American Association defectors, the champion Brooklyn Bridegrooms and a strong Cincinnati Reds club.

- The financially troubled Baltimore and Kansas City franchises folded, and into the void stepped two new New York teams, the Rochester Hop Bitters and the Syracuse Stars. Also joining the Association were the Toledo (Ohio) Maumees and the Brooklyn Gladiators. (The Brooklyn club transferred to Baltimore in mid-season.)

- Harry Decker, a journeyman catcher, invented the Decker Safety Catching Mitt, an oversized, padded glove and the forerunner of modern catching mitts.

Buck Ewing, Jake Beckley, and Pud Galvin—and a dozen others who probably should be in Cooperstown.

Twelve members of the pennant-winning 1889 New York Giants moved to the Players' League, leaving only outfielder Mike Tiernan and pitcher Mickey Welch in the National League. In contrast, only one member of the 1889 American Association champion Brooklyn Bridegrooms, Joe Visner, jumped his contract. Twenty of the twenty-seven participants in the 1888 World Series left their respective leagues for the new organization.

All Players' League members were given three-year contracts at a figure no less than what they had earned in 1889. A $25,000 prize fund, contributed by the clubs, would be distributed at the conclusion of the season, based on the final standings; the team which won the pennant was to receive seven thousand dollars. The first ten thousand dollars in club profits would go to the investors, the next ten thousand to the players, and anything over that amount was to be divided among all the players in the League. Visiting clubs would share equally in game receipts, as opposed to National League and American Association rules, which gave sixty percent of the take to the home club.

The Players' League attempted to right all the injustices, real or imagined, that ballplayers had suffered under the tyrannical domination of the reserve rule, which bound a player to his club for life.

It was a grand and noble plan, but like most grand and noble plans, it was doomed from the outset.

The National League went head-to-head with the Players' League in Boston, Brooklyn, Chicago, Cleveland, New York, Philadelphia, and Pittsburgh. The American Association went head-to-head with the PL in Brooklyn and Philadelphia. The only one-team cities in the National League and Players' League were Cincinnati and Buffalo. The American Association had exclusivity in Louisville, Columbus, St. Louis, Toledo, Rochester, and Syracuse, and with franchises in so many small cities, found itself virtually relegated to the stature of a high minor league. Fan interest in Association contests dropped to such a low point that many newspapers refused to print box scores of the games.

Teams in all three leagues lied shamelessly about their attendance figures. At the conclusion of the 1890 season, the Players' League claimed to have drawn 980,888 fans; the National League, 813,678; and the American Association, about 500,000. All three figures are inflated, but it is a safe bet the order is correct. Only the

Players' League could lay a genuine claim of offering major league baseball in the 1890 season.

At season's end, the Players' League had suffered estimated losses of just under $400,000. With payrolls severely reduced, National League losses were around $250,000, but the senior circuit had the capital and the resources to hang on. The Players' League did not, and it folded.

Spalding's Official Base Ball Guide 1891 commented:

> Not in the twenty years' history of professional club organizations was there recorded such an exceptional season of financial disaster and general demoraliztion [sic] as characterized the professional season of 1890 . . . Two hundred thousand dollars would not compensate the eight clubs of the National League alone for the cost of the base ball war of last year, incurred in individual club expenses, and in the loss of the customary receipts of previous years; and fully double that amount was lost by the Players' League Clubs, not one of which rendered actual expenses.

Unfortunately for major league baseball, the demise of the Players' League had the effect of throwing the baby out with the bath water. The brief existence of the league had so severely weakened the fabric of competition that the American Association, already strapped with severe financial problems, would meet its own death following the 1891 season.

The Players' League pennant race promised the most excitement and, in many respects, provided the least drama as the Boston Reds took an early lead and held on throughout the summer months. The surprise of the American Association was the Louisville Cyclones, the worst team in the major leagues the previous year. (In early 1890, a tornado struck the city of Louisville, killing seventy-five and causing hundreds of thousands of dollars' damage. In an unusual tribute, the Louisville ballclub was re-nicknamed the Cyclones for the upcoming season.) Although top-heavy with youngsters, Louisville suffered fewer player defections than other Association clubs and cruised to the pennant, a comfortable ten games ahead of the Columbus Colts.

The Brooklyn Bridegrooms had jumped from the American Association to the National League and, in the process, became the first and only team to win pennants in two leagues in successive years. Brooklyn moved into the lead in early July and held on to the title for dear life, withstanding an assault from the surging Chicago Colts, winners of forty-one of their last fifty-six games.

At no time did National League or American Association owners consider inviting Players' League involvement in the 1890 World Series.

The Brooklyn Bridegrooms and Louisville Cyclones came into the 1890 World Series about evenly matched, offensively and defensively. As a team, the Bridegrooms had led the National League in runs scored (884), slugging average (.369), stolen bases (349), and fielding percentage (.940), while finishing second in runs allowed (620), home runs (43), and team ERA (3.05). The Cyclones had led the Association in fewest runs allowed (588), batting average (.279), fielding percentage (.933), and ERA (2.58), and were second in slugging average (.350) and shutouts (13).

Brooklyn's Thomas "Oyster" Burns (so nicknamed because of a former job opening crates of oysters in Baltimore) led the National League in runs batted in (128), was second in home runs (13), and third in slugging average (.468). Leadoff batter George Hubbert "Hub" Collins was coming off one of his finest seasons, a year in which he topped all National League batters in runs scored (148), and finished second in doubles (32) and stolen bases (85). Darby O'Brien, despite injuries which had kept him on the bench for some fifty games during the season, finished fourth in the league in batting average (.314). Converted first baseman Dave Foutz had one of his best seasons at the plate, scoring 106 runs and finishing fifth in the league in RBIs (98).

The Cyclones were led by an outfielder-third baseman with the rather improbable name of William Van Winkle Wolf. Wolf had joined the Louisville club in 1882, the first year of its existence, and was instantly nicknamed "Chicken" by teammate Pete Browning. In his decade with the Cyclones, Wolf would prove to be the most durable player on the team, playing a full schedule of games in five seasons, 1883–85, 1887, and 1890. He was the only man to play in the American Association for each season of its ten-year existence. In addition to having a potent bat, one of Wolf's virtues was his defensive versatility. Mainly an outfielder, Wolf nonetheless put in thirty-eight games at first base, fifteen games at second, twenty-five games at third, sixty-four games at short, and thirty-nine games behind the plate in his career. For fun, he also made three appearances over the years as a pitcher. In Louisville's ill-fated season of 1889, Wolf had even managed the club for sixty-six games, compiling the best winning percentage of any of the team's four managers that year.

When Pete Browning left the club following the 1889 season (forfeiting the only chance in his career to play on a pennant winner), Wolf's nickname of Chicken went with him, and his teammates began calling him Jim or Jimmy, for reasons unknown. After he retired, Wolf would join the Louisville fire department and in 1894, was thrown from a horse-drawn fire engine, suffering head injuries that caused brain damage. Wolf and Browning were reunited when Wolf was institutionalized at the Lakeland Insane Asylum two years before his death. He died in 1903 and was buried in Cave Hill Cemetery in Louisville. Browning joined him two years later.

Wolf enjoyed an MVP-like season in 1890, and was the offensive catalyst of the Louisville Cyclones. He led the American Association in batting average (.363), hits (197), and total bases (260), and finished second in doubles (29), and third in slugging average (.479).

On the mound, on paper at least, the Cyclones held a clear edge over Brooklyn. Louisville had three top starting pitchers in rookie George Meakim (12-7), Red Ehret (25-14), and Scott Stratton (34-14), all of whom had career years.

In 1890, the lanky Meakim made twenty-eight appearances and was fourth in the Association in winning percentage (.632). Possessed of a blazing fastball, he finished third in most strikeouts per nine innings (5.77). This was Meakim's only successful year in the majors, as his lifetime win-loss record of 15-13 would attest.

Phillip "Red" Ehret—called "Red" more for his complexion than for the color of his hair—was a native of Louisville and despite playing on several pennant-contending teams in his career, never fulfilled the potential he showed in 1890. He finished second in earned run average (2.53) and fewest walks per nine innings (1.98), tied for second in shutouts (4), and was third in winning percentage (.641).

Scott Stratton, the Association's ERA leader (2.36), was the bulwark of the Louisville staff. Stratton led the league in fewest walks per nine innings (1.27), finished second in victories (34), tied for second in shutouts (4), and was third in complete games (44) and innings pitched (431). But the four-hundred-inning workload had extracted a terrible toll on Stratton. His arm blew out and he was never the same pitcher again.

If this Louisville pitching staff had a weakness that Brooklyn manager Bill McGunnigle might exploit, it was its inexperience. Twenty-five-year-old George Meakim was the eldest, although just a rookie. Red Ehret had turned twenty-two six weeks before the season ended, and Scott Stratton had reached the age of majority just two weeks before the World Series began.

The Bridegrooms had three top starting pitchers in Tom Lovett, Adonis Terry, and Bob Caruthers. Lovett had appeared briefly with the 1885 Philadelphia Athletics but did not return to the big leagues until 1889, when he joined the Bridegrooms. He was a pitcher of some promise, as a 77-48 record over his first four years would seem to indicate, but an arm injury in 1891 would virtually finish his career. He would retire with a career record of 88-59. Lovett was 17-10 with the pennant-winning Bridegrooms in 1889 and improved his record to 30-11 this year, his best season ever. He led all National League hurlers in winning percentage (.732) and was third in victories.

Adonis Terry, the veteran of the staff, might have been one of the best ever had it not been for alternate seasons of overwork. When he burst upon the American Association scene in 1884, his manager, George Taylor, saw fit to let the rookie work 485 innings, a decision which accomplished little more than to ruin his arm. The following year, Terry made half the number of appearances and saw his victory output drop from twenty to six. In 1890, Terry had his finest year, finishing with a record of 26-16 and completing thirty-eight of his forty-four starts. His 2.94 ERA was sixth best in the league.

Last on the Brooklyn staff was Bob Caruthers. Caruthers was nearing the end of a distinguished career and this was the last season he would win twenty games. His 23-11 record was a shade or two removed from his glory days with St. Louis, but his 3.09 ERA was still respectable, and he completed thirty of thirty-three starts. Caruthers was only twenty-six years old, but an average of 391 innings pitched in each of the past six seasons had abused his strong right arm beyond repair.

◆ ◆ ◆

Final arrangements for the 1890 World Series were not completed until October 7, a mere nine days before the scheduled opening date. Because of the superiority of the Players' League teams, disenchanted fans around the country paid little attention to the Series. The fact that Louisville was the southernmost site of any Series to date may also have had something to do with fan disinterest. The Philadelphia *Evening Bulletin* commented, "There is scarcely enough interest in the series to induce the people to read the scores."

It was decided to hold the first eight games in the home parks of both clubs with a ninth and deciding game, if necessary, played in Boston. The first four games would be played in Louisville, the next four in Brooklyn.

Louisville's season had ended October 14, but Brooklyn had finished its playing schedule a week before the Series was due to begin. To keep sharp, the Bridegrooms played four exhibition games with the St. Louis Browns, two in Kansas City and two in St. Louis. Adonis Terry won the first game at Kansas City, 16-9, and Tom Lovett lost the second, 8-7. Bob Caruthers was victorious in the first contest at St. Louis but sprained his ankle and was unavailable to pitch in the World Series. Dave Foutz made a rare start in the second game at St. Louis and earned a come-from-behind 9-7 victory when his teammates scored three runs in the ninth inning.

The Bridegrooms arrived in Louisville for the Series opener on October 16, but they needn't have hurried—a blinding rain forced cancellation of the contest. Game One was played the next day at tiny Eclipse Park, which featured one of the longest left-field distances in the major leagues—360 feet. Dead-center field was a staggering 495 feet from home plate and a batter could hit a home run out of the park only if it cleared the twelve-foot high fence. Left-handed hitters had a sizable advantage: The right-field fence was only 320 feet away. Billboards on the outfield walls loudly advertised: "CHEW HOLD FAST TOBACCO," "CHEW THE BEST: COLGANS," and "RB GEOGHEGAN, THE HATTER."

Excursion trains ran from all the large towns around Louisville, and Eclipse Park was filled past its five-thousand-seat capacity long before the scheduled 3:15 starting time. The sun shone and, although winter was fast approaching, it was an ideal day for baseball, with no visible traces of the previous day's heavy rain. When Brooklyn took the field for pre-game practice, it was greeted with polite applause from the Louisville partisans.

John McQuaid was the plate umpire, Wesley Curry worked the bases, and the starting pitchers for Game One of the 1890 World Series were Scott Stratton and Adonis Terry.

Hub Collins, a Louisville native, was the first batter for Brooklyn and was greeted with a prolonged ovation as he stepped into the box. When he singled to center and stole second, the crowd applauded somewhat less enthusiastically. The next batter, Darby O'Brien, sent an easy grounder to Louisville third baseman Harry Raymond, but Raymond booted the ball and the Bridegrooms had a first-and-third opportunity with none out. It wasn't the best of starts for the Cyclones. Things got worse when Oyster Burns singled to center to drive in Collins. George Pinckney grounded to sore-shouldered Phil Tomney* and the twenty-seven-year-old shortstop bobbled the ball for the Cyclones' second error. O'Brien scored on the muff and Burns came home when Dave Foutz grounded into a double play. Adonis Terry slapped a grounder to short for what should have been the third out of the inning, but the nervous Tomney booted the ball for his second error. Terry brought the three-run frame to a close a moment later when he was thrown out stealing second.

There was no more scoring until the fifth when Brooklyn raked Stratton for another three runs. The Bridegrooms' team captain, Germany Smith, reached base on Harry Raymond's second error and came around when slow-footed Bob Clark legged out a triple to left-center on Stratton's next delivery. Phil Tomney dropped Hub Collins's high popup in short center for his third error of the game and Clark trotted home with Brooklyn's fifth run. An RBI double by Oyster Burns gave the Bridegrooms a 6-0 lead.

Brooklyn removed all doubt as to the outcome of the contest with a third three-run burst in the seventh. Bob Clark reached on an error when rookie first baseman Harry Taylor lost Raymond's throw in the sun. Clark raced to second as the ball rolled to the bleachers. A Hub Collins single made the score 7-0 and two sacrifice bunts added another run. When the speedy George Pinckney legged out a triple and came home on a wild pitch, the Bridegrooms led, 9-0.

In the bottom of the seventh, Brooklyn's starting catcher Bob Clark split his right thumb and his services were lost for the

---

* Phil Tomney would be dead in less than two years, at the age of twenty-nine. Several of the participants in the 1890 World Series would meet with premature deaths within three years. Hub Collins would die of typhoid fever at his home in Brooklyn in May 1892. Pitcher Ed Daily would succumb to consumption in 1891, a year to the day after Game Four of the 1890 Series. Brooklyn catcher Ned Bligh died six days after the 1892 baseball season began and Darby O'Brien passed away in June of 1893.

rest of the Series. At the conclusion of the eighth inning, with the score 9-0 Brooklyn, umpire McQuaid called the game because of darkness.

Adonis Terry finished with a two-hit masterpiece, one of the best pitching performances of the nineteenth-century World Series. Scott Stratton gave up eleven hits and a walk but deserved a better fate—only one of the nine Brooklyn runs was earned.

After the game, Louisville manager Jack Chapman said, "Of course, everyone knows the Brooklyns are the strongest team, but we'll give 'em a good tussle yet."

The next morning, the Louisville *Courier-Journal* put a happy face on the outcome, saying:

> It was only courtesy to our visitors to give them the first of the series, anyhow. Louisville is in Kentucky, and Kentuckians would not be true to themselves if they were not hospitable.

The Louisville *Commercial Gazette* more accurately summed up the game:

> Some clubs are born to win; some achieve winnings and some have winnings thrust upon them. Brooklyn was given the game yesterday . . . The whole secret of their [Louisville's] poor playing lies in the two words "over anxious." The boys were too anxious to win and played too hard . . . Today there will probably be a very different tale told . . . The boys will not be so nervous and consequently will give the visitors a hard tussle.

As it developed, the *Commercial Gazette* was correct; but the paper was a couple days early on its prediction.

Because the weather had turned bitterly cold overnight, Game Two, on October 18, was played before a crowd numbering about half that of the previous day—2,860. Tom Lovett and Ed Daily were the starting pitchers.

Daily fanned Brooklyn's Hub Collins and Darby O'Brien on a diet of fastballs to start the game, then induced Oyster Burns to ground weakly to second. With the crowd chanting, "Daily! Daily!" the teams changed positions. Louisville broke through for its first run of the Series in the bottom of the first as the lanky Harry Taylor coaxed a walk from Lovett, went to second on Harry Raymond's sacrifice bunt, and scored on William "Farmer" Weaver's single to center. For the first time in the Series, the Louisville crowd had something to cheer about.

The Bridegrooms nailed Daily for the tying and lead runs in the next half-frame as the youthful Cyclones put on another exhibition of World Series jitters. George Pinckney lifted a high pop fly which fell untouched between Phil Tomney and Harry Raymond on the infield. Pinckney went to second on a passed ball and to third on Adonis Terry's infield single. Terry bluffed a steal, and when catcher John Ryan's throw went through second baseman Tim Shinnick's legs, Pinckney raced in with the tying run. Terry stopped at second, was sacrificed to third by Tom Daly, and trotted home on a wild pitch to give Brooklyn a 2-1 lead.

The Cyclones tied the score in the bottom of the inning when Harry Taylor singled on the infield, stole second, and scored on Farmer Weaver's line single to left.

But the Bridegrooms were not to be denied. In the top of the fourth, George Pinckney led off with a base on balls and one out later, Adonis Terry reached first on Harry Raymond's fourth error of the Series. Tom Daly grounded into an apparent inning-ending double play, but umpire John McQuaid blew the call at first and Daily, instead of being delivered from the inning, was faced with a first-and-third situation and two out. (For the balance of the game, the crowd cheered McQuaid sarcastically on every putout at first base. The decision upset Louisville catcher John Ryan so much that he stopped McQuaid after the game and accused him of robbing the Cyclones of victory.) Daly surprised everyone in the park by stealing second, and both baserunners came around to score on Germany Smith's single. The Bridegrooms added their final run of the day in the sixth when Dave Foutz doubled and later scored on an error by shortstop Phil Tomney.

Many of the fans had already left the park when Louisville mounted a rally in the ninth. Tomney drew a base on balls, Lovett's fourth of the game, raced to third on John Ryan's single, and scored on Ed Daily's sacrifice fly. But Harry Taylor popped to short and Harry Raymond ended the game when he became Lovett's seventh strikeout victim. Brooklyn was a 5-3 winner, and had a two-games-to-none lead in the Series.

Sunday, October 19, was an off-day in the Series, but the Cyclones played a benefit game against former Louisville ballplayers, including Tommy McLaughlin, Monk Cline, Joe Crotty, and

Phil Reccius. Herb Goodall, an 8-5 performer for the Cyclones in 1890, pitched for Louisville.

The Series resumed at Eclipse Park on Monday, October 20, at 3:15. A crowd of only 1,253 braved thirty-degree temperatures and bitter winds to see a rematch of Scott Stratton and Adonis Terry. Brooklyn's George Pinckney, having taken ill, had to sit this game out, and further damaging the Bridegrooms' chances was the loss of Bob Caruthers and Bob Clark. Clark left for home in the evening and Caruthers would not play again until the fifth game.

In the second inning, a hard-hit grounder off the bat of Dave Foutz took a funny hop and hit the unlucky Phil Tomney squarely on his bad right shoulder, forcing his retirement from the game and the Series. It was the fourth major injury for Tomney during the 1890 season. Harry Raymond moved to short, Jimmy Wolf took over duties at third, and Ed Daily entered the game in right field. To make matters worse for the Cyclones, Brooklyn scored in the inning to take a 2-0 lead.

Louisville cut the margin in half in the bottom of the third when Stratton doubled, took third on Harry Taylor's single, and scored on a Harry Raymond sacrifice. The Bridegrooms got that run back in the top of the fourth when Adonis Terry reached on a fielder's choice, stole second, advanced a base on a missed third strike, and scored on a passed ball. To add to Louisville's woes, Scott Stratton's pitching arm began bothering him and he, too, was forced to leave the game. George Meakim came on in relief and the catching duties were passed from John Ryan to Ned Bligh. In the bottom of the fourth, Louisville closed the gap to 3-2 when Jimmy Wolf tripled and scored on Charlie Hamburg's single.

The Bridegrooms took what appeared to be a commanding 6-2 lead in the top of the fifth when singles by Dave Foutz and George Pinckney, a Germany Smith triple, and a wild pitch netted three runs. But Louisville wasn't about to concede yet—doubles by Wolf and Tim Shinnick sandwiched a Charlie Hamburg triple in the bottom of the inning and the Cyclones closed to within two runs. In the top of the seventh, Brooklyn's Darby O'Brien singled to center, stole second, took third on an infield out, and scored when Tim Shinnick booted Dave Foutz's grounder.

With darkness rapidly approaching, both managers agreed to end play at the conclusion of the eighth inning. Brooklyn failed to score, but Louisville rallied to tie the game. Jimmy Wolf drew a base on balls and went to second on Charlie Hamburg's base hit. Tim Shinnick's second double of the day made the score 7-5, Brooklyn, and gave the crowd cause for hope. Ed Daily drove the next delivery from Adonis Terry to the left-field wall for a sacrifice fly. Shinnick advanced to third and Hamburg came home, pulling the Cyclones to within a run. With the weak-hitting Ned Bligh at the plate, Terry uncorked a wild pitch and Shinnick scored the tying run. After Bligh grounded out, George Meakim laced a single to right and stole second, but Harry Taylor grounded to third, leaving the potential winning run stranded in scoring position. The contest ended with the scored tied at seven.

With this tie, the Cyclones seemed to come together as a team after showing a severe case of World Series nerves in the first two games. A look at the ages of the Louisville starting eight tells the story: Rookies Tim Shinnick, Harry Taylor, and Charlie Hamburg were twenty-two, twenty-four, and twenty-six, respectively. John Ryan had just recently reached the age of majority and was enjoying his first full year in the majors. Farmer Weaver, Phil Tomney, and Harry Raymond were twenty-five, twenty-seven, and twenty-eight, respectively, but all three were playing in only their second full year in the big leagues. Jimmy Wolf was three weeks younger than Harry Raymond, but still the veteran of the group with nine years' experience behind him. Playing the Bridegrooms to a tie and more important, coming from behind with three runs in the final inning, gave the Cyclones a shot of badly needed confidence and let them stand on equal footing with Brooklyn. The final four games of the Series would prove this dramatically.

The Bridegrooms still held a two-games-to-none advantage in the Series as the clubs met for the final game at Louisville on October 21. Because of the increasingly bad weather, attendance dropped off to 1,050 for the fourth game. Righthander Red Ehret made his first appearance for the Cyclones and his teammates struck early against Brooklyn starting pitcher Tom Lovett. With one out in the first, Harry Raymond lined an infield single off shortstop Germany Smith's glove, and Farmer Weaver followed with a double to plate the first run of the game. Jimmy Wolf's line drive glanced off Oyster Burns's glove at third and rolled into short left field. By the time Burns could get to the ball, Wolf was standing at second base and Weaver had scored. Wolf stole third and came home on catcher Doc Bushong's wild throw. The Cyclones led, 3-0.

Brooklyn tied the score in the next half-frame. Dave Foutz singled and moved to second when Adonis Terry drew a base on balls from Red Ehret. Germany Smith singled off Jimmy Wolf's glove at third to drive in Foutz and when Smith broke for second, Wolf panicked and threw the ball away into right field. Terry came home to make the score 3-2, Louisville, and rookie Patrick "Patsy" Donovan's single drove in Smith with the tying run.

Brooklyn took the lead in the top of the third when Hub Collins singled, went to second on a sacrifice bunt, and scored on Oyster Burns's single to left. Undeterred, the Cyclones tied the score in the bottom of the inning, then took a 5-4 lead in the seventh. Leadoff hitter Tim Shinnick launched a triple into right field and the next batter, John Ryan, hit a sharp grounder, fair by inches, down the first-base line. Dave Foutz made a dazzling stop of the ball, scrambled to his feet and cocked his arm, but Lovett had forgotten to cover the bag. Hub Collins raced over from second and took Foutz's throw for the putout, but the damage had been done. Shinnick trotted home with what proved to be the winning run.

Louisville fans, who had been crying, "Too dark! Too dark!" as the game entered the ninth, changed their chant to "Ehret! Ehret!" as the Cyclones' hurler retired Dave Foutz on a popup to start the inning. Adonis Terry struck out on three straight fastballs and Germany Smith lifted a little pop fly into short left field for what looked like a certain Texas leaguer. After a hard run, Jimmy Wolf hauled the ball in, his back to the plate, and the Cyclones had captured their first victory of the Series. They had finally jelled as a team, and were playing like the champions they were.

After a rocky start, Red Ehret pitched a terrific game, stifling the Bridegrooms' offense on only two hits from the third inning on. Ehret finished with a seven-hitter, walked two, and struck out five. Two double plays helped bail him out of serious jams. Losing pitcher Tom Lovett gave up nine safeties and struck out five in absorbing the loss.

The teams left Kentucky at 2:50 the next morning in two private Pullman cars of the Louisville and Nashville line, both decorated with flags, bunting, and streamers, and pulled into the Jersey City Depot at 8:10 a.m. The Cyclones went immediately to the Grand Central Hotel in New York, but the Brooklyn contingent was met at the depot by a welcoming committee and escorted across the Brooklyn Bridge.

Former Louisville outfielder Pete Browning had a rather gloomy and self-serving prediction on the outcome of the Series, as reported in the Louisville *Courier-Journal*.

> They ain't no telling how these games will come out. All the Brooklyns might get killed in a wreck and then the Louisvilles will have to win; not that I mean that's the only way Pete's old club could win. You see when Pete was here he wasn't nobody, and he had to go away from Kentucky to get recognition from the people. Now Pete comes back here, and everybody calls him 'Mr. Browning' and tell him he's fine as silk . . . In 1882 and 1885 Pete was something here. But the papers pulled him down, and people called him 'Red Eye' and 'Distillery Pete' and hadn't no respect for him. But when he got with good people he got to be good people himself . . . In Cleveland, we all was the people and Al Johnson's the boy to have at the head of a club. Look at this [displaying a wad of money]; every one of them 'long greens' is a fiver or tenner, and it's as big around as my arm. That's what the Brotherhood did.

Browning, who had no love for the city of Louisville, had just spent the year with the Cleveland Infants, leading the Players' League with a .387 batting average. He would return to the Louisville club in 1892, but would spend only twenty-one games with the team before finishing out the season with Cincinnati. (Curiously, although he singled out his title years of 1882 and 1885 as his two best seasons, Browning hit a resounding .402 in 1887, his highest batting mark and the best year of his career.)

Wednesday, October 22, was an open date in the schedule and heavy rains prevented play the next two days. After lunch on October 25, the Bridegrooms met the Cyclones at the New York end of the Brooklyn Bridge and, led by Conterno's full band, the clubs proceeded by horse-drawn carriage to Washington Park for Game Five. The weather was bitter and a raw, cold wind swept through the park. The field, which according to the New York *Daily Tribune*, was "full of malaria, mud and water," required the spreading of several hundred pounds of sawdust and sand before it was playable. Before the contest, Brooklyn management hoisted the National League championship pennant, and after the flag-raising ceremonies, Conterno's band gave a concert which lasted until game time at 3:00. Because of the miserable weather, only a thousand fans were on hand. What they lacked in numbers, however, they more than made up for in enthusiasm.

The Bridegrooms were still hampered by the illness of George Pinckney, and added to their list of walking wounded was the name of center fielder Darby O'Brien, also under the weather. The starting pitchers were Tom Lovett and Ed Daily.

Daily got off to a poor start in the bottom of the first when he walked leadoff batter Hub Collins and one out later, served up a curveball which Oyster Burns lofted over the distant left-field fence for a two-run homer. Burns, the leading home run hitter for the Bridegrooms during the previous season with thirteen, doffed his pillbox-type hat to the hometown crowd several times while circling the bases.

Louisville cut the lead in half in the top of the second on John Ryan's sacrifice fly, but Brooklyn neutralized that run in the bottom of the inning. With two out, Irish-born Patsy Donovan beat out a slow roller to third. Tom Lovett lifted a pop fly to second baseman Tim Shinnick in short right field, but Shinnick dropped the ball and Donovan, on the move with two out, raced home ahead of the throw.

In the fourth, Donovan started another Brooklyn rally when he reached first on Jimmy Wolf's error and stole second. Catcher John Ryan's throw bounded into the outfield and Donovan continued on to third. Daily walked Hub Collins and picked him off, but first baseman Harry Taylor dropped the ball and, amid the confusion, Donovan trotted home. Dave Foutz followed with a triple and the Bridegrooms led, 5-1.

Louisville scored a single run in the fifth when pitcher Ed Daily's triple was followed with a sacrifice fly from Harry Taylor. Brooklyn closed out the scoring in the seventh with back-to-back RBI doubles from Adonis Terry and Tom Daly.

Tom Lovett got the 7-2 victory by holding the Cyclones to five hits—none over the last four innings. Ed Daily gave up only seven safeties in the loss, but three of the six men he walked eventually scored. The Bridegrooms now had a commanding three-games-to-one lead in the Series.

Sunday, October 26, was another off-day in the Series and attendance fell for the fifth straight game as only six hundred people turned out at Washington Park for the sixth and hardest-hitting contest. The wind was raw and cutting and the mercury was in the twenties. Players wore overcoats on the benches and it was so cold the New York *Herald* commented:

Managers Chapman and McGunnigle sat on the benches with the players until they resembled the ossified man, while the players blew on their fingers and kept out of the reach of hard grounders.

Brooklyn's Darby O'Brien and George Pinckney were back in the lineup and the Bridegrooms touched Scott Stratton for a two-out run in the first when Oyster Burns doubled and ambled home on Pinckney's triple. An RBI double by John Ryan tied the score in the second and Louisville rocked Lovett for two more runs in the third. Harry Raymond coaxed a base on balls, Farmer Weaver singled, and both men advanced a base on a passed ball. Ed Daily's base hit to right scored both men and gave the Cyclones a 3-1 lead. Louisville added a single run in the fourth and scored again in the sixth before the Bridegrooms broke out of their offensive doldrums in the bottom of the inning. With the bases loaded, Adonis Terry drew a base on balls from Stratton for the first run of the inning. Singles from Germany Smith and George Pinckney sent three more men home and tied the score in the four-run inning.

Louisville tallied two runs in the seventh and two more in the eighth to widen its lead to 9-5 with six outs to go. By now, Red Ehret had replaced the struggling Scott Stratton on the mound for the Cyclones. Brooklyn failed to score against Ehret in the seventh but raked the right-hander in the eighth. Singles by Dave Foutz, Germany Smith, and Patsy Donovan, coupled with a throwing error by Jimmy Wolf, brought home three runs and cut Louisville's lead to one. Ehret set the Bridegrooms down in order in the ninth and the Cyclones had their second victory of the Series.

Louisville's Ed Daily was fined twenty-five dollars in the game for "ungentlemanly talk" to umpire Curry, the first such penalty in a World Series game.

What proved to be the final game of 1890 was played the next day before the smallest crowd of the Series. The weather was worse than ever, and only three hundred fans turned out at Washington Park to watch Red Ehret and Tom Lovett pitch in Game Seven. Before the clubs took the field, managers McGunnigle and Chapman agreed to finish the championship the following spring, making this the last game of the Series.

George Pinckney was ill again and could not play, and Adonis Terry was sick enough that Bob Caruthers, bad ankle and all, was called upon to take his place in the outfield. Louisville's starting catcher Ned Bligh split a finger in the opening inning and was replaced by rookie Pete Weckbecker.

The Cyclones took a first-inning lead when Harry Taylor singled, went all the way to third on Harry Raymond's sacrifice bunt, and scored on Farmer Weaver's sacrifice fly to right. Brooklyn tied the score in the bottom of the inning when Oyster Burns singled and came home on Dave Foutz's double down the right-field line. After Germany Smith drew a base on balls, Tom Daly grounded to second baseman Tim Shinnick. Shinnick booted the ball, then picked it up and threw over first baseman Harry Taylor's head as Foutz trotted in with the lead run.

In the third, Louisville tied the score on a 495-foot RBI triple by Harry Raymond. Farmer Weaver walked and stole second, and both Weaver and Raymond came home on Jimmy Wolf's single over second base. The Cyclones added two insurance runs in the eighth to make the score 6-2. Harry Taylor started the inning with a double, moved to third on Harry Raymond's sacrifice and scored when the hobbled Bob Caruthers dropped Farmer Weaver's fly ball in left after a long run. Jimmy Wolf sacrificed Weaver to second from where he scored on Ed Daily's single to right.

Red Ehret pitched masterfully in earning his second victory of the Series, holding the Bridegrooms to four hits and striking out five. Lovett evened his record in the championship Series to 2-2.

Because of friction between the American Association and National League, the spring championship was never held. Thus, the last true World Series of the nineteenth century ended—not with a bang, but a whimper.

GAME ONE—October 17, 1890, at Eclipse Park, Louisville, Kentucky

BROOKLYN	AB	R	H	PO	A	E		LOUISVILLE	AB	R	H	PO	A	E
Collins, 2b	5	3	2	1	1	0		Taylor, 1b	4	0	0	8	0	1
O'Brien, cf	4	1	0	2	0	0		Raymond, 3b	4	0	0	0	2	2
Burns, lf-rf	4	1	2	1	0	0		Weaver, cf	3	0	1	0	0	0
Pinckney, 3b	4	1	1	1	3	0		Wolf, rf	3	0	0	0	1	0
Foutz, 1b-lf	4	0	1	2	0	0		Hamburg, lf	3	0	0	2	0	0
Terry, p	3	0	0	1	1	0		Shinnick, 2b	2	0	0	3	2	0
Daly, 1b-c	4	0	1	9	0	0		Tomney, ss	1	0	1	3	5	3
Smith, ss	4	1	1	4	4	0		Ryan, c	3	0	0	8	3	0
Clark, c	3	2	2	3	1	1		Stratton, p.	2	0	0	0	1	0
Lovett, rf	1	0	1	0	0	0			25	0	2	24	14	6
	36	9	11	24	10	1								

```
BKN   3 0 0   0 3 0   0 3 - 9
LOU   0 0 0   0 0 0   0 0 - 0
```

Earned runs: BKN 1. 2B: Burns. 3B: Pinckney, Clark. SH: O'Brien, Burns. SB: Shinnick 2, Tomney, Collins 2. BB: Stratton 1, Terry 3. Struck out: Terry 5, Stratton 2. PB: Clark 2, Ryan 1. WP: Stratton. Umpires: Wesley Curry and John McQuaid. Time—1:45. Att: 5,563.

GAME TWO—October 18, 1890, at Eclipse Park, Louisville Kentucky

BROOKLYN	AB	R	H	PO	A	E		LOUISVILLE	AB	R	H	PO	A	E
Collins, 2b	4	0	1	1	1	1		Taylor, 1b	4	2	1	12	1	1
O'Brien, cf	4	0	0	0	0	1		Raymond, 3b	4	0	0	0	2	2
Burns, lf	4	0	0	2	0	0		Weaver, cf	4	0	3	1	0	0
Pinckney, 3b	3	2	1	0	4	0		Wolf, rf	3	0	1	0	0	0
Foutz, 1b	4	1	1	14	0	1		Hamburg, lf	4	0	0	4	0	0
Terry, rf	3	1	0	0	0	0		Shinnick, 2b	3	0	0	3	3	1
Daly, c	4	1	0	8	0	0		Tomney, ss	3	1	0	2	6	1
Smith, ss	4	0	2	2	3	0		Ryan, c	4	0	1	4	0	0
Lovett, p	4	0	0	0	2	0		Daily, p	4	0	0	1	2	0
	34	5	5	27	10	3			33	3	6	27	14	5

```
BKN   0 2 0   2 0 1   0 0 0 - 5
LOU   1 0 1   0 0 0   0 0 1 - 3
```

Earned runs: Lou 1. 2B: Foutz. 3B: Smith. SB: Taylor, Weaver 2, Daly. SH: Raymond 2, Wolf, Shinnick, Daly, Smith. BB: Lovett 4, Daily 2. Struck out: Lovett 7, Daily 3. PB: Daly, Ryan 2. WP: Daily, Lovett. Umpires: Curry and McQuaid. Time—1:45. Att: 2,860.

GAME THREE—October 20, 1890, at Eclipse Park, Louisville, Kentucky

BROOKLYN	AB	R	H	PO	A	E	LOUISVILLE	AB	R	H	PO	A	E
Collins, 2b	5	1	3	0	1	0	Taylor, 1b	4	0	1	9	0	0
O'Brien, cf	5	2	1	4	0	0	Raymond, 3b-ss	4	0	0	2	4	0
Burns, lf	4	0	0	0	1	0	Weaver, cf	4	0	0	1	0	0
Pinckney, 3b	3	0	1	3	2	0	Wolf, rf-3b	3	2	2	2	2	1
Foutz, 1b	3	1	1	7	0	0	Hamburg, lf	4	2	2	3	0	0
Terry, p	4	1	0	0	0	0	Shinnick, 2b	4	2	2	4	2	1
Daly, c	4	0	1	8	0	0	Tomney, ss	1	0	0	1	1	0
Smith, ss	4	0	2	2	4	2	Daily, rf	2	0	1	1	1	1
Donovan, rf	4	2	1	0	0	0	Ryan, c	1	0	0	1	2	0
	36	7	10	24	8	2	Stratton, p	1	1	1	0	0	0
							Bligh, c	3	0	0	0	0	0
							Meakim, p	3	0	1	0	0	0
								34	7	10	24	12	3

```
BKN    0 2 0   1 3 0   1 0 - 7
LOU    0 0 1   1 0 2   0 3 - 7
```

Earned runs: BKN 3, LOU 3.   2B: Wolf, Shinnick 2, Daily, Stratton.   3B: Wolf, Hamburg, O'Brien, Smith.   SH: Raymond, Weaver, Hamburg, Daily, Bligh, Donovan. Struck out: Meakim 2, Terry 3.   BB: Meakim 2, Terry 2.   PB: Ryan 2, Bligh.   WP: Meakim, Terry.   Umpires: McQuaid and Curry.   Time—1:50.   Att: 1,253.

GAME FOUR—October 21, 1890, at Eclipse Park, Louisville, Kentucky

BROOKLYN	AB	R	H	PO	A	E	LOUISVILE	AB	R	H	PO	A	E
Collins, 2b	4	1	1	1	1	1	Taylor, 1b	4	1	2	10	0	0
O'Brien, cf	4	0	0	2	0	0	Raymond, ss	4	1	1	0	1	0
Burns, 3b	4	0	1	1	1	1	Weaver, cf	4	1	1	2	0	1
Foutz, 1b	4	1	1	2	0	0	Wolf, 3b	4	1	2	1	3	1
Terry, lf	2	1	0	8	1	0	Daily, rf	4	0	0	0	0	0
Smith, ss	4	1	1	1	4	0	Hamburg, lf	3	0	1	3	0	0
Donovan, rf	3	0	3	1	0	0	Shinnick, 2b	3	1	1	5	3	0
Lovett, p	3	0	0	0	1	0	Ryan, c	3	0	0	6	2	0
Bushong, c	3	0	0	8	0	0	Ehret, p	3	0	1	0	0	0
	31	4	7	24	8	2		32	5	9	27	9	2

```
BKN    0 3 1   0 0 0   0 0 0 - 4
LOU    3 0 1   0 0 0   1 0 x - 5
```

Earned runs: LOU 4, BKN 4.   2B: Weaver, Wolf.   3B: Shinnick.   SH: Raymond, Weaver, O'Brien, Ryan.   SB: Taylor.   DP: LOU 2.   BB: Ehret 2.   Struck out: Ehret 5, Lovett 5.   PB: Bushong.   Umpires: McQuaid and Curry.   Time—1:45.   Att: 1,050.

◆ ◆ ◆

GAME FIVE—October 25, 1890, at Washington Park, Brooklyn

LOUISVILLE	AB	R	H	PO	A	E	BROOKLYN	AB	R	H	PO	A	E
Taylor, 1b	4	0	0	14	1	0	Collins, 2b	5	2	1	1	3	0
Raymond, ss	4	0	1	2	7	0	Foutz, 1b	4	0	1	16	0	0
Weaver, cf	4	0	0	3	0	1	Bruns, 3b	4	2	1	1	4	0
Wolf, 3b	4	0	0	0	2	1	Terry, cf	4	1	1	4	0	0
Stratton, rf	4	1	1	0	0	0	Daly, c	4	0	2	2	0	0
Hamburg, lf	3	0	2	1	0	0	Smith, ss	4	0	0	2	6	0
Shinnick, 2b	3	0	0	0	1	0	Caruthers, lf	4	0	0	0	0	0
Ryan, c	3	0	0	3	0	1	Donovan, rf	4	2	1	1	0	0
Daily, p	3	1	1	1	2	0	Lovett, p	4	0	0	0	2	0
	32	2	5	24	13	3		37	7	7	27	15	0

```
LOU   0 1 0   0 1 0   0 0 0 – 2
BKN   2 1 0   3 0 0   1 0 x – 7
```

Earned runs: BKN 2, LOU 1.   2B: Terry, Daly 2, Raymond.   3B: Foutz, Daily.   HR: Burns.   BB: Daily 6, Lovett 1.   Struck out: Daily 3.   PB: Ryan.   Umpires: McQuaid and Curry.   Time—1.50.   Att: 1,000.

◆ ◆ ◆

GAME SIX—October 27, 1890, at Washington Park, Brooklyn

LOUISVILLE	AB	R	H	PO	A	E	BROOKLYN	AB	R	H	PO	A	E
Taylor, 1b	5	1	2	11	1	0	Collins, 2b	5	0	0	3	4	0
Raymond, ss	5	3	1	3	5	0	O'Brien, cf	5	0	2	3	0	0
Weaver, cf	5	1	2	1	2	0	Burns, lf	5	2	1	0	0	0
Wolf, 3b	5	1	3	2	3	1	Pinckney, 3b	5	1	2	1	2	0
Daily, rf	5	0	0	2	0	0	Foutz, 1b	5	2	2	12	0	1
Hamburg, lf	5	1	2	2	1	0	Terry, p	5	1	0	0	4	0
Shinnick, 2b	5	0	0	0	1	0	Smith, ss	5	1	2	4	10	1
Ryan, c	5	0	3	6	0	2	Donovan, rf	4	1	3	1	1	0
Stratton, p-rf	4	2	0	0	3	0	Bushong, c	3	0	0	2	1	0
Ehret, p	0	0	0	0	1	0	Daly, c	4	0	0	1	0	1
	44	9	13	27	17	3		46	8	12	27	22	3

```
LOU   0 1 2   1 0 1   2 2 0 – 9
BKN   1 0 0   0 0 4   0 3 0 – 8
```

Earned runs: LOU 4, BKN 4.   2B: Wolf, Hamburg, Burns, Donovan.   3B: Pinckney. BB: Stratton 3, Terry 4.   Struck out: Ehret 2.   Umpires: Curry and McQuaid. Time—1:50.   Att: 600.

GAME SEVEN—October 28, 1890, at Washington Park, Brooklyn

LOUISVILLE	AB	R	H	PO	A	E	BROOKLYN	AB	R	H	PO	A	E
Taylor, 1b	4	2	2	14	0	1	Collins, 2b	4	0	1	1	1	0
Raymond, ss	4	1	1	3	4	0	O'Brien, cf	4	0	0	0	0	0
Weaver, cf	4	2	0	3	1	0	Burns, 3b	4	1	1	2	6	0
Wolf, 3b	4	0	1	0	2	1	Foutz, 1b	4	1	2	19	0	0
Daily, rf	4	0	1	0	0	0	Smith, ss	4	0	0	1	6	0
Hamburg, lf	4	0	0	1	0	0	Daly, c	4	0	0	3	1	0
Shinnick, 2b	4	0	1	0	4	3	Donovan, rf	4	0	0	1	1	0
Bligh, c	0	0	0	0	0	1	Caruthers, lf	4	0	0	0	0	1
Weckbecker, c	4	0	0	6	0	0	Lovett, p	3	0	0	0	5	0
Ehret, p	4	1	2	0	1	0		35	2	4	27	20	1
	36	6	8	27	12	6							

```
LOU    1 0 3    0 0 0    0 2 0 – 6
BKN    2 0 0    0 0 0    0 0 0 – 2
```

Earned runs: LOU 1, BKN 1.   2B: Collins, Foutz, Taylor.   3B: Raymond, Ehret.   SB: Weaver 2, O'Brien, Foutz, Daly.   DP: LOU 2.   Struck out: Lovett 3, Ehret 5.   BB: Ehret 4, Lovett 1.   Umpires: McQuaid and Curry.   Time—1:30.   Att: 300.

· 9 ·

THE SPLIT SEASON
OF 1892

◆

I t was back to business in 1891.
Following the demise of the
Players' League, dozens of con-
trite ballplayers rejoined their
former clubs for the 1891 season. The disappointing Louisville
Colonels not only failed to repeat as pennant winners, but plummeted all the way to seventh place. They were replaced atop the
Association standings by the Boston Reds, who were fielding a team
in the Association for the first time. In the National League, experts
predicted New York would unseat the incumbent Brooklyn Bridegrooms, but injuries to key players Buck Ewing and Jack Glasscock
devastated the Giants, and the club finished a distant third. The
Bridegrooms' pitching staff slumped terribly; Brooklyn dropped off
to sixth place, while the Boston Beaneaters mounted a strong, late-
season comeback, edging the Chicago Colts for the title.

Boston Reds manager Art Irwin challenged Beaneaters manager Frank Selee to a post-season championship, but Selee declined
the offer. The chance for an all-Boston post-season confrontation
was lost, and for the first time since 1883—and in the last year of
the American Association—there was no World Series.

Over the winter of 1891, the American Association quietly
passed away.

1892

The Changing Game

- *Teams could substitute players at any point in a game, not just at the end of an inning.*

- *A ball hit over the fence was a ground-rule double if the distance from the plate to the fence was less than 235 feet.*

- *On June 7, New York's Jack Doyle became the first successful pinch-hitter in the history of the game.*

- *The National League absorbed the St. Louis Browns, Washington Senators, Baltimore Orioles, and Louisville Colonels.*

◆ ◆ ◆

National League owners, enjoying a monopoly on major league baseball for the first time since 1881, were poised to recoup some of their losses from the baseball wars of the past two seasons. They set about this task feverishly in 1892 by reducing club rosters from fifteen to thirteen players and slashing salaries by thirty to forty percent. Players refusing to take a cut in pay could be released outright, and it was an open secret that no owner would approach a released player.

To help stimulate fan interest, the magnates decided to split the 1892 season into two parts. The *Reach Guide* had this to say about the idea:

> To add to the novelty which a 12-club league might have, the season was divided into two championships, the first to end on

July 15 and the second to terminate late in October. At the same time the complement of championship games was increased from 140 games to 154. So the season began two weeks early and ended ten days later than 1891. The result was that the opening games were played in weather which was far from being inducive to enthusiasm and that fact threw a damper upon the year's sport from the beginning.

That the fans cared little for the split-season arrangement was beyond argument: League-wide, attendance was down by over three hundred thousand in the second half. (For the owners, at least, the split season was a popular, if short-lived, idea. In 1892, the experiment was also tried in the Eastern League, Southern League, Pacific Northwestern League, Pennsylvania State League, the Illinois and Iowa League, and the Wisconsin and Michigan League. The novelty was such a spectacular failure in the Western League that the organization disbanded shortly after the second half began.)

Led by a strong pitching staff, the Boston Beaneaters won eleven of their first thirteen games, played at a .700 clip for the first three months of the season, then clinched the first-half pennant by the end of June, with two weeks remaining in the first half. The Beaneaters took the title largely by drubbing the three first-half tailenders in nineteen of twenty-one games.

Halfway through the season, Boston management slashed salaries, released King Kelly and Harry Stovey, and when John Clarkson balked at having his salary cut, he, too, was given his release. Demoralized, the Beaneaters started slowly in the second half, only to find themselves accused by fans and management of "hippodroming" to force a playoff at the end of the season. The Cleveland Spiders played at a torrid pace through August, winning twenty-three while losing only five, and by the end of the month, held an 8½-game lead over Boston. Midway through the second half, the Beaneaters re-signed King Kelly and named the big Irishman team captain. Boston's fortunes improved immeasurably and the club won twenty-eight of its last thirty-seven contests to finish just three games behind Cleveland. Many National League owners were of the opinion that the pennant should summarily be awarded to Boston (neatly sidestepping the issue of hippodroming), but the Cleveland Spiders insisted on a playoff and a best-of-nine Series was agreed upon. The post-season playoffs would do little to allay charges of dishonesty when Boston, after playing to a scoreless tie in the first contest, went on to sweep the next five straight games.

Boston finished the season with a combined record of 102-48; Cleveland was 93-56. Despite the disparity in winning percentages, an argument could be mounted that, overall, the two clubs were equally matched, at least on paper. The only offensive area in which the Beaneaters truly outclassed their opponents was stolen bases, 338 to 225. The Beaneaters scored seven more runs than the Spiders, had seven more doubles, eight more home runs, four more shutouts, and thirty-seven more pitcher strikeouts, but that was where their superiority, if it could be called such, ended. The Spiders had forty-four more triples, a higher team batting (.254 to .250) and slugging average (.340 to .327), and a better fielding percentage (.935 to .929), with forty-seven fewer errors. Cleveland pitchers allowed thirty-six fewer runs, forty-seven fewer walks, and their team ERA was 0.45 run per game less than Boston.

The Beaneaters had three regulars who hit above .280—Tommy Tucker (.282), Herman Long (.286), and Hugh Duffy (.301).

The mellifluously named Tommy Tucker was one of the finest-fielding first basemen of the 1890s. Although he had never hit higher than .281 in the minors, Tucker would compile a lifetime .290 batting average in the major leagues and, in 1889, had led the American Association with a .372 mark. Never more than a free-swinging singles hitter, Tucker was an aggressive baserunner and, in the early years of his career, an excellent basestealer.

Herman Long was born in Chicago of German immigrants and was given the unavoidable nickname "Germany" by his teammates. Long had begun his professional career in 1887 and was sold to the Boston Beaneaters in 1890 for $6,500, a considerable sum for a light-hitting, erratic-fielding shortstop. A crafty baserunner, Long stole 534 bases in his career and earned himself a second nickname of "The Flying Dutchman," long before the time of Honus Wagner.

Hugh Duffy had broken into organized baseball with a .278 batting average while roaming the outfield for Hartford in the Eastern League in 1886. In 1887, playing for three minor league teams, Duffy had hit .412, earning himself a contract with the Chicago White Colts. Meeting the five-foot, seven-inch Duffy for the first time, Chicago manager Cap Anson asked, "Where's the rest of you?" "That's all there is," Duffy replied.

Duffy was never able to convince Anson that he was a ballplayer, despite hitting .302 in two seasons for the Colts and playing an aggressive game. (Early in his career, Duffy's combative nature earned him the nickname "Angel Child" for the same reason a fat man is called "Slim.") In 1890, Duffy jumped to the Chicago Pirates of the Players' League, and by 1892, he was with the Beaneaters. He would finish his career with a lifetime .328 batting average. Following his retirement, Duffy became the playing manager for the 1901 American League Milwaukee Brewers, managed the Milwaukee entry in the Western League in 1902 and 1903, then joined the Philadelphia Phillies, where he was player-manager from 1904 through 1906. From Philadelphia, he would become owner and manager of Providence in the Eastern League from 1907 through 1909; he managed the Chicago White Sox in 1910 and 1911, and Milwaukee of the American Association in 1912. He was president and manager of Portland in the New England League from 1913 through 1916, manager of Toronto in the International League in 1920, and manager of the Boston Red Sox in 1921 and 1922. He scouted for the Boston Red Sox from 1917 through 1919, resumed scouting in 1924, and continued in that position until his death in 1954 ended a baseball career which spanned sixty-nine years. As a manager, Duffy never had the horses to win anything at the major league level and never finished higher than fourth place. Nine years before his death, he was inducted into the Hall of Fame.

The Spiders had only one regular who hit .300, Cupid Childs (.317), but they also had future Hall of Famer Jesse Burkett.

Clarence Childs, nicknamed Cupid for his pudgy resemblance to the cherub, was a lifetime .313 hitter at the time of the 1892 World Series. He was coming off a season in which he had established lifetime highs in games played, at bats, hits, home runs, runs scored, and bases on balls. A solid-fielding second baseman with good range, Childs would bat leadoff during the Series and often proved to be the spark plug of the club.

Jesse Cail Burkett had made his organized baseball debut in 1888 and had shown absolutely no indication of the hitter he would become when he hit .226 for Scranton of the Central League. Burkett exhibited enough promise the next year at Worcester (.280) that the New York Giants brought him up and converted him from a second baseman-pitcher to a full-time outfielder. Burkett was sold to Cleveland in 1891 and farmed out to Lincoln until the Spiders recalled him in mid-August. He hit only .269 in forty-seven games for Cleveland, but the club liked what it saw and brought him back for 1892. Burkett wouldn't hit his stride as a batter until 1893, when he would reel off successive averages of .348, .358, .423, .410, .383, .345, .402, .363, and .382—his best years at the major league level. He was transferred to the St. Louis Cardinals in 1899, jumped to the American League St. Louis Browns in 1902, and was traded to the Boston Red Sox in 1905, his last year in the majors. Following his exile from the big leagues, Burkett went on to hit .325 in the high minors for the next eight seasons. In 1916, at the age of forty-six, he played for three teams in the Eastern League, hit .211 in twenty-four games, and managed the Lawrence and Hartford clubs.

Nicknamed "The Crab" for his less than genial personality and his fabled short temper, Burkett often waged war on umpires and opposing players. As he once noted, "Other players are bigger and huskier. I have to make up for the difference somehow." The only major leaguer other than Ty Cobb and Roger Hornsby to hit for a .400 average three times, Burkett was elected to the Hall of Fame in 1946.

Also on the Spiders' roster was Ed McKean, destined to be Cleveland's regular shortstop from 1887 to 1898—"regular" being a chronological indicator, not a presumption of talent. From all available evidence, McKean was a catastrophe at his position. In 1887, his rookie year in the majors, his ninety-nine errors had led all American Association shortstops. Inexplicably, his errors total plummeted to just thirty-six the following year, and from 1889 through 1891, he averaged only sixty errors a year, about normal for the time. Never possessed of much range at short, McKean's weight had ballooned twenty pounds by 1892, when he made ninety-three errors, and for the next four years, McKean made over a hundred fumbles a season. His work with the stick kept him in the major leagues. A good clutch hitter, McKean had ninety or more RBIs in eight of his twelve seasons with Cleveland.

A comparison of the ace pitchers on the two staffs shows Boston's Charles "Kid" Nichols (33-13, 3.52) and Cleveland's Cy Young (32-16, 3.36) to be evenly matched.

Charles Augustus "Kid" Nichols (so named for his boyish looks) was in his third full year as a major league pitcher, with a lifetime record of 92-52. After spending three years in the minor leagues, Nichols had been brought up by Boston in 1890, and in his rookie year, he won twenty-seven games and lost nineteen. It was the first of ten consecutive seasons in which Nichols would win twenty or more games, seven in which he would win thirty or more. Nichols is the youngest pitcher ever to win three hundred games, reaching the mark nine months and twenty-three days past his thirtieth birthday. He finished with 360 wins but might have won four hundred had he not taken two years out to become the player-manager for Kansas City of the Western Association in 1902-03. In his two years at Kansas City, Nichols won forty-eight games. A fastball pitcher with an amazing repertoire of changeups, Nichols would live to be inducted into the Hall of Fame in 1949, four years before his death.

Denton True Young was nicknamed "Cy," short for cyclone. While with Canton of the Tri-State League, the Ohio farm boy had attracted the attention of Davis Hawley, secretary-treasurer of the Cleveland Spiders, when he pitched a no-hitter against McKeesport on July 25, 1890. Young made his major league debut against the Chicago Colts twelve days later, pitched a three-hitter, and struck out the legendary Cap Anson twice. According to baseball lore, Anson offered Cleveland management a thousand dollars for the big right-hander following the game and when he was rebuffed, haughtily announced that Young was "no good, just another big farmer."

Young worked the first nine years of his career for Cleveland before he was transferred to the St. Louis Cardinals in 1899. Two years later, he jumped to the Boston club in the newly formed American League and, after eight years with Boston, returned to Cleveland in 1909. His last eleven games were spent with the National League Boston Braves. Beaten in his last start by rookie Grover Cleveland Alexander, Young retired following the 1911 season because he was no longer young enough or slim enough to field his position.

In his long and distinguished career, Cy Young pitched a perfect game, two no-hitters and, at age thirty-seven, a record twenty-three consecutive hitless innings. He led the league in shutouts seven times; in victories, four times; in complete games, three times; in winning percentage, earned run average, appearances, and innings pitched, twice; and in games started, once. He was the most remarkable control pitcher in the history of baseball, leading the league in least walks per innings pitched thirteen times in the years

1893 to 1906. On the all-time lists, Young is first in wins (511), losses (313), games started (815), complete games (751), and innings pitched (7,356). He is fourth in shutouts (76) and fifth in appearances (906). Young stepped on the mound more often than any other starting pitcher, but relievers Hoyt Wilhelm, Lindy McDaniel, Rollie Fingers, and Kent Tekulve now top the all-time list in most appearances. Wilhelm was the first to pass Young, fifty-seven years after Young's retirement. Young lived long enough to enjoy his induction into the Hall of Fame in 1937.

Once you got past Nichols and Young, the Beaneaters held a clear edge in pitching. Boston's two other top starters—Jack Stivetts (35-16) and Harry Staley (22-10)—had a combined 57-26 record, a vastly superior edge on any two of Cleveland's next best pitchers John Clarkson (17-10 with the Spiders), Nig Cuppy (28-13), and George Davies (10-16), who were a combined 55-39. (Davies, with a sore shoulder, would see no action in the Series.)

"Happy Jack" Stivetts (so nicknamed because of his genial disposition) was a strikeout pitcher with plenty of speed but little control. In 1892, his best year on the mound, Stivetts supplemented his 35-16 record with some excellent work at the plate—three home runs, thirty-six RBIs, and a batting average of .296. (With a lifetime .297 batting average, Stivetts was the best-hitting pitcher of his day.) In August 1892, playing left field, he had broken up a scoreless game with Brooklyn by slugging a twelfth-inning home run. Working the mound the next day, he no-hit the Dodgers, 11-0, and on the final day of the season, threw a five-inning no-hitter against Washington. Stivetts had a tendency to tire in the late innings, but still won twenty or more games five times and finished his career with a lifetime 207-131 record.

Cleveland's George "Nig" Cuppy was a rookie sensation in 1892, with a sparkling 2.51 earned run average and twenty-eight wins in forty-one decisions. In his first five seasons, Cuppy would compile a record of 120-66 (a winning percentage of .645) before overwork ruined his pitching arm.

Boston's pitching figured to win the day in the World Series.

◆ ◆ ◆

Cleveland, also known as the Forest City, was first surveyed in 1796 by Moses Cleaveland, for whom the city is named. Two centuries later, the city had many mining, shipping, and manufacturing concerns and in the Flats, miles of narrow streets and alleys lay under a film of smoke and cinders from the great ironworks located near League Park, the Spiders' new home and the site of the first three games of the 1892 World Series.

League Park had formally opened on May 1, 1891, when ten thousand spectators jammed every inch of the structure to watch Cy Young down Cincinnati 12-3. Owners of a nearby saloon and two homes had refused to sell their property, so the park was constructed around the buildings, resulting in some unusual dimensions. Center field was 460 feet from the plate and the left-field foul line was 375 feet, but the distance to the right-field stands was only 290 feet, a feature which would prove to be a boon for twentieth-century sluggers. A twenty-foot-high wooden fence in right field made League Park a sort of mirror image of today's Fenway Park. There was a covered pavilion that rose behind first base, a single deck of seats behind the plate, and a small bleacher section.

The park's site was chosen by club owner and streetcar magnate Frank D. Robison, whose streetcar line dropped passengers off a few feet from the main entrance. League Park would be demolished by the city of Cleveland in 1951 and is today the site of a playground.

National League President Nick Young appointed Bob Emslie, Charles Snyder, John Gaffney, and John McQuaid to umpire the Series. Emslie and Snyder umpired the first and third games, while John Gaffney and John McQuaid umpired the second, fourth, and last games.

Cleveland team captain and manager Oliver Wendell "Patsy" Tebeau, employing a bit of reverse psychology, said before Game One, "We are not claiming to be equal to the big task of beating the Bostons, but we will do our best."

The Series opened at 3:00 on October 17 with one of the most exciting championship games ever played. Through the years, the legend has persisted that the starting pitchers for Game One were Cy Young and Kid Nichols, but Nichols didn't make his first appearance until the fourth game of the Series. Boston's starting pitcher for the first contest was Jack Stivetts.

There were six thousand fans in the stands, and hundreds more stood behind ropes stretched around the playing field, eagerly awaiting Stivetts's first pitch and Cleveland's first at bats. Cupid Childs stepped to the plate for the Spiders and rose to the occasion by coaxing a base on balls, delighting the crowd. Childs streaked for second a moment later as Jesse Burkett squared around to bunt. But the ball tipped off the top of Burkett's bat, straight into Stivetts's waiting hands, and Childs was doubled off first. George Davis followed with a fly ball to left and the Beaneaters took their places on the players' bench.

Cy Young always believed he had only a finite number of pitches in his arm and so took only a few warmup tosses before facing Boston in the bottom of the inning. Herman Long was the first to face the rawboned pitcher and he lined a pitch cleanly into left for a single. Tommy McCarthy, the former St. Louis Browns star, was jammed with a fastball and lifted a harmless pop foul for catcher Chief Zimmer for the first out of the inning. As Young worked to the next batter, Hugh Duffy, Zimmer, from his squatting position, made a snap throw to first. Jacob Virtue tagged a surprised Herman Long for the second out. Duffy followed with a single to right, but Zimmer threw him out stealing, collecting his third chance of the inning.

In the fourth, Duffy reached base on an error, stole second, and made third when Zimmer's throw went into center field, but King Kelly struck out to end the threat. Boston's Bobby Lowe reached third with two out in the fifth, but was stranded when Joe Quinn grounded out. Both clubs had two-out singles in the sixth but neither scored, and each side went down in order in the seventh and eighth.

The Spiders muffed an opportunity to win the game in the ninth inning. Jesse Burkett's bunt went for an infield single and he took second on George Davis's infield hit. When Ed McKean forced Davis, Burkett never even slowed down rounding third. But second sacker Joe Quinn launched a strong throw to the plate and Kelly put a hard tag on Burkett to complete the double play.

In the bottom of the inning, Kelly put on a grand display of poor sportsmanship when teammate Jack Stivetts, first man up for the Beaneaters, lifted a high pop fly above the plate. As Chief Zimmer circled under the ball, Kelly shouted from the bench for first baseman Jacob Virtue to make the catch. Confused, the two fielders collided and went down. Zimmer held the ball but the Cleveland bench emptied and manager Patsy Tebeau demanded that Kelly, King or not, be ejected. Kelly received a ten-dollar fine, but was allowed to remain in the game.

Neither team mounted a threat over the next two innings, and at the conclusion of the eleventh, umpire Bob Emslie ended the game because it was too dark to continue. Cy Young finished with a five-hitter, struck out six, and walked none. Stivetts surrendered four hits, struck out seven, and walked four. Although the hometown team had failed to win, everyone leaving the park agreed they had witnessed a history-making game.

Game Two was played the next day with over seven thousand fans taking advantage of perfect fall weather to watch a contest which, if not quite as well played as the first, was equally exciting. Starting pitchers were Cleveland's John Clarkson and Boston's Harry Staley.

The Beaneaters jumped off to a first-inning lead. Leadoff batter Herman Long lined a single into center field, inches in front of Jimmy McAleer, and went to third on Tommy McCarthy's hit. With King Kelly at the plate, McCarthy broke for second base. Kelly knocked the ball from Zimmer's hand as he started to throw, and McCarthy, glancing over his shoulder, trotted into second standing up. Cleveland captain Patsy Tebeau raised a terrible fuss and umpire McQuaid called Kelly out for interference. Hugh Duffy launched one of Clarkson's next deliveries into deep center field and McAleer, at the sound of the crack of the bat, turned his back on the diamond and raced to the wall. Turning just in time, he pulled down the long drive, preventing an inside-the-park home run and three scores. Long trotted home on the sacrifice fly.

The Beaneaters increased their lead to 2-0 in the third when Long reached on an error and scored on Duffy's triple. The Spiders tallied their first run of the Series in the bottom of the inning when, with the bases loaded, Jesse Burkett lined a sacrifice fly to deep left field. In the fourth, Jimmy McAleer's RBI double plated Ed McKean and tied the score at two-all.

With one out in the fifth, Boston took a 3-2 lead as Tommy McCarthy reached base on Patsy Tebeau's boot and came around on Hugh Duffy's double. The Beaneaters regained their two-run lead in the eighth when Duffy tripled and walked home on Billy Nash's single.

The score remained 4-2 as Harry Staley worked to the Spiders in the bottom of the ninth. Leadoff batter Jacob Virtue began the inning with a tremendous drive to the deepest part of center field, some 450 feet from the plate. But Virtue's blast fell ten feet short as Hugh Duffy raced to the wall and made a dazzling over-the-shoulder catch to save the run. Jimmy McAleer gave Duffy a much easier chance with a soft pop fly, but Duffy muffed the chance and McAleer, running hard, pushed his luck and tried to make second. Duffy nailed him with a strong throw to Joe Quinn. Manager Patsy Tebeau argued the call with Gaffney but then, as now, the umpire's decision was final and Cleveland was within one out of suffering its first loss of the Series. (In a creative bit of second-guessing, the Cleveland *Leader* commented the next day that had "McAleer stayed on first . . . the game would have been tied, but base ball is like the stream that flows through the mill sluice. The stones never grind with the water that is past.")

Jack O'Connor was the last hope for the Spiders and he came through in the clutch with a clean single to center. As Chief Zimmer came to the plate, excited fans peppered him with shouted offers of five, fifteen, twenty, and fifty dollars to hit a home run. Zimmer was a dangerous right-handed hitter with excellent bat control and, with the short right-field fence beckoning, Staley knew better than to throw him anything on the outside corner. Jammed with a pitch, Zimmer nonetheless met the ball squarely and lined a triple over the head of Bobby Lowe in left. O'Connor scored and, suddenly, the Spiders had the tying run on third. Pitcher John Clarkson was the next batter and when he lined a pitch off Staley's glove, the cheers of seven thousand Cleveland fans were deafening. But it was a short-lived euphoria as the ball caromed straight into the hands of shortstop Herman Long, who threw Clarkson out with room to spare, preserving the 4-3 Boston victory. The *Cleveland News* attributed the loss to "hard luck and Angel Child Hugh Duffy." Duffy, who drove in the first three Boston runs and scored the fourth, was the undisputed offensive star of the game.

The starting pitchers for Game One, Stivetts and Young, were rematched on October 19 for the third and final contest of the 1892 season at League Park. While the Spiders were taking fielding practice, a group of gamblers approached the Boston bench, hoping to obtain some inside information on which way to bet. Coldly rebuffed by the players, the gamblers were left to their own devices.

Cleveland took its first lead of the Series in the top of the first. Leadoff batter Cupid Childs started the uprising with a single and went to third when Jesse Burkett lined a double down the left-field line, fair by inches. Ed McKean's single scored both runners and put the Spiders up, 2-0.

In the bottom of the inning, Cy Young surrendered his first run of the Series when Tommy McCarthy reached on a fielder's choice, stole second, and came home on Charlie Ganzel's RBI single. The Beaneaters tied the score in the second. Bobby Lowe singled, was bunted to second by Tommy Tucker, and the next batter, Joe Quinn, rocketed a Young fastball into left. When Jesse Burkett misjudged the liner, it fell in for an RBI double.

Neither team mounted any kind of scoring threat over the next four innings but the Beaneaters took the lead in the seventh. Good-hitting pitcher Jack Stivetts laced a Cy Young fastball over Burkett's head in left field. The ball rolled to the wall for a one-out double. Herman Long popped out to second and it looked as though Young might escape the inning unharmed, but he got behind in the count to Tommy McCarthy and had to lay a fastball over the plate. McCarthy met the pitch squarely and drove the ball into center to put the Beaneaters up, 3-2.

The Spiders had a chance to tie the game in the ninth when leadoff batter Jimmy McAleer singled and was sacrificed to second by Jack O'Connor. On Chief Zimmer's shallow fly ball to right, McAleer daringly advanced to third. Cy Young (lifetime batting average: .156) was due to bat, but Cleveland manager Patsy Tebeau sent pinch-hitter George Davis to the plate instead. Tebeau's failure to pinch-hit for John Clarkson (a lifetime .220 hitter) in Game Two may have cost the Spiders the game and he was determined not to make the same mistake twice. Davis had been sidelined in the Series with a lame tendon and he took Stivetts's first pitch for a called strike as the crowd groaned in disbelief. Stivetts's second delivery was wide of the plate for ball one and the fans cheered optimistically. The next offering was a sharp-breaking curveball and Davis swung so hard he splintered his bat, grounding weakly to Tommy Tucker at first. Tucker carefully squeezed the ball, trotted to the bag, and Boston had a two-games-to-none advantage in the Series. (Davis's turn at bat was historic because he was the first batter to pinch hit in a World Series. Pinch-hitters were still a rarity, even during the regular season.)

After his shaky start, Stivetts had surrendered only four hits, shutting out the Spiders the rest of the way for his first victory of the Series.

The *Cleveland News*, still lamenting the Spiders' run of hard luck, said:

> Even the bats were against the Cleveland team in yesterday's game with Boston. This may seem like a strange statement to make, but

it is the fact in the case. In the ninth inning of the third game of the series for the world's championship it came to an angle where the victory depended on the wood in George Davis' bat. The wood was poor and Cleveland lost the game.

The baseball season had ended for the city of Cleveland with two straight losses to the champion Beaneaters. The clubs left late that evening on two special Pullman cars and arrived in Boston at 3:40 on October 20, an off-day.

Boston. According to Oliver Wendell Holmes and most Bostonians (if no one else), The Hub Of The Universe. Located on an inlet of Massachusetts Bay at the mouth of the Charles River, Boston was the leading seaport and undisputed capital of New England, having achieved international status in finance, education, and medicine. To the south, running eastward, the harbor enclosed the city; to the north was the Charles, with a large inner basin known as the Back Bay. The North End was a land of poverty, the West End was politically corrupt. The South End was a melting pot for immigrants. Boston could boast the luxury of Beacon Street, the elegant shopping district on Winter Street, and one of the finest symphony orchestras in the world. Narrow streets were rich in history with the Paul Revere House, the Old North Church, Faneuil Hall, the Old State House, and the Boston Common, set aside as public grounds in 1634. With a population of well over half a million—many of them rabid baseball fans—the city was also the site of South End Grounds, the home field of the Boston Beaneaters.

South End Grounds, located on Walpole Street adjacent to the Boston and Providence Railroad tracks, was one of the more unusually shaped rectangular parks of the nineteenth century. The foul lines in left and right field were, respectively, 250 and 255 feet from the plate. The power alley in left-center field (445) was, incongruously, five feet farther from the plate than the power alley in right-center and the deepest part of center field. Topped with flags of all nations, the South End Grounds Grand Pavilion was the only double-decked grandstand in Boston and the highest of its day. Twin spires rose majestically above the stands behind home plate and the bleachers extended down both foul lines.

Boston was Mike Kelly's stomping grounds and its fans were among his favorites, as shown in this tribute from his autobiography, *Play Ball!*:

> I always received the very best treatment at the South End Grounds in Boston. This is saying a great deal considering the fact that I was a member of a visiting club and had the reputation of being a tricky man on the field. How a Boston audience would shout and roar, with mingled feelings of anger and joy, when I would cut the third bag on my way home. It almost reminded me of hundreds of insane people on the loose.

The weather was cold and raw when the Series resumed on October 21. Boston's Kid Nichols and Cleveland's Nig Cuppy made their first starts in a game which had to be stopped several times because smoke from nearby factories blew across the field, obscuring the players' vision and stinging everyone's eyes. Nichols walked the first man he faced, Cupid Childs, and the crowd booed umpire John Gaffney, who was calling balls and strikes. The umpiring crew got into more hot water in the second. Cleveland's Jimmy McAleer led off the inning with a ringing single, then broke for second on Nichols's second pitch to Jack O'Connor. McAleer appeared to slide in under Quinn and in the eyes of most spectators, had his hand on the base when umpire John McQuaid called him out. Even the Boston fans felt this was unfair. From the grandstands could be heard the chant of "Robber! Robber!"

Nig Cuppy retired the first two Boston batters in the third, then lost his control momentarily and issued a base on balls to Tommy McCarthy. Hugh Duffy was the next batter and when Cuppy made a fastball a little too good, Duffy dinked it over the short right-field fence for a 2-0 Boston lead. In the sixth, the Beaneaters struck again. Billy Nash reached on an error, stole second, and went to third on Bobby Lowe's hit. After Lowe stole second, Joe Quinn laced a single into center to put Boson ahead, 4-0.

The Spiders failed to mount a serious scoring threat until the seventh inning when, with one out, Ed McKean stroked a hit to left. Jimmy McAleer's line drive fell into right field and McKean sprinted around second as Tommy McCarthy unloaded a strong throw to third baseman Billy Nash. Nash gloved the ball but McKean upended him at the bag. Umpire McQuaid cried, "Out!"

even though Nash had tagged McKean with his bare hand and not the ball.

Kid Nichols, who already had three more runs than he needed, finished with a seven-hit shutout, struck out eight, and walked only Childs. Hugh Duffy was a perfect 3-for-3 in the game and now had a .563 batting average, with nine hits in sixteen at bats, including two game-winning hits. His slugging average was a neat 1.063.

In general, neither team was altogether happy with the umpiring crew of Gaffney and McQuaid. The Cleveland *Leader*, which up to this time had merely hinted at the umpires' mediocrity, said

> It doesn't do any good to cry over spilled milk, and it is enough to tire one's brain to constantly expostulate hard luck, but if the Cleveland club isn't getting the ragged end of the meanest work ever done against a base ball club it is no fault of the brilliant— more or less—galaxy of umpires that [National League] President Young has ever afflicted the public with. There were three close decisions in to-day's game. In each of them Cleveland had a chance to score. Every single decision was rendered against the visiting team. Cleveland has not had the benefit of a play since the series began . . . Umpire Gaffney umpired behind the bat and his decisions on balls and strikes were about the worst that ever were seen on any ball field . . . On the bases, McQuaid was just as bad, or a little more so, and it must have caused a thrill of pride in President Young's breast as he watched his appointees at work.

The *Cleveland News* agreed wholeheartedly, but in fewer words:

> . . . for the sake of honesty and justice, McQuaid was the man to blame today, so to describe his work in a few words, it is but necessary to say that it was vile.

The sports correspondent for the Cleveland *World*, Mr. Bates, allowed as how the game was "chiefly distinguished by rotten umpiring."

Of course, it all depends on whose ox is being gored. The only comment the Boston *Herald* had to offer on the umpiring was to say, "Umpires Gaffney and McQuaide [sic] officiated most satisfactorily." (In fairness, the *Herald* reporter may have had his mind on other things during the game, having noticed a gentleman in "the right field bleachers who wore two overcoats [and] had a very long head.")

Through the first four games, Cleveland had been shut out twice and its offense amounted to an anemic five runs. Cy Young was scheduled to start the fifth game for the Spiders but complained of soreness in his arm, so John Clarkson, who had, including the regular season, now lost four straight decisions to the Beaneaters, was substituted. His opposition was Jack Stivetts.

The Spiders broke out of their offensive slump in convincing fashion as they pummelled Stivetts in a wild second inning. After McAleer and O'Connor had been retired, Chief Zimmer doubled to right. Patsy Tebeau hit an easy grounder to Herman Long which should have retired the side, but Long fumbled the ball. The right-handed hitting Clarkson followed with an opposite-field three-run homer to give the Spiders a 3-0 lead. Childs singled and Burkett gave Long another opportunity to retire the side, but the little shortstop booted his second chance of the inning. After Stivetts issued a base on balls to Jacob Virtue, Ed McKean lined a long single off the top board of the right-field fence for two more runs. Virtue and McKean then worked the double steal successfully and Cleveland had a seemingly insurmountable 6-0 lead. To all outward appearance, Clarkson had finally overcome his Boston jinx.

Through the first three innings, the Beaneaters had no hits at all off Clarkson, but the famine ended in the fourth when Tommy McCarthy opened the frame with a single. Hugh Duffy sacrificed and McCarthy wisely held up at third on Charlie Ganzel's single to right. Jack O'Connor's throw to the plate was strong and accurate and McCarthy would have been out easily. Billy Nash followed with a double to plate the first two Boston runs and after Bobby Lowe walked, Tommy Tucker singled, driving in Nash with the final run of the inning.

After Cleveland scored a single tally in the top of the fifth, Boston struck again. Herman Long reached on an error and scored on McCarthy's double. After Duffy sacrificed, Billy Nash's long fly ball put the Beaneaters within two runs of a tie. The Spiders and Clarkson were fading fast.

The Beaneaters turned the game into a rout in the sixth. With one out, Joe Quinn lined a Clarkson fastball into left for a hit and trotted home on Jack Stivetts's triple. Herman Long redeemed himself for his sloppy defensive play earlier in the game with an RBI single, tying the score. The partisan crowd was wild with delight. Tommy McCarthy was the next batter and grounded slowly to Tebeau at third. Tebeau hurried his throw and the ball sailed past first baseman Jacob Virtue. Virtue scrambled after the ball and threw Long out at the plate while McCarthy steamed into third. Before Hugh Duffy stepped to the plate, he looked into the stands, searching for his girlfriend, Dolly McVey. He found her and the two exchanged the "sweetest smiles." Thus refreshed, Duffy took up his bat and slammed an RBI double, bringing home what proved to be the winning run. The unthinkable had happened: Boston led, 8-7. When Charlie Ganzel popped a soft liner into center, Duffy scored and the Beaneaters moved ahead by a 9-7 margin.

Cleveland failed to score in the seventh, and Clarkson dispiritedly took the mound in the bottom of the inning. Just lobbing the ball over the plate, Clarkson sent in a slow pitch to leadoff batter Tommy Tucker. Tucker's eyes grew wide at the fat delivery and he belted it over the right-field fence for a home run. Singles by Joe Quinn and Jack Stivetts, a sacrifice bunt, and a muffed fly ball by center fielder Jimmy McAleer brought in two more insurance runs and put the game out of Cleveland's reach.

The Cleveland *Leader,* by now completely disgusted, said the way the Spiders were playing "would be a disgrace to an organization of knock-kneed and pigeontoed school boys." Cy Young was asked if he had anything to say, and he vowed to win the next game or spend the winter "splitting rails by the hundred."

Sunday, October 23, was an open date, and what proved to be the Series finale was played the next day. Cold weather and a sense of the inevitable kept the crowd down to only 1,812. Boston, going for the sweep, had Kid Nichols on the mound. The Cleveland club was trying to salvage what little dignity it could from the Series with sore-armed Cy Young. The Spiders were beaten before they even took the field, but they made a game of it in the early going.

Cy Young himself started the last Cleveland rally of the Series in the third when he lined a leadoff single and went to third on Cupid Child's base hit. When right fielder Tommy McCarthy fumbled the ball, Young came in to score. Jesse Burkett singled Childs to third, stole second, and Ed McKean plated both baserunners with a single to center. The Spiders led, 3-0.

Boston then set about winning the game with a determination matched only by Cleveland's haplessness. The sore-armed Young no longer had anything on the ball, and in the bottom of the third gave up a single to his Cleveland counterpart, Kid Nichols, then moved Nichols along to second and third on consecutive wild pitches. After Herman Long popped out, Tommy McCarthy drew a walk. Young picked McCarthy off and first baseman Jacob Virtue began chasing him toward second. Nichols, watching the rundown closely, edged down the line toward home. Virtue planted his feet and threw the ball across the diamond to third baseman Patsy Tebeau. Nichols stopped short, began scrambling back to the bag, then watched in delight as the ball sailed high over Tebeau's head. He scored easily and McCarthy went all the way to third. Hugh Duffy's double pulled the Beaneaters within one.

There were two out in the fourth when Kid Nichols came to the plate with two runners in scoring position and a chance to put Boston ahead. With a line single between center fielder Jimmy McAleer and right fielder Jack O'Connor, Nichols gave the Beaneaters their first lead of the game, 4-3. By now, Young was pitching from memory. Bobby Lowe's RBI grounder plated another run in the fifth and a solo homer by Charlie Bennett put the Beaneaters ahead, 6-3, after six. Joe Quinn's seventh-inning RBI triple made the score 7-3 in the seventh and the Beaneaters closed out the scoring with an unearned run in the eighth. The Spiders went out in order in the ninth and at 4:30 on the afternoon of October 24, the 1892 World Series officially came to an end.

Visiting the Boston clubhouse, National League president Neal Young said that, though he would have enjoyed seeing Cleveland win a game or two, the Series had definitely been worth the trip, just to watch the Beaneaters play such a grand game. Boston manager Frank Selee, usually a taciturn, colorless man, graciously told reporters that no club had battled the Beaneaters as hard as the Spiders and that his club played just well enough to win. Cleveland president Frank Robison took the sweep good-naturedly, telling the Boston players, "Never mind, boys, we'll go at you harder in 1893."

Boston president Soden presented his championship club with one thousand dollars to be divided thirteen ways. This left each member with the princely sum of $76.92 for his club's victory over Cleveland. Looked at another way—dividing the $76.92 by six games—the resulting figure of $12.82 was about as much as a Boston regular would have earned per game during the regular season.

With a .462 batting average and nine runs batted in, Boston's Hugh Duffy was the batting star of the Series. Kid Nichols and Jack Stivetts won two games apiece, and Harry Staley won his only start. Ed McKean led all Cleveland hitters with a .440 mark and six RBIs, while Cupid Childs hit .409.

The Boston *Journal* taunted the Spiders by saying, "They're all right in a minor league, but when they make pretensions of capturing the gay bit of bunting which signifies champions of the world, from the champion Bostons, they overstepped the mark."

The Cleveland *Leader* summed up the Spiders' performance more succinctly: "They came, they saw, they got licked."

Cy Young, presumably, spent the off-season "splitting rails by the hundreds."

GAME ONE—October 17, 1892, at League Park, Cleveland

BOSTON	AB	R	H	BI	E	CLEVELAND	AB	R	H	BI	E
Long, ss	4	0	1	0	0	Childs, 2b	3	0	0	0	1
McCarthy, rf	4	0	1	0	0	Burkett, lf	4	0	2	0	0
Duffy, cf	4	0	2	0	0	Davis, 3b	4	0	1	0	0
Kelly, c	4	0	0	0	0	McKean, ss	3	0	1	0	0
Nash, 3b	4	0	1	0	0	Virtue, 1b	4	0	0	0	0
Lowe, lf	4	0	0	0	0	McAleer, cf	3	0	0	0	0
Tucker, 1b	4	0	0	0	0	O'Connor, rf	4	0	0	0	0
Quinn, 2b	4	0	1	0	0	Zimmer, c	4	0	0	0	1
Stivetts, p	4	0	0	0	0	Young, p	4	0	0	0	0
	36	0	6	0	0		33	0	4	0	2

```
CLE   0 0 0   0 0 0   0 0   0   0 0 – 0
BOS   0 0 0   0 0 0   0 0   0   0 0 – 0
```

SB: Duffy, McAleer.   SAC: Virtue.   DP: BOS 2.   LOB: BOS 3, CLE 4.   PB: Zimmer. BB: Stivetts 4, Young 0.   Struck out: Stivetts 7, Young 6.   Umpires: Emslie and Snyder. Time—2:00.   Att: 6,000.

GAME TWO—October 18, 1892, at League Park, Cleveland

BOSTON	AB	R	H	BI	E	CLEVELAND	AB	R	H	BI	E
Long, ss	5	2	1	0	0	Childs, 2b	3	0	0	0	0
McCarthy, rf	5	1	2	0	0	Burkett, lf	4	0	1	1	0
Duffy, cf	5	1	3	3	1	Davis, 3b	1	0	0	0	0
Kelly, c*	4	0	0	0	0	Tebeau, 3b	3	0	0	0	1
Nash, 3b	4	0	1	1	0	McKean, ss	4	1	2	0	0
Lowe, lf	4	0	1	0	0	Virtue, 1b	4	0	1	0	1
Tucker, 1b	4	0	2	0	0	McAleer, cf	4	0	1	1	0
Quinn, 2b	3	0	0	0	0	O'Connor, rf	4	1	1	0	0
Staley, p	4	0	0	0	0	Zimmer, c	4	1	3	1	0
	38	4	10	4	1	Clarkson, p	4	0	1	0	0
							35	3	10	3	2

* Kelly called out for interference

```
BOS   1 0 1   0 1 0   0 1 0 – 4
CLE   0 0 1   1 0 0   0 0 1 – 3
```

D: Duffy, McAleer, Zimmer.   T: Duffy 2, Zimmer.   SB: Kelly.   SAC: McCarthy, Virtue. SF: Duffy, Burkett.   LOB: CLE 6, BOS 8.   DP: BOS.   BB: Clarkson 1, Staley 1. Struck out: Clarkson 4.   Umpires: Gaffney and McQuaid.   Time—1:35.   Att: 7,000.

GAME THREE—October 19, 1892, at League Park, Cleveland

BOSTON	AB	R	H	BI	E	CLEVELAND	AB	R	H	BI	E
Long, ss	4	0	1	0	1	Childs, 2b	3	1	1	0	0
McCarthy, rf	4	1	2	1	0	Burkett, lf	4	1	2	0	0
Duffy, cf	4	0	1	0	0	Tebeau, 3b	4	0	0	0	0
Ganzel, c	4	0	2	1	0	McKean, ss	4	0	2	2	0
Nash, 3b	4	0	0	0	1	Virtue, 1b	4	0	1	0	0
Lowe, lf	4	1	1	0	0	McAleer, cf	4	0	1	0	0
Tucker, 1b	3	0	0	0	1	O'Connor, rf	4	0	1	0	0
Quinn, 2b	3	0	1	1	0	Zimmer, c	4	0	0	0	0
Stivetts, p	3	1	1	0	0	Young, p	3	0	0	0	0
	33	3	9	3	3	Davis, ph*	1	0	0	0	0
							35	2	8	2	0

* pinch hit for Young in the ninth.

```
CLE   2 0 0   0 0 0   0 0 0 – 2
BOS   1 1 0   0 0 0   1 0 x – 3
```

D: Stivetts, Burkett, Quinn.   SB: McCarthy.   SAC: Tucker, O'Connor.   LOB: CLE 7, BOS 6.   BB: Stivetts 1.   Struck out: Stivetts 6.   Umpires: Snyder and Emslie. Time—1:30.   Att: 7,500.

GAME FOUR—October 21, 1892, at South End Grounds, Boston

CLEVELAND	AB	R	H	BI	E	BOSTON	AB	R	H	BI	E
Childs, 2b	3	0	2	0	0	Long, ss	4	0	1	0	0
Burkett, cf	4	0	1	0	0	McCarthy, rf	1	1	0	0	0
Virtue, 1b	4	0	0	0	0	Duffy, cf	3	1	3	2	0
McKean, ss	4	0	2	0	1	Nash, 3b	4	1	0	0	0
McAleer, lf	4	0	2	0	0	Lowe, lf	3	1	1	0	0
O'Connor, rf	3	0	0	0	0	Tucker, 1b	3	0	0	0	0
Zimmer, c	3	0	0	0	0	Quinn, 2b	2	0	1	2	0
Tebeau, 3b	3	0	0	0	1	Bennett, c	3	0	0	0	0
Cuppy, p	3	0	0	0	0	Nichols, p	3	0	0	0	0
	31	0	7	0	2		26	4	6	4	0

```
CLE   0 0 0   0 0 0   0 0 0 – 0
BOS   0 0 2   0 0 2   0 0 x – 4
```

T: Childs. HR: Duffy. SB: Nash, Lowe, Duffy. SAC: Tucker, Quinn. DP: CLE. BB: Cuppy 4, Nichols 1. Struck out: Nichols 8, Cuppy 1. Umpires: McQuaid and Gaffney. Time—1:40. Att: 6,546.

GAME FIVE—October 21, 1892, at South End Grounds, Boston

CLEVELAND	AB	R	H	BI	E	BOSTON	AB	R	H	BI	E
Childs, 2b	5	1	4	0	0	Long, ss	5	1	1	1	2
Burkett, lf	5	1	0	0	0	McCarthy, rf	4	3	2	1	1
Virtue, 1b	3	1	0	0	0	Duffy, cf	5	1	1	2	0
McKean, ss	5	1	2	2	1	Ganzel, c	4	1	2	1	0
McAleer, cf	4	0	0	0	1	Nash, 3b	4	1	1	3	0
O'Connor, rf	4	0	0	0	0	Lowe, lf	4	0	0	0	1
Zimmer, c	4	1	2	1	0	Tucker, 1b	5	1	3	2	0
Tebeau, 3b	4	1	0	0	2	Quinn, 2b	5	2	2	0	0
Clarkson, p	4	1	1	3	0	Stivetts, p	5	2	2	1	0
	38	7	9	6	4		41	12	14	11	4

```
CLE   0 6 0   0 1 0   0 0 0 –  7
BOS   0 0 0   3 2 4   3 0 x – 12
```

Earned runs: BOS 6, CLE 1. 2B: McCarthy, Duffy, Nash. 3B: Stivetts, Childs. HR: Tucker, Clarkson. SH: Long, McCarthy, Duffy 2, Ganzel, Quinn 2, McAleer 1. SB: Burkett 2, Virtue, Tebeau. BB: Clarkson 4, Stivetts 2. Struck out: Clarkson 2, Stivetts 5. WP: Clarkson. PB: Zimmer. Umpires: Snyder and Emslie. Time—1:50. Att: 3,376.

◆ ◆ ◆

GAME SIX—October 24, 1892, at South End Grounds, Boston

CLEVELAND	AB	R	H	BI	E	BOSTON	AB	R	H	BI	E
Childs, 2b	5	1	2	0	0	Long, ss	5	1	1	0	1
Burkett, lf	4	1	2	0	0	McCarthy, rf	3	2	1	0	1
Virtue, 1b	5	0	1	0	0	Duffy, cf	5	0	2	1	0
McKean, ss	5	0	2	2	2	Nash, 3b	4	1	1	0	0
McAleer, cf	3	0	0	0	0	Lowe, lf	4	0	0	1	1
O'Connor, rf	3	0	1	0	0	Tucker, 1b	4	1	1	0	0
Zimmer, c	4	0	1	0	0	Quinn, 2b	4	0	1	1	0
Tebeau, 3b	4	0	0	0	2	Bennett, c	4	2	2	1	2
Young, p	4	1	1	0	0	Nichols, p	4	1	2	2	0
	37	3	10	2	4		37	8	11	6	5

```
CLE   0 0 3   0 0 0   0 0 0 - 3
BOS   0 0 2   2 1 1   1 1 x - 8
```

Earned runs: BOS 6, CLE 2.   2B: Duffy, McCarthy.   3B: Quinn.   HR: Bennett.   SB: McCarthy, Nichols, Burkett, Zimmer, Tucker, Long.   SH: McAleer, O'Connor, McCarthy, Lowe 2, Tucker 2.   DP: BOS 1, CLE 1.   BB: Young 3, Nichols 2.   Struck out: Young 3, Nichols 8.   PB: Bennett.   WP: Young 3.   Umpires: McQuaid and Gaffney.   Time—1:55.   Att: 1,812.

· 10 ·

THE DEBUT OF THE TEMPLE CUP

◆

The Boston Beaneaters and Baltimore Orioles were the two most dominant teams in baseball in the final decade of the nineteenth century, and the Orioles were *the* dominant team of the Temple Cup games, appearing in each of the four championships. The O's did not develop the hit-and-run style of baseball, as is widely thought (Boston did), but if it wasn't their invention, they were the team that perfected it. After he watched Baltimore turn thirteen hit-and-run plays in a four-game series, New York's Monte Ward said "They weren't playing baseball, but a new game."

That they were. The Orioles ushered in the era of scientific play. After the pitching distance was increased, the club took constant bunting practice to capitalize on the extra hitting room. The Orioles perfected cut-off plays, the "Baltimore chop" (the art of hitting the ball into the ground, resulting in a high bounce over infielders' heads), the bluffed steal, and the defensive strategy of having infielders cover bases other than their own. Ned Hanlon became the first manager in the history of baseball to employ platooning consistently: When a southpaw took the mound for the other side, Hanlon often benched himself in favor of a right-handed hitter.

1894

The Changing Game

♦ ♦ ♦

• *The pitcher's box was replaced with a slab twelve inches long by four inches wide.*

• *The distance from the pitcher to home plate was extended to sixty feet, six inches.*

• *The sacrifice rule, written in 1893 but not widely used until the 1894 season, was rewritten so that when a bunt resulted in advancing a baserunner and the batter was, or could have been, put out, the batter was credited with a sacrifice hit and no time at bat. The new rule was not uniformly recognized by official scorers until 1897.*

• *To curb bat-control artists like Willie Keeler (who would intentionally bunt pitch after pitch into foul territory until he got one to his liking), a batter was now charged with a strike if he bunted the ball foul.*

• *Louisville Colonels third baseman Jerry Denny retired. Denny was the last man to play baseball without the aid of a fielder's glove.*

And when all else failed—and even if all else was successful—the Orioles weren't averse to a little cheating, subtle or otherwise. Baltimore infielders loved to turn the phantom double play, or trip opposing players running the bases. John McGraw's favorite trick was grabbing a runner's belt as he rounded third. The team was famous for hiding baseballs in the outfield's long grass, the better to put into play at propitious moments of the game. Groundskeeper Tom Murphy kept the infield rock-hard for the Baltimore chop, and let the grass grow long near the foul lines to make sure the Baltimore bunts would not roll into foul territory.

Boston had won the pennant in 1893, but for the second time in three years, there was no post-season championship series and this time there was no talk of one. National League owners, remembering the bitter disaster of the split season of 1892 and the charges of hippodroming, were content to leave well enough alone. This situation would change in 1894. At the annual National League meetings in the winter of 1893, William Chase Temple, ex-president of the Pittsburgh Pirates and a fervent sportsman, announced the offering of a silver loving cup to the winner of a post-season championship of not less than four games between the National League pennant winner and the second-place club. According to Temple's plan, the Series would be scheduled under League rules, governed by League discipline, and umpired by League umpires. Playing grounds would be donated free of charge by the owners involved and the winning team would receive sixty-five percent of the net profits.

A gaudy, silver loving cup was ordered from New York jeweler A.E. Thrall. Standing two feet high, valued at approximately five hundred dollars, the Temple Cup was heavily ornamented and featured a bas-relief figure of a player in the act of throwing a ball. During the 1894 season, the cup was sent around the league and placed on exhibit in each city.

Leading the band of Baltimore outlaws was manager Edward Hugh "Ned" Hanlon. Hanlon had broken into the major leagues with the Cleveland Spiders in 1880 and spent the next eight years with Detroit, compiling a lifetime .260 batting average. He was the field captain of the 1887 Wolverines and, according to most accounts, deserved more credit for winning the pennant and World Series than the club's nominal manager, Bill Watkins. Hanlon's first official taste of managing came when he took over a seventh-place Pittsburgh club in 1889 and improved its record to fifth. After piloting the Players' League Pittsburgh Burghers in 1890 and the National League Pirates the next year, Hanlon came to Baltimore in 1892. Inheriting a record of 1-16, Hanlon and his new club finished the season right where they started—in last place. The 1892 Orioles made 584 errors, the most in baseball, so their new manager drilled the club relentlessly in fundamentals.

In 1893, the O's cut their miscues by an even two hundred and improved from last place to sixth. Hanlon helped trim another 101 errors in 1894 and Baltimore streaked to its first of three consecutive pennants.

But to say the Orioles climbed to the 1894 championship on the strength of their defense would be misleading. Hanlon built the club and Hanlon alone was the reason for its success. In his first three years at the helm, he traded George Van Haltren to Pittsburgh for Joe Kelley, signed rookie second baseman Heinie Reitz, and traded outfielder Tim O'Rourke to Louisville for Hughie Jennings. In January 1894, Hanlon made his most important swap, sending Billy Shindle and George Treadway to Brooklyn for Willie Keeler and the aging Dan Brouthers. Brouthers's best years were behind him, and most people in the Brooklyn organization thought Keeler was just too small to make good in the majors, even though he sported a .318 batting average in his two seasons with the club. (Treadway, a dark-skinned man rumored to have Negro blood, lasted only four years before leaving the major league scene following the 1896 season.) Of the eight starting Orioles most often on the field in 1894, only two— Heinie Reitz and Steve Brodie—failed to make the Hall of Fame. Only one of the 1892 regulars, catcher Wilbert Robinson, had survived Hanlon's massive rebuilding efforts.

Following three consecutive pennants in 1894 through 1896, the Orioles finished second in 1897 and 1898. After the franchise was transferred to Brooklyn, Hanlon won pennants in 1899 and 1900, finished third in 1901, and second in 1902. Somewhat of a dandy, Hanlon frequently managed the club in street clothes from his place on the bench, wearing a silk top hat and spats. Appearances aside, Ned Hanlon was an unerring judge of talent who developed such players as John McGraw, Wilbert Robinson, Hughie Jennings, Kid Gleason, Willie Keeler, and Fielder Jones.

Weighing in at only 155 pounds, John McGraw, nicknamed the Little Napoleon, was one of the best-hitting third basemen of his day. Born just outside Truxton, New York, the son of John and Ellen Comerfort McGraw, John Joseph McGraw was named after his grandfather back in Ireland. The eldest of eight children, John was eleven years old when he lost his mother and four siblings to typhoid. The family moved from their farm to a frame house in Truxton proper where McGraw, a well-liked child who served in the local parish as an altar boy, clashed often with his father, who considered the boy's preoccupation with baseball a waste of time. Young John moved next door to Mary Goddard's boarding house where he did odd jobs in return for his room and board. McGraw pitched for the Truxton Grays and was good enough to catch the eye of the manager of the club from East Homer, a small town five miles down the road. The East Homer pilot offered the young pitcher two dollars to start a game and McGraw, after winning, told his skipper if he wanted him to pitch again, he would require a raise to five dollars and a horse-drawn hack to bring him to and from the town.

For sixty dollars a month plus board, the teenager joined Olean in the New York-Penn League and was installed at third base by manager Bert Kenney. On May 18, 1890, in his organized baseball debut against Erie, John McGraw made seven errors in ten chances and had a lone single to show for his trouble. After six games, he was benched. After two weeks, he was released.

McGraw turned up at Wellsville of the Western New York League, where he worked hard on his defense and hitting. Appearing in twenty-four games from June until the season ended in early October, he pitched occasionally and played all infield and outfield positions. Still making plenty of errors, he had nevertheless cut down on his bad throws and was hitting .365, a batting average which allowed for a large margin of error defensively. The next season, McGraw moved to Cedar Rapids of the Three-I (Illinois, Indiana, and Iowa) League. Bill Gleason (then with Rockford in the Three-I), told McGraw that Baltimore manager Bill Barnie had written to ask about him. How good did McGraw think he was, asked Gleason. "You can tell Barnie," answered the cocky eighteen-year-old, "I'm just about as good as they come."

Later in the season, Cedar Rapids played an exhibition game against Cap Anson's Chicago Colts. McGraw taunted the veteran Anson unmercifully about his age and Anson was so impressed by the youngster's talent and audacity that he asked if he would like to join the club someday. McGraw hit .275 for Cedar Rapids and finished the 1891 season in the major leagues when his contract was bought by the Orioles. In and out of the lineup during his first two years, McGraw was installed at short in 1893 and shifted to third the following year.

Usually the team's leadoff hitter, McGraw began to develop the superb bat control that would make him one of the nineteenth century's hardest outs. Standing upright in the box, McGraw, like

Keeler, would foul off pitch after pitch until, his hands choked up on the bat, he'd find a delivery to his liking and punch the ball into play somewhere. On the field, John McGraw was mean-spirited, cruel, and he cheated. Former St. Louis great Arlie Latham, working as an umpire years later, would say, "McGraw eats gunpowder every morning and washes it down with warm blood." Anyone who called him "Muggsy," his indelicate (and much-hated) nickname, would have a fight on his hands. Off the field, this fierce battler was, inexplicably, a soft touch for a loan or a favor.

McGraw retired from baseball with a lifetime .334 batting average and 436 stolen bases, but his playing talent was later overshadowed by his work as manager. As the iron-fisted strategist of the Giants for many years, McGraw won ten pennants for New York and finished second eleven other times. His managing career spanned thirty-four years, from 1899 through 1932, and he was elected to the Hall of Fame in 1937, three years after his death.

Wilbert Robinson, the only player Ned Hanlon liked enough to keep, was an excellent handler of pitchers. Team captain of the Orioles, "Uncle Robbie" began his professional career with Haverill of the New England League in 1885. The Philadelphia Athletics brought him to the major leagues as a catcher/first baseman in 1886, but he struggled with the bat and was traded to Baltimore in 1890. Robinson finished his career with a .273 batting average and 1,316 games behind the plate, the most by any catcher up to that time. He first managed Baltimore in 1902 and was Brooklyn's manager from 1914 through 1931, winning pennants in 1916 and 1920, but losing the World Series both years. Robinson was elected to the Hall of Fame in 1945.

The shortstop of the 1894 Orioles, Hugh "Hughie" Ambrose Jennings, made his organized baseball debut in 1890 for Allentown, where he hit .320. Baseball was a method of getting out of the coal fields of northeastern Pennsylvania for this freckled, carrot-topped youngster with deep blue eyes. The Louisville Colonels bought Jennings's contract in 1891 and brought him to the American Association. Jennings was a foot-in-the-bucket hitter with a lifetime .240 batting average until Ned Hanlon corrected the fault in 1894. The shortstop responded with consecutive averages of .335, .386, .398, .355, and .328 and became an accomplished clutch hitter in the mid-1890s. After his retirement, Jennings became the manager of the Detroit Tigers in 1907. He won American League pennants in his first three years at the helm but despite holding his job through

1920, never won another. Competitive and high-strung, Jennings was inducted into the Hall of Fame in 1945.

William J. "Kid" Gleason was a perfectly average pitcher (lifetime record, 134-134) with the Philadelphia Phillies and St. Louis Browns before Hanlon made him the Orioles' full-time second baseman in 1895. Gleason played only two years for Hanlon, but those were two of the only three seasons he hit above .300. After his retirement as an active player in 1912, he went on to become a rookie manager with the Chicago White Sox of 1919. The revelations of the Black Sox Scandal in the World Series came out in September of the following year. The Sox finished second in 1920 and, deprived of its best players, the team and Gleason subsequently dropped into the second division. Gleason retired as the club's pilot after the 1923 season and never managed again.

William Henry "Wee Willie" Keeler is perhaps the most recognized name from nineteenth-century baseball. People who know nothing about the game of baseball, then or now, are familiar with the phrase "Hit 'em where they ain't" and the man who uttered it. A tremendous talent, Keeler was a choke left-handed batter and a rarity, a left-handed third baseman and second baseman. Keeler hit .373 with Binghamton of the Eastern League until the Giants bought his contract. He hit .321 at New York in 1892, moved to the Brooklyn Bridegrooms, then found himself back in Binghamton in 1893. Keeler was traded to Baltimore in 1894 and, under Ned Hanlon's tutelage, began to forge his considerable reputation. A tiny man—he stood five feet, four inches and weighed only one hundred forty pounds—Keeler stood at the plate with his legs straight and body bent slightly, bat cocked behind his ear. His forty-four-game hitting streak remained a baseball standard until broken by Joe Dimaggio in 1941, and his 243 hits in 1897 were a National League record until Rogers Hornsby topped the mark with 250 in 1922.

Keeler scored more than a hundred runs and made more than two hundred hits in each of his first eight full seasons in baseball. A consistent basestealer, he drew a great number of walks (524) for his era. Keeler fell shy of becoming the second man to break the three-thousand-hit barrier by a mere thirty-eight safeties, and his lifetime batting average of .345 is fifth on the all-time list.

Somewhat of a pariah on his own club, Keeler was a loner on and off the field. He rarely argued with umpires and seemed to lack the fiery reputation the swashbuckling Orioles tried so hard to maintain. But he did appreciate a practical joke. During a game against the New York Highlanders late in his playing career, Keeler set off a string of firecrackers behind him in left field. While umpire Silk O'Laughlin berated the bleacher bums, Keeler was chuckling behind his back.

Years later, John McGraw paid Keeler the highest praise possible. "With the possible exception of Ty Cobb," said McGraw, "Willie Keeler was the greatest player of all time. He was the most expert batter I ever saw. There was nothing he could not do in place hitting. He was the fastest man I ever saw on the bases and one of the headiest baserunners." Keeler, the man who Cy Young once said was the hardest batter for him to get out, was elected to the Hall of Fame in 1939.

Two other members of this distinguished band were also elected to baseball's Hall of Fame—Dan Brouthers and Joe Kelley.

Dennis Joseph "Dan" Brouthers was winding down a long and distinguished career. The left-handed, clean-living power hitter was much travelled—he spent two seasons with Troy, five with Buffalo, three with Detroit, one year with the Boston Beaneaters, a year with the Players' League Boston Reds, a year with the American Association Boston Reds, two years with Brooklyn, a year and a half with Baltimore, half a season with Louisville, one season with the Phillies, and five at bats with the New York Giants in 1904, seven years after he retired as an active major league player. His uniforms alone could occupy an entire wing of the Baseball Hall of Fame. Brouthers is eighth on the all-time list with 206 triples and ninth on the all-time list with a .343 batting average. The first player to win back-to-back batting titles, Brouthers was still playing ball in the high minors at age forty-one and was forty-six when he took his five at bats with the Giants. Dan Brouthers was inducted into the Hall of Fame in 1945.

Joe Kelley started his professional career with Lowell of the New England League in 1891, hit .357 in fifty-seven games, and compiled a 10-3 record in fourteen appearances as a pitcher. Kelley came to the Boston Beaneaters late in the year, hit .244, and was traded to Pittsburgh. He showed no offensive ability for the Pirates and in 1892 was sent to Baltimore for George Van Haltren. A career .234 hitter at the time, Kelley, like so many of Ned Hanlon's charges, magically began to hit. In his years under Hanlon, he batted .343. Kelley is ninth on the all-time triples list with 194 and had a lifetime batting average of .319. He managed the Cincinnati

Reds from 1902 through 1905 and the Boston Braves in 1908, and was elected to the Hall of Fame in 1971.

Most experts expected the Boston Reds to repeat as pennant winners for the fourth consecutive year, but the club entered the final month of the campaign in a virtual tie with Baltimore. The Orioles finished strong, winning eighteen in a row in September, and wrested the title from Boston. Nearly eighteen hundred fans jammed into Ford's Theatre in Baltimore to get a telegraph play-by-play of the Orioles' pennant-clinching victory over Cleveland at the close of September. With such a stretch drive, it was not surprising that the Orioles were an overwhelming favorite to win the Temple Cup Series with the Giants.

The Orioles returned to Baltimore from their last series in Chicago by special train on the evening of October 2. Enthusiastic crowds were on hand to greet the team at many whistle stops along with way, and by the time the train arrived at Baltimore's Camden Station, thousands of loyal fans were waiting. The players, accompanied by floats and decorated wagons and led by a platform wagon shooting off fireworks (lest anyone miss the excitement), headed a procession of horse-drawn carriages through the business district of the city. Many private residences and all the prominent office buildings were decorated with pennants or orange and black bunting, the team colors. A mounted police escort delivered the parade to the Fifth Regiment Armory where governor Brown, mayor Latrobe, and a dozen other state and city officials made appropriate addresses. The Armory reception droned on for almost two hours, after which the club and its officers were taken to the Hotel Rennert for a ten o'clock banquet. The next evening, benefit performances at local theaters netted several thousand dollars, which was divided among the grateful Orioles.

Baltimore was known in the 1890s as Mob Town, a legacy from the city's violent reputation which had been cultivated over the past half-century. The reputation was well deserved. In the presidential elections of 1856, eight persons had been killed and nearly three hundred injured by hoodlums engaged in electioneering. Competition between fire companies to see which engines could get to a fire first often ended in free-for-alls, while a house or building raged nearby. In April 1861, when the 6th Massachusetts Infantry marched through Baltimore on its way to Washington, the

Yankee troops were set upon by an angry throng of Southern sympathizers. In the melee which followed, thirteen Baltimoreans and four men of the 6th were killed. A month later, Union General Benjamin F. Butler seized Baltimore's Federal Hill and trained its guns on the town. Until the end of the Civil War, the city was essentially held captive, although many of its citizens continued to proclaim their loyalties to the South and to Maryland, a slave-holding state prior to the war.

From Camden Station, the Baltimore of 1894 looked, at first glance, like a dreary place. Winding northwestward from the bay, the Patapsco River was already dead, polluted by canneries and factories situated nearby. (Heavy industrialization would not begin until 1897 with the opening of the Sparrows Point steel mill.) Dozens of dilapidated one- and two-story ramshackle dwellings (with scores of pigs, chickens, and other livestock wandering aimlessly about) crowded as many disease-ridden avenues.

The Orioles reflected the city's rough exterior, and they came into the first Temple Cup Series confident of a quick and easy victory over the Giants. In most areas, on paper at least, the Giants offered no challenge at all. Baltimore had outscored New York by a wide margin (1171 to 940); the Orioles' team batting average of .343 was 42 points better than the Giants'; and the club's gaudy slugging average of .483 outstripped New York by seventy-four points. In addition, the Orioles were the best-fielding team in the League, having committed one hundred fifty fewer errors than the Giants. The only item of concern was the stark contrast in pitching between the two clubs: The O's had a bloated team earned run average of 5.00, while New York's team ERA of 3.83 was the best in the League. Indeed, Baltimore was the first team in the history of major league baseball to win a pennant with a team earned run average in excess of 4.50.

Sadie McMahon had the League's second-best winning percentage (.758) and led the Baltimore pitching staff with a 25-8 record and a 4.21 ERA. Unfortunately for the Orioles, McMahon was hampered by a sore arm and would be unavailable for the Series. Following McMahon in the rotation were Kid Gleason (15-5, 4.45), Bill Hawke (16-9, 5.84), and Charles "Duke" Esper (15-12). Hawke was working his last year in the major leagues. Esper had come over from the lowly Washington club in mid-season and, after starting the year 5-10 with the Senators, became a considerable factor down the stretch as he went 10-2 with the Orioles. (His teammates thought Esper looked like a lame horse when he ran the bases, and this is thought to be the most likely derivation of the phrase "charley horse.") Rounding out the Baltimore staff was George Hemming, a refugee from the last-place Louisville club. Hemming had compiled a perfect 4-0 record in six late-season appearances with the Orioles.

The Giants had two quality starters—the big right-handed duo of Jouett Meekin and Amos Rusie. Meekin had kicked around with Louisville and Washington and was a ten-game winner in each of his first three seasons before he came to the Giants. This was his best year in the majors, and what a sensational year it was. The big Indianan went 36-10, led the league in winning percentage (.786), tied for the league lead (with Rusie) in victories, finished second in earned run average (3.70), third in strikeouts (133) and innings pitched (409), and fourth in complete games (40). Were it not for his teammate, Meekin would have been the league's best pitcher in 1894.

Amos Wilson Rusie, the Hoosier Thunderbolt, also hailed from Indiana and was noted throughout his career for two things—overpowering speed and an utter inability to find the plate. Rusie's speed was one of the reasons the pitching distance had been increased—he once hit Hughie Jennings with an errant fastball and the Baltimore shortstop was unconscious for three days—and even then, the few extra feet gave his dazzling curveball more time to bend. The 210-pound right-hander led the league in strikeouts five times in his ten-year career and, discounting an aborted comeback attempt with the Cincinnati Reds in 1901, averaged 217 Ks a season. As for his wildness, well, the Thunderbolt was legendary. He led the league five straight years in bases on balls, each time with two hundred or more, and even today stands seventh on the all-time list in walks. (Rusie averaged 4.10 bases on balls per nine innings pitched throughout his career; by contrast, Bill Donovan, nicknamed "Wild Bill" for his lack of control, averaged 3.21 walks per nine innings pitched.) Three times in his career, Rusie committed the ultimate pitching sin of walking more men than he struck out. In each of his eight seasons with the Giants, he won twenty or more games and he finished his career with a lifetime 243-160 record.

Discounting his rookie season in the majors, Rusie had worked an average of sixty starts and five hundred innings per year when 1894 ended. "The pitchers were under too hard a strain in

my day to last many years," he would say years later. "In New York
especially, the practice prevailed of working a winning pitcher as
much as he would stand. The crowd demanded it. I was young. I
didn't think my arm would ever wear out, and I even asked to be
allowed to work sometimes when not called upon. Later I paid the
price." The price was his career. Three more years of three hundred or more innings would follow before Rusie's arm burned out.
His career was effectively ended at the age of twenty-seven. On
December 15, 1900, Rusie was traded to the Cincinnati Reds for a
young man with six major league appearances and an unimpressive
0-3 record—Christy Mathewson.

Connie Mack described the Nolan Ryan of his day as "the
fastest, without a doubt. Maybe that's because I had to hit against
him. They [Rusie's pitches] looked like peas as they sailed by me.
All I saw of them was what I heard when they went into the
catcher's mitt."

Sportswriter O.P. Caylor said the Giants "without Rusie
would be like *Hamlet* without the Melancholy Dane."

Thirty-five years after his death in 1942, Amos Rusie, the man
responsible for the new pitching distance—the last major rules
change in baseball and the one which made the game what it is
today—was belatedly inducted into baseball's Hall of Fame.

In 1894, the year of the first Temple Cup Series, Rusie was the
dominant pitcher of the National League. Tied for the league lead in
shutouts (3) and wins, he led all pitchers in earned run average
(2.78), strikeouts (195), fewest hits per nine innings (8.64), and most
strikeouts per nine innings (3.95). He was second in innings pitched
(444), complete games (45), and appearances (54), and third in winning percentage (.735).

Meekin and Rusie had won six of eight starts against the
Orioles during the regular season and, with the pennant already
lost, New York manager Monte Ward rested his two best hurlers
for the Series. Sure, Meekin and Rusie were the best the League
had to offer, but on the other hand, thought Baltimore manager
Ned Hanlon, how dominant could pitching be in a short series?
He was soon to find out.

◆ ◆ ◆

At noon on October 4, eager fans began pouring through the
ticket gates into Baltimore's Union Park and by 1:30, over eight
thousand people were in the stands. Included among the early

birds was an army of ticket speculators who had bought up as many pasteboards as they could stuff into their pockets. Fans who alighted from street cars shortly before game time paid double the face value for an illegal ducat, only to discover moments later that the ticket offices were still open and working efficiently.

The front of Union Park resembled nothing so much as a circus. The national flag and the championship pennant waved overhead and everywhere a person turned could be seen the gaudy club colors of black and orange. Vendors were peddling an assortment of baseball trinkets, books about the champion players, Oriole badges and pennants, pink lemonade, and peanuts.

The Giants dressed at the Eutaw House—there were no lockers in the clubhouse—and made the trip to the park in one of George Kinnier's buses, a fabulous contraption of unbelievable length, drawn by four horses. Longitudinal seats provided room for thirty or more passengers and it took a skillful driver to handle the mighty vehicles in the narrow streets of Baltimore. When the Giants entered the grounds at Union Park, they were enthusiastically jeered by the partisan crowd. Monte Ward's men carried a white pennant, bearing the inscription "TO VICTORY, NEW YORK, 1894," which they planted near their bench amid no small ceremony.

John Ward and Ned Hanlon had met at the Eutaw House earlier in the morning and agreed, on behalf of their teams, to play the Series under Temple Cup committee rules; several Baltimore players, most notably John McGraw and Willie Keeler, objected to the receipts being split 65/35. They were under the erroneous impression that the Orioles were to receive sixty-five percent of the Series profits, no matter who won. McGraw's suggestion that the clubs split the stakes evenly was rejected out of hand by the Temple Cup principals on the grounds that an even split would be an inducement for both clubs to prolong the Series by hippodroming. Under the rules of competition, if the Orioles defaulted, the second-place New York Giants would defend the Temple Cup against the third-place Boston Beaneaters.

National League president Nick Young was in the ballpark. While Baltimore was taking practice, Monte Ward visited his box to inform him that unless the Orioles agreed to play the Series under Temple Cup rules, the contest would be of an exhibition nature and no more games would follow. Ward made one other demand: If the Giants agreed to abide by the rules, he wanted the umpires to announce that fact to the crowd. Wilbert Robinson called Keeler in from shagging fly balls in right field and the pair made their way to McGraw, fielding grounders at third base. The angry eyes of each Baltimore ballplayer were on the trio as Robinson pleaded with Keeler and McGraw to give in. Keeler acquiesced almost immediately, but McGraw petulantly strolled down the left-field foul line, apparently giving the matter some careful thought. When he turned toward Robinson and saw the contempt in his teammate's eyes, he gave in. Even if the Orioles lost, the third baseman reasoned, thirty-five percent of something was better than sixty-five percent of nothing. (McGraw later announced he was persuaded to play against his will and flatly stated he had appeared in his last game of the Series. This resolution would last only until Game Two began.)

Umpires Tim Hurst and Robert Emslie approached the grandstands and announced to the crowd, "It is for the Temple Cup," then proceeded down the foul lines repeating the same words to everyone else in the park. The fans, somewhat confused by the goings-on, roundly booed the New Yorkers.

Because of the large crowd, ropes had been strung behind the foul lines and in the outfield. Many of the 11,720 spectators overflowed onto the field or stood in the aisles; the playing rules for this game (indeed, for all games of the Series) stated that any ball hit into the crowd would go for a ground-rule triple, no more.

Baltimore's Union Park, located at Barclay Street and Huntingdon Avenue (later called Twenty-Fifth Street), just north of the business district, had a seating capacity of about eight thousand. Local vendors were hawking a German-style sausage called Wecke, but known as "weckers." Served in a split bun, weckers were popular with Baltimore fans long before the hot dog was supposedly first sold at New York's Polo Grounds.

Union Park was quite an experience for visiting right fielders. The field sloped sharply downhill near the sixteen-foot-high fence and stream water from nearby Brady's Run often created swamp-like conditions after a hard rain. It had stormed the night before the Series opener and black clouds that afternoon promised more of the same. Tim Hurst was behind the plate and Robert Emslie on the basepaths when Emslie called for play to begin at 3:00. Duke Esper was the Orioles' starter. The Giants had Amos Rusie on the mound. Rusie was a tough enough opponent on sunny days, but under cloudy conditions, with limited visibility, his overpowering fastball was virtually unhittable.

The game was scoreless until the Giants batted in the fifth. Eight-year veteran George Van Haltren, in his first year with New York, sent the ball over the ropes in right field for a ground-rule triple and scored the first run of the Series when William "Shorty" Fuller skied a sacrifice fly to Joe Kelley in deep left field. The Giants added a run in the next inning when switch-hitting George Davis grounded a triple down the line and into the left-field crowd, and scored on Jack Doyle's grounder. In the seventh, Amos Rusie doubled to right and scored on Eddie Burke's single. One inning later, the Giants scored their final run of the day. Jack Doyle skied a high fly into left field and Joe Kelley, who first misjudged the ball, watched helplessly as the ball rolled into the crowd. Doyle broke stride at second base and trotted into third with his gift triple. As Doyle danced off third, Monte Ward executed a perfect squeeze bunt to give the Giants a 4-0 lead.

Baltimore's lone tally came in the ninth inning. John McGraw singled and went to second on a groundout by Steve Brodie (christened Walter Scott Brodie, but nicknamed Steve, after the legendary man who allegedly jumped from the Brooklyn Bridge). McGraw promptly stole third and scored on a single by second-year man Heinie Reitz. In this same inning, Robert Emslie blew an easy decision when he called Hughie Jennings out on a not-so-close play at first base. Jennings planted himself on the bag and refused to leave until teammate Wilbert Robinson unloaded on him for his childish tantrum. Emslie's gaffe caused bitter feelings among a few fanatics in the crowd, and both umpires needed a police escort from the park after the 4-1 New York victory.

Feelings ran close to the surface in the first game of the 1894 Temple Cup Series and there were several incidents of near-violence. Early in the contest, Steve Brodie was coaching at first base and quite by accident struck Jack Doyle, causing both benches to empty. In the seventh, John McGraw slid high into second base, spikes flashing, and knocked the ball from Monte Ward's hands. Ward shouted at McGraw and the two nearly came to blows. When Hugh Jennings forced Steve Brodie at second a moment later, McGraw rounded third and kept running. Ward's throw home caught McGraw a full ten feet from the plate, but "Muggsy" slammed into catcher Duke Farrell, then intentionally tore off Farrell's mask. Farrell held onto the ball for the out and immediately went after McGraw, but players on both clubs separated the two combatants. In the ninth, Steve Brodie and Jack

Doyle exchanged a few harmless punches before Monte Ward stepped in.

When it was all over, losing pitcher Esper had given up thirteen hits, walked one, and struck out three. (If not for the unusual ground rules, he might have fared a bit better.) The well-rested Amos Rusie spun a seven-hitter, struck out three, and gave up two bases on balls as he earned a 4-1 victory. None of the Baltimore hits went for extra bases and only John McGraw had reached Rusie for more than one hit. The undisputed batting star of the day was Eddie Burke, with a 4-for-5 performance.

Later that evening—much later that evening; in fact, it was almost daybreak the next morning—a Judge Cullom from New York was celebrating the Giants' victory with a party of friends when he was approached by a rabid Orioles fan who wanted nothing more than to buy the good judge a drink. Cullom, being a judge and sober after all, demurred, offering the unlikely explanation that he was a confirmed teetotaler. The Baltimorean shouted, "You can't lie to a Maryland gentleman and escape the consequences," produced a pistol, and fired two rounds. Both volleys missed their mark and, given the jurist's rather generous girth, many Baltimore residents made light of the episode, saying that no man who had actually aimed at the judge could have missed him. Many New Yorkers also poked fun, pointing out that Baltimore's marksmanship apparently equalled its ability at baseball.

The next day, an even larger crowd of eleven thousand fans turned out for what proved to be the final baseball game of the 1894 season in Maryland. After the rowdy behavior on the field the day before, the mayor of Baltimore, expecting trouble, had mustered over two hundred policemen for duty at Union Park. His farsightedness paid off during pre-game practice. New York ballplayers arrived on the field for practice and again planted their pennant near the bench, antagonizing the early arrivals at the park. Eddie Burke took his place in left field and began shagging fly balls. A number of men and boys were on the field while the Giants took practice and as Burke was chasing a fly ball, he ran headlong into an Orioles fan, Mr. W.H. Heist. Heist took umbrage and lunged at Burke, but the left fielder merely shoved him aside. Then, to add insult to injury, Burke threw a baseball at Heist's face. Nearly a hundred fans rushed the outfielder, but police intervened and a near-riot was averted. Heist later appeared before Justice Murray at the central police station to swear out a warrant for assault against the New York ballplayer, but a police captain named Toner persuaded him to drop the charges.

The starting pitchers for Game Two were Kid Gleason and Jouett Meekin. Meekin had not lost to the Orioles all year long and not even the sight of the fickle John McGraw at his familiar third-base station could lessen the New Yorkers' conviction of victory. The game began at 3:30 and was "broadcast" via the telegraph wires to eager fans at Ford's Theatre. It was an ideal day for baseball and the home team immediately took advantage of the favorable playing conditions.

In the bottom of the second, Steve Brodie drew a walk, went to third on Heinie Reitz's bunt single, and scored on Wilbert Robinson's sacrifice fly. Kid Gleason then helped his own cause by depositing a fly ball into the left-field crowd for a ground-rule triple and a 2-0 Baltimore lead.

New York came roaring back in the top of the third. With two out and Jouett Meekin and Mike Tiernan on base, George Davis lined his second cheap triple of the Series into the crowd in right, and the score was tied. Jack Doyle followed with an infield single to drive in Davis and give the Giants the lead, stole second, and scored himself on Monte Ward's safety. The Giants had a two-run margin, but not for long. In the bottom of the inning, consecutive singles by Dan Brouthers, John McGraw, Steve Brodie, and Heinie Reitz netted two runs, and the score was once again tied. That's where matters stood until the bottom of the seventh when Baltimore's Joe Kelley lofted a high fly ball into the crowd behind the center-field ropes for a ground-rule triple. He scored a moment later when Shorty Fuller dropped Willie Keeler's easy pop fly in short center field.

In the New York eighth, Mike Tiernan singled, was advanced to third on sacrifice bunts by Davis and Doyle, and scored the tying run on Monte Ward's safety.

A wild ninth inning decided the contest. For the Giants, Shorty Fuller and Duke Farrell hit back-to-back singles, before Jouett Meekin fanned for the first out of the inning. Eddie Burke, the hitting star of the previous day, but hitless in four at bats today, smacked an easy double-play ball to Hughie Jennings at short. A horrified Baltimore crowd gasped as Jennings dropped the ball, loading the bases. Seconds later, Mike Tiernan capitalized on Jennings's defensive lapse when he slammed a 2-1 pitch from Gleason into the right-field crowd for a ground-rule triple, emptying the bases. Tiernan scored on George Davis's single to right and the Giants had a 9-5 lead with three outs to go.

But the Orioles weren't willing to give up the ghost just yet. In the bottom of the ninth, Meekin issued walks to Wilbert Robinson, Joe Kelley, and Dan Brouthers, sandwiched around two harmless fly balls. The tying run came to the plate in the person of John McGraw. The Little Napoleon grounded weakly to third and George Davis fired the ball across the diamond, but first baseman Jack Doyle dropped the throw for an error. Robinson scored to make it 9-6. Steve Brodie was the next batter, 2-for-3 on the day and representing the winning run. He grounded softly to Meekin, who threw to first. This time the ball stayed in Doyle's glove, ending the game. Hughie Jennings, depressed over his ninth-inning error, sat motionless in the clubhouse for half an hour before he even began taking off his uniform.

In earning the victory, Jouett Meekin walked five, struck out two and, like Rusie the day before, pitched a seven-hitter. Kid Gleason gave up thirteen hits, walked one, and struck out four in a losing effort. Every batter in the New York lineup hit safely except Eddie Burke, the hitting star of the day before.

Through the first two games, the National League champion Orioles had looked like anything but. Baltimore hitters were struggling along with a .203 batting average, compared with the Giants' .347. The Baltimore team slugging average was an even more embarrassing .261, compared with New York's .493. Baltimore pitchers had allowed thirteen runs; New York's Meekin and Rusie had surrendered just seven, two of which were unearned. The Orioles had been in the lead just twice, and neither lead had lasted longer than it took for the Giants to bat in the next half-inning.

The clubs took separate trains to New York and the Series resumed the next day at the "new" Polo Grounds, which was the old Brotherhood Park. The Polo Grounds seated sixteen thousand, including over five thousand in the grandstands and the center-field bleachers, named Burkville for the Irish immigrant fans who sat there.

A line for tickets began forming early that morning and by 2:00 in the afternoon, the stands were well filled. It looked as if Game Three would be witnessed by the biggest New York crowd of the season. An hour later, the grandstand and bleacher seats were filled to capacity as the crowd began to spill over behind the out-field and the foul lines. Hundreds of fans perched on Coogan's

Bluff, which rose from behind the home plate grandstand, and the playing field was surrounded by a fringe of spectators a dozen deep. Over a hundred carriages were parked on the running track behind the ropes stretched across the outfield.

The Catholic Protectory Brass Band played the two clubs onto the field at 2:30, and the Orioles were given a warm reception by the New York fans, in stark contrast to the treatment the Giants had received in Baltimore. The Giants left their clubhouse sixteen abreast and marched proudly up the field to the strains of "Hail to the Chief." Monte Ward held down one end of the line, Yale Murphy the other, and pitcher Huyler Westervelt carried the team pennant. When Ward and Murphy broke ranks near home plate, the applause rose to an ear-splitting crescendo. The crowd numbered twenty-two thousand and was almost certainly the largest of the year.

Umpire Tim Hurst took his place behind the plate and Bob Emslie worked the basepaths. Amos Rusie, pitching with one day of rest, was given a thunderous standing ovation as he took his place on the mound and retired Baltimore one-two-three in the top of the first. In the bottom of the inning, the Orioles acted as if they were seeing a baseball for the first time. With one out, Mike Tiernan grounded to first baseman Dan Brouthers, who made a nice play and flipped to pitcher George Hemming covering the bag. Hemming got his feet tangled trying to find the base and dropped the ball for an error. George Davis followed with a line single to left and when the ball skittered off Joe Kelley's glove for the second error of the inning, Tiernan came around to score the first run of the game. Center fielder Steve Brodie was backing up the play and prevented any further damage by gunning Davis out at third.

The Orioles tied the score in the fourth. Fooled by one of Rusie's bullets and trying to avoid a strikeout, Dan Brouthers desperately threw his bat at the ball and hit a slow roller toward George Davis, playing deep at third. Brouthers beat the throw for an infield single and as he returned to the bag, laughed out loud at his good fortune. He stopped laughing long enough to steal second base. One out later, batter Steve Brodie was hit on the foot by one of Rusie's curveballs and while catcher Duke Farrell scrambled for the ball, Brouthers, illegally, scored all the way from second. (With a hit batsman, the ball would have been dead.) When he saw Brouthers come home, the quick-thinking Brodie tried to convince umpire Emslie that Rusie had uncorked a wild pitch. Emslie was not persuaded, however, and sent Brouthers back to second. John McGraw unleashed an inventive string of obscene comments at this turn of events, and Emslie, full of fury, flew at the Orioles' third baseman. Duke Farrell restrained the ump as McGraw haughtily turned his back and walked away. The crowd booed McGraw lustily for the balance of the game. Rusie resumed his place on the mound and proceeded to walk Heinie Reitz, loading the bases. When shortstop Monte Ward fumbled Hughie Jennings's grounder, Brouthers came home to tie the score.

But not for long. The Giants moved into the lead for good in the fifth. Shorty Fuller drew a base on balls and was forced at second by Duke Farrell. Second baseman Heinie Reitz's return throw to first was wild and Farrell motored on to third, later scoring on Amos Rusie's groundout. New York added two insurance runs in the sixth. George Davis reached on an infield single and came home on Jack Doyle's double. Monte Ward bunted Doyle over and when catcher Wilbert Robinson tried to pick off Doyle at third, the ball hit him in the back and bounced into left field. He trotted home with the Giants' fourth run. George Van Haltren was the next batter and he lifted a difficult pop fly for Steve Brodie in center field. Brodie caught the ball at his shoetops, but many of the New York partisans shouted at Monte Ward, pointing to an object which appeared to be a baseball laying in the grass near Brodie. Van Haltren strolled into the outfield and picked up the discarded core of an apple that some unthinking fan had thrown onto the field.

There were no more runs scored in the game, but that is not to say there was no more excitement. In the top of the seventh, a pair of horses in left field became frightened by the fans and bolted. One was caught immediately, but the other broke harness, jumped the ropes, and galloped onto the playing field. Center fielder George Van Haltren didn't stop running until he reached the clubhouse steps, but left fielder Eddie Burke was somewhat less fortunate. His retreat cut off, Burke made a mad dash for the elevated stands in right field where, finding no help from the New York fans, he scurried under the bleachers until several local policemen finally corralled the mare. No one was seriously injured, but a number of fans standing outside the playing field were bruised as they fell over each other in their efforts to escape.

Indeed, it was a difficult game for horses, fans, players, and umpires alike. A small section of the bleachers gave way during the game and, although no one was seriously injured, more than two dozen people fell to the ground. Umpire Tim Hurst was knocked unconscious by a foul tip from an Amos Rusie fastball which raised a lump as big as a walnut on his head. Upon recovering, Hurst observed that Rusie "certainly had his speed with him."

In the eighth, the band struck up "John Brown's Body," and the crowd joined in the singing. It was already growing dark when the inning began, but the umpires saw the contest through as the Giants won their third straight game, this one by the margin of 4-1. The Catholic Protectory Band played "Carry the News to Mary" in post-game celebrations. The Orioles had put men on base in every inning save the first, but were never able to break through against Rusie, who held the club to eight hits. Rusie walked two and struck out nine in recording the victory. George Hemming gave up ten hits and took the loss. Through the first three games, the Giants had stolen six bases off the weak arm of Wilbert Robinson.

After a day off, the teams took the field at the Polo Grounds for what proved to be the Series finale. Because it was very nearly a foregone conclusion as to who would win the championship, only twelve thousand fans turned out—a very good gate, but ten thousand fewer than the game before. Those who did were rewarded at the entrance to the Polo Grounds with miniature replicas of the Temple Cup. A slight sprinkle of rain before game time caused some unrest among the spectators, but the sun came out again just as the teams marched onto the field in double lines. The Catholic Protectory Band, on hand again, played "Hail to the Chief" and "Maryland, My Maryland." It was exactly 3:00 when plate umpire Bob Emslie called for play to begin. The starting pitchers were Jouett Meekin and Bill Hawke. Hawke was widely acknowledged as Baltimore's most uncertain pitcher, and his selection for such a crucial game was a definite indicator that the Orioles had thrown in the towel.

Baltimore struck first, as Willie Keeler singled on the infield, following a walk to leadoff batter Joe Kelley. Dan Brouthers's bunt sacrifice moved both runners into scoring position from where they raced home on John McGraw's single to center. The Giants halved the two-run margin in the bottom of the first. Eddie Burke walked, stole second, and continued to third as Wilbert Robinson's throw went into the outfield. When a Hawke fastball eluded Robinson for a passed ball, Burke came home. The Orioles tallied another run in the third when John McGraw singled, moved to third on a throwing error by George Davis, and scored on Heinie Reitz's single. The Giants got that run back in the bottom of the inning. Jouett Meekin singled and moved to second on Mike Tiernan's safety. Tiernan was forced at second by George Davis, but Meekin scored when Jack Doyle reached on John McGraw's error.

Reacting to complaints from the fans on ball and strike counts, umpires Emslie and Hurst changed positions in the Baltimore fourth. In the bottom of the inning, the Giants broke through against Hawke. With one out, consecutive singles by George Van Haltren, Shorty Fuller, and Duke Farrell tied the score, and a bunt single by Jouett Meekin put the Giants on top, 4-3. Eddie Burke's sacrifice fly drove in Farrell to round out the three-run inning. Happy Giants fans clambered onto the field to hug their favorite players and the game was delayed for a few minutes.

The New Yorkers made a shambles of the contest, and the Series, in the fifth, when Kid Gleason came on in relief of Bill Hawke. Gleason walked leadoff batter George Davis, who immediately scored on Jack Doyle's double. Monte Ward reached on a fielder's choice when he forced Doyle at third, and George Van Haltren kept the rally alive by coaxing a base on balls. Shorty Fuller singled to right to score Ward, and Willie Keeler dropped Duke Farrell's fly ball in right, allowing Van Haltren to score and Fuller to advance to third. The Orioles were coming apart at the seams. Jouett Meekin's single drove in Fuller and Farrell with the fourth and fifth runs of the inning to give New York a commanding 10-3 lead.

The Giants struck again in the sixth as two players were forced to leave the game because of injury. With one out, Jack Doyle singled, stole second, and scored on Van Haltren's base hit. Van Haltren tried to take an extra base on the hit and, seeing that he was going to be out by a wide margin, made no attempt to slide, but tried to dodge Hughie Jennings instead. Unprepared for the evasive move, Jennings ran full-tilt into Van Haltren and was rewarded with a two-inch cut over his left eye. A doctor stitched the wound and Frank Bonner took Jennings's place at short. Van Haltren thought his nose was broken—it wasn't—and was forced to leave the game as well. Yale Murphy took over center-field duty for the Giants.

With Gleason just lobbing the ball over the plate, New York sent nine men to the plate in the seventh and scored five times. After Shorty Fuller grounded out, Duke Farrell singled to left. Jouett Meekin popped out on the infield but Eddie Burke singled Farrell to third, then stole second. Gleason walked Mike Tiernan and George Davis, forcing in Farrell with the inning's first run. Jack Doyle's single to right—his tenth hit of the Series—scored Burke and Tiernan and gave the Giants a 14-3 lead. A Monte Ward single plated Davis and when the throw from the outfield eluded John McGraw at third, Doyle trotted home with the Giants' sixteenth run of the game. Yale Murphy finally ended the inning with a deep fly to Steve Brodie in center.

In the top of the eighth, with two men out and no one on base, Baltimore's popular Wilbert Robinson came to the plate for his last at bat of 1894. The New York crowd broke into a cheer:

What's the matter with Robbie?
He's all right!
Who's all right?
Why, Robinson!

Flattered and embarrassed, Robinson struck out, but the fans gave him a rousing three cheers anyway. The ovation to this most gentlemanly of ballplayers was, of a sort, a backhanded insult to his teammate John McGraw, who had so incensed the fans with his roughhouse style of play.

After the Giants batted in the eighth, darkness and umpire Tim Hurst halted play with the final score 16-3, New York. The crowd surged past the ropes onto the playing field and carried the Giants in triumph to their clubhouse. A speech was demanded from Monte Ward, who leaned over the balcony and shouted, "My friends, we'll all drink from the Temple Cup together." The idea was greeted with a roar of approval.

Jouett Meekin had his second victory of the Series, a six-hitter in which he walked three and struck out four. Bill Hawke took the loss. Eddie Burke stole two bases; Jack Doyle, Duke Farrell, and Monte Ward swiped one each; and the Giants finished the Series with the rather remarkable total of eleven thefts.

As a team, the Orioles had mounted an anemic .207 for the Series, compared with New York's robust average of .389, and had been outscored by a three-to-one margin, thirty-three runs to eleven. The leading batters for the Orioles were Joe Kelley and

Heinie Reitz, with five hits in fifteen times at bat for a .333 mark. For the Giants, a .300 average was considered the mark of a poor Series. Jack Doyle led all regulars with ten hits in seventeen at bats, for a .588 mark, followed by George Van Haltren (seven-for-fourteen, .500), Duke Farrell (six-for-fourteen, .429), and Eddie Burke (seven-for-seventeen, .412). The New York pitchers joined in the offensive spirit as well, batting the ball around for a .500 average. Jouett Meekin was five-for-nine (.556) and Amos Rusie was three-for-seven (.429). On the mound, Rusie had given up only one earned run in eighteen innings for a sparkling 0.50 earned run average and two wins; Meekin had allowed three earned runs in his two victories for a 1.59 ERA.

That evening, many of the players on both squads gathered at the Broadway Theatre for a performance of the play *Dr. Syntax*. George Van Haltren was presented with a solid-silver bat for being voted New York's most popular ballplayer. The following week, at the same theatre, the Giants were the guests at a benefit performance which netted each player a little over three hundred dollars. For the Series, each member of the New York club took home $768. (Except for George Davis. Alfred Saloman, a Philadelphia jeweler, had successfully attached Davis's World Series share for twenty-five dollars, an amount Davis still owed on a diamond ring.) Each share for the Orioles was worth $360. It was later disclosed that, prior to the Series, five members of the Giants had agreed to split their shares with as many Orioles. When the New Yorkers refused to honor their part of the agreement, the story became public knowledge.

All things considered, the debut of the Temple Cup had been a rousing success. Attendance for the four games exceeded 56,000, an average of fourteen thousand fans per contest. The games themselves had been exciting. The Giants, having dominated the Orioles by taking the Series in the minimum number of games, were ecstatic and somewhat better off financially. The Orioles were left to lick their wounds and wait until next year.

GAME ONE—October 4, 1894, at Union Park, Baltimore

NEW YORK	AB	R	H	BI	E	BALTIMORE	AB	R	H	BI	E
Burke, lf	5	0	4	0	0	Kelley, lf	4	0	1	0	1
Tiernan, rf	5	0	0	0	0	Keeler, rf	4	0	1	0	0
Davis, 3b	4	1	1	0	0	Brouthers, 1b	4	0	0	0	0
Doyle, 1b	4	1	2	1	0	McGraw, 3b	4	1	2	0	0
Ward, 2b	4	0	1	0	1	Brodie, cf	4	0	0	0	0
Van Haltren, cf	3	1	1	0	0	Reitz, 2b	4	0	1	0	0
Fuller, ss	4	0	0	0	1	Jennings, ss	3	0	1	1	0
Farrell, c	4	0	2	0	0	Robinson, c	4	0	1	0	0
Rusie, p	4	1	2	0	0	Esper, p	2	0	0	0	0
	37	4	13	1	2		33	1	7	1	1

```
NY    0 0 0   0 1 1   1 1 0 – 4
BAL   0 0 0   0 0 0   0 0 1 – 1
```

D: Rusie.   T: Van Haltren, Davis, Doyle.   SF: Fuller.   SAC: Ward.   SB: Doyle, McGraw.   DP: BAL 1, NY 1.   BB: Esper 1, Rusie 2.   Struck out: Esper 3, Rusie 3. Umpires: Hurst and Emslie.   Time—2:00.   Att: 11,720.

GAME TWO—October 5, 1894, at Union Park, Baltimore

NEW YORK	AB	R	H	BI	E	BALTIMORE	AB	R	H	BI	E
Burke, lf	5	1	0	0	0	Kelley, lf	3	1	1	0	0
Tiernan, rf	5	3	3	3	0	Keeler, rf	5	0	2	0	0
Davis, 3b	5	1	1	3	0	Brouthers, 1b	4	1	1	0	1
Doyle, 1b	5	1	2	1	1	McGraw, 3b	5	0	0	1	0
Ward, 2b	4	0	2	2	0	Brodie, cf	4	2	0	0	0
Van Haltren, cf	4	0	1	0	0	Reitz, 2b	4	1	2	2	0
Fuller, ss	3	1	1	0	1	Jennings, ss	4	0	0	0	1
Farrell, c	3	1	1	0	0	Robinson, c	3	1	0	1	0
Meekin, p	4	1	2	0	0	Gleason, p	4	0	1	0	2
	38	9	13	9	2		36	6	7	4	4

```
NY    0 0 4   0 0 0   0 1 4 – 9
BAL   0 2 2   0 0 0   1 0 1 – 6
```

T: Davis, Tiernan, Gleason, Kelley.   SB: Doyle, Brodie.   SAC: Davis, Doyle.   SF: Robinson, Davis.   DP: BAL 1, NY 1.   BB: Gleason 1, Meekin 5.   Struck out: Meekin 2, Gleason 4.   Umpires: Hurst and Emslie.   Time—2:00.   Att: 11,000.

GAME THREE—October 6, 1894, at the Polo Grounds, New York

BALTIMORE	AB	R	H	BI	E	NEW YORK	AB	R	H	BI	E
Kelley, lf	5	0	1	0	1	Burke, lf	4	0	2	0	0
Bonner, rf	4	0	0	0	0	Tiernan, rf	3	1	0	0	0
Brouthers, 1b	4	1	2	0	0	Davis, 3b	4	1	2	1	0
McGraw, 3b	4	0	1	0	0	Doyle, 1b	3	1	2	1	1
Brodie, cf	4	0	0	0	0	Ward, 2b	4	0	1	0	0
Reitz, 2b	3	0	1	0	1	Van Haltren, cf	4	0	2	0	0
Jennings, ss	4	0	1	1	0	Fuller, ss	2	0	0	0	1
Robinson, c	4	0	1	0	2	Farrell, c	3	1	0	0	0
Hemming, p	3	0	1	0	1	Rusie, p	3	0	1	1	0
	35	1	8	1	5		30	4	10	3	2

```
BAL   0 0 0   1 0 0   0 0 0 – 1
NY    1 0 0   0 1 2   0 0 x – 4
```

D: Kelley, Davis, Burke 2.   SB: Brouthers 2, Van Haltren, Burke, Davis, Doyle.
SAC: McGraw, Rusie, Ward.   HBP: Brodie (Rusie).   DP: NY 2.   BB: Hemming 3,
Rusie 2.   Struck out: Rusie 9, Hemming 2.   PB: Farrell 2.   Umpires: Hurst and
Emslie.   Time—2:06.   Att: 22,000.

GAME FOUR—October 8, 1894, at the Polo Grounds, New York

BALTIMORE	AB	R	H	BI	E	NEW YORK	AB	R	H	BI	E
Kelley, lf	3	1	2	0	1	Burke, lf	4	2	1	1	0
Keeler, rf	3	1	0	0	0	Tiernan, rf	4	1	1	0	0
Brouthers, 1b	4	0	0	0	0	Davis, 3b	3	2	1	1	1
McGraw, 3b	3	1	1	2	2	Doyle, 1b	5	2	4	3	0
Brodie, cf	3	0	0	0	0	Ward, 2b	5	1	1	1	0
Reitz, 2b	4	0	1	1	1	Van Haltren, cf	3	2	3	1	0
Jennings, ss	3	0	0	0	0	Fuller, ss	5	2	3	2	1
Robinson, c	4	0	2	0	1	Farrell, c	4	3	3	0	0
Hawke, p	2	0	0	0	0	Meekin, p	5	1	3	3	0
Bonner, ss	1	0	0	0	0	Murphy, cf	1	0	0	0	0
Gleason, p	1	0	0	0	0		39	16	20	12	2
	31	3	6	3	5						

```
BAL   2 0 1   0 0 0   0 0 – 3
NY    1 0 1   3 5 1   5 0 – 16
```

D: Davis, Van Haltren, Doyle.   SB: Burke, Doyle 2, Farrell, Ward.   SAC: Brouthers.
SF: Burke.   HBP: McGraw (Meekin).   DP: NY 1, BAL 2.   BB: Meekin 3, Hawke 1,
Gleason 5.   Struck out: Meekin 4.   Umpires: Hurst and Emslie.   Time—1:55.
Att: 12,000.

· 11 ·

THE TEMPLE CUP RIOTS

◆

Pitching, hitting, defense—the three requirements for winning. And the 1895 Baltimore Orioles had all three.

The season shaped up as a four-team horse race among Baltimore, Boston, Cleveland, and the champion New York Giants. But the Giants broke from the gate with a disappointing 15-17 record and quickly dropped from sight. Came August, and the Spiders held a slim lead over Baltimore, with Boston not far behind. In mid-month, the Beaneaters were handed their hats when the Orioles swept a crucial four-game series and, entering the final month of the season, Baltimore had narrowed the gap with Cleveland to a half-game. Cleveland failed to match the O's 20-7 mark in September and Hanlon's crew had captured its second straight title.

The Orioles had supplemented their baseball talent with spikes and fists as they fought and clawed their way to a second straight pennant. The team was assisted, intangibly at least, by ferocious home crowds which intimidated visiting clubs so much that some opposing players were afraid to come to the park. A listless team on the road (33-29), at Union Park the Orioles rode to the sound of the guns, compiling a stunning 54-14 mark.

1895

The Changing Game

◆ ◆ ◆

- *The infield fly rule was adopted.*

- *Foul tips caught on the fly were counted as strikes.*

- *The pitcher's rubber was enlarged to twenty-four inches long by six inches wide.*

- *The diameter of the bat was enlarged from 2½ inches to 2¾ inches.*

- *Mitts—oversized gloves—were abolished for all fielders except catchers and first basemen.*

- *Players using vulgar, indecent, or other improper language saw fines for these indiscretions raised from $5 and $25 to $25 and $100. National League rules forbade a club from paying its players' fines.*

The club led the league in team fielding percentage (.946), as George "Scoops" Carey at first, Hughie Jennings at third, Willie Keeler in right, and Wilbert Robinson behind the plate, led all regulars at their respective positions.

On the mound, the Orioles had a strong pitching staff in Billy Hoffer (30-7), George Hemming (20-13), Sadie McMahon (10-4), Arthur "Dad" Clarkson (12-3), and Duke Esper (10-12).

Rookie Billy Hoffer was the team's best pitcher and the league leader in winning percentage (.811). A slender, almost frail right-hander, Hoffer was a workhorse who relied mainly on his fastball. Although he had two good years left, after 1895, Hoffer's career would go neatly downhill. In successive years, his win-loss record went to 25-7, 22-11, 3-4, 8-10, and 3-8 before he retired. Arm trouble in 1898 would eventually put a halt to a very promising career. On April 21, 1901, the twenty-nine-year-old Hoffer would achieve a distinction of some dubious note when he became the losing pitcher in the American League's first game.

Vagabond right-hander George Hemming, a six-year veteran of five teams, was coming off his best year on the mound, having compiled a 20-13 record and the lowest ERA (4.05) of his career. Known for an economy of motion in his delivery, Hemming was sometimes nicknamed "Old Wax Figger."

John "Sadie" McMahon had been on the roster in 1894 but had been idle in the previous year's Temple Cup games. He had made his major league debut in 1889, and was 45-30 in two years with the financially troubled Philadelphia Athletics before the franchise bowed to economics and sold the talented right-hander to Baltimore, along with Wilbert Robinson and Curt Welch. McMahon had won twenty or more games in each of the five preceding seasons, but a shoulder injury in August 1894 had kept him out of action until August 1895. When he returned, he won a dramatic 1-0 game, the first entry in an eight-game winning streak which helped propel the Orioles back into first place.

Baltimore manager Ned Hanlon judiciously used McMahon as a spot starter in the remaining two months of the 1895 season— six of his fifteen starts came in doubleheader nightcaps when the fading light made his fastball more effective—and the right-hander came through with ten wins in fourteen decisions. Four of the victories were shutouts, tying him for the league lead in that category. McMahon would pitch effectively in 1896 (12-9, 3.48 ERA), but after getting off to an 0-5 start with Brooklyn in 1897, the twenty-nine-year-old hung up his spikes for good. McMahon was unconsciously overworked early in his career. After turning in 255 innings in his rookie career, he endured workloads of 509, 503, 397, and 346 innings before his arm blew out.

Early in his career McMahon had possessed a blazing fastball, but by 1895, he had turned into a control pitcher with an excellent curve. He rarely got rattled on the mound, fielded his position well, and liked to pitch behind in the count.

Filling out the staff were Dad Clarkson and Duke Esper. Clarkson had begun the season with the St. Louis Browns, where he was a dismal 1-6. In his twenty appearances for the Orioles, he rang up a 12-3 mark in relief and several spot starts. Esper, who had compiled a 10-2 record after coming to the Orioles in the middle of the 1894 season, was unable to build on his good beginning. Easily the least effective hurler in the Baltimore rotation, Esper's record for 1895 was 10-12. Four of his losses came in relief, a figure which led the league.

Neither Hemming nor Clarkson would see action in the 1895 Temple Cup Series.

The Orioles' team ERA of 3.80 narrowly topped the second-place Spiders' 3.90. And while the Spiders gave up 106 fewer runs than any other team in the league, the Orioles were even stingier, allowing seventy-four fewer than Cleveland.

Offensively, the Orioles were nothing to be sneered at. Scoring 1,009 runs (second only to Cleveland's 1,068), Baltimore banged out 235 doubles (second to Cleveland's 272), stole 310 bases (second to Cincinnati's 326), had a team batting average of .324 (second to Cleveland's .330), and compiled a team slugging average of .427 (second to Cleveland's .450).

The Baltimore lineup featured six .300 hitters—right fielder Willie Keeler (.391), shortstop Hughie Jennings (.386), third baseman John McGraw (.369), left fielder Joe Kelley (.365), center fielder Steve Brodie (.348), and second baseman Kid Gleason (.309). Reserve second baseman Heinie Reitz batted .294 and reserve catcher William "Boileryard" Clarke hit .290. Keeler's batting average was fifth best in the League, and his 162 runs scored were second only to the era's greatest basestealer, Billy Hamilton. Keeler's 211 hits tied him for second place with Philadelphia's Sam Thompson. Joe Kelley had ten home runs, good enough to be included among the League's five best totals, and he finished fifth in the League in slugging average (.546), and fourth in total bases (283). When there were men on base, the Orioles had no trouble bringing them home: Kelley, Steve Brodie, and Hughie Jennings were three of the four best RBI men in baseball.

This team could hit.

Cleveland's success could be traced, in the main, to two men: Left fielder Jesse Burkett and pitcher Cy Young.

With a league-leading total of 235 hits, Burkett's .423 batting average—the first of back-to-back .400 seasons for the left-handed slugger—was twenty-four points higher than his closest competition, Philadelphia's Ed Delahanty. (From 1893 through 1901, his best seasons in the majors, Burkett would average .379, a nine-year run better than anyone in baseball history except Ty Cobb and Rogers Hornsby.) One of the game's most feared hitters, Burkett, with an .884 fielding percentage, was also one of the shakiest outfielders in the National League.

Cleveland had three other regulars with averages above the coveted .300 mark—shortstop Ed McKean (.342), catcher Chief Zimmer (.340), and the club's first baseman and player-manager, Patsy Tebeau (.318).

On the mound for the Spiders, Cy Young (35-10) had led all National League pitchers in victories (including a perfect 7-0 record in seven relief appearances), tied for the league lead in shutouts (4), finished second in winning percentage (.778), fourth in appearances (47), fifth in strikeouts (121), and sixth in earned run average (3.24). At twenty-eight years of age, Young still had 347 wins left in his strong right arm.

George "Nig" Cuppy was a much improved version of the young man who had been shut out by Boston and Kid Nichols in the fourth game of the 1892 World Series. With ninety-five wins in his first four major league seasons, Cuppy was now being favorably compared with Cy Young. In 1895, he had posted a 26-14 mark and a 3.54 earned run average, a full run per game lower than in his two previous seasons.

Rounding out the Cleveland staff were second-year man Bobby Wallace (12-14) and the much travelled Phil Knell. Roderick John "Bobby" Wallace would convert to the infield after the 1895 season and eventually become the prototypical good-field, no-hit shortstop. Wallace was the first to abandon the straight-up style of playing shortstop and field the ball in the scoop-and-toss style familiar today. In a career which spanned twenty-five years, Wallace was a lifetime .267 hitter who topped the .300 mark just three times. He was inducted into the Hall of Fame in 1953, the first American League shortstop so honored.

In his six-year career, Phil Knell had spent time with eight teams. He began the 1895 season with an 0-6 mark for the Louisville Colonels, and finished the year 7-5 with the Spiders, his last gasp as a major league pitcher. Neither Knell nor Wallace would see action in the 1895 Temple Cup games.

The Series opened on October 2 at Cleveland's League Park with perfect weather and a cloudless sky. The crowd numbered between six and seven thousand and was unusually boisterous, tooting tin horns, jangling cow bells, shaking rattles, and throwing garbage at the Orioles, third baseman John McGraw proving a popular target. The Orioles must have felt right at home.

A portion of the reporters' row had been sold to garner more income for the home club, and members of the fourth estate were so badly crowded that one visiting newspaperman, forced to work where there was no protective screen, was hit by a ball before the game even began. Cleveland management sought to add a few more dollars to its profits by refusing to post the score on the scoreboard; this, it was thought, would cause patrons to buy more scorecards. (The baseball moguls of the period were cheap down to the very last detail.)

The umpiring staff would change twice during the playing of the 1895 World Series. The umpires for the first two games were John McDonald and the recently retired pitcher, Timothy Keefe. John McQuaid and Tim Hurst worked Game Three. Hurst and Keefe worked the final two games of the Series.

Testimonials and presentations were the order of the day for Game One. Cleveland manager Patsy Tebeau was presented with a diamond ring as he led off the second inning, and Jesse Burkett, noted for his hunting as well as his ability at the plate, received a double-barrelled shotgun in the third. Cy Young was given a floral tribute in the shape of a shotgun in the fifth.

Young and Baltimore's Sadie McMahon were the starting pitchers for the opener. The game started slowly, neither team able to advance a man past second base through the first four innings. Cleveland scored the first run of the Series in the fifth. Nine-year veteran Chippy McGarr, leading off, singled to left, and Cy Young followed with a bunt safety. After Jesse Burkett sacrificed both runners over, Ed McKean hit a little pop fly into short right-center field. Second baseman Kid Gleason made a fine running catch with his back to the infield but his throw to the plate was too late to get McGarr and the Spiders led, 1-0.

Baltimore got on the board (figuratively speaking) in the top of the sixth. John McGraw singled, took second on Willie Keeler's groundout, moved to third when Hughie Jennings flew out to center, and scored the tying run on Joe Kelley's infield single. But Cleveland regained the lead in the bottom of the inning. Patsy Tebeau started the rally with an infield single. As Chief Zimmer strode to the plate, an Orioles fan tossed a potato in his direction, an omen of far worse things to come. Zimmer legged out a slow grounder to short and when Harry Blake doubled off the left-field fence, Tebeau scored and the Spiders led, 2-1.

The Orioles tied the score in the eighth inning when McGraw singled, took second on Keeler's groundout, and came home on a Hughie Jennings single. Joe Kelley then followed with a safety to center, sending Jennings to third. Steve Brodie grounded into a forceout at second, but the Cleveland infield couldn't turn the double play and Jennings scored to put the Orioles ahead, 3-2. The Spiders rallied for a tie in the bottom of the inning. Patsy Tebeau was hit by a pitch, but Sadie McMahon protested that he had made no effort to get out of the way, so Tebeau was sent back to the plate. When he doubled to left a moment later, McMahon was left to debate the wisdom of his protest. One out later, Harry Blake's single knotted the score at three-all.

The ninth inning provided a wild conclusion to the game. In the top half, Baltimore took a 4-3 lead when Wilbert Robinson doubled and scored on John McGraw's clutch two-out single. In the bottom of the ninth, everyone expected a bunt from Cleveland's leadoff batter Jesse Burkett, but Burkett straightened up and punched an opposite-field double into left. Fooled on an outside pitch, Ed McKean somehow managed to slap a single into right, sending Burkett home with the tying run. Cupid Childs moved McKean to second with a single and when Jimmy McAleer bunted safely, the Spiders had the bases loaded with none out. The Orioles brought the infield in, a move which paid dividends when Patsy Tebeau forced McKean at the plate for the first out of the inning. Chief Zimmer then grounded to second for what looked to be an inning-ending double play, but Kid Gleason's return throw to first was late and Childs crossed the plate with the winning run. The crowd poured onto the field and carried the victorious Spiders off on their backs.

Quite an exciting start for the 1895 Temple Cup Series.

Neither Young nor McMahon had been at his best. Young had given up twelve hits and a walk in recording the victory and

McMahon had allowed fourteen hits and two walks in taking the loss. None of the bases on balls figured in the scoring. The hitting star for the day was Ed McKean, three-for-four, with a double, a triple, a sacrifice fly, and two runs batted in.

The second game of the Series, the next day, was a sellout long before play was called. About ten thousand fans arrived at League Park, crowding ten-deep behind ropes which stretched all the way from the outfield to the foul lines. This group was even noisier and more demonstrative than the fans the day before, thanks, in part, to one sadistic fan who brought a specially made eight-foot horn with extra tubes through which seven fans could blow a one-note melody. The horn's owner propped his monstrosity on a railing and, with the aid of his neighbors, proudly and loudly serenaded the ballplayers for the full nine innings. During the game, some of the more obnoxious fans threw pop bottles and garbage at the Orioles, and one particularly obstreperous spectator set off fire-crackers before the police politely asked him to leave the park. Cleveland management attempted to head off any more ill will between the two clubs by offering a twenty-five-dollar reward to local policemen who arrested rowdies in the act of throwing any kind of missile at the players.

Shortly before game time, word reached the two clubs that Harry Wright, chief of the National League umpires, had died. Born in Sheffield, England, in 1835, the son of a cricket-playing father, Wright and his parents had emigrated to the United States in 1836. In 1857, he'd been a member of the fabled New York Knickerbockers, and later had helped organize the Cincinnati Reds, baseball's first professional club. Wright has been credited with the introduction of hand signs in coaching, pre-game batting practice, fungo hitting, and the concept of team play. As a manager, he had led the Boston Reds to back-to-back pennants in 1877 and 1878. He had managed the National League Philadelphia Phillies (sometimes called the Quakers) from 1884 through 1893. At various points in their careers, Series participants Kid Gleason, Duke Esper, Phil Knell, and Tim Keefe had all played for Wright, and the moment of his passing must have made this a sad day.

Game Two, unlike the Series opener, was decided in the first inning. Nig Cuppy retired the Orioles one-two-three on ground-outs in the top of the inning, and the Spiders began pounding Bill Hoffer as soon as they came to the plate. Jesse Burkett started the uprising with a single and went to second on a wild pitch. Ed

McKean's hit scored Burkett with the first run of the game and when the throw from Keeler went to the plate, McKean kept running and wound up on second. He made third on a sacrifice bunt by Cupid Childs and, after Jimmy McAleer was hit by an errant pitch from Hoffer, scored on Patsy Tebeau's sacrifice fly. McAleer came home on Chief Zimmer's double and the Spiders had what proved to be an insurmountable 3-0 lead.

Aided by two Cleveland errors, Baltimore scored its first run of the game in the second. The Orioles returned the favor in the fifth by giving the Spiders a run, courtesy of fumbles by Hoffer and Hughie Jennings. Baltimore pulled within two again in the top of the sixth. Jennings singled and went to third on Steve Brodie's hit. Brodie attempted a steal and, while the Cleveland infield was busy running him down between first and second, Jennings raced home with a run. That was all the offense Baltimore would muster on the day. The Spiders added two insurance runs in the sixth on a walk to Zimmer and two-out doubles by Nig Cuppy and Jesse Burkett. A run in the Cleveland eighth made the final score 7-2.

Bill Hoffer had exhibited none of the ability that made him one of the league's leading pitchers during the 1895 season. He had walked two men, hit one, made a wild pitch, and allowed eleven hits, four of them doubles. Cuppy, on the other hand, had scattered five hits and might have finished with a shutout had his teammates been a little more capable in the field.

After a day off, the Series continued at League Park. By noon, there were more people in line for tickets than usually attended a game. An hour later, the stands were filled and the ticket line reached halfway down Lexington Avenue. By game time, there were twelve thousand people on hand. Most of the fans were in their seats, but some were on the roof of the grandstand, some sat astride the outfield fences, and an enterprising (and daring) two dozen or so spectators were perched on the scoreboard. Ropes stretched completely around the field, and the crowd was twenty-deep in places. Outside the park, fans peered through second-story house windows, stood on rooftops, and climbed trees to get a free view of the game. Several more clung precariously to telegraph pole rungs.

The sound level rose to a new high in Game Three. Ticket-holders were admitted through the gate with any old noisemaker at all—gongs, cow bells, tin horns, and homemade rattles filled with rocks. Several small impromptu bands struck up off-key melodies, and brass horns could be heard clearly throughout the park with a tuba now and again adding a mournful note to the proceedings.

Before the game began, admiring friends presented Chief Zimmer with a diamond ring and a plaque displaying the emblem of the Knights of Pythias. Ed McKean was given a diamond stick-pin, valued at five hundred dollars, and Nig Cuppy received a hammerless shotgun. According to an account in the Cleveland *Plain Dealer*, Cuppy "brought the gun to his shoulder and pulled both triggers. A moment later a boy ran out of the crowd from the direction in which he fired and placed a dead pigeon in the pitcher's hand."

One comes to the almost inescapable conclusion that the reporter for the *Plain Dealer* made this story up.

The contest itself was a virtual carbon copy of Game Two. In the top of the first, John McGraw and Hughie Jennings roughed up starting pitcher Cy Young for a single and double, respectively, but Young escaped intact when McGraw was thrown out stealing before Jennings came to the plate. The Spiders, as they had the game before, scored three times in the first. With one out and Ed McKean on first, consecutive singles by Cupid Childs, Jimmy McAleer, and Patsy Tebeau put Cleveland up 2-0. McAleer scored the final run of the inning on a groundout.

Cy Young escaped a bases-loaded, two-out jam in the third when he induced Joe Kelley to foul out, then rolled along for the next four innings without allowing a baserunner. The Spiders added to their 3-0 lead in the seventh when second-year man Harry Blake doubled, moved to third on Chippy McGarr's single, and scored on Young's single. After Burkett moved both runners along with a sacrifice bunt, McKean plated McGarr with a deep fly to left. When Joe Kelley's throw to the plate sailed past catcher Wilbert Robinson, Young came home to make the score 6-0. Both teams traded tallies in the eighth, and the final score was 7-1, Cleveland. Cy Young had his second victory of the Series and Sadie McMahon his second loss.

The Spiders had swept the first three games at League Park in convincing fashion—convincing enough for Cleveland manager Patsy Tebeau to tell his players before leaving for Baltimore, "We'll be back Wednesday morning, no need to take more than one shirt along."

The Cleveland *Plain Dealer* couldn't resist taking the opportunity to poke a little fun at the city of Baltimore:

If, as stated by the Baltimore papers, nobody but thugs and rowdies attend ball games in Cleveland the town must be pitied, for then, it certainly has a large representation of those classes. If all the people who filled League Park yesterday were thugs and rowdies, why, Cleveland has a better supply than Baltimore itself and that city will have to give up its title to having the worst audiences in the league . . . The fact is, a better audience was never seen in any ball park than the one that saw the Spiders literally wipe up the ground with the champion Baltimores yesterday afternoon.

But the *Plain Dealer* took pains to point out that spectators in no way interfered with the action on the field:

With all the crowd and all the noise nothing occurred that need be regretted by the audience or management. Never in the slightest degree was a visiting player interfered with. Once, when Brodie backed up, to take Tebeau's long fly, the crowd gave way and gave him room to catch it, while had they chosen to hold their places, a two-base hit would have resulted.

The sixth of October was an off-day for travel, and the Series resumed on the 7th at Union Park in Baltimore. Maryland governor Brown and Baltimore mayor Latrobe, reeking of misplaced optimism, had festivities planned for their team—on the eighth and ninth, benefit performances by the Digby Bell Opera Company and on the evening of the tenth, a parade and grand ball at which Brown and Latrobe, assisted by officers of the Maryland militia in full uniform, were to formally receive the Orioles.

Fans in Baltimore had been stirred up by reports of the shabby treatment given their team in Cleveland and turned out determined to give the Spiders a dose of the same. When the club started from the Carrollton Hotel, a crowd of several hundred people was waiting. As the Spiders entered their large, horse-drawn wagon for the journey to the ballpark, they were pelted with rotten apples, potatoes, eggs, and an occasional pebble or stone. Matters didn't improve any when the team arrived at Union Park. Many fans had brought small baskets of rotten eggs, but were required to leave them at the entrance gates. At game time, long lines of policemen were stationed along the bleachers, behind the ropes with the fans, and among the crowd in the stands. Baltimore Orioles president Von Der Horst and players John McGraw, Joe Kelley, and Boileryard Clarke pleaded with the spectators not to disrupt the game, but during the bottom of the first inning, several fans threw small pieces of brick at some of the Cleveland players. Third baseman Chippy McGarr, reaping the whirlwind of abuse hurled at his Oriole counterpart, John McGraw, came in for the most attention. Manager Patsy Tebeau was roundly hissed as he stepped to the plate in the second inning, but turned the hisses into applause when he stepped out of the batter's box and made a great show of tipping his hat to the crowd.

Baltimore's Duke Esper got his first start of the Series in Game Four, as Nig Cuppy took the mound for Cleveland. This game, following the same pattern as the two which preceded it, was decided in the early innings. With Steve Brodie on base in the bottom half of the second, George "Scoops" Carey doubled to right center for the first run of the game. (Carey had an unusual career. He had been a National League rookie in 1895, played no big league ball again until he joined Louisville in 1898, then didn't play in the majors again until joining Washington for the 1902 and 1903 seasons.) The Orioles widened their lead in the third when McGraw, Keeler, and Jennings banged out consecutive singles, McGraw scoring. A base on balls to Joe Kelley filled the bases, and Steve Brodie's sacrifice fly put the O's up, 3-0. Baltimore plated two insurance runs in the seventh and won handily, 5-0. Duke Esper pitched a nifty five-hitter, striking out three and walking no one. Cuppy, whose teammates had now been shut out in two of his three Series starts, including the fourth game of 1892, took the loss.

The only thing the police feared more than a Baltimore loss was a Baltimore victory. To avert as much violence as possible, constables sneaked the Spiders under the grandstand and out through the home-team entrance, completely bypassing the visitors' gate. Despite this precaution, a mob of fifteen hundred strong was waiting. Ten of Baltimore's finest surrounded the Cleveland players, while the rest of the small force did what it could to subdue the angry crowd. It took a full five minutes to make the fifteen-foot journey from the home-club entrance to the team wagon. The mob pelted players and police with potatoes, eggs, and fruit the entire time, but the real trouble began when the angry crowd ran short of produce and began picking up anything within reach—chunks of dirt, rocks, slag, sticks, and bricks. The Spiders covered their heads with baseball mitts and bat bags, and sought shelter on the floor of the wagon. The stoning continued for ten minutes as police tried to push the crowd back and make room for the wagon to leave. When the frenzied mob attempted to unhitch the wagon, the horses grew skittish and galloped down the street, the wagon careening wildly. The crowd followed as long as it could, picking up missiles it had thrown just a few moments before. No fewer than ten arrests were made by the Baltimore police. Three of the men taken into custody were made to pay a stiff fine of five dollars and court costs.

When all was said and done, damage to the Cleveland players was slight. Cupid Childs suffered the only injury—a lump on the side of his head from a large rock. Back at the Carrollton Hotel, Jesse Burkett nervously fingered an impressive piece of slag he had found in the wagon bed after the excitement had died down. When placed on the scales later that evening, the chunk weighed in at eighteen ounces.

The Cleveland papers were outraged. The *Plain Dealer* trumpeted, "CLEVELANDS BOMBARDED BY TOUGHS GOING AND COMING" in its headline, and said that "the wonder now is that the Cleveland players are alive and able to tell the story and not in either hospital or morgue." The headline in the Cleveland *Leader* stated flatly, "AN EXHIBITION OF ROWDYISM BY A BALTIMORE MOB." The Cleveland *Press* was more to the point: "RIOT." Even *The New York Times* called the ruckus "almost a riot," and referred to the mob as "hoodlums." The Baltimore *Sun*, on the other hand, predicted that Cleveland newspapermen were sure to make a row over the incident, "and all because a few stones were thrown at the Spiders."

Cleveland manager Patsy Tebeau was not discouraged by the loss. "One swallow don't make a summer," he said after the game, "and we'll get the cup yet . . . Young will pitch tomorrow, and we think the trophy will come our way, of course."

Over fifteen hundred fans crowded into the Cleveland Music Hall the next afternoon to watch little figures representing ballplayers reenact each play of Game Five, seconds after the telegraph report reached the hall. But they weren't exactly breaking down the doors for tickets at Union Park and at game time, there were only 4,100 fans on hand to watch the two aces, Cy Young and Bill Hoffer, square off against each other.

Cleveland threatened in the second when Patsy Tebeau singled and went to third on Harry Blake's double, but Tebeau was thrown out at the plate when McGarr grounded to second baseman Kid Gleason. The Orioles put two men on in the bottom of the inning but they, too, failed to score. The wily catcher for the Spiders, Chief Zimmer, helped keep the game scoreless in the fourth. With Steve Brodie on third and Boileryard Clarke on first, the Orioles attempted a double steal. Clarke pulled into second unmolested as Zimmer bluffed a throw, then fired the ball to third instead, trapping Brodie in a rundown.

The death knell for the Orioles sounded in the seventh when Cleveland broke through against Hoffer for three runs. Appropriately, Cy Young started the inning with a double to the fence in left center. Jesse Burkett singled to right, but Willie Keeler's strong throw to third baseman John McGraw kept Young from scoring. One out later, Cupid Childs lifted a high fly ball for Kelley in left field. Anticipating a play at the plate, Kelley had one eye on the baserunner at third and one eye on the ball, and dropped the routine fly. Young dashed home with the first run of the game. In the Cleveland Music Hall, men rose and threw their hats in the air, and the ladies cheered with equal abandon. Subsequent hits by Jimmy McAleer and Patsy Tebeau gave the Spiders a 3-0 lead.

The Orioles tallied their first run of the game in the bottom of the seventh. Boileryard Clarke singled, stole second, and took third on Bill Hoffer's groundout to first. As Hoffer was crossing the bag, Patsy Tebeau threw out his leg and tripped him. Hoffer shoved Tebeau to the grass, then claimed interference, but umpire Tim Hurst ruled Hoffer was out and separated the two to prevent any further trouble. A moment later, John McGraw grounded to short and, seeking revenge, slid into first with his spikes high. Tebeau touched the bag with his foot and nimbly sidestepped McGraw, but Clarke scored easily on the play.

Cleveland put the game out of reach with two runs in the top of the eighth, and the Orioles again showed their roughhouse style of play when they took the field for the ninth. Patsy Tebeau reached base when Joe Kelley dropped his fly ball. Chief Zimmer singled to left and Kelley redeemed himself somewhat with a strong throw to third. John McGraw put a forceful tag on the sliding Tebeau, bloodying his lip, while the small but rowdy crowd cheered its approval.

Baltimore's last gasp came in the bottom of the inning. Boileryard Clarke was retired on a weak grounder to short and Hoffer on a foul pop to the catcher, but Young faltered and issued walks to McGraw and Keeler. When he hit Hughie Jennings with a pitch, the bases were loaded and the winning run was standing at the plate in the person of the fumble-fingered Joe Kelley. Kelley grounded to short for what looked to be the last out of the game, but Ed McKean kept the inning alive by booting the ball, allowing McGraw to score. Steve Brodie then hit a one-hopper back to Young and the 1895 Temple Cup Series was history.

Cleveland management was eager to avoid a repeat of any post-game disturbances and had stationed mounted police around the Spiders' wagon. A solid wall of foot police held the crowd at a distance of some fifty feet. Several stones were thrown at the wagon but the violence was nothing like the day before.

The headline in the Cleveland *Plain Dealer* again cried foul: "CHAMPIONS PLAY DIRTY BALL AND SHOW A YELLOW STREAK WHEN THEY SEE THE GAME SLIPPING FROM THEM." With the Temple Cup victory safely in the bag, the *Plain Dealer* went on to taunt the Orioles in the body of the article:

> The Temple cup belongs to Cleveland and the champions' pennant is all smeared with mud. The Spiders went at 'em today, and for a time the Orioles kept up to the clip, but then the streak of "yellow" showed and it was all over . . . There was not a shout for the Temple cup winners, while the crowd filed out of the grounds like a funeral procession and Baltimore is sore, very sore, and this only makes the victory more glorious.

In the first two years of Temple Cup competition, the second-place team had won the championship in convincing fashion over first-place Baltimore, whose record in the two Series stood at 1-8.

Each of the sixteen Cleveland players received $528.33 for winning the Series, a paycheck made that much sweeter because they had refused any sort of agreement with the Orioles to share the money. The Orioles netted $316 per man.

The Baltimore *American* had this to say about the Series:

> We hope for the sake of baseball and the reputations of citizens and cities that this will be the last year of the Temple Cup series. The events in Cleveland and the proceedings which followed the opening game here illustrate the bad effects of a contest which is in reality little more than a money-making opportunity for the players. The series clouds the title of any championship, and does more to bring the game into bad repute than all the other misfortunes of the season. The natural climax of the playing is the

winning of the championship, and to add a second competition is to discount and confuse the whole fight.

While the *American* was certainly biased in its opinions toward the Orioles, the writer made a good point. Most people clung to the belief that the strongest team was the one that won the most often in the 132-game season. Of what value, then, was a postseason championship between the first- and second-place clubs, other than for lining the pockets of the participants? While interest and attendance had run high for the first nine games of the Temple Cup Series, the fans had begun to tire of the artificial championship.

GAME ONE—October 2, 1895, at League Park, Cleveland

BALTIMORE	AB	R	H	BI	E	CLEVELAND	AB	R	H	BI	E
McGraw, 3b	4	2	3	1	0	Burkett, lf	4	1	1	0	0
Keeler, rf	5	0	1	0	0	McKean, ss	4	0	3	2	1
Jennings, ss	4	1	1	1	0	Childs, 2b	5	1	1	0	1
Kelley, lf	4	0	3	1	0	McAleer, cf	5	0	1	0	0
Brodie, cf	4	0	0	1	0	Tebeau, 1b	5	2	2	0	1
Gleason, 2b	4	0	2	0	0	Zimmer, c	4	0	2	1	0
Carey, 1b	4	0	0	0	0	Blake, rf	4	0	2	2	0
Robinson, c	4	1	2	0	0	McGarr, 3b	4	1	1	0	0
McMahon, p	4	0	0	0	0	Young, p	4	0	1	0	0
	37	4	12	4	0		39	5	14	5	3

```
BAL   0 0 0   0 0 1   0 2 1 – 4
CLE   0 0 0   0 1 1   0 1 2 – 5
```

D: Robinson, McKean, Blake, Tebeau, Burkett.   T: McKean.   SAC: Burkett.   SF: McKean.   DP: CLE.   BB: McMahon 2, Young 1.   Struck out: McMahon.   PB: Robinson.   Umpires: Keefe and McDonald.   Time—2:15.   Att: 6,500.

GAME TWO—October 3, 1895, at League Park, Cleveland

BALTIMORE	AB	R	H	BI	E	CLEVELAND	AB	R	H	BI	E
McGraw, 3b	4	0	0	0	0	Burkett, lf	5	1	4	1	0
Keeler, rf	3	0	1	0	0	McKean, ss	4	1	1	1	1
Jennings, ss	4	1	1	0	1	Childs, 2b	3	1	0	0	0
Kelley, lf	3	1	0	0	0	McAleer, cf	3	1	0	1	1
Brodie, cf	4	0	1	0	0	Tebeau, 1b	4	1	1	1	0
Gleason, 2b	4	0	0	0	0	Zimmer, c	3	1	2	1	0
Carey, 1b	3	0	2	0	1	Blake, rf	4	0	0	0	0
Clarke, c	3	0	0	0	0	McGarr, 3b	4	0	2	0	0
Hoffer, p	3	0	0	0	1	Cuppy, p	3	1	1	1	0
	31	2	5	0	3		33	7	11	6	2

```
BAL   0 1 0   0 0 1   0 0 0 – 2
CLE   3 0 0   0 1 2   1 0 x – 7
```

D: Zimmer, McGarr, Cuppy, Burkett.   SB: Jennings, Burkett, McKean.   SAC: Childs, Cuppy.   SF: Tebeau.   BB: Hoffer 2, Cuppy 2.   Struck out: Hoffer 1, Cuppy 3.   WP: Hoffer.   PB: Clarke.   HBP: McAleer (Hoffer).   Umpires: Keefe and McDonald. Time—2:15.   Att: 10,000.

GAME THREE—October 5, 1895, at League Park, Cleveland

BALTIMORE	AB	R	H	BI	E	CLEVELAND	AB	R	H	BI	E
McGraw, 3b	4	0	2	0	0	Burkett, lf	3	0	2	1	0
Keeler, rf	4	1	0	0	0	McKean, ss	4	1	0	0	1
Jennings, ss	3	0	2	0	0	Childs, 2b	4	1	2	1	0
Kelley, lf	4	0	1	1	1	McAleer, cf	4	1	3	1	0
Brodie, cf	4	0	0	0	0	Tebeau, 1b	4	0	1	1	0
Gleason, 2b	4	0	0	0	0	Zimmer, c	3	1	1	0	0
Carey, 1b	4	0	1	0	0	Blake, rf	3	1	1	1	0
Robinson, c	4	0	1	0	0	McGarr, 3b	4	1	2	1	0
McMahon, p	3	0	0	0	0	Young, p	4	1	0	0	0
	34	1	7	1	1		33	7	12	6	1

```
BAL   0 0 0   0 0 0   0 1 0 – 1
CLE   3 0 0   0 0 0   3 1 x – 7
```

D: Jennings, Blake, Childs, Zimmer, McGarr.   SAC: Blake, Burkett.   SF: McKean. BB: Young 1, McMahon 1.   Struck out: Young 1, McMahon 1.   Umpires: McQuaid and Hurst.   Time—1:45.   Att: 12,000.

GAME FOUR—October 7, 1895, at Union Park, Baltimore

CLEVELAND	AB	R	H	PO	A	E	BALTIMORE	AB	R	H	PO	A	E
Burkett, lf	4	0	0	4	0	0	McGraw, 3b	4	1	1	1	2	0
McKean, ss	4	0	1	1	1	0	Keeler, rf	3	2	1	3	0	0
Childs, 2b	4	0	0	3	4	0	Jennings, ss	4	1	3	2	2	0
McAleer, cf	4	0	1	2	0	0	Kelley, lf	3	0	2	4	0	0
Tebeau, 1b	4	0	1	6	1	0	Brodie, cf	4	1	1	3	0	0
Zimmer, c	3	0	0	3	0	1	Gleason, 2b	3	0	0	4	4	1
Blake, rf	3	0	1	4	0	0	Carey, 1b	4	0	1	6	1	0
McGarr, 3b	3	0	1	0	2	0	Robinson, c	4	0	0	3	0	0
Cuppy, p	3	0	0	1	0	0	Esper, p	3	0	0	1	0	0
	32	0	5	24	8	1		32	5	9	27	9	1

```
CLE   0 0 0   0 0 0   0 0 0 – 0
BAL   0 1 2   0 0 0   2 0 x – 5
```

Earned runs: BAL 3.   2B: Carey, Jennings.   SB: Jennings, Kelley.   DP: BAL 1.   BB: Cuppy 2.   Struck out: Esper 3, Cuppy 3.   PB: Zimmer.   Umpires: Keefe and Hurst. Time—1:55.   Att: 9,100

GAME FIVE—October 8, 1895, at Union Park, Baltimore

CLEVELAND	AB	R	H	BI	E	BALTIMORE	AB	R	H	BI	E
Burkett, lf	5	1	3	1	0	McGraw, 3b	4	1	2	1	1
McKean, ss	4	0	1	0	0	Keeler, rf	4	0	1	0	1
Childs, 2b	4	1	1	2	1	Jennings, ss	4	0	0	0	0
McAleer, cf	5	0	1	1	0	Kelley, lf	5	0	1	0	2
Tebeau, 1b	4	0	1	1	1	Brodie, cf	4	0	2	0	0
Zimmer, c	5	0	1	0	0	Gleason, 2b	4	0	0	0	1
Blake, rf	5	0	1	0	0	Carey, 1b	4	0	1	0	0
McGarr, 3b	4	1	1	0	1	Clarke, c	4	1	2	0	0
Young, p	4	2	1	0	0	Hoffer, p	4	0	0	0	1
	40	5	11	5	3		37	2	9	1	6

```
CLE   0 0 0   0 0 0   3 2 0 – 5
BAL   0 0 0   0 0 0   1 0 1 – 2
```

D: Blake, Young, McGraw.   SB: McGraw, Clarke.   SAC: Young, Keeler.   BB: Young 2, Hoffer 4.   Struck out: Hoffer 3, Young 1.   HBP: Brodie and Jennings (by Young).   Umpires: Hurst and Keefe.   Time—2:30.   Att: 4,100.

· 12 ·

A Sweep for the Orioles

◆

One pitch was all it took to decide the 1896 World Series.

One pitch, one line drive, one injured Cy Young.

Nobody seemed to want the 1896 National League pennant, as no fewer than five teams vied for the lead in the opening weeks of the season. An early battle between Pittsburgh and Philadelphia was transformed into a bruising race between Baltimore and Cleveland. Then the Cincinnati Reds surprised all the experts, winning twenty-five of thirty games and establishing a six-game lead by the end of July.

The Reds, hampered by injuries to their infielders and (it was rumored) drunkenness, faltered and were soon passed by the Spiders. The Orioles caught fire, passed everyone, and sailed through the final month of the season to capture their third National League title in as many years. For the year, Baltimore again sported a sizzling record at home (47-14).

Baltimore and Cleveland personnel had changed very little since 1895. For the Orioles, George "Scoops" Carey was back in the minor leagues despite an impressive rookie season of 1895 which saw him hit .261 with 75 RBIs and lead all National League

1896

The Changing Game

♦ ♦ ♦

• *The home club was required to have at least a dozen baseballs ready for use at the start of a ballgame.*

• *Only the club president, manager, and players in uniform could occupy the players' bench during a game.*

first basemen in fielding percentage. Baltimore manager Ned Hanlon had acquired Jack Doyle from the Giants, a good-hitting, wide-ranging infielder with a scrappy reputation that had earned him the nickname "Dirty Jack." Second baseman Kid Gleason had gone to the Giants, his duties being assumed by reserve infielder Heinie Reitz. Jim Donnelly, after a four-year sabbatical from the major leagues, was filling in for the ailing John McGraw at third. (McGraw had missed most of the season with recurring bouts of malaria.) The starting eight for the Cleveland Spiders was unchanged, but Zeke Wilson had replaced Phil Knell in the pitching rotation.

Baltimore was the dominant club, having led the twelve-team league in runs scored (995), triples (100), batting average (.328), slugging average (.429), and stolen bases (441). The Orioles finished second in the league in doubles (207) and team earned run average (3.67).

Individually, shortstop Hughie Jennings, with a .398 batting average, had narrowly lost the batting title to Jesse Burkett (.410), but Jennings had finished second in the league in RBIs (121), and third in hits (208). Wee Willie Keeler had finished second in hits (214) and had tied for second in runs scored (153). Joe Kelley, second in stolen bases (87), had tied for second in triples (19), been third in the league in doubles (31) and total bases (282), and fourth in slugging average (.543).

When the Orioles came to town, opposing pitchers knew they were in for a hard day's work. While the team itself hit for a .328 batting average, the regular eight starters had a combined .346 mark alone! Hughie Jennings (.398), Willie Keeler (.392), Joe Kelley (.364), Wilbert Robinson (.347), Jack Doyle (.345), and Jim Donnelly (.328) all topped the .300 plateau, while Steve Brodie (.297), backup catcher Boileryard Clarke (.297), and Heinie Reitz (.287) narrowly missed the mark. Four of the club's regulars had one hundred or more runs batted in for the season—Jennings (121), Reitz (106), Doyle (101), and Kelley (100).

The Cleveland Spiders had finished the season second in fielding percentage (.949) and tied for second in doubles (207). The club was third in batting average (.301) and slugging average (.391). The Spiders' pitching staff had the best control of any National League team, had tied for second with Baltimore in shutouts (9), and had led the league in earned run average (3.46).

Jesse Burkett had had another fine year for the Spiders, hitting .400 for the second straight season and leading the league in hits (240), total bases (317), and runs scored (160). Other than Burkett, only Cupid Childs (.355) and Ed McKean (.338) had topped the .300 mark, but those two batters had combined for 218 RBIs. In Chief Zimmer, the Spiders had the league's best defensive catcher, and it was practically impossible to ground a ball through the right side of the infield. Patsy Tebeau had finished third in fielding percentage but led all first basemen in putouts (1,340) and total chances (1,415). Second sacker Cupid Childs had achieved a near sweep in each defensive category, leading the league in putouts (375), assists (487), total chances (862), and double plays (73). Childs handled nearly 150 more chances than any other National League second baseman.

On the mound, the Spiders appeared to have the edge, particularly in a short series. Cy Young (29-16, 3.24 ERA) and Nig Cuppy (25-14, 3.12) were followed in the rotation by Zeke Wilson (17-9, 4.01) and Bobby Wallace (10-7, 3.34). Young had tied for the league lead in strikeouts (137) and shutouts (5), and finished second in victories, innings pitched (414), appearances (51), and complete games (42). Nig Cuppy was third in ERA and fifth in victories. Cuppy was coming off his fifth major league season, was a consistent winner with a lifetime win-loss record of 120-66 and, although he would remain in the major leagues for five more years, this would be his last full season on the mound.

The Orioles were led by Bill Hoffer (25-7, 3.38 ERA), Arlie Pond (16-8, 3.49), George Hemming (15-6, 4.19), Duke Esper (14-5, 3.58), and Sadie McMahon (12-9, 3.48). Hoffer had led the league for the second straight year in winning percentage (.781), and George Hemming had tied for second in the same category (.714). If, as it is said, good pitching stops good hitting, the Spiders, with Young and Cuppy, looked like they would be difficult to beat. One out after the Series began, all that would change.

The Orioles were the superior team, offensively, at nearly every position, holding a clear edge at first base (Jack Doyle over Patsy Tebeau), shortstop (Hughie Jennings over Ed McKean), third base (Jim Donnelly over Chippy McGarr), right field (Willie Keeler over Harry Blake), center field (Steve Brodie over Jimmy McAleer), and catcher (Wilbert Robinson over Chief Zimmer). The Spiders were slightly stronger at second base, with Cupid Childs a better hitter than Heinie Reitz, although both batters had 106 RBIs for the year. The teams were more evenly matched in left field. Jesse Burkett (.410) hit for a higher average than Joe Kelley (.364), but Kelley had twenty-eight more runs batted in.

Fans and press alike expected an exciting Series, despite the apparent mismatch. During the regular season, the Spiders had easily taken the measure of the Orioles, winning eight of the eleven games they had played. (Cy Young had beaten the O's in four of his five starts against the club.) With this memory still fresh in their minds, the Spiders hoped again to defeat the Orioles, the same club they had nearly swept in the 1895 Temple Cup Series. Baltimore was eager to prove the 1895 losses had been nothing more than an aberration.

The 1896 Temple Cup Series began on Friday, October 2, at Baltimore's Union Park. In preparation, the Orioles had played exhibition games nearly every day for the week prior to the Series, and the club was at its peak. In contrast, the Spiders were somewhat rusty, having been unable to play since the preceding Saturday after bad weather had forced the cancellation of three exhibition games. Cy Young was scheduled to pitch Game One for the Spiders but because of illness, looked doubtful until shortly before game time, when the veteran right-hander answered the bell. His opponent was right-hander Bill Hoffer, looking for vindication after losing both starts in the 1895 Series.

Ticket prices, normally a quarter, had been doubled for the first three games and, though it was a clear and balmy day, only 3,995 turned out for Game One, nowhere near a capacity crowd for Baltimore's Union Park. Play began at 3:30, with umpire Robert Emslie stationed at first and John Sheridan behind the plate.

It didn't take long to see which way the ball was rolling in the Series. The first batter, Baltimore third baseman John McGraw, hit a screaming line drive off Cy Young's right wrist. Young recovered in time to retire McGraw at first, but for a few moments it appeared as though the big right-hander would be lost for the rest of the game. Eventually the pain in his wrist subsided and Young resumed his place in the box. (Only manager Patsy Tebeau knew how seriously injured his ace was. When the game ended, Young's pitching hand was so badly swollen and stiff he could barely bend his fingers.) Hughie Jennings started a two-out rally with a line single to right but it looked as though third baseman Chippy McGarr would close the inning out when he made a terrific stop of Joe Kelley's hard grounder. But McGarr threw the ball away and the Orioles had a first-and-third scoring threat. Jack Doyle's line drive spun Cupid Childs around and knocked him to the dirt, but the game infielder crawled to second base just ahead of Joe Kelley for the forceout. The Spiders had held, just barely, and Cy Young appeared to be in for a hard day.

Cleveland mounted a threat in the bottom of the inning when leadoff batter Jesse Burkett singled and Ed McKean drew a base on balls. Childs sacrificed both runners over. Jimmy McAleer's hot grounder was headed for left field, but John McGraw made a fine stop of the ball, and Burkett was run down between third and home. McKean made third on the play and McAleer stole second a moment later, but Chief Zimmer stranded both runners when he struck out.

In the bottom of the second, Patsy Tebeau wrenched his back with an awkward swing at one of Hoffer's nasty curveballs. Tebeau, who required a doctor's attention and a hospital stay, was lost to the Spiders for the balance of the Series. (He later said he would rather give up five hundred dollars than miss the games.) Nine-year veteran utility player "Peach Pie" Jack O'Connor took Tebeau's place at first base.

The Orioles struck for the first runs of the Series in the third. John McGraw singled and raced to third on Hughie Jennings's safety. Cy Young took the relay from outfielder Harry Blake and fired the ball to shortstop Ed McKean to catch Jennings who, thinking the throw was going through to third, was steaming for second. But McKean took his eye off the ball and it skittered off his glove. Second baseman Cupid Childs picked it up and, with Mc-Graw heading for home, unleashed a terrible throw to the plate, ten feet over catcher Chief Zimmer's head. McGraw scored easily and Jennings reached third. (Running the bases had taken its toll on John McGraw, still suffering the effects of malaria. Too weak to continue, he was replaced in the lineup by reserve second baseman and twelve-year veteran Joe Quinn.) Joe Kelley, the next batter, handcuffed Cy Young with a hard line drive and Jennings came home with the second run of the inning.

The clubs traded runs in the sixth, and the Orioles touched Young for some insurance in the seventh. With one out, Willie Keeler legged out an infield single. Hughie Jennings blooped a pop-fly double just inside the left-field foul line, sending Keeler to third from where he scored on Joe Kelley's groundout. Because of the injury to his wrist, Young no longer had anything on the ball, and Jack Doyle slashed one of his deliveries to the bleachers in left for two bases. A single by Heinie Reitz gave Baltimore a command-ing 6-1 lead. Willie Keeler's RBI triple in the eighth accounted for the final run and the Orioles had taken the Series opener by a convincing 7-1 score.

Bill Hoffer had scattered five hits and walked four in record-ing the easy victory. The offensive star of the game was shortstop Hughie Jennings, with a 3-for-5 performance at the plate.

Because of his first-inning injury, Cy Young had been roughed up for thirteen hits, four for extra bases, and had suffered a sting-ing defeat in this, his only start of the Series. The loss of Young would prove to be fatal to the Spiders.

The Baltimore *American* summed the game up neatly:

> Deprived at once of their gingery captain [Tebeau] and their usual matchless box strength, the Spiders were not at all terrible . . .
> With their trump card (pitching) not working and Tebeau in the hospital, it was easy enough to take the Spiders, bag and baggage, into camp.

The Cleveland *Leader* noted that Baltimore manager Ned Hanlon's "smile has extended until it threatens to engulf his ears, and he says it hasn't got a good start yet, at that." The *Leader*

also took a swipe at Baltimore fans when it said "the attendance . . . was about as expected. Baltimore people think base ball
is a 25-cent game and that's all they will pay."

There was an overcast sky and a threat of rain for Game Two
the next day, and another small crowd of 3,200 turned out. Because
of the poor attendance, talk had begun of playing the third game in
Pittsburgh or Cincinnati to increase gate revenues.

Baltimore manager Ned Hanlon, confident of victory now
that his Orioles were hitting, bypassed the rest of his usual starters
(Arlie Pond, George Hemming, Duke Esper, and Sadie McMahon)
and showed his contempt for the Spiders by selecting second-year
pitcher Joe Corbett to work Game Two. Corbett's major league
experience consisted of just sixty innings and eleven starts over the
previous two seasons. He was 3-0 with the Orioles in eight appearances in 1896, but Hanlon had high hopes for the twenty-year-old.
Patsy Tebeau went with right-handed hurler Bobby Wallace.

An offensive rampage by Baltimore and defensive lapses by his
teammates plagued Wallace in the opening inning. Leadoff batter
John McGraw grounded to Ed McKean, whose wild throw to first
baseman Jack O'Connor let McGraw reach second. Willie Keeler
lashed a single to center to score McGraw and, after Wallace hit
Hughie Jennings with a pitch, Joe Kelley followed with another
run-scoring single. When center fielder Jimmy McAleer booted
the ball, Kelley went to second and Jennings to third. Jack Doyle
beat out a Baltimore chop, sending Jennings home with the third
run of the inning, and Kelley later scored on a groundout to give
the Orioles a four-run first. Doyle was thrown out stealing to end
the rally, but the Orioles were in the catbird seat.

Singles by Hughie Jennings, Joe Kelley, and Jack Doyle, and a
Steve Brodie groundout gave Baltimore two more runs in the
third. The Spiders got on the board in the bottom of the inning
when Bobby Wallace beat out an infield hit and scored on Ed
McKean's double. The Orioles scored their final run in the fifth
and Cleveland notched an unearned run in the sixth to round out
the day's official offense. Baltimore plated two more runs in the
ninth, but darkness prevented the final half-inning from being
played and the score reverted to the eighth, making the O's 7-2
victors. This marked the first time Baltimore had managed to win
two games in a World Series.

Despite the pressure of pitching in post-season competition,
the youngster Corbett had performed well, scattering seven hits,

walking two, and striking out four in recording his first victory of the Temple Cup games. Cleveland's Bobby Wallace had surrendered ten hits, two walks, and hit three batters, Jennings twice. Four of the seven Baltimore runs—six of nine, including the aborted ninth inning—were unearned.

Hoping to draw a larger crowd, Baltimore management rolled back the price of admission to twenty-five cents for Game Three on October 5. It did little good. Despite perfect weather, attendance improved only to 4,240 for the final game at Union Park.

Patsy Tebeau, released from the hospital but still unable to get into the game, was wrapped in a heavy winter overcoat and seated on the bench, directly in front of super-fan DeWolf Hopper. Hopper was the stage actor famous for reciting Ernest Thayer's "Casey at the Bat." The Baltimore *American* stated that Tebeau's wrenched back

> . . . is giving him excruciating pain, and a fear has come to the game little man that he will never be the Pat Tebeau of old. The complete refusal of the injured muscles to heal has thoroughly frightened him, and he looks on the future with gloom. To a friend on parting he said he feared he would never be as good a man as he was.

Tebeau's fears that his best playing days were over were well grounded. Only thirty-two years old and a lifetime .287 hitter, he would never again hit higher than .270.

Ned Hanlon rewarded pitcher Bill Hoffer for his excellent performance in Game One with his second start in four days. Tebeau went with his veteran, Nig Cuppy. Cuppy was hampered by a split finger on his pitching hand.

The Orioles continued their pattern of drawing first blood. In the top of the second, Joe Kelley got the Baltimore offense untracked with an infield single to short. On a hit-and-run play, Jack Doyle grounded to Ed McKean, who had moved over to cover second. McKean stepped on the bag for the forceout, but Kelley's hard slide broke up any chance for the double play. Doyle then stole second and came home on Steve Brodie's single to right. Baltimore scored again in the third when Bill Hoffer tripled to the left-field fence and ambled home on Willie Keeler's deep sacrifice fly.

Cleveland narrowed the margin in the bottom of the inning. Jesse Burkett and Ed McKean singled, and Burkett scored on Cupid Childs's groundout. In the fifth, the Spiders pulled into a tie for the first time in the Series. With two out, Hoffer issued a walk to Cupid Childs, then surrendered back-to-back singles to Jimmy McAleer and Jack O'Connor. O'Connor's hit tied the score at two-all, but Baltimore regained the lead in the next half-frame when John McGraw singled, stole second, went to third on a wild pitch, and scored on Willie Keeler's second sacrifice fly of the game.

The O's put the contest away with three insurance runs in the eighth. Team captain Wilbert Robinson doubled and scored on John McGraw's single. With Willie Keeler at the plate, Baltimore again employed its favorite offensive tactic, the hit-and-run. Keeler's single sent McGraw to third, from where he scored the Orioles' fifth run of the day on Hughie Jennings's sacrifice fly. Keeler stole second and subsequently came home on Chippy McGarr's throwing error. Still pitching strongly, Bill Hoffer retired the top of the Cleveland lineup in the ninth and Baltimore had its third straight victory, a 6-2 triumph.

Hoffer had allowed ten hits and a walk in the game. The Spiders had had numerous scoring opportunities but were unable to produce with men on base and had stranded ten runners. Nig Cuppy had allowed only four hits through the first seven innings but three of those were to leadoff batters, all of whom eventually scored.

The Cleveland *Leader* bemoaned the poor luck of the Spiders:

> As for the Clevelands, they hit the ball harder and oftener by far than in either of the other two games, but the hardest drives were right at somebody, and the safe hits came pretty much all the time except when men were on bases . . . The Clevelands' rustiness alone was responsible for the first two defeats, to-day's was bad luck, and the players are sure that they can win every game at home.

The *Leader* also crabbed that umpires Emslie and Sheridan favored the Orioles on all the close plays and were particularly hard on the Spiders on balls and strikes. But the Spiders hadn't lost three straight because of a few close decisions on the basepaths; nor were the umpires at fault. Through the first three games, the Orioles had scored twenty runs to Cleveland's five, and baseball teams rarely win ball games when they are outscored by a four-to-one margin.

The clubs left Baltimore on the sixth of October and played exhibition games in Newark, Scranton, Wilkes-Barre, and Cantonville before arriving in Cleveland for the fourth game of the Series on October 8. With a three-game lead, Hanlon again disdained the services of his five best pitchers and went with Joe

Corbett. Patsy Tebeau tapped Nig Cuppy, who was pitching on two days' rest. The weather had taken a turn for the worse. The mercury dipped down into the forties and only twelve hundred people turned out at League Park in Cleveland. Patsy Tebeau had hoped to play, but the frigid temperature made his back ache even more, and Jack O'Connor again filled in at first.

In many ways, the finale was the most interesting contest of the Series. The game was a pitchers' battle for the first six-and-a-half innings and there were no scoring opportunities until the Cleveland fifth. Leadoff batter Chippy McGarr singled and went to second when Hughie Jennings booted an easy double play grounder off the bat of Harry Blake. With Nig Cuppy at bat, the rest of the Cleveland players came on the field and stood behind the plate, encouraging the baserunners and Cuppy, while taunting Corbett. Umpire Emslie stopped the game and ordered the Spiders back to their bench, but as soon as he put on his mask, manager Tebeau led them back out.

Cuppy struck out, but McGarr and Blake worked the double steal, putting runners on second and third with only one down. Jesse Burkett grounded to Jennings, who redeemed himself by throwing a perfect strike to the plate to nail McGarr. When Ed McKean grounded out to end the inning, Cleveland fans showed their good sportsmanship by applauding Corbett's clutch pitching.

Through the first six frames, Cuppy had pitched marvelously, allowing only five hits, two each to Willie Keeler and Joe Corbett and one to Heinie Reitz. Two of the safeties were of the infield variety. But in the seventh, Cuppy blew up. His downfall began when Joe Kelley doubled to left center and scored a moment later on Jack Doyle's single. After Heinie Reitz flew out, Doyle stole second and went to third when Chief Zimmer's throw sailed over the bag and bounced into center field. Steve Brodie grounded to Childs for the second out of the inning, but Doyle came home and the Orioles led, 2-0, with six outs to go.

The Spiders mounted their last threat of the Series against Corbett when they put men on second and third with two outs in the top of the eighth. Corbett was equal to the task, fanning Jimmy McAleer—a lifetime .258 hitter, but two-for-fifteen (.133) in the Series—to end the inning. Baltimore then proceeded to put the Series on ice, scoring three times in the bottom of the inning. Corbett beat out an infield single for his third hit of the game and, one out later, Willie Keeler doubled him to third.

Hughie Jennings's two-bagger scored both men and a Jack Doyle single gave Baltimore a 5-0 lead.

With the championship on the line in the ninth, young Corbett got a little excited and walked two batters. But pinch-hitter Bobby Wallace hit a soft come-backer to secure the 5-0 Baltimore victory, and the 1896 Temple Cup games were over.

Corbett had finished with a four-hit shutout, walking five and striking out eight, in garnering his second win of the Series. Cleveland's Nig Cuppy had gone down to a fourth defeat in this, his fifth World Series start. In three of the losses, his teammates had been shut out.

"WHO NOW DISPUTES THE FACT THAT THE ORIOLES ARE THE GREATEST BASEBALL TEAM IN THE WORLD?" read the headline in the Baltimore *American* the next morning. Indeed, there could be little doubt. The Baltimore Orioles, swept 4-0 by the Giants in 1894 and beaten 4-1 by the Spiders in 1895, had taken their first Temple Cup championship. "Methodical" would be an accurate assessment of the Orioles' play in the Series. So decisive were the Baltimore victories that, at no time in any of the four games, did Cleveland ever hold a lead. The Orioles had scored twenty-five runs on forty-two hits, to Cleveland's five runs on twenty-six hits. As a team, the O's had batted .298 with a slugging average of .404. The Spiders had hit a sluggish .195, with a weak .226 slugging average.

The Orioles left Cleveland by train at midnight and arrived at Camden Station in Baltimore at dinnertime on Friday, October 9. A small crowd greeted their arrival. From Camden, the players were taken to the Ganzhorn Hotel, where a banquet was held in their honor. The players were so elated with their Temple Cup victory that they raised ninety dollars for pitcher Jerry Nops, who had seen no action in the Series. The four exhibition games had netted each man about forty-eight dollars, and a benefit at Ford's Theatre increased his individual purse by another thirty-one dollars. Each winner's share of the gate receipts came to $194.88, making each player's total draw approximately $274. The Spiders received about $115 per man.

The four-game sweep had been viewed by fewer than thirteen thousand people, a piddling total for what was supposedly championship-caliber major league baseball.

Poor attendance coupled with lackluster play would soon make the Temple Cup nothing more than part of baseball history.

GAME ONE—October 2, 1896, at Union Park, Baltimore

CLEVELAND	AB	R	H	BI	E	BALTIMORE	AB	R	H	BI	E
Burkett, lf	3	0	1	0	1	McGraw, 3b	2	1	1	0	0
McKean, ss	3	0	1	0	1	Quinn, 3b	3	1	0	0	0
Childs, 2b	3	1	1	0	1	Keeler, rf	5	1	2	1	0
McAleer, cf	3	0	0	0	0	Jennings, ss	5	2	3	0	1
Zimmer, c	3	0	1	1	0	Kelley, lf	5	0	2	1	0
McGarr, 3b	4	0	0	0	1	Doyle, 1b	5	1	1	1	0
Tebeau, 1b	1	0	0	0	0	Reitz, 2b	4	0	1	1	0
O'Connor, 1b	3	0	1	0	0	Brodie, cf	4	1	0	0	0
Blake, rf	4	0	0	0	0	Robinson, c	4	0	2	1	0
Young, p	3	0	0	0	0	Hoffer, p	4	0	1	0	0
Wallace, ph*	1	0	0	0	0		41	7	13	5	1
	31	1	5	1	4						

* pinch hit for Johnson in ninth

```
BAL    0 0 2    0 0 1    3 1 0 – 7
CLE    0 0 0    0 0 1    0 0 0 – 1
```

Earned runs: BAL 6, CLE 1.   LOB: BAL 8, CLE 8.   2B: Zimmer, Jennings, Doyle.
3B: McKean, Hoffer, Keeler.   SH: Childs.   SB: Kelley 2, Brodie, McAleer.   DP: BAL.
BB: Hoffer 4, Young 1.   Umpires: Sheridan and Emslie.   Time—1:40.   Att: 3,995.

◆ ◆ ◆

GAME TWO—October 3, 1896, at Union Park, Baltimore

CLEVELAND	AB	R	H	BI	E	BALTIMORE	AB	R	H	BI	E
Burkett, lf	3	0	2	0	0	McGraw, 3b	5	1	1	0	0
McKean, ss	4	0	2	1	2	Keeler, rf	4	1	2	1	0
Childs, 2b	3	0	0	0	0	Jennings, ss	2	2	1	0	3
McAleer, cf	4	0	0	0	1	Kelley, lf	4	2	3	1	0
O'Connor, 1b	4	1	1	0	0	Doyle, 1b	4	0	2	2	0
Zimmer, c	4	0	1	0	0	Reitz, 2b	3	1	0	0	0
McGarr, 3b	4	0	0	0	0	Brodie, cf	4	0	0	2	0
Blake, rf	3	1	0	0	0	Robinson, c	4	0	1	1	0
Wallace, p	3	0	1	0	0	Corbett, p	3	0	0	0	0
	32	2	7	1	3		33	7	10	7	3

```
BAL    4 0 2    0 1 0    0 0 – 7
CLE    0 0 1    0 0 1    0 0 – 2
```

D: McKean.   SB: McGraw 2, McGarr.   SAC: Reitz.   DP: CLE 1, BAL 1.   BB: Wallace
2, Corbett 2.   Struck out: Wallace 4, Corbett 4.   HBP: Jennings 2, and Reitz (Wallace).
WP: Wallace, Corbett 2.   PB: Zimmer.   Umpires: Emslie and Sheridan.   Time—2:00.
Att: 3,200.

GAME THREE—October 5, 1896, at Union Park, Baltimore

CLEVELAND	AB	R	H	BI	E	BALTIMORE	AB	R	H	BI	E
Burkett, lf	5	1	2	0	0	McGraw, 3b	4	2	2	1	0
McKean, ss	5	0	1	0	0	Keeler, rf	4	1	1	2	0
Childs, 2b	4	1	1	1	0	Jennings, ss	4	0	0	1	1
McAleer, cf	4	0	2	0	0	Kelley, lf	4	0	2	0	0
O'Connor, 1b	4	0	2	1	0	Doyle, 1b	4	1	0	0	1
Zimmer, c	4	0	1	0	1	Reitz, 2b	4	0	0	0	0
McGarr, 3b	4	0	0	0	1	Brodie, cf	4	0	1	1	0
Blake, rf	4	0	1	0	0	Robinson, c	4	1	1	0	0
Cuppy, p	4	0	0	0	0	Hoffer, p	3	1	1	0	0
	38	2	10	2	2		35	6	8	5	2

```
BAL   0 1 1   0 0 1   0 3 0 – 6
CLE   0 0 1   0 1 0   0 0 0 – 2
```

Earned runs: BAL 6, CLE 1.   LOB: BAL 2, CLE 10.   2B: Robinson.   3B: Hoffer.
SB: McGraw 2, Keeler, Doyle.   BB: Hoffer.   Struck out: Hoffer 5, Cuppy 2.
Umpires: Sheridan and Emslie.   Time—2:00.   Att: 4,240.

GAME FOUR—October 8, 1896, at League Park, Cleveland

BALTIMORE	AB	R	H	BI	E	CLEVELAND	AB	R	H	BI	E
McGraw, 3b	4	0	0	0	0	Burkett, lf	4	0	0	0	0
Keeler, rf	4	1	3	0	0	McKean, ss	4	0	1	0	0
Jennings, ss	4	1	1	0	1	Childs, 2b	2	0	1	0	0
Kelley, lf	4	1	1	0	0	McAleer, cf	4	0	0	0	0
Doyle, 1b	4	1	2	2	0	O'Connor, 1b	4	0	0	0	0
Reitz, 2b	4	0	1	0	0	Zimmer, c	3	0	0	0	1
Brodie, cf	3	0	0	1	0	McGarr, 3b	4	0	1	0	0
Robinson, c	3	0	0	0	0	Blake, rf	3	0	0	0	0
Corbett, p	3	1	3	0	0	Cuppy, p	3	0	1	0	0
	33	5	11	3	1	Wallace, ph*	1	0	0	0	0
							32	0	4	0	1

* pinch hit for Cuppy in the ninth

```
CLE   0 0 0   0 0 0   0 0 0 – 0
BAL   0 0 0   0 0 0   2 3 x – 5
```

D: Corbett, Kelley, Keeler, Jennings.   SB: McKean, McGarr, Blake, Childs, Doyle.
DP: CLE.   BB: Corbett 5.   Struck out: Corbett 8, Cuppy 2.   Umpires: Sheridan and
Emslie.   Time—2:00.   Att: 1,200.

• 13 •

THE END OF
AN ERA

◆

If pitching is seventy-five percent of baseball, then how can
one explain the 1897 Temple
Cup Series?

The Series was a non-stop slugfest between the two most
powerful teams in baseball, the Baltimore Orioles and Boston
Beaneaters.

The Orioles, who entered the 1897 season with three successive pennants and their strongest team ever, were picked by most
experts to take a fourth. Their closest competition was considered
to be the Beaneaters and the Cleveland Spiders.

Boston began the season by dropping six of its first seven
games, three of those to Baltimore. The Orioles settled comfort-
ably into the lead, and many people prematurely assumed the race
had been decided. But the Beaneaters quickly regained their stride,
winning twenty-two of twenty-four games in June, and swept into
the lead. Throughout the final month of the season, the margin
separating the two clubs never grew larger than one game.

A late September three-game series between the two teams,
played up in the papers as a clash between good (Boston) and evil
(Baltimore), decided the pennant. Boston moved into sole posses-
sion of first place when Kid Nichols won the opener, slamming the

1897

The Changing Game

♦ ♦ ♦

• *The modern stolen-base rule went into effect, crediting the runner with a theft when he reached a base he had attempted to steal without the aid of a fielding error or a hit by the batter.*

• *An error was no longer charged to a catcher for a poor throw on a stolen-base attempt, unless the runner was able to take an extra base.*

• *An error was not charged to a fielder who failed to complete a double play, unless the runner took an extra base.*

---

door on the Baltimore offense in the ninth inning with the tying runs on base. But Baltimore regained the lead the next day with a 6-3 win that was as close as one run in the seventh inning. In the series finale, the Orioles pounded Kid Nichols with five early runs, but Boston rang the bell nine times in the seventh and eventually cruised to a 19-10 victory, earning a split in the twelve games of head-to-head competition. The series drew 57,025 fans, a remarkable total for the era.

For the year, at home, Boston had played at an incredible .821 clip (55-12), overshadowing even Baltimore's excellent 53-15 (.779). Boston had led the league in runs scored (1,025) while giving up the fewest runs (665) of any team, an almost impossible combination to beat. On average, Boston had outscored its opposition by 2.73 runs per game. The Beaneaters had also finished first in home runs (45), slugging average (.426), and shutouts (8), and tied for first place with Baltimore in team fielding average (.951). Boston was second in the league in doubles (230) and batting average (.319), and third in team ERA (3.65).

Individual leaders for the Beaneaters included Hugh Duffy, who had topped the league in home runs (11) and finished third in runs batted in (129), just behind teammate Jimmy Collins (132). League honors in runs scored (152) and walks (105) had gone to Billy Hamilton, who had also finished second in stolen bases (70).

Billy Hamilton, the nineteenth century's most prolific base-stealer, had broken in with the Kansas City Blues of the American Association in 1888, hitting a modest .264, but giving an indication of things to come when he stole twenty-three bases in thirty-five games. "Sliding Billy" became a full-time player the next year and stunned the Association with 117 thefts in 137 games, a major league record which would stand until broken by St. Louis Cardinals left fielder Lou Brock in 1974. Two years later, Hamilton set the National League record by stealing 115 bases with the Philadelphia Phillies. This small (5'6", 165 pounds) left-handed batter stole one hundred bases or more three straight years, from 1889 through 1891, a record which held up for almost a century until equalled by another St. Louis Cardinal left fielder, Vince Coleman, from 1985 through 1987. Hamilton scored one hundred or more runs in each of his first ten full seasons and reached base on a hit or walk an average of 2.10 times a game in his career. (To put this statistic in perspective, Ted Williams reached base an average of 2.04 times per game; Babe Ruth, 1.97; and Pete Rose, 1.63.)

In 1894, Hamilton had set a National League standard which may never be approached, much less beaten, when he scored 196 runs. That same year, he had fallen shy of a .400 batting average by one hit. Hamilton would retire from the majors after the 1901 season and accept a managerial post with Haverhill of the New England League the next year. He played and managed in the minor leagues for the next nine years until turning in his glove at the age of forty-four in 1910. He continued to manage in the high minors through 1916 and was inducted into the Hall of Fame in 1961.

Billy Hamilton may have been Boston's biggest offensive threat, but Baltimore's Willie Keeler was the most dangerous hitter in all of baseball in 1897 with a league-leading .432 batting average. Keeler had finished first in hits (243), second in slugging average (.553), total bases (311) and runs scored (145), and fifth in stolen bases (64). Teammate Jake Stenzel had led the league in doubles (43) and had finished third in stolen bases (69). Joe Kelley's batting mark of .388 had been good enough for third best in the league and he finished fifth in runs batted in.

As a team, the Orioles had led the league in doubles (243), batting average (.325), and stolen bases (401), tied for the league lead in fielding percentage, and finished second in team ERA (3.55).

Since the pitching distance had been increased to sixty feet, six inches, no major league club had had more than two twenty-game winners on its staff in the same season. Boston and Baltimore could each boast three twenty-game winners. The Beaneaters had Ted Lewis (21-12), Fred Klobedanz (26-7), and Kid Nichols (30-11). Lewis, a Welshman, was a second-year man, having appeared in six games for Boston in 1896. Klobedanz, a huge left-hander, had led all pitchers in winning percentage (.788) and was third in the league in victories. Right-hander Kid Nichols (30-11) had been the league's best hurler in 1897, finishing first in victories and innings pitched (368), and tying Cleveland's Cy Young for the most appearances (46). Jack Stivetts, winding down a distinguished career, had rounded out the starting rotation with a 12-5 record in eighteen appearances.

The Orioles' twenty-win trio was composed of Bill Hoffer (22-11), Jerry Nops (20-6), and Joseph Corbett (24-8). Baltimore's fourth starter, Arlie Pond (18-9), had narrowly missed the twenty-victory circle.

Although he was the sixth-winningest pitcher in the National League, Hoffer was Baltimore's least effective starter, sporting a bloated 4.30 earned run average. Left-hander Jerry Nops had a career year, finishing third in the league in winning percentage and ERA (2.81).

The O's leading pitcher was 21-year-old Joseph Corbett. In only his second season with the Orioles, he had just enjoyed the most successful year of his career. Just a few years earlier, young Joe had accompanied his older brother, boxer "Gentleman Jim" Corbett, on his travels around the country and, as a stunt to draw fans, the boxer would play first base for the home team of the city he was visiting, while Joe would play shortstop. Eighteen-year-old Joe was given a tryout by the Washington Senators in 1895 and went 0-2 in three appearances, then joined the Orioles in 1896 and was 3-0 during the regular season with two victories in the Temple Cup Series. In 1898, disenchanted by his contract offer,

Corbett would leave the Orioles, never to pitch for the club again. After a six-year layoff, Corbett attempted a comeback with the St. Louis Cardinals in 1904, but was 5-9 in fourteen appearances before he requested his release in early August.

The night before the Series opened, popular stage actress May Irwin presented a silk pennant to the Boston club before a packed crowd at the Tremont Theatre. The pennant, inscribed "CHAMPIONSHIP, 1898" was given to manager Frank Selee following a short speech by Boston mayor Quincy at the end of the second act of *The Swell Miss Fitzwell.* The mayor said, in part, "I think Boston's victory this year was earned by hard work. The contest was a remarkable one, Boston starting out very low down on the list and fighting themselves to the front." Manager Frank Selee said a few words of thanks and the applause had no sooner died down than the audience began calling for a speech from team captain Hugh Duffy. Embarrassed, Duffy declined. *The Swell Miss Fitzwell* made several allusions to the pennant-winning Boston club and was enthusiastically received by the crowd.

The final Temple Cup Series of the nineteenth century opened on October 4 at the "new" South End Grounds in Boston. The old park, decaying and underinsured, had been razed by a fire on May 15, 1894. The new South End Grounds was smaller than its predecessor because not enough money was available from the insurance claim to build a park of equal size.

Saint Augustine's brass band played "Maryland, My Maryland" and "Yankee Doodle Dandy" as nearly ten thousand spectators filed into the park. They overflowed onto the field, and the ground rules specified that anything hit into the crowd would be an automatic double. The weather was perfect—a mild Indian summer day with no wind and a clear sky. A 300-page history of the Boston baseball club, written by George V. Touhey and illustrated with halftone photographs, was on sale at the gate and fans eagerly bought up all copies. Receipts of the sale went to the players.

Robert Emslie and Tim Hurst, both seven-year veterans and a study in contrasts, were the umpires for this game and the Series. Hurst took very little abuse on the field and was often as quick with a curse as the players he supervised. The Canadian-born Emslie wore a wig because frayed nerves had cost him premature baldness.

Willie Keeler had a sore finger on his throwing hand which was lanced before game time; nevertheless, he took his usual place in right field. Boston outfielder Jimmy Collins was late, arriving just a few minutes before the contest began, and was roundly booed by the crowd. Baltimore team captain Wilbert Robinson, hospitalized with malaria, was lost for the Series.

Starting pitchers for the Series opener were Kid Nichols and Jerry Nops. The first inning set the tone for the game. After John McGraw and Willie Keeler had legged out infield singles, Baltimore's Hughie Jennings doubled to right for the first run of the game. Joe Kelley followed with a soft grounder to Boston third baseman Jimmy Collins and Keeler was trapped in a rundown between third and home. But Collins's throw to the plate was wild and both Keeler and Jennings raced home. Jake Stenzel reached on an error and when Jack Doyle singled, the Orioles had the bases loaded and none out. Kid Nichols settled down and retired the next three batters, but Kelley scored on Boileryard Clarke's groundout to put the Orioles up 4-0. All nine men in the Baltimore lineup had come to the plate and it looked like it might be a very long game and a very short Series for Boston.

But the Beaneaters had blood in their eyes, rebounding to nearly tie the score in their half of the first. After Billy Hamilton walked, Fred Tenney bunted to John McGraw, who bobbled the ball for an error. Bobby Lowe hit a ground-rule double into the crowd behind third base and Hamilton did what he did more often than any other baserunner in 1897—he scored a run. Rookie Chick Stahl squeezed Tenney home with a sacrifice bunt, and Hugh Duffy's RBI single gave the Beaneaters their third run of the inning.

When Duffy came to the plate in this inning, a Mr. John E. Good of Providence, Rhode Island—Duffy was Rhode Island-born—rushed onto the field with a large package wrapped in tissue paper. Upon opening the parcel, Duffy found a golden emblem shaped like a baseball, supported by three bats resting on a wooden base. The inscription on the testimonial read, "PRESENTED TO CAPTAIN HUGH DUFFY, CAPTAIN OF THE BOSTON BASEBALL CLUB, BY AN ADMIRER OF THE NATIONAL GAME." Good also presented the Boston left fielder with a beribboned broom, symbolic of a sweep in the Series. Later in the same inning, Herman Long was given a basket of flowers which stood almost as tall as he. Long popped out to first, the bouquet apparently having an unnerving effect.

The Orioles widened their margin to 5-3 on a double by Joe Kelley and a Heinie Reitz single in the third, but Boston got that run back in the fourth on singles by Long and catcher Marty Bergen* and a run-scoring groundout by Kid Nichols.

Both clubs scored twice in the fifth and, entering the sixth inning, the score was 7-6, Baltimore. And what a sixth it was. The Orioles started the fun when John McGraw singled and went to second on a passed ball. One out later, Hughie Jennings singled to right, sending McGraw home. Joe Kelley's double to center made the score 9-6 and when Jack Doyle's single went through right fielder Chick Stahl's legs for an error, Kelley came home and the Orioles had regained their original four-run lead.

But Boston hadn't won the pennant for nothing. Kid Nichols grounded out to start the bottom of the sixth, but the next five men reached base. Billy Hamilton bunted safely, Fred Tenney coaxed a base on balls, and Bobby Lowe singled to drive in Hamilton for the first run of the inning. Chick Stahl doubled, scoring Tenney, and Hugh Duffy's single brought home Lowe and Stahl. Center fielder Jake Stenzel made a dazzling catch of Jimmy Collins's soft liner and looked up to see Duffy a few feet from second base. All Stenzel needed to do to complete the double play and retire the side was make an accurate toss to first, but his throw was well off the mark and Duffy toured the bases with the fifth run of the inning. The Beaneaters now had the lead for the first time in the game, 11-10. Neither team was exactly showing championship form.

After six innings, Kid Nichols was forced to leave the game with a sore arm. After the contest, Nichols was quoted in the *Boston Daily Globe* as saying, "My arm grew lame in the second [September] game at Baltimore, and I will let some of the other boys finish the season as I want to be right next season." The ace of the Boston staff would see no action for the balance of the Series.

---

* In two years, Bergen would become one of baseball's most tragic figures. Shortly after the 1899 season opened, his son Willie died. Bergen jumped the club on two separate occasions during the season to return to his family and, over the winter months, became silent and withdrawn. In the early-morning hours of January 19, 1900, at his farm in Brookfield, Massachusetts, he murdered his wife, his six-year-old daughter, and his three-year-old son with an axe, then took his own life by slashing his throat with a razor. Bergen's fit of insanity was of such fever pitch that it was rumored his head had nearly been severed from his neck. No one seemed terribly surprised by the tragedy. For months, Bergen's batterymate, Ted Lewis, had admitted to being frightened by his catcher. Boston manager Frank Selee said, "I knew Bergen was not in his right mind." And club president Arthur Soden, questioned by reporters after being told of Bergen's death, said calmly, "I am not surprised. Bergen has shown signs of insanity for two years."

Boston manager Frank Selee replaced Nichols with Welsh-born Ted Lewis, a small man in his second year in the majors. In the early going, Lewis had no more luck than his predecessor. With one out in the seventh, pitcher Jerry Nops reached on a Baltimore chop. McGraw singled him to second, but Nops was forced at third. Jennings and Kelley followed with singles and Baltimore had a 12-11 lead with just three innings remaining. Nops retired the Beaneaters in the bottom of the seventh, escaping a one-out, second-and-third jam, and the Orioles went down one-two-three to Lewis in the eighth.

In the bottom of the eighth, Nops quickly got into another jam. After issuing a base on balls to leadoff batter Chick Stahl, Nops surrendered a single to Hugh Duffy. With a first-and-third opportunity, Herman Long stroked a clutch double, plating Stahl. The score was tied at twelve-all. When Marty Bergen executed a perfect squeeze bunt, Duffy came home and the Beaneaters led, 13-12, with three outs to go.

Boston manager Frank Selee, fearing a Baltimore uprising in the ninth, pleaded with umpire Tim Hurst to call the game because of darkness. The sun had already set, and the game was being played by blue moonlight and the fading rays of the sun. Gnats were so thick on the field that players and umpires alike kept waving their hands to clear the air. Hurst shouted, "Play it out!" and Jerry Nops fanned on three pitches to start the ninth. John McGraw lifted a high fly to Duffy in center for the second out of the inning, and the Orioles were down to their last hope, Willie Keeler. Always a gamer, Keeler rapped a hit to center. Hughie Jennings lined a fastball into right for an apparent single, but when Chick Stahl had trouble locating the ball in the dark, Jennings steamed into second base with a double. Joe Kelley came to the plate with the tying run on third and the lead run on second. A base hit would have won the game for the Orioles. Kelley grounded a slow roller to shortstop Herman Long and appeared to beat the throw to first, but umpire Emslie ruled him out on a decision which could only be called a gift to Boston.

Jerry Nops was tagged with a well-deserved loss, as he surrendered thirteen hits and seven walks in eight innings, and was anything but effective. By contrast, the Boston duo of Kid Nichols and Ted Lewis allowed twenty hits—among them, six doubles—yet emerged smelling like roses with a first-game victory. Ted Lewis was the winning pitcher.

Everyone in the Baltimore lineup had hit safely, with McGraw, Keeler, Jennings, Kelley, and Doyle enjoying multiple-hit performances. Hughie Jennings had been 5-for-6 with two doubles and three singles, the first man ever to collect five hits in a World Series game. (His record would stand until Paul Molitor banged out five safeties for the Milwaukee Brewers in the first game of the 1982 World Series.) On the Boston side, Hamilton, Lowe, Long, and Bergen all had collected two hits, and Hugh Duffy had rapped out three.

Game Two was played the following day—same game, same script, but a different winner. Boston management expected a record attendance after the home team's victory in the Series opener, but only 6,000 fans turned out. Ropes that had been strung along the foul lines to restrain spectators were hurriedly taken down. The brass band was missing and so were the ground rules. National League president Nick Young occupied a front row seat in the grandstand.

A few moments before game time, the bat boy, a tall young man dressed in a red sweater, carried out two loads of bats. The crowd soon learned this gangly right-hander was twenty-one-year-old pitcher Vic Willis from Syracuse, New York. (Willis would make his debut in the majors in 1898 and go on to win 247 games, an unusually high total for a pitcher who was never elected to the Hall of Fame.)

Starting pitchers for Game Two were phenom Joe Corbett and the wily left-hander, Fred Klobedanz.

Baltimore's John McGraw tripled and later scored in the top of the first, and the Orioles added three more runs for a 4-0 lead in the second. In the Boston third, Klobedanz singled and Joe Corbett suddenly hit a wild streak. After walking Billy Hamilton and Fred Tenney to load the bases, Corbett hit Bobby Lowe above the heart with a fastball. The wind left Lowe's lungs in a rush and he dropped like a stone to the dirt. Concerned players from both squads crowded around the prostrate batter, but he recovered after a few minutes and took his base, forcing in Klobedanz with the first Boston run of the game. When Hamilton scored on Chick Stahl's sacrifice fly, the Beaneaters had cut their deficit in half.

Baltimore scored a singleton in the fourth, but Boston exploded for six runs off Corbett in the bottom of the inning to take an 8-5 lead. With one out, reserve catcher George Yeager singled to center. Klobedanz grounded a sure double play ball to Hughie

Jennings, but Jennings slipped and fell before making the toss to second baseman Heinie Reitz and everybody was safe. Billy Hamilton's single to left loaded the bases and Corbett traded an out for a run when Fred Tenney's sacrifice fly scored Yeager. The next batter, Bobby Lowe, took a full swing at Corbett's first delivery but, unbelievably, umpire Tim Hurst missed the swing entirely and called the pitch a ball. Lowe took two more called strikes for what should have been the third out of the inning, but because of Hurst's inattention, Lowe still stood at the plate. His sharp single to left seemed to take the heart out of Corbett, as Jake Stahl, Hugh Duffy, and Jimmy Collins followed with safe blows, Duffy's hit a double. Germany Long finally ended the inning with a pop fly on the infield.

The Baltimore pitching staff was finding it difficult to contain the Beaneaters.

As Fred Klobedanz worked to the Orioles in the top of the fifth, he discovered a dismaying addition to his pitching repertoire—a hanging curveball. Two walks, an RBI single, and a three-run homer by Heinie Reitz drove him to an early shower, trailing 9-8. Happy Jack Stivetts came on in relief, but Boileryard Clarke drilled his first pitch over the left-field fence to put the Orioles up by two. Matters didn't improve any when Corbett doubled and McGraw singled him home to make the score 11-8, Baltimore. The hometown fans reacted angrily, stamping their feet and booing Stivetts for several minutes.

Joe Corbett continued to fall apart in the bottom of the fifth, surrendering two runs and allowing Boston to close the gap to 11-10. Miraculously, neither team scored in the sixth. Corbett's two-out home run in the top of the seventh widened the Orioles' margin to 12-10. (According to the *Baltimore American*, Corbett's blast was hit "over the left-field fence into the tender of a passing locomotive.") Herman Long led off the Boston half of the seventh with a towering home run over the left-field fence. Long was so impressed with his drive he took a slow, showy trot around the bases, much to the delight of the partisan crowd. Boston failed to score again in the inning and Baltimore struck once in the eighth.

The Orioles held a 13-11 lead as Joe Corbett faced the Beaneaters in the bottom of the ninth inning. With the crowd chanting, "Two runs to tie, three to win," and the late-afternoon sun nearing the horizon, Herman Long went down swinging on a pitch well outside the strike zone. George Yeager struck a clutch double to keep Boston's hopes alive, but Stivetts flew out and the Beaneaters were down to their last batter. Billy Hamilton legged out an infield hit and unaccountably, Yeager held second. A passed ball sent the tying runs to second and third, but Fred Tenney hit an easy one-hopper to second baseman Heinie Reitz and the Orioles had dodged the bullet.

Joe Corbett, although walking four, making two wild pitches, hitting a batter, and giving up sixteen hits, had been the winning pitcher in the 13-11 victory. He surely had earned his pay. Fred Klobedanz had taken the loss for Boston. Klobedanz and Stivetts had given up five bases on balls and seventeen hits—nine singles, three doubles, two triples, and three home runs. Klobedanz and Stivetts had earned their pay too.

Through the first two games, Baltimore had scored twenty-five runs on thirty-seven hits, and Boston had scored twenty-four runs on twenty-nine hits—not exactly tight baseball.

Later that evening, a banquet was held for the ballplayers at Faneuil Hall in Boston. Nineteen Beaneaters and twenty-one Orioles attended, joined by Massachusetts congressmen John F. Fitzgerald and Charles J. Lavis. Faneuil Hall was decorated with flags and streamers, amid which were two banners inscribed, "WELCOME, BOSTON'S CHAMPIONS, 98" and "NOW LET THE EAGLE SCREAM." From the center of the ceiling hung a stuffed American eagle. Everyone made speeches, including umpires Tim Hurst and Bob Emslie, Hurst throwing in a few unnecessary comments about Hugh Duffy being the only ballplayer who had given him any trouble all year. Emslie, somewhat more aware of the locale, said even Duffy had been a gentleman.

The baseball season came to a close for Bostonians the next day with an easy Baltimore victory, the closest thing to a pitchers' duel the Series would offer. Boston's reserve catcher, Fred Lake, was picked to start the contest behind the plate. He was the third backstop in as many days for the Beaneaters, and as unpopular a choice with the fans as the selection of Fred Lewis as the starting pitcher. Sportswriter Tim Murnane, writing in the *Boston Daily Globe*, said:

> When the crowd saw Lake and Lewis in the points it was all off. This has been Boston's jonah battery and manager Selee must have turned them out as a huge joke, and so it proved, the visitors having all the fun . . . The crowd on the bleachers got back at

Sir Frederick Lake until he turned and shot a few hot words at his tormentors.

The final crowd of the year at South End Grounds numbered four thousand, including 958 fans who had purchased phony fifty-cent tickets on which the counterfeiters had misspelled the word "Grounds" as "Gronds."

Neither team scored in the first, but Baltimore sent ten men to the plate and tallied four runs off starting pitcher Ted Lewis in the second. Lewis, who had begun throwing sidearm for some reason, walked leadoff batter Jake Stenzel, who scored the first run of the game on Jack Doyle's double. Heinie Reitz singled Doyle to third and Boileryard Clarke was hit by a pitch to load the bases with none out. Pitcher Bill Hoffer forced Clarke at second but the Beaneaters failed to turn the double play and Doyle came home to put the Orioles ahead, 2-0. A single by John McGraw scored Reitz and when the ball went off left fielder Hugh Duffy's glove, the baserunners moved to second and third. Hoffer was forced at the plate on Willie Keeler's grounder, but Hughie Jennings drew a base on balls to load the bases again. A walk to Joe Kelley forced in McGraw with the fourth run of the inning.

The Orioles replayed this performance in the third when they sent ten more men to the plate for another four-run inning. Jack Doyle singled and stole second, but two outs later had not advanced any farther than third. Lewis might have escaped the inning unharmed but he surrendered an RBI single to Bill Hoffer, then walked John McGraw. Both runners moved up on a wild pitch and Willie Keeler sent them home with a base hit. The Orioles led, 7-0. Hughie Jennings walked and Joe Kelley's single drove in Keeler with the eighth Baltimore run of the game. Boston pilot Frank Selee had seen enough and changed pitchers, bringing on Fred Klobedanz in relief. Considering the less than marvelous job Klobedanz had done just twenty-four hours earlier, this managerial brainstorm seemed a little like throwing gasoline on a fire. When Klobedanz's first act was to hit Jake Stenzel with a pitch, loading the bases, matters looked grim indeed. But Jack Doyle flew out to right and the inning was over.

The Beaneaters rounded out the day's official scoring in the bottom of the inning. Singles by Klobedanz, Hamilton, and Tenney loaded the bases with none out. Klobedanz scored on a force-out and Hamilton came home on Chick Stahl's single. Hugh

Duffy walked to load the bases again, and Jimmy Collins's sacrifice fly to left drove in Tenney. Herman Long drew a base on balls to load the bases for the third time in the inning, but weak-hitting substitute catcher Fred Lake struck out and Boston's last scoring threat fizzled.

Both Klobedanz and Hoffer held the line, as neither team was able to score for the next four innings. But nine men faced Klobedanz in the top of the eighth and Baltimore scored four more runs to go up 12-3. In the Boston half of the inning, Lake and Klobedanz were retired when, with Billy Hamilton at the plate, it began to rain. The umpires, seeing little need to prolong Boston's agony, mercifully called the game, and the score reverted to the end of the seventh, 8-3.

Tim Murnane commented:

> There was considerable disappointment with the ball put up by the new champions. The patrons of the game in this part of the country know good playing and were not able to find anything brilliant in the work of Boston yesterday, even with the aid of a powerful [magnifying] glass.

The New York Times agreed, saying:

> The third game of the Temple Cup series was as dull and uninteresting a contest as has been seen here for many a day . . . The enthusiasm to-day, which in the two previous games was a marked feature, was utterly lacking, the "rooters" being apparently disheartened with the ease with which the Baltimores disposed of the Boston pitchers.

The Orioles had taken two of three on opposition turf and, more significantly, had that all-important intangible, momentum, on their side. A Series which most observers thought would be a tightly contained affair had now degenerated into a free-for-all, resulting in sixty runs and eighty-five hits in three games.

On October 7, en route by train to Baltimore, the Orioles and Beaneaters stopped to play an exhibition game at Worcester, Massachusetts, before a crowd of 3,500. During the contest, admirers from Holy Cross College presented Hughie Jennings with a gold-headed ebony cane. Both clubs played listlessly in the field and savagely at the plate, much as they had in the first three official games of the Temple Cup Series. The exhibition slate continued the next day at

Hampden Park in Springfield, Massachusetts, the site of Hugh
Duffy's first professional baseball game more than a decade earlier.
Built in 1853 on sixty-three acres of pasture, Hampden Park featured a horse racing track, and had no fences to contain the ballplayers' long drives. A capacity crowd of three thousand fans turned out
to see the Orioles take a second exhibition victory. During the
game, Jack Doyle was presented with a gold watch by fellow citizens
from Holyoke, Massachusetts. The teams left at 6:30 that evening
for Baltimore.

Including the exhibition contests, the Orioles had now won
four straight from Boston and were supremely confident of taking
the Temple Cup. Also apparently convinced was the city of Baltimore—only 2,626 fans turned out for the fourth game of the
Series at Union Park on October 9. With Jerry Nops and Jack
Stivetts on the mound, spectators who looked for another slugfest
were not disappointed. Boston failed to score in the top of the first
but the Orioles came at Stivetts hell-bent-for-leather in the bottom
of the inning. With two out and Hughie Jennings and Joe Kelley on
base, Jake Stenzel's pop fly fell between second baseman Bobby
Lowe and shortstop Herman Long for a single, scoring Jennings
and advancing Kelley to third. A double by Jack Doyle, singles by
Frank Bowerman and John McGraw, and walks to Heinie Reitz
and Nops netted five more runs. In the bottom of the second, the
Orioles strengthened their grip on the Temple Cup when two
walks, doubles by Stenzel and Doyle, a triple by Bowerman, and a
Jerry Nops single accounted for five more runs and an 11-0 lead.
Boston manager Frank Selee came to the stark realization that Jack
Stivetts might not be the man for the job and brought on Ted
Lewis in the third.

Given a seemingly insurmountable 11-0 lead, Jerry Nops began to let down. In the Boston fifth, Herman Long's triple was
followed by a Ted Lewis double and a Fred Tenney single to make
the score 11-2. In the sixth, consecutive hits by Chick Stahl, Hugh
Duffy, Jimmy Collins, Long, and George Yeager—with a passed
ball and hit batsman thrown in for good measure—brought home
four more Boston runs. The Beaneaters now trailed by a more
manageable 11-6 score.

The Orioles scored their final run in the sixth. Jack Doyle
reached on an error and Heinie Reitz singled him to third.
Doyle came home on Hugh Duffy's errant throw back to the
plate, described by sportswriter Tim Murnane in the *Boston Daily*

Globe as "the wildest throw made this year, as well as the most senseless."

In the Boston seventh, Bobby Lowe doubled and scored on Chick Stahl's single. When the ball eluded center fielder Jake Stenzel, Stahl went to second. Hugh Duffy drove a liner to left and when Willie Keeler fumbled the ball, Stahl scored and Duffy took the extra base. A walk to Yeager and another hit by Ted Lewis made the score 12-9, Baltimore. Orioles manager Ned Hanlon replaced Nops with Joe Corbett to prevent any further damage, but the Beaneaters continued their come-from-behind attack in the eighth. Fred Tenney and Bobby Lowe singled, and both men advanced a base when catcher Frank Bowerman lost the handle on strike three as Chick Stahl struck out. Hugh Duffy's sacrifice fly scored Tenney, and Jimmy Collins's single scored Lowe. Unbelievably and against all odds, Boston had closed to within one run.

The Orioles failed to pad their lead in the eighth and George Yeager drew a base on balls to lead off the Boston ninth. Ted Lewis's third hit of the day moved him to second and the Beaneaters had the tying and winning runs on base. Billy Hamilton and Fred Tenney were retired, but Corbett walked Bobby Lowe to load the bases. A hit by the next batter, Chick Stahl, might have put the Beaneaters ahead and tied the Series at two games apiece. Pitching carefully to Stahl, Corbett sent in a 2-2 curveball and the Boston right fielder, fooled on the pitch, could only manage a weak pop fly to third. John McGraw circled around third base and squeezed the ball at the foul line. The Orioles had hung on for a thrilling 12-11 victory.

Ted Lewis had allowed only one run in six innings of relief—far and away the best pitching performance on either side in the Series—but that run provided the deciding margin as Boston went down to its fifth straight defeat.

Six men in the Boston lineup—Tenney, Lowe, Stahl, Duffy, Long, and Lewis—had collected two hits or more. Doyle and Bowerman banged out three hits apiece for the Orioles, and Jake Stenzel turned in a 4-for-5 performance. The day's offensive totals included twenty-one singles, seven doubles, two triples, fourteen walks, two hit batsmen, and five stolen bases—hardly championship play at its best.

A persistent rumor had begun to spread that the Orioles and Spiders had split their winnings from the 1896 championship, a clear violation of the Temple Cup rules. The rumor also maintained that the Orioles and Beaneaters were doing the same this year,

accounting for the ragged and indifferent style of play. William
Chase Temple, for whom the Cup was named, was furious. He said:

> The rumors that the games were fixed are not pleasant to me, and
> I will demand a thorough investigation of the matter. If it can be
> proved that there has been any arrangement among the players, I
> will attend the annual meeting of the league, make a demand that
> the Boston and Baltimore players be blacklisted and that the cup
> be returned to the league. The cup was not given altogether as a
> means of making money for the ball players. One of its objects
> was to stimulate the game and increase the interest in it among the
> people . . . But if an agreement has been made among the
> players by which they all equally divided the receipts, whether
> they win or lose, then all the objects of the cup contests are
> frustrated . . . The series has not been a good one by any means,
> and there has been general disappointment.

Game Five was little more than a formality. Pleasant weather
greeted the teams upon their arrival at Union Park but despite
balmy temperatures, the audience was so small that management
refused to announce a total. (The crowd was estimated at 750.)

Apparently, neither team took the contest seriously, as both
clubs fielded patchwork lineups. For the Orioles, rookie Tom
O'Brien replaced Joe Kelley in left field, and catcher Frank Bowerman played first instead of Jack Doyle. Boston hurler Jack Stivetts
replaced Billy Hamilton in center field, and Piano Legs Hickman
was the starting pitcher. Hickman was about as rookie as a rookie
could get. During the regular season, he had appeared in two games,
both in relief, for only seven and two-thirds innings pitched. He had
no record and was 1-for-3 at the plate. One might infer that manager
Frank Selee was conceding the championship.

In the second, Boston took an early lead when four successive
hits brought in two runs. In the bottom of the inning, the Orioles
scored their first run of the game when Jake Stenzel beat out a
bunt, stole second, took third on a groundout, and came home
when first baseman Fred Tenney tried to pick him off third. Boileryard Clarke bunted safely and scored the tying run when Jack
Stivetts muffed an easy fly ball to center.

Baltimore moved ahead to stay in the third. After Willie
Keeler hit safely and Hughie Jennings drew a base on balls, Tom
O'Brien's single gave the Orioles a 3-2 lead. Heinie Reitz's triple
plated two insurance runs and the Orioles led by three. Two runs

in the seventh and two more in the eighth gave Baltimore a 9-2 lead heading into the final frame of the 1897 Temple Cup Series.

By now, the pressures of the long season had eased and players on both teams were loosening up. Umpires Emslie and Hurst jovially encouraged each Boston batter to do his best, and a few spectators strayed onto the field to join in a little mock coaching. The distinction of scoring the final run in the 1897 Temple Cup championship went to the Beaneaters when George Yeager tripled and Piano Legs Hickman doubled him home.

Hickman took the loss and Bill Hoffer, with a nifty fifteen-hitter, was the winning pitcher. Boston had out-hit the Orioles for the third straight game, but finished on the wrong end of the score for the sixth time in eight days.

The Series finale took only eighty minutes to play and the defensive star of the game was second baseman Heinie Reitz. Reitz was involved in all four Baltimore double plays, nearly turning a triple play in the third. With Bobby Lowe on second and Chick Stahl on first, Hugh Duffy sent a liner straight into Reitz's hands. He touched second base to catch Lowe off the bag for the second out and threw to Bowerman at first in plenty of time to double off Stahl, but the throw went into the dirt and Bowerman couldn't dig it out.

Press reports of the Series were not kind. Writing in the *Boston Daily Globe*, Tim Murnane said, "As a burlesque it was a grand success, and plainly proved that the Temple cup games have very little interest for the players when the crowd is not paying."

The New York Times said the audience, so "utterly devoid of enthusiasm that scarcely a ripple of applause occurred, witnessed the downfall of the champions, and appeared to be glad that the game . . . was over and the season ended." The paper also echoed Murnane's observations on the quality of play, commenting that "the series just ended has been a fizzle from almost the word go, and even at Baltimore and Boston but little interest was taken in the games." The *Times* went on to label the action "the worst series for the Temple cup on record."

The players' individual shares for the Series amounted to $310 for the Orioles and $207 for the Beaneaters. The exhibition games netted each man an extra $77.

For the third time in four years, the National League pennant winner had been defeated by the second-place club, a circumstance which probably surprised the Cup's founder. At the post-season

National League meetings, a resolution was introduced to abolish the championship. Orioles manager Ned Hanlon cast the only dissenting vote and the Cup was returned to its owner, William Chase Temple. It can be seen today at the Baseball Hall of Fame in Cooperstown, New York—now only a curious artifact of the nineteenth-century World Series.

Glory fades away . . .

GAME ONE—October 4, 1897, at South End Grounds, Boston

BALTIMORE	AB	R	H	BI	E	BOSTON	AB	R	H	BI	E
McGraw, 3b	6	3	3	0	1	Hamilton, cf	3	2	2	0	0
Keeler, rf	6	2	2	3	0	Tenney, 1b	2	3	0	0	1
Jennings, ss	6	2	5	2	0	Lowe, 2b	5	2	2	2	1
Kelley, lf	6	4	3	0	0	Stahl, rf	3	3	1	1	1
Stenzel, cf	5	1	1	2	1	Duffy, lf	5	2	3	3	0
Doyle, 1b	5	0	3	1	0	Collins, 3b	5	0	1	0	1
Reitz, 2b	5	0	1	1	0	Long, ss	4	1	2	1	0
Clarke, c	5	0	1	0	0	Bergen, c	4	0	2	0	0
Nops, c	5	0	1	0	1	Nichols, p	3	0	0	1	0
	49	12	20	9	3	Lewis, p	2	0	0	0	0
							36	13	13	8	4

```
BAL   4 0 1   0 2 3   2 0 0 – 12
BOS   3 0 0   1 2 5   0 2 x – 13
```

D: Jennings 2, Kelley 2, Lowe, Stahl, Long.   SB: Stahl, Tenney.   SAC: Stahl.   BB: Nops 7.   Struck out: Nichols 3, Lewis 1, Nops 2.   PB: Bergen, Clarke.   WP: Nops. Umpires: Hurst and Emslie.   Time—2:10.   Att: 9,600.

BALTIMORE	AB	R	H	BI	E	BOSTON	AB	R	H	BI	E
McGraw, 3b	5	1	1	1	2	Hamilton, cf	4	3	4	0	1
Keeler, rf	5	0	2	0	0	Tenney, 1b	4	0	0	1	0
Jennings, ss	5	1	1	0	0	Lowe, 2b	4	1	2	4	2
Kelley, lf	4	1	1	0	0	Stahl, rf	4	1	2	2	0
Stenzel, cf	4	1	1	1	0	Duffy, lf	5	1	2	2	0
Doyle, 1b	5	2	2	1	0	Collins, 3b	5	0	1	1	0
Reitz, 2b	5	2	2	3	0	Long, ss	5	1	1	1	0
Clarke, c	4	3	3	3	0	Yeager, c	5	1	2	0	0
Corbett, p	5	2	4	2	0	Klobedanz, p	2	2	2	0	0
	42	13	17	11	2	Stivetts, p	2	1	0	0	0
							40	11	16	11	3

```
BAL    1 3 0    1 6 0    1 1 0 - 13
BOS    0 0 2    6 2 0    1 0 0 - 11
```

Earned runs: BAL 8, BOS 7.   2B: Keeler, Kelley, Corbett, Hamilton, Duffy, Yeager. 3B: McGraw, Clarke.   HR: Reitz, Clarke, Corbett, Long.   SB: Doyle, Hamilton, Stivetts.   DP: BOS.   BB: Corbett 4, Klobedanz 4, Stivetts 1.   Struck out: Corbett 3. HBP: Lowe (by Corbett).   PB: Clarke.   WP: Corbett 2.   Umpires: Emslie and Hurst. Time—2:13.   Att: 6,000.

BALTIMORE	AB	R	H	BI	E	BOSTON	AB	R	H	BI	E
McGraw, 3b	4	2	1	1	0	Hamilton cf	4	1	2	0	0
Keeler, rf	3	1	1	2	0	Tenney, 1b	3	0	1	0	0
Jennings, ss	3	0	0	0	1	Lowe, 2b	4	1	0	1	0
Kelley, lf	2	0	1	2	0	Stahl, rf	4	0	1	1	0
Stenzel, cf	3	1	0	0	0	Duffy, lf	3	0	2	0	1
Doyle, 1b	4	2	2	1	0	Collins, 3b	3	0	1	1	0
Reitz, 2b	4	1	1	0	0	Long, ss	3	0	0	0	1
Clarke, c	3	0	2	0	0	Lake, c	4	0	0	0	1
Hoffer, p	4	1	1	2	1	Lewis, p	0	0	0	0	0
	30	8	9	8	2	Klobedanz, p	3	1	3	0	0
							31	3	10	3	3

```
BAL    0 4 4    0 0 0    0 - 8
BOS    0 0 3    0 0 0    0 - 3
```

Earned runs: BAL 2, BOS 2.   2B: McGraw, Doyle.   SB: Doyle, Tenney, Stenzel. DP: BOS.   BB: Hoffer 4, Lewis 5, Klobedanz 4.   Struck out: Hoffer 1.   Umpires: Hurst and Emslie.   Time—1:55.   Att: 4,000.

GAME FOUR—October 9, 1897, at Union Park, Baltimore

BOSTON	AB	R	H	BI	E	BALTIMORE	AB	R	H	BI	E
Hamilton, cf	5	0	0	1	1	McGraw, 3b	1	0	1	2	0
Tenney, 1b	6	1	2	1	0	Keeler, rf	4	1	1	0	0
Lowe, 2b	5	2	2	0	0	Jennings, ss	4	1	0	0	0
Stahl, rf	5	2	3	1	0	Kelley, lf	4	2	0	0	0
Duffy, lf	5	2	2	3	1	Stenzel, cf	5	2	4	2	1
Collins, 3b	5	1	1	1	0	Doyle, 1b	5	3	3	4	0
Long, ss	5	2	2	0	1	Reitz, 2b	3	1	1	0	0
Yeager, c	3	0	1	2	1	Bowerman, c	4	2	3	2	1
Stivetts, p	0	0	0	0	0	Nops, p	2	0	1	1	0
Lewis, p	4	1	3	2	0	Corbett, p	1	0	0	0	0
	43	11	16	11	4		33	12	14	11	2

```
BOS   0 0 0   0 2 4   3 2 0 – 11
BAL   6 5 0   0 0 1   0 0 x – 12
```

Earned runs: BAL 12, BOS 6.   2B: Stenzel, Doyle, Keeler, Lewis, Lowe, Stahl, Duffy. 3B: Long, Bowerman.   SB: Stahl, Long, Tenney, Lowe, Stenzel.   DP: BAL 1, BOS 1. BB: Nops 2, Corbett 3, Stivetts 6, Lewis 3.   Struck out: Nops 1, Lewis 3, Corbett 2. PB: Bowerman 3.   Umpires: Hurst and Emslie.   Time—2:30.   Att: 2,626.

GAME FIVE—October 11, 1897, at Union Park, Baltimore

BOSTON	AB	R	H	BI	E	BALTIMORE	AB	R	H	BI	E
Stivetts, p	5	0	0	0	1	McGraw, 3b	5	0	0	0	0
Tenney, 1b	5	0	3	0	1	Keeler, rf	5	1	3	1	0
Lowe, 2b	5	0	3	0	1	Jennings, ss	4	1	1	0	1
Stahl, rf	4	0	1	0	0	O'Brien, lf	5	2	2	1	0
Duffy, lf	3	1	2	0	0	Stenzel, cf	4	2	2	1	0
Collins, 3b	4	1	1	0	0	Bowerman, 1b	4	0	1	1	0
Long, ss	4	0	1	1	0	Reitz, 2b	3	0	0	2	1
Yeager, c	4	1	3	1	0	Clarke, c	4	2	3	0	0
Hickman, p-lf	4	0	1	1	0	Hoffer, p	4	1	1	1	0
Sullivan, p	1	0	0	0	0		38	9	13	7	2
	39	3	15	3	3						

```
BOS   0 2 0   0 0 0   0 0 1 – 3
BAL   0 2 3   0 0 0   2 2 x – 9
```

Earned runs: BAL 2, BOS 3.   2B: O'Brien, Clarke, Hoffer, Hickman.   3B: Stenzel, Yeager.   SB: Stenzel.   DP: BAL 4.   BB: Hickman 2.   Struck out: Hoffer 1.   PB: Yeager.   WP: Hickman.   Umpires: Hurst and Emslie.   Time—1:20.   Att: 750 (estimated).

AFTERWORD

*Before the World Series started in 1903 there were
other post-season championships which took place
as early as 1884. Although they are not officially
recognized as part of World Series history, they
provided a basis for the establishment
of the World Series.*

THE BASEBALL ENCYCLOPEDIA

◆

Nonsense.
I first discovered the
existence of the nineteenth-
century World Series when I
read Bob Tiemann's book, *Cardinal Classics*, in 1983. Like most
fans, I'd never heard of any World Series games before 1903, so I
looked through my Macmillan *Baseball Encyclopedia* and found no
significant mention of the nineteenth-century World Series. Well,
if Macmillan didn't see fit to include those games in the *Encyclopedia*, that was good enough for me.

My interest in the origins of the Series was further stimulated
when the Society for American Baseball Research (SABR) sent out
its special pictorial issue on nineteenth-century baseball in the
spring of 1984. Seeing pictures of these old ballplayers in the flesh,
as it were, made me realize for the first time that these were real
men playing real baseball. Their reputations were at stake, their
pride, the pride of their teams, and the honor of their leagues.

When I dipped back into the *Encyclopedia* again, I read that
baseball officialdom grants major league status to the American
Association for the years of its existence—indeed, no less an authority than baseball historian David Q. Voigt calls this period
baseball's golden age. So why, exactly, do the powers that be

continue to treat the nineteenth-century World Series as a bastard child and claim, instead, that the 1903 Series was the first "official" championship? I wrote to the Macmillan Publishing Company, asking if it could explain its reasons in more detail. The answer I got was quite simple: 1903 was the first time the games were referred to as the World Series.

Were those games of the nineteenth-century so vastly different from the ones played in 1903? Indeed, were they so different from the ones played last year?

Dismissing, for the moment, the 1882 World Series as games of exhibition, and discounting the 1892 National League Championship Series and the Temple Cup games of 1894 through 1897, let us examine only the World Series matchups of 1884 through 1890 to see what differences existed between the nineteenth- and twentieth-century games.

In 1884, New York Metropolitans manager Jim Mutrie challenged the League-leading Providence Grays to a championship game to be played on an off-day during the regular season. Providence declined, but later consented to a three-game series at the home grounds of the Mets and under American Association rules. The clubs posted purse money and Providence swept the Series in three games.

In 1885, the St. Louis Browns and Chicago White Stockings scheduled a twelve-game series, most of the games to be played under Association rules and, excepting Game One, in Association parks. Both teams put up five hundred dollars as a purse.

In late September of 1886, St. Louis Browns owner Chris Von Der Ahe wrote Chicago White Stockings president Al Spalding, challenging him to a "series of contests to be known as the World's Championship Series." Von Der Ahe expressed indifference toward the length of the championship, but suggested all games be played at the clubs' home fields. A best-of-seven series was arranged, winner-take-all, with both teams to pay their own expenses. The victor was responsible for paying the umpires.

In 1887, Detroit owner Fred Stearns challenged Von Der Ahe to a best-of-fifteen series for the championship of the world, the winning club to receive 75 percent of the net gate receipts. With so many games and so little competition—the Wolverines won eight of the first eleven meetings—the 1887 World Series was a financial disaster and so, in 1888, the Browns and Giants elected to shorten the number of games to a best-of-eleven championship. A year later, the format was further refined when Giants manager Jim Mutrie declared he would end the Series when either team won the deciding game. This established a tradition which has lasted for more than a century.

Arrangements for the 1890 World Series were not settled until a little more than a week prior to the scheduled opening date. Because the Players' League Boston Reds were widely acknowledged as baseball's best team in 1890, fan interest in the Brooklyn-Louisville series was minimal, and the format reverted to best-of-nine. The first four games were played in Louisville, the next four were to be played in Brooklyn, and a seventh game, had it been necessary, would have been played for a neutral park.

Now let's turn to the World Series of 1903, the first "official" Series, according to Macmillan and see how it differs from its predecessors.

In February of 1903, the National and American Leagues reached a shaky peace treaty in which they agreed, among other things, not to raid each other's clubs for players. By August, the Pittsburgh Pirates were leading the National League, and owner Barney Dreyfuss decided it would be a fine (and profitable) idea if his club played the American League pennant winner in a post-season competition. He broached the subject with Henry J. Killilea, the Milwaukee lawyer who owned the first-place American League Boston Pilgrims. Killilea went straight to the office of American League president Ban Johnson to see what he thought of the idea. The irascible Johnson, keenly aware that many of the National League magnates still looked upon his charges as little more than a minor league, asked one question of Killilea, "Do you think you can beat them?" The last thing Johnson wanted was to reinforce the American League's weak image with a post-season drubbing.

Killilea and Dreyfuss agreed that the best-of-seven format left over from the Temple Cup games was too short and struck a deal for a best-of-nine series. They further agreed to use no players signed or otherwise acquired after September 1, to split the gate receipts, and to make their own financial arrangements with their own ballplayers. This presented no problem for Dreyfuss. The series was scheduled to begin October 1, and the Pirates were under contract through the fifteenth. Killilea, however, was faced with a dilemma. The Boston contracts expired on the first of October and the Pilgrims immediately threatened to strike unless their owner forked over the receipts. Killilea resolved the conflict by giving everyone an extra two weeks' pay and a share of the receipts. The 1903 World Series, won by the Boston Pilgrims in eight games, was the inauguration of post-season championship play between the National and American Leagues and the first World Series of the twentieth century. *Although the games were not played under National Commission rules,* they have come to be recognized, erroneously, as the first "official" World Series.

As you can see, in no important respect was this series any different from those played between 1884 and 1890.

Late in the 1904 season, the newly installed president of the Boston Pilgrims, John I. Taylor, challenged John McGraw's New York Giants to a post-season series for the championship of the world. McGraw, whose avocation was the full-time hatred of Ban Johnson, had stated publicly as early as August 5 that his Giants would not participate in any such series. "Why should we play this upstart club, or any other American League team, for any post-season championship?" McGraw said. "When we clinch the National League pennant, we'll be champions of the only real major league."

Giants owner John T. Brush said his club was "content to rest on its laurels," and supported his manager with a statement in early September, saying, "There is nothing in the constitution or playing rules of the National League which requires its victorious club to submit its championship honors to a contest with a victorious club in a minor league." National League president Pulliam stood firmly behind Brush, pointing out that the 1903 Series had been played by voluntary agreement and no further obligations had ever been reached. "Playing of games outside the regular schedule," Pulliam said, "is left to the discretion of individual clubs." The president of the National League clearly was of the opinion that there was nothing official about the 1903 World Series.

McGraw and Brush had their horns out for Ban Johnson and, as a result, there was no World Series in 1904. The ballplayers held a team meeting and requested Brush's permission to play the Pilgrims, but Brush refused, so the Giants went on a two-week barnstorming tour instead. *The Sporting News* called the Boston Pilgrims "World's Champions by default."

At their annual winter meeting, National League owners re-elected Harry Clay Pulliam as their president and endorsed the idea of holding a World Series in future seasons. In 1905, John Brush drew up a playing code for the World Series containing these four main points: First, the games would be played under National Commission rules—unlike the 1903 Series—in a best-of-seven format. Second, umpires, official scorers, and playing dates would be determined by the National Commission. Third, 60 percent of the receipts of the first four games would be set aside as the players' pool of prize money; the winning team would receive 75 percent of this sum. Finally, the site of the first game and seventh, if a seventh was necessary, would be determined by coin toss.

After reviewing the facts, it is clear the 1903 World Series cannot lay any rightful claim to being an "official" World Series. That distinction, if a distinction even needs to be made, must go to the 1905 games, the first to be played under the auspices of the National Commission—*if* baseball officialdom is to abide by its own arbitrary rules.

Finally, Macmillan's claim that the 1903 games were the first to be called the World Series is nothing but semantics. The *New York Clipper* called the 1884 series the "United States Championship;" *The Sporting News* called the Providence Grays the "champions of the world," and referred to the Series itself as "the world's championship;" the *Boston Journal*, another impartial observer, called the series the "championship of the country." The *New York Clipper* referred to the 1885 St. Louis Browns as the "world's champions," and *Spalding's Official Base Ball Guide 1886* called the series "the United States championship." The *Reach Baseball Guide* called the 1886 games "The Great World's Series," the first such use of the modern phrase I was able to locate in an objective source. *Spalding's Official Base Ball Guide 1887* recognized the importance and the tradition of the annual event by moving its account of the World Series from its traditional place in the back of the book all the way up to page twenty-one. By 1887, there wasn't a newspaper in the country that didn't use the phrase "world's championship," and by 1886, *The Sporting News* was, for the first time, referring to the games as "The World's Series."

Enough said.

It is true that most of the nineteenth-century World Series did not follow the now-familiar best-of-seven format, but this was also the case in 1903, 1919, 1920, and 1921. I daresay no one has suggested to Macmillan that its editors expunge those four Series from the *Encyclopedia*. (For that matter, one might wonder, and with good cause, why the 1919 World Series is still in the book.) It is also true that the nineteenth-century World Series were often played under American Association rules. But if baseball grants both the National League and American Association equal status, it should make no difference under which rules the games were played.

It is also true that none of the nineteenth-century World Series games were played under today's rules. On the other hand, a third-strike bunt was still just a foul ball in 1908, Burleigh Grimes was throwing the spitball as late as 1932, and the strike zone has been tampered with three times since 1963 alone. Where does one draw the line? Well, Macmillan clearly draws its line with the twentieth-century and the formation of the American League.

Sure, the rules may have stated a hundred years ago that it took six or even seven bad pitches before a batter drew a base on balls; and maybe that same base on balls was credited as a hit; and maybe, early on, pitchers were required to throw underhand. But the point is, the nineteenth-century World Series games were played under the rules as they were written. The game wasn't Australian-rules football, it wasn't rounders, and it wasn't cricket. It was baseball. The team that had the most runs at the end of nine innings was the winner. Just as it is today. Nobody wore blindfolds, no one had to hop on one foot while fielding his position, pitchers took their cuts at the plate, and they *didn't* use aluminum bats.

The game was baseball.

The nineteenth-century brand.

REFERENCES

BOOKS

Allen, Lee. *The National League Story: The Official History.* New York: Hill & Wang, 1961.

_____. *The World Series: The Story of Baseball's Annual Championship.* New York: G.P. Putnam's Sons, 1969.

Astor, Gerald, ed. *The Baseball Hall of Fame 50th Anniversary Book.* New York: Prentice Hall Press, 1988.

Benson, Michael. *Ballparks of North America: A Comprehensive Historical Reference to Baseball Grounds, Yards and Stadiums, 1845 to Present.* Jefferson, North Carolina: McFarland & Company, 1989.

Broeg, Bob, and William J. Miller, Jr. *Baseball From a Different Angle.* South Bend, Indiana: Diamond Communications, 1988.

Carter, Craig, ed. *The Complete Baseball Record Book.* St. Louis: The Sporting News Publishing Company, 1988.

Curran, William. *Mitts: A Celebration of the Art of Fielding.* New York: William Morrow and Company, 1985.

Durso, Joseph. *Baseball And The American Dream.* St. Louis: The Sporting News Publishing Company, 1986.

Frommer, Harvey. *Primitive Baseball: The First Quarter Century of the National Pastime.* New York: Atheneum, 1988.

Hynd, Noel. *The Giants of the Polo Grounds: The Glorious Times of Baseball's New York Giants.* New York: Doubleday, 1988.

James, Bill. *The Bill James Historical Baseball Abstract.* New York: Villard Books, 1988.

Kaese, Harold. *The Boston Braves.* New York: G.P. Putnam's Sons, 1948.

Kennedy, MacLean. *The Great Teams of Baseball.* St. Louis: The Sporting News Publishing Company (reprint), 1988.

Lanigan, Ernest J., ed. *The Baseball Cyclopedia.* New York: The Baseball Magazine Company, 1922.

Leptich, John, and Dave Baranowski. *This Date In St. Louis Cardinals History.* New York: Stein and Day, Publishers, 1983.

Levine, Peter. *A.G. Spalding and the Rise of Baseball: The Promise of an American Sport.* New York: Oxford University Press, 1985.

Lewis, Dottie L., ed. *Baseball in Cincinnati: From Wooden Fences to Astroturf.* Cincinnati: Cincinnati Historical Society, 1988.

Lewis, Franklin. *The Cleveland Indians.* New York: G.P. Putnam's Sons, 1949.

Lieb, Frederick G. *The Boston Red Sox.* New York: G.P. Putnam's Sons, 1947.

_____. *The Detroit Tigers.* New York: G.P. Putnam's Sons, 1946.

_____. *The St. Louis Cardinals: The Story of a Great Baseball Club.* New York: G.P. Putnam's Sons, 1947.

Lowry, Phillip J. *Green Cathedrals.* Cooperstown, New York: Society for American Baseball Research, 1986.

Macfarlane, Paul. *Daguerreotypes of Great Stars of Baseball.* St. Louis: C.C. Spink & Son, 1971.

Nadel, Eric, and Craig Wright. *The Man Who Stole First Base: Tales From Baseball's Past.* Dallas: Taylor Publishing Company, 1989.

Obojski, Robert. *Bush League: A History of Minor League Baseball.* New York: Macmillan Publishing Company, 1975.

Orem, Preston. *Baseball (1845–1881) From the Newspaper Accounts.* Altadena, California, Private issue, 1961.

Phillips, John. *The Fall Classics of the 1890s.* Cabin John, Maryland: Capital Publishing Company, 1989.

_____. *The Baseball Encyclopedia: The Complete and Official Record of Major League Baseball.* New York: Macmillan Publishing Company, 1988.

_____. *The Great All-Time Baseball Record Book: A Unique Sourcebook of Facts, Feats, and Figures.* First, fourth, and seventh editions. New York: Macmillan Publishing Company, 1981.

Reidenbaugh, Lowell. *100 Years of National League Baseball.* St. Louis: The Sporting News Publishing Company, 1976.

Scully, Gerald W. *The Business of Major League Baseball.* Chicago: The University of Chicago Press, 1989.

Seymour, Harold. *Baseball: The Early Years.* New York: Oxford University Press, 1960.

Thorn, John, and John Holway. *The Pitcher: The Ultimate Compendium of Pitching Lore: Featuring Flakes and Fruitcakes, Wildmen and Control Artists, Strategies, Deliveries, Statistics, and More.* New York: Prentice-Hall Press, 1987.

Thorn, John, and Pete Palmer, eds. *Total Baseball.* New York: Warner Books, Inc., 1989.

Tiemann, Robert. *Cardinal Classics.* St. Louis: Baseball Histories, Inc., 1982.

Tiemann, Robert L., and Mark Rucker, eds. *Nineteenth Century Stars.* Cleveland: The Society for American Baseball Research, 1989.

Turkin, Hy, and S.C. Thompson. *The Official Encyclopedia of Baseball.* New York: A.S. Barnes, 1951.

Voigt, David Quentin. *American Baseball, Volume One.* University Park, Pennsylvania: The Pennsylvania State University Press, 1983.

_____. *Baseball: An Illustrated History.* University Park, Pennsylvania: The Pennsylvania State University Press, 1987.

Wheeler, Lonnie, and John Baskin. *The Cincinnati Game.* Cincinnati: Orange Frazer Press, 1988.

Wright, Craig, and Tom House. *The Diamond Appraised.* New York: Simon and Schuster, 1989.

Zoss, Joel, and John Bowman. *Diamonds In The Rough: The Untold History of Baseball.* New York: Macmillan Publishing Company, 1989.

PERIODICALS

Ahrens, Arthur R. "An Assist for Jimmy Ryan." *Baseball Research Journal.* Twelfth Annual Historical and Statistical Review of the Society for American Baseball Research: 1983.

_____. "Baseball's Biggest Inning." *Baseball Research Journal.* Sixth Annual Historical and Statistical Review of the Society for American Baseball Research: 1977.

_____. "The Daily Dahlen of 1894." *Baseball Research Journal.* Sixth Annual Historical and Statistical Review of the Society for American Baseball Research: 1977.

_____. "Fred Pfeffer: Stonewall Second Baseman." *Baseball Research Journal.* Eighth Annual Historical and Statistical Review of the Society for American Baseball Research: 1979.

Eddleton, Oscar. "Under The Lights." *Baseball Research Journal.* Ninth Annual Historical and Statistical Review of the Society for American Baseball Research: 1980.

Gerlach, Larry. "Umpire Honor Rolls." *Baseball Research Journal.* Eighth Annual Historical and Statistical Review of the Society for American Baseball Research: 1979.

Haas, Alex J. "A Woman Official Scorer." *Baseball Research Journal.* Fifth Annual Historical and Statistical Review of the Society for American Baseball Research: 1976.

Ivor-Campbell, Frederick. "1884: Old Hoss Radbourn and the Providence Grays." *The National Pastime: A Review of Baseball History.* A publication of the Society for American Baseball Research: 1985.

_____. "Sweeney's Whiff Feat of 1884 Rates No. 1." *Baseball Research Journal.* Fourteenth Annual Historical and Statistical Review of the Society for American Baseball Research: 1985.

Liebman, Ronald. "Highest Scoring Games." *Baseball Research Journal.* Ninth Annual Historical and Statistical Review of the Society for American Baseball Research: 1980.

_____. "Schedule Changes Since 1876." *Baseball Historical Review.* Compiled By The Society for American Baseball Research: 1981.

Kermisch, Al. "From A Researcher's Notebook." *Baseball Research Journal*. Historical and Statistical Review of the Society for American Baseball Research: Seventh through Fourteenth Annuals, 1978–85.

McConnell, Robert. "Hitting Three Triples In One Game." *Baseball Historical Review*. Compiled By The Society for American Baseball Research: 1981.

O'Malley, John O. "The Great Pennant Race of 1885." *Baseball Research Journal*. Sixth Annual Historical and Statistical Review of the Society for American Baseball Research: 1977.

_____. "Mutrie's Mets of 1884." *The National Pastime: A Review of Baseball History*. A publication of the Society for American Baseball Research: 1985.

Overfield, Joseph. "James 'Deacon' White." *Baseball Research Journal*. Fourth Annual Historical and Statistical Review of the Society for American Baseball Research: 1975.

Schwartz, John. "History of the Sacrifice Fly." *Baseball Research Journal*. Tenth Annual Historical and Statistical Review of the Society for American Baseball Research: 1981.

Smith, James D., III. "Honest John Kelly: He Was One Of A Kind." *Baseball Research Journal*. Fourteenth Annual Historical and Statistical Review of the Society for American Baseball Research: 1985.

Thorn, John, and Mark Rucker. *The National Pastime: A Review of Baseball History*. Special Pictorial Issue: The Nineteenth Century. A publication of the Society for American Baseball Research: 1984.

Voigt, David Q. "A Century of Baseball Strife." *Baseball Historical Review*. Compiled By The Society for American Baseball Research: 1981.

"Jim Corbett Playing First Base." *Baseball Research Journal*. Twelfth Annual Historical and Statistical Review of the Society for American Baseball Research: 1983.

"The 1892 Split Season." *Baseball Research Journal*. Eighth Annual Historical and Statistical Review of the Society for American Baseball Research: 1979.

Reach's Official Base Ball Guide. Philadelphia: A.J. Reach & Bros., 1887–92.

Spalding's Official Base Ball Guide. Chicago: A.G. Spalding and Bros., 1882–97.

NEWSPAPERS

Baltimore American, Baltimore News, The Boston Daily Globe, Boston Herald, Boston Journal, Brooklyn Eagle, Chicago Tribune, Cincinnati Enquirer, Cleveland Leader, The Cleveland Plain Dealer, Cleveland News, Louisville Courier-Journal, Louisville Commercial, Louisville

Evening Post, New York Clipper, The New York Times, Providence Journal, St. Louis Globe-Democrat, St. Louis Post-Dispatch, and *The Sporting News.*

MISCELLANEOUS

Orem, Preston. "Baseball (1882) From the Newspaper Accounts." Private issue. Altadena, California, 1961.

_____. "Baseball (1883) From the Newspaper Accounts." Private issue. Altadena, California, 1961.

_____. "Baseball (1884) From the Newspaper Accounts." Private issue. Altadena, California, 1961.

_____. "Baseball (1885) From the Newspaper Accounts." Private issue. Altadena, California, 1961.

Tattersall, John C. "Baseball: The Early World Series: 1884-1890." Private issue. Havertown, Pennsylvania, 1976.

INDEX